Bookvan

Bookvan

D0949759

FOR AARON JOSEPH

The criticism of religion is the prerequisite of all criticism.
—Karl Marx,
*A Contribution to the Critique
of Hegel's Philosophy of Right*

If thou art in the mood I will discourse.
—Thomas Lake Harris,
"Nu. VII," *White Roses for the Pall*

CONTENTS

THREE: THE GREAT COSMIC EGG

FOUR: THE GLO-RAYS OF GOD

FIVE: FALL OF THE SKY GOD

Epilogue 352

FOREWORD

My SECOND TRIP TO HEAVEN was more propitious than the first.
I wasn't alone this time, but accompanied by my friend Shannon, who
works as a historic preservationist in Philadelphia. Shannon lent some
professional credibility to our Sunday tour of Woodmont, also known
as the Mount of the House of the Lord. Woodmont is an impecca-
bly preserved nineteenth-century manor in Gladwyne, Pennsylvania,
situated within one of the wealthiest zip codes in the Northeast cor-
ridor. At the time of our visit, Woodmont was the residence of Sweet
Angel Mother Divine, the geriatric regent of a nationwide religious
movement founded by her husband, Father Divine, more than three-
quarters of a century prior. The preservation of historic buildings in
and around Philadelphia, a city that has hemorrhaged wealth and
population since the 1960s, was a cause near to Mother Divine's heart.
For decades she managed a vast network of Victorian-era mansions
and hotels across the Northeast. Stewardship of these structures had
made Mother Divine a celebrated proponent of historic preservation,
and the recipient of awards from the Philadelphia City Council and
the Commonwealth of Pennsylvania in recognition of her work.

Beginning in the second decade of the twentieth century, Father
Divine's followers have lived in communes known alternately as "heavens" or "extensions" of the International Peace Mission Movement.
Once scattered from coast to coast and housing tens of thousands of
believers, Peace Mission extensions have slowly been emptied and sold
ever since Father Divine "sacrificed" his earthly body in September

1965. Woodmont is one of the last and most majestic of the Movement's once-legendary real-estate holdings, and it is still occupied by a coterie of (mostly) elderly followers. The denizens of Peace Mission heavens used to be known as "angels," so called because of the sanctified lifestyle they adopted. Believers in Father Divine's divinity do not usually describe themselves this way anymore, but they still follow the same severe moral code Father Divine enforced while he was alive. The code includes celibacy, a stricture that all but guarantees the eventual demise of the movement.

My first visit to a Peace Mission extension, a former hotel located on the corner of Broad and Catharine Streets in Center City Philadelphia, was thwarted by my own failure to abide by the International Peace Mission Modesty Code. I knew about the code, and was prepared not to swear, smoke, drink, tip, bribe, or engage in any "undue mixing of the sexes" during the Holy Communion banquet I wished to attend. I was only in town for a few days and put together the finest outfit I could assemble from my suitcase. I was turned away nonetheless, on account of my red shoes, and told to return when I was wearing my "Sunday best." I packed accordingly for my next trip to Philly, and sent Shannon the Modesty Code before I picked her up. We turned up at Woodmont looking like frumpy substitute teachers.

Shannon and I weren't the only visitors to the estate. A row of sedans had completely occupied the small parking lot at the end of the long lane that leads from the road to the mansion. I stopped short of the lot and pulled in behind a black SUV parked on the edge of the lane. A film crew was threading its way across a nearby garden.

There was no indication of where visitors should begin the tour, so Shannon and I made straight for the mansion's porte cochere. Beneath it, the front door was thrown wide open. We showed ourselves in. Just as we crossed the threshold into a lavishly wood-paneled interior, the sound of voices, singing or chanting in unison, suddenly reverberated in the adjacent room. From where we stood in the mansion's grand two-story foyer, Shannon and I could see through an archway into the dining room, where the Divinites appeared to be gathered around the table for worship over an elaborate meal: a tradition known in the Peace Mission as Holy Communion. Two silver-haired butlers in pale-blue tuxedo jackets and gloves wavered in the archway to the dining room but did not appear disposed to greet us. We ducked back out.

The film crew was eating lunch near one of the outbuildings when we approached. They were gathering footage for a documentary, and today, we learned, was a special day to do it: without realizing it, Shannon and I were visiting the annual feast held to mark Mother and Father Divine's wedding anniversary. Mother Divine and the resident followers were hosting a full table, the crew explained; otherwise, we'd have been invited to sit down. After I mentioned that we'd called ahead to confirm our tour, members of the crew encouraged us to go back and request one from someone at the banquet.

We hovered in the mansion's lobby while Father Divine's voice crackled on recordings playing in the next room. Occasionally the sermon elicited a unified response from those assembled. None of the worshipers at the table who saw us enter made the slightest move to alert anyone else of our presence. Eventually, one of the guests emerged from the dining room to use the bathroom and sent for our tour guide. Miss Sibyl Child entered the hall wearing a knee-length navy-blue skirt, a white blouse, and a red blazer with a white *V* for "victory" embroidered on the breast. I recognized her attire as the patriotic uniform of the Rosebuds, an elite corps of angels Father Divine had organized in the 1940s. Miss Sibyl was, to my eyes, a black woman in her golden years. But in the Peace Mission, which denies racial categories, she was merely considered dark-complected, whereas Shannon and I happened to be light-complected.

Our tour began in the foyer, under a nearly life-size portrait of Father and Mother Divine. I knew the spot from old photos I'd seen of one of the first wedding banquets. After we introduced ourselves as admirers of historic architecture, Shannon stepped forward with knowledgeable questions about Woodmont's construction and maintenance as we proceeded through several rooms on the ground floor. One of these was Father Divine's office, which is kept exactly as he left it in 1965. Miss Sibyl spoke to Father as though he were seated at his desk.

As we meandered, Miss Sibyl narrated the history of the Peace Mission, starting with Father Divine's appearance in New York in the 1920s. Beginning in this manner, with the man fully formed, prompted Shannon to ask an obvious question: where was Father Divine originally from? Miss Sibyl said she didn't know, nobody did. Her reply was crisp, delivered in the manner of someone who's answered the question many times before.

As I'd feared, the dining room proved to be the most awkward segment of the tour. The followers and their guests were still eating when we entered. But after pointing out the room's architectural features, Miss Sibyl insisted we take a turn about the room to inspect it more closely. An enormous table occupied almost the entire chamber. Thirty-odd diners of varied complexions filled all but one place at the table. Shannon and I squeezed behind the chairs of the faithful, moving along the edges of the room as silver clattered against china. Conversation was kept to a minimum while Father Divine's voice continued over the loudspeaker. Mother Divine, in her nineties, was seated by herself at the end of the table. She was wearing a white wedding dress.

Miss Sibyl then guided us outdoors, around a small outbuilding called the Brothers' Quarters, and across the mansion's handsome grounds. We stopped for a while in a garden on the edge of the property, where the ridge dropped to the Schuylkill River valley below. The tour inevitably led to a mausoleum on the edge of the estate, a structure known as the Shrine to Life. Here was where Father Divine's earthly remains lay entombed. Miss Sibyl explained that although he had decided to abandon the body in which he'd conducted his marvelous career, Father Divine was by no means dead. This is because she, like the angels who came before her, believed Father Divine to be God.

AMERICAN MESSIAHS

THE MESSIANIC IMPULSE IN AMERICA

F ATHER DIVINE was far from the first American to be worshiped
by his followers as the embodiment of the living God returned to
Earth. Over the course of two and a half centuries, numerous Americans have laid stakes to the claim of a divinely ordained salvational
mission.

Among them was the holy family of the Walla Walla Jesus, known
to terrestrial authorities as Arthur Davies. This American messiah
did not take up the mantle for himself, but was proclaimed to be the
reincarnation of Jesus of Nazareth by his father, William W. Davies.
The elder Davies was a Welsh convert to Mormonism who emigrated
in 1855 to join his people's exodus to Utah. After arriving in Mormon territory, he became disenchanted with the authoritarian bent of
Mormon society under the leadership of the church's new president,
Brigham Young. Davies was particularly dismayed by the Mountain
Meadows Massacre, which revealed the violent means to which the
church would resort to preserve its control of the region. In this 1857
tragedy, a Utah militia murdered more than 100 Arkansas migrants
whose wagon train had stopped to camp in Mountain Meadows en
route to California. The caravan had only stopped for rest, but tensions
between the Mormons and the federal government had reached the
point of armed insurrection, and the militiamen alleged the Arkan-
sans were part of a federal plot to overthrow Brigham Young and
impose martial law on the territory.

After this slaughter of innocent pioneers, Davies and other disillusioned converts broke away from the church under the leadership of James Morris, an apostate who began to receive communications directly from God around the time of the massacre. One of the most exotic revelations he received concerned the doctrine of reincarnation, and the corresponding disclosure that Morris possessed the gift of identifying the prior identities of disaffected Mormons, who presumably learned of their glamorous past lives through him.

This was already an absurd heresy against Mormon theology, but it was not the revelation that church authorities found to be the most offensive. Morris claimed that although Brigham Young was indeed the legitimate political successor to Joseph Smith, he was not Smith's prophetic heir: this, God instructed through his newly minted prophet, was none other than James Morris himself.

The Mormon Church based its legitimacy on the claims of latter-day prophets, so Morris saw no reason why he should not mention that God had made this revelation unto him. Brigham Young was of a much different opinion, and desired for the heretic to be executed. He sent a sheriff to apprehend Morris, who had led several hundred of his followers out of Mormonism and into the wilderness. When the Mormon posse arrived at the apostate camp, they found the heretics armed and prepared to defend their new faith. The sheriff thought it wise to tire them out with a siege. But after three days produced no surrender, it was the sheriff who became impatient. Unfortunately for the besieged encampment, an item of light artillery had arrived on the scene, and the sheriff considered it the most expedient way to end the standoff. An exploding shell killed numerous Morrisites, and the prophet was shot and killed in the melee that ensued.

Satisfied with the bloody end of James Morris, Mormon authorities allowed his deluded converts to disperse without another massacre. Davies was among the surviving apostates, and he prudently escaped to Idaho. He later relocated to Montana, where he experienced mystic visions he would later recount in sworn court testimony. The Montana revelations led him to Washington territory, where he led approximately forty of the followers he'd gathered in the meantime. In 1867, the faithful settled near the municipality of Mill Creek, in Walla Walla County, on land that Davies declared the Kingdom of Heaven.

The following February 11, Davies's wife gave birth to Arthur Davies, who was announced to be the reincarnation of Jesus Christ. After a second son was born on September 28, 1869, he was declared to contain the spirit of God the Father. The residents of the kingdom worshiped accordingly. Not long after the second holy birth, the elder Davies revealed a final secret: that his own body carried the Holy Spirit.

Like other small and embattled religious minorities, the Daviesites lived communally, emulating the example set by Christ's apostles and recorded in the Book of Acts. In addition to managing communal affairs, Davies administered a stern moral policy that allowed for no impropriety or insobriety. The kingdom's subjects fluctuated in number between 40 and 70 souls over the course of the next decade. The commune was never self-sufficient, but missionaries dispatched by the Holy Spirit to Portland and San Francisco yielded new converts, who arrived with their liquidated assets and kept the kingdom in the black.

In the fall of 1879, Mrs. Davies suddenly died, posing an inconvenience to the community's belief that Davies could work miracles, one of which was the banishment of death and disease from their ranks. A worse calamity befell them in February 1880, when diphtheria reached the Kingdom of Heaven. The disease killed God the Father, age ten, on February 15. The same epidemic claimed the life of Jesus, age twelve, less than one week later.

As the kingdom mourned, some of its denizens began murmuring their discontent. Obviously the death of two-thirds of the Trinity was not an auspicious sign for the community. Nor did it augur well for the Holy Spirit. Finally, three of Heaven's residents filed suit against Davies after he declined to refund their contributions to the colony. The case went to trial in January 1881, when the Holy Spirit took the stand to testify that the spirit of God that descended into his body had authorized his sole control of the kingdom's financial affairs. Numerous witnesses confirmed Davies's testimony that everyone who entered Heaven's domain agreed to the practice of communal living. The plaintiffs emphatically disagreed, and the court, disliking the whole arrangement, ordered they be paid $3,200. The Holy Ghost could not produce this sum, having spent most of the community's cash on land, expensive missionary trips, and the construction of homes, a church, and a school. The judge instructed the sheriff to sell the kingdom's belongings in order to award the judgment, which effectively wiped Heaven off the map.

Davies's career as a holy messenger came to an abrupt halt when he and his followers became homeless. Most of them disbanded, and Davies later ended up in San Francisco, married to a follower named Miss Perkins. The Holy Spirit justified his remarriage on the grounds that Miss Perkins was the reincarnation of the first Mrs. Davies. This injured the sensibilities of those followers who remained, and the movement drifted into obscurity.[1]

. . .

UNLIKE THE PEACE MISSION, the Walla Walla Kingdom of Heaven did not influence the history of American religion in a meaningful way. Nor was it influential, or even original, to the history of American messianism. But as a case study, it is instructive for the number of characteristics it shares with previous and subsequent American messianic movements. Reincarnation, for example, is one of the very un-Christian teachings these movements often teach; it reappears in Father Divine's Peace Mission, whose followers believe Mother Divine to be the reincarnation of Father Divine's first wife. Yet although some American messianic movements eschew reincarnation in favor of a dispensational framework wherein each civilizational age will have its own unique savior, another feature unites American messianic sects with near universality: the practice of communal living derived from biblical accounts of the apostolic church.

Communalism represents the ultimate repudiation of the values and institutions that Americans historically hold dear: it rejects not only the sacrosanct individualism on which American culture thrives, but also the nuclear family unit that evolved alongside industrial capitalism. In each of the most successful American messianic movements, including those analyzed in the pages to follow, communalism, often in conjunction with celibacy, was elaborated as a rejection of marriage, childbearing, and traditional kinship structures. Far more than for their heretical beliefs, the communistic and anti-family leanings of American messianic movements pose a threat to the prevailing socioeconomic order. For this reason, messianic movements find reliable opponents in the press, in law enforcement, and in the courts, which often sympathize with any complaint made against them for the sake of preserving public decency and morality.

The arousal of public opposition sometimes leads to a swift demise, as it did for the Walla Walla Kingdom of Heaven. But aversion to these groups, their lifestyles, and their actions has also led to their exclusion from historical narratives in which they played important roles. For although Father Divine was the most well-known and influential civil rights leader on the national stage between the deportation of Marcus Garvey and the emergence of Martin Luther King Jr., he usually goes unmentioned in accounts of the American civil rights movement, having been blotted from history for the embarrassment he caused black and liberal elites. Like many other messianic movements, the Peace Mission has been called a "cult" and given little historical consideration. The lacunae that result from these banishments have meant that the historical continuity of American messianic thought has gone unrecognized. And yet a direct lineage connects Ann Lee, the Shaker messiah who arrived to American shores in 1774, to Jim Jones, the holy-rolling Marxist who in 1978 led more than 900 of his congregants in mass suicide at their Promised Land commune in Guyana.

The mass suicide of Jim Jones and Peoples Temple led many Americans to conclude that the United States was afflicted by a dangerous cult epidemic. Loud proponents of this view, including many from the twentieth-century evangelical movement, persuaded the public that separatist religions were dangerously un-American. Yet the impulse to purify the group through separation from mainstream society, now regarded as the signature of a cult, could not be more fundamental to the nation's history. In the opinion of their contemporaries in England, the Pilgrims who landed at Plymouth Rock were members of an undesirable and heretical religious cult; they were Separatist Puritans, so called because they believed that the Church of England was so corrupt that it could never be reformed from within—hence their desire to divorce themselves from it.

The Pilgrims' decision to leave the Old World for America was made not only as a result of persecution at the hands of those who found their views too much to bear; it also originated from their optimistic desire to reestablish an uncorrupted Christian church. They took as their inspiration the apostolic or "primitive" church: those first communities of believers gathered in Christ's name by his apostles. As described in the Book of Acts, the primitive Christian church was founded on ideals of charity, mutual aid, and the equal and impartial acceptance of every member—including the weak, the poor, and the sick. These first Christians forsook private property and held all things in common, a practice Jim Jones would later call "apostolic socialism."

Such a church would never have been allowed to flourish in seventeenth-century Europe, but the English king allowed the Separatists to have a go of it in America. The Pilgrims knew that for the new church to remain pure, they would need to create a society unpolluted by the temptations associated with unchecked economic and political power. Commonly described by historians as a theocracy, the resulting colony at Plymouth was a utopian community crafted by religious deviants who believed they were founding God's kingdom on Earth by restoring the primitive church. They meant for their experiment to inspire others to take up their virtuous ways. In a famous speech aboard the *Arabella* before their final departure, John Winthrop told his fellow Pilgrims they would build a "city upon a hill" for all to see. The Puritans believed that if they were successful maintaining a society in which the "true" church could flourish, they would bring about the Second Coming by demonstrating to the Lord that his people were ready to receive him. A more ambitious variant of this belief teaches that humankind must maintain God's kingdom on Earth for a millennium before Christ will return. This theological orientation is known as postmillennialism.

Few today would consider the Puritans' goal, or the theocracy that resulted from it, a liberal endeavor. But the complaints the Separatists lodged against the Church of England were animated by what were, at the time, progressive ideas about land reform. Radical Puritans in England would later start and win a civil war over the same concerns: the English Church, they believed, had not been meaningfully reformed following its break from Rome. The king had preserved the Catholic bishopric hierarchy, which left the medieval power structure more or less intact. English bishops continued to consort with lords and kings to control the distribution of property and productive lands. In the Radical Puritan view, the church behaved as a usurious corporate landlord—and not as a community of charity and faith, as Christ commanded.[2]

It was no coincidence that the rising capitalist merchant class and the emergent bourgeoisie joined with the Puritans when they took up arms in 1642: the Puritanical rhetoric of answering only to God and one's conscience squared with ascendant liberal ideas about the free market and individual liberty. When the Interregnum finally ended with the restoration of the Stuarts to the throne, Charles II took pleasure in persecuting the Puritans who remained in England, which encouraged greater numbers to embark for America. There they combined with that other notable category of émigré: fortune seekers who saw America not as the kingdom of God on Earth but a place where they might make themselves rich.

For the Puritans, these were never countervailing impulses: the

Calvinist belief that earthly wealth resulted from God's favors easily resolved whatever inconvenience capitalist greed might have posed to Puritan theocracy. This theological principle made each individual responsible for his or her own salvation, and made a virtue of financial success. In this way, the Protestant ethic, as Max Weber famously called it, wormed its way to the core of the American ethos.

The history of American politics and religion—which is a single intertwined history—is a record of the battle for the survival of this idea. It has triumphed in the sphere of religion: as Harold Bloom has observed, American evangelical Christianity hinges on the individual's personal and intimate relationship to God.[3] Individualism carried the day in political economy, as well: the Calvinist mandate to be a responsible steward of one's own soul secularized into the familiar American ideology of bootstrapping personal accountability.

After doctrinaire Calvinism succumbed to wave after wave of democratizing evangelical revivals unleashed by the American Protestant obsession with religious reform, the obvious contradictions between capitalism and Christian values have returned to the fore during periods of social unrest. As occurred in seventeenth-century England, the more radical responses to perceived social injustice sometimes emerge in the form of intentional communities. Not all are religious in nature: the Brook Farm commune founded by New England Transcendentalists and the New Harmony community built by Welsh industrialist Robert Owen in Indiana are two of the many examples of intentional communities based on socialist principles only loosely connected to religion. Often inspired by scientific advances, secular socialist communes attempt to light the path of progress and point the way to a more perfect human society.

In other instances, intentional communities wishing to enact immediate social reform find reason to look backward and forward simultaneously. Like the Pilgrims, they believe that a return to the egalitarian lifestyle of the primitive church will heal a society wallowing in the sins of greed, and thereby bring about the salvation of mankind. Although less common, religiously oriented intentional communities are more robust and enduring than their secular counterparts. The reason for this inheres in the lexicon: *religion* derives from the Latin word for bonding and obligation. Religion supplies the ties to bind a community together, and obliges adherents to have faith and express devotion. Left-wing social movements are notoriously fractious because they rely on tenuous alliances between vulnerable and disenfranchised members of society. Movements helmed by a messianic prophet overcome these divisions with the bonds of religion, allowing those disillusioned and oppressed by the status quo to band together, and create a new society within the shell of the old.

American messiahs tend to arise from progressive movements within left-wing politics because they identify capitalism and exclusionary social hierarchies as sources of evil that will inevitably damn the nation to perdition. They seize on social injustices that directly contradict the primitive church that Christ's apostles built, and position themselves against American racism, class oppression, and the subjugation of women. Although anarchist and socialist movements have briefly flourished on the basis of similar opposition, they have tended to make religion their opponent. However, until the Third Great Awakening at the turn of the twentieth century, American evangelical Christianity was a socially liberal and democratizing force in national politics—it was nothing like the reactionary and revanchist movement that it has become today. This is because until the Third Great Awakening, postmillennialism remained a strong current in evangelical discourse: evangelicals believed that humankind would have to prove it was worthy of salvation in order to attain it. Today's evangelicals, by contrast, hold the pre-millenarian view that Christ will return before the kingdom of God is restored on Earth, that the reason for the Second Coming is for Christ to establish it himself, and that only those who aren't destroyed or hauled off to hell in the apocalypse will be around to enjoy it.

American messianic movements do not abide by the dichotomy of pre- or post-millennialism. They instead combine the two views to suggest a more generous and humanistic approach: namely, that the Messiah might return in order to lead humankind through the process of reform and regeneration. For this reason, messianic movements arise at the radical fringe of nearly every major American reform movement, including the movements for women's liberty and the abolition of slavery, the temperance and antimonopoly movements, and the modern civil rights movement. Like the Pilgrims, American messianic sects hold up the revolutionary microsocieties they establish as a shining example for all to follow. But because none has succeeded in eliminating the evils of capitalism or resolving the contradictions at the core of the American religion, American messiahs continue to arise. A nearly unbroken trajectory of messianic leadership links Jim Jones and Father Divine to America's first messiahs—both of whom were women. This is the story of their collective attempts to save the American soul.

ONE

WOMEN
IN THE
WILDERNESS

1. THE PERSON FORMERLY KNOWN AS JEMIMA WILKINSON

MERE MONTHS AFTER the signing of the Declaration of Independence, a strange figure on horseback began to circulate throughout the New England colonies. The body atop the horse responded to the name of Public Universal Friend, and the double column of riders who followed behind their leader all believed that the Friend's body housed the Spirit of God, sent to Earth to deliver an urgent message. Paying little heed to worldly skirmishes between Revolutionaries and Redcoats, the Friend galloped across the countryside announcing the apocalypse was drawing nigh. The Public Universal Friend exhorted audiences to heed heaven-sent warnings meant to save those who would listen, believe, and endeavor to live righteously—that is, according to the Friend's advice.

God had selected a handsome female body for the Universal Friend to inhabit, one that had recently belonged to Jemima Wilkinson of Cumberland, Rhode Island. Jemima was known as an intelligent and attractive twenty-three-year-old woman when she was struck by fever on October 5, 1776. Her family summoned a doctor when her condition worsened, but there was little to be done; the patient seemed doomed by the tenth, when her illness climaxed in babbling delirium.

Miraculously, the fever broke and the body calmed. According to family lore, Jemima's body had chilled in death before it warmed and revived. The other Wilkinsons were astonished when her body arose from the bed on October 11. But if the family at first rejoiced that Jemima had been spared, they were mistaken: the newly risen patient announced that Jemima had died, and that her body had been requisitioned by God for no less holy a purpose than the salvation of humankind.

Unusually for a woman of her age, Jemima Wilkinson was unwed at the time of her illness; in their early twenties, most of her peers were married mothers. She was born November 29, 1752, the eighth child of Jeremiah and Amey Whipple Wilkinson, and was named after one of Job's daughters.[1] Amey would go on to have four more children, but the last of these deliveries killed her in 1764. Jemima was only about twelve years old when this occurred, but would later understand that her mother had spent her entire adult life pregnant and nursing.

Jeremiah Wilkinson did not remarry, and carried on with the family by himself. Like any young woman of farmer's stock, Jemima was expected to help with chores and raise her younger siblings. Formal education was out of the question: at the time, women bore much of the responsibility of instructing their children, their daughters in particular. Lacking a mother and expected to labor in the home, Jemima turned to books, proving herself a prodigious autodidact. Aside from the Bible, she read deeply from the work of esteemed Quakers, including George Fox, William Penn, and the martyr Marmaduke Stephenson, one of three Quakers executed in Boston in 1659.[2]

Although they were a simple farming family, the Wilkinsons were not the poor bumpkins that many of the Friend's critics would later make them out to be. Jemima and her siblings were fourth-generation Americans who traced their origins to the first Wilkinson's arrival to New England in 1650. They were connected to prominent families in Rhode Island, including Jeremiah's first cousin Stephen Hopkins, a colonial governor and signatory of the Declaration of Independence. Jeremiah Wilkinson had inherited his farm in Cumberland, but his family more or less resembled the modest but self-sufficient sort of yeoman farmers so adored by Thomas Jefferson. His principal crop was cherries, and he was fondly called "Cherry Wilkinson" by the villagers in Cumberland.[3]

Although Jeremiah was a successful farmer with aristocratic relations, there was nothing extravagant about the Wilkinson family before the autumn of 1776. However, reports of Jemima's alleged death and resurrection caused her to become infamous across New England and the Middle Colonies, leading to considerable embellishment of the Universal Friend's words and deeds, and to the invention of numerous apocryphal childhood anecdotes meant to demonstrate that the Friend's public ministry had resulted from the inherently corrupt character of a girl who had always been headstrong, lazy, arrogant, and manipulative. The folktale of Jemima's girlhood was concocted largely by adversaries, including her first biographer, David Hudson, whose unflattering 1821 biography of Jemima Wilkinson was meant to influence the outcome of a lawsuit that would determine the ownership of valuable lands belonging to the communal society the Friend had founded in upstate New York—a suit from which Hudson stood to gain.[4]

Although Hudson's biography was obviously a work of character assassination, his claim to be personally acquainted with the Friend, albeit accurate, allowed the stories he invented and the tall tales he repeated to pass into the historical record unchallenged for more than a century. Hudson and other detractors portray Jemima as an exceptional young woman, though not in any ways becoming to a Quakeress. She was called a "a fine blooming girl" who was "spritely in her manners," but possessed of "an unconquerable aversion to labor, an unusual cunning in shifting upon others the tasks assigned to her, an imperious will, and a strong propensity to dictate and rule, together with a love for idleness, finery, pomposity, and superiority"—all supposedly well in evidence by her seventeenth birthday.[5] Even more fantastic lies adhered to the Friend's decades-long career as an itinerant prophet.

. . .

THE TRUTH IS THAT little is known about Jemima's youth and young adulthood beyond what might be surmised from her later activities. She was, for example, a skilled horsewoman by the time the Friend occupied her body. Her robust physique, often described as masculine by those who went to hear the Friend preach, suggested that Jemima did her fair share of chores on the family farm. Jemima's command of the Bible and knowledge of Quaker theology were likewise in evidence by the time of her illness, and indicate that far from being an indolent girl who was scornful of work, she was industrious and even excelled in the few activities available to an unmarried woman.[6]

The Friend's assumption of Jemima's body transpired at a time of great confusion and turmoil in Rhode Island generally, and in the Wilkinson family in particular. The months preceding Jemima's illness in October 1776 had been far from calm in Cumberland: hostilities with the British, begun the preceding year, had transformed New England into one of the principal battlegrounds in the fight for independence. British forces were besieged in Boston and then evacuated in March 1776, but loomed off the coast in naval vessels, which were used to launch surprise attacks on coastal New England villages. Members of the Society of Friends, to which the Wilkinson family belonged, found themselves in a quandary when they were forced to choose between faith and country: patriotic Quakers who wished to be involved in the independence movement faced excommunication from the Society if they dared to take part in defense-training exercises with the local militia. This was the case for three of the Wilkinson brothers: Benjamin, Stephen, and Jeptha were all expelled from the Smithfield Friends monthly meeting for the un-Quakerly act of taking up arms. To these dismissals, another was added in 1776, when Jemima's sister Patience was disciplined for the disgrace of having a child out of wedlock. All of them were disowned by the time of their sister's metamorphosis.[7]

Jemima had likewise been booted from the Smithfield Friends meeting in the summer of 1776, mere weeks before her illness. The cause in her case was not sex or guns, but religious unorthodoxy: Jemima was disciplined when it became known among the Smithfield Friends that she was attending the revival meetings of New Light Baptists in the region.

The New Light revivals in New England resulted from the religious enthusiasm that had spread across the colonies in the preceding decades in reaction to declining satisfaction with the Puritan interpretation of Calvinist doctrine. Collectively known as the Great Awakening, the revivals of 1730–1770 gathered up disaffected Christians from the several Reformed churches that had already established themselves in the colonies. The New Light Stir of the 1770s saw a resurgence of this activity in rural New England communities that were distressed by the tumult of war. New Lights believed that individual inspiration and personal enlightenment from God were not only possible, but held priority over the worldly authorities in the established churches. They accepted the Puritan teaching that conscience reigned in matters of the spirit, but rejected the belief that abiding by church traditions and hierarchies while awaiting the final judgment was the way to steer clear of error and vouchsafe salvation. Saving grace, the New Lights believed, was a prize to be sought and gained. This democratic attitude struck an unmistakable contrast to the elitism that had become entrenched within the Congregational churches, as the Puritan congregations became known.

Like the other Protestant sects that placed an emphasis on individual conscience, Quakerism found itself on the defensive when the New Light ignited in its vicinity. The Quakers already taught a relatively liberal doctrine, one that affirmed the existence of a God-given "inner light" universally present in all humankind; this was one of the principal reasons why the Quakers opposed slavery. A crucial difference between New Light and Quaker orientations, however, was the Quaker belief that God's will becomes apparent only through dialogue among the enlightened. Members rise to speak in meetings when the Spirit moves them to do so, and the opinion of the congregation is forged by arriving at consensus.

New Light theology was more unruly than this, and held that

God's truth was available to anyone at any time—there need be no consensus. Similar views on individual inspiration and spiritual authority later became commonplace in twentieth-century American evangelical communities, whose members believe they can literally speak to God through prayer and receive his responses through signs, intuition, or biblical passages that God brings to their personal attention. At the close of the eighteenth century, however, such beliefs invited the censure of traditional Calvinist clergy, who rightly understood the evangelical movements as a challenge to their authority. New Light flirtation with antinomianism threatened to overturn the doctrines that distinguished the established denominations from one another, and to divide them from within along this new cleavage of individualism.

If the young Jemima Wilkinson was half as rebellious as her detractors claimed, then it is easy to see why antinomian currents in the New Light evangelical movements would have drawn her to investigate them for herself. It is just as likely that she merely sought a new religious community, one that was not already in the process of expelling her family. With several siblings already disowned by the Quakers, and with revolutionary fervor upending political and religious orders in New England, Jemima had little to lose and much to gain by associating with the New Lights.

But Jemima did not stop with association. After being seized by the New Light, she stood before the Smithfield Friends to hold forth her opinions and refused to take her seat when consensus demanded it be so.[8] The Friends regarded her outbursts as disrespectful and uncouth. Quakers were used to being censured for speaking their minds in public, particularly when it came to their pacifist convictions in a time of war. But Jemima's garrulousness extended to political concerns in ways that went beyond the pale of accepted opinion among the Quakers when she spoke at length about the war. Her views were not recorded, but she likely spoke in defense of her brothers and against their punishment.

Following Quaker custom, the Friends' disciplinary committee first requested that Jemima reform her conduct and cease attending New Light meetings. This she would not do. By August, Jemima remained insubordinate, and became the fourth of her siblings to be expelled from the Smithfield Quaker meeting. She spent the next weeks brooding at home, avoiding the company of others by spending long hours reading the Bible and praying. Her fever followed this interval of solitude.

Although no one ever doubted that Jemima's religious conversion was sincere, her illness was the subject of malicious conjecture. The Friend's later account of Jemima's sickness and death described the illness as the result of the "Columbus fever," an outbreak of typhus named for a colonial warship that had inadvertently contaminated Providence by transferring contagious British sailors to shore as prisoners.[9] In the Friend's retelling, the malady struck on "the seventh day of the week" and worsened for several days until "She appear'd to meet the Shock of Death."[10]

In her hour of mortal anguish, Jemima experienced a vision. Although not yet embodied, the Public Universal Friend was already present in spirit, and later transcribed the vision for posterity:

> The heavens were open'd And She saw too Archangels
> descending from the east, with golden crowns upon there
> heads, clothed in long white Robes, down to the feet; Bring-
> ing a sealed Pardon from the living God; and putting their
> trumpets to their mouth, proclaimed saying, Room, Room,
> Room, in the many Mansions of eternal glory for Thee and
> for everyone . . .

The angels explained to the expiring young woman, "The time is at hand, when God will lift up his hand, a second time, to recover the remnant of his People." The "Spirit of Life from God," the angels continued, had returned once more to Earth "to warn a lost and guilty, perishing dying World, to flee from the wrath which is to come." The Spirit was "waiting to assume the Body which God had prepared, for the Spirit to dwell in." This, of course, was the body of Jemima Wilkinson. [11]

Thenceforth, Jemima's body ceased recognizing her father and siblings as relatives, began to prefer male pronouns, and responded only to the names of "Public Universal Friend," "the All-Friend," "Friend of Sinners," and "the Comforter."[12] The transformation was later complemented by the Friend's preference for wearing men's clothing when he began his public ministry, a quirk that became one of his most remarked-upon characteristics.

2. THE UNIVERSAL FRIENDS

B Y SUNDAY the illness had retreated. Finding himself comfortably accommodated in Jemima's body, the Friend of Sinners decided to attend services at the Elder Miller Baptist meetinghouse that Jemima had been rebuked for attending. The other congregants soon learned that although Jemima Wilkinson's body had returned to their midst, it was the Public Universal Friend who replied to their greetings. Those who were not repelled by this sudden transformation gathered after the service to hear the Friend deliver his first public sermon under a shade tree near the meetinghouse. Thereafter, the Friend began to hold meetings in the Wilkinson family home. The four Wilkinson sisters and Jemima's brother Stephen became the Friend's first followers. Patience and Stephen had already been ejected from the Smithfield Friends; the other three girls were forced out by 1779 for indulging their sister's delusions.

Meanwhile, tongues began to wag. In eighteenth-century New England, proclaiming oneself a vessel for the Spirit of God was both risky and ridiculous. But the countryside rumbled with troubles deadlier than any heresy, offering a distraction that supplied considerable latitude for religious idiosyncrasies that might have been unthinkable in calmer days. Even so, the Friend's declarations horrified those who believed Jemima Wilkinson's transformation to be a grandiose stunt carried off by a woman who considered herself too clever to end up an old maid. Biographer David Hudson later disseminated the belief that Jemima was a fake prophet but a natural actress, a view that was no doubt shared by some of the Wilkinsons' neighbors. But if Jemima's transformation was only an act, it was one she kept up until the end of her life: the "actress" never publicly broke from her character. Rather, the next forty-three years of the Friend's career provide satisfying evidence that his belief in his holy mission was sincere.

By springtime, the Friend was ready to begin his itinerant ministry, having spent the winter practicing his sermons on the Wilkinson siblings. Villagers who had already been converted during visits to the Wilkinson home began to open their doors to the Friend's meetings, as did other New Lights and errant Quakers who had been dismissed from the Society of Friends for one or another transgression. To this ragtag set of mostly ex-Quakers, the Friend thundered his opposition to the inquisitorial and punitive meetings in which Quakers were censured, and demanded an end to the practice. He continued to insist on the right of every person to preach his or her conscience.[1]

When moving between the homes of his new followers, the Friend usually traveled with a retinue numbering between twelve and twenty adherents, and relied on the hospitality of converts and friendly listeners for victuals and lodging. Jeremiah escorted the Friend on his travels abroad. For this he received a stern warning from the Smithfield Friends, instructing him to cease "going about" with his heretic daughter. He disobeyed, prompting the Friends to initiate disciplinary proceedings that concluded with yet another expulsion from the Smithfield meeting.[2]

Over the next two years, the Public Universal Friend's celebrity spread across lower New England as a wave of rumor followed by visitations in the flesh. Opponents greatly aggrandized the Friend's reputation by spreading lies about his blasphemous assertions to be Jesus Christ in a female body—a claim the All-Friend was careful to avoid making directly—and by inventing stories about his attempts to raise the dead and walk on water. Fantastic tales of the Friend thus preceded his ministrations throughout New England, not least due to his singular appearance. Nearly every contemporary account remarks upon the dark beauty of the Comforter's androgynous countenance: a well-apportioned female body cloaked in black robes along with a white or purple cravat, topped by a wide-brimmed hat made of gray beaver fur.[3]

Although some regarded the Friend as demented, others were curious enough to hear him preach. The All-Friend's dramatic predictions of impending apocalypse impressed his listeners; they seemed to square with the chaos raging in New England and slowly enlarged his following. During this early phase of his ministry, the Comforter also went out of his way to attend funerals as a way to attract new adherents: those who came to pay their respects to the departed included members of rival meetings and churches who were unlikely to seek him voluntarily. Another tactic of recruitment was to follow Christ's advice to comfort soldiers taken as prisoners of war. When describing this aspect of his mission, the Friend cited Isaiah 61:1–2, in which the biblical prophet writes of his duty "to bind up the broken hearted; to proclaim liberty to the captives, and the opening of the prison to them that are bound."[4] The All-Friend's ministry to the sick, poor, imprisoned, and wounded continued to yield converts while the war lasted, including several former soldiers.

The Comforter appeared to have little concern for the hazards of gallivanting across occupied Rhode Island. Regarding this period, one of the Friend's secretaries later wrote:

> The Friend of Sinners began to speak in the Year 1777. When
> this Nation was all in arms; and America had imbru'd her
> hands in human blood. . . . The Friend was not stayed by
> guards of armed men, but went through; to visit the poor and
> condem'nd prisoners in their Chains: naked swords shook
> over The Friend's head, was no terror because of the mighty
> Power of the Lord.[5]

As he moved among the ranks of soldiers, the Comforter loudly denounced all war, except for the holy battle he was waging for humankind's salvation. Although some Patriots regarded this as a tacit rebuke of their cause, the Friend was generally considered unthreatening and was permitted to preach to British captives.

The All-Friend became known for his solemn and admonishing sermons, and for the spectacles of religious enthusiasm that sometimes burst forth during the meetings over which he presided. When seized by enthusiasm, the Universal Friends would sometimes shake and convulse. In keeping with Quaker tradition, the Friend allowed anyone moved to speak to stand and deliver, but amplified this practice by teaching his followers that the message he had come to share might be transmitted through the visions, dreams, and intuitions of any who obeyed his instructions. Thus to the Quaker inner light was added the kerosene of New Light evangelism blended with folk Christian mysticism.

During the New England phase of his ministry, the Friend would predict stunning events across the globe, such as earthquakes, and demonstrated powers of clairvoyance that allowed him to see directly into the hearts and minds of his audience.[6] This, critics alleged, was a talent the Friend maintained only by relying on a network of informants who brought him information useful for putting on a show of divine omnipotence.[7] According to accusations made by Abner Brownell, a follower excommunicated for the disloyalty of publishing his own prophecies against the Friend's wishes, the Comforter's spies would disclose transgressions perpetrated by his followers, so that the Friend could inspire wonder in his omniscience when he confronted wrongdoers and traitors with their sins. These were techniques later adopted by Jim Jones.

Brownell had been a follower of the Public Universal Friend for more than three years. After becoming disenchanted, he published an exposé about the Friend's ministry, titled *Enthusiastical Errors, Transpired and Detected*. In this 1783 pamphlet, Brownell promised to embarrass the fraudulent movement to which he'd fallen prey. Chief among the schemes he alleged was one that convinced him of the Friend's imposture: this was the 1779 publication of a short text, titled *Some Considerations, Propounded to the Several Sorts and Sects of Professor of This Age*, published under the Friend's name.

Following its publication, Quakers immediately recognized the pamphlet to be little more than a compendium of unattributed passages taken from works by Isaac Penington and William Sewel. When confronted with this fact, the Friend's devoted followers stated their belief that it was possible for the same divine source to have found several earthly representatives. But Brownell confirmed the plagiarism was deliberate, having done it himself. He also asserted that the Universal Friend had sent two followers to steal his verboten prophetic manuscript from its publisher's office. Although Brownell recovered the document, he claimed that it was conveyed to the Friend before it was returned, so that the Comforter could ridicule its contents and pretend divine omniscience when he summoned Brownell to appear before him.

Like any apostate narrative, *Enthusiastical Errors* is a blend of truth and lies; the exposé is likely based on Valentine Rathbun's famous anti-Shaker narrative, first printed in 1781.[8] Nevertheless, Brownell's pamphlet offers one of the few unofficial firsthand accounts of the Friend's early ministry. By explaining how he became "attach'd to her Doctrine," Brownell desired to show how it "prevails upon others" to convince them to join the Universal Friends.[9] His description of the effectiveness of the Friend's persuasions is credible and sincere.

Although Brownell hoped to destroy the Friend's ministry, he refuted assertions that the Comforter claimed to be Jesus returned, explaining that the All-Friend considered his ministry a continuation of Jesus Christ's. As subsequent American messiahs would do, the Friend relied on a distinction between the Christ spirit, which is immortal, and Jesus of Nazareth, its temporary mortal host. During sermons, the Friend told his listeners that the Christ spirit had returned to lift Jemima's body in the same way that he had lifted Jesus's body many centuries before, and that his dwelling within a woman's body represented the fulfillment of the prophecies of Jeremiah 31:22, which ambiguously states, "the Lord hath created a new thing in the earth, A woman shall compass a man." Because it reinforced his claim to be a divine male spirit inhabiting a female human body, this verse was one of the Friend's favorite passages of scripture. Similarly, Brownell asserts that the Friend was often inclined to read

> a Description that she has, that the Turks gave antiently
> concerning our Lord Jesus Christ's outward Appearance, his
> Shapes, Stature, Features and Complexion, and Hair, with a
> long loose Gown, and his Hair being black, and curled in his
> Neck, or upon his Shoulders, and parted upon the Top, after
> the Manner of the Nazarenes, and then that they may look
> upon her and see how near she resembles those Descriptions.[10]

Such heavy-handed insinuations, Brownell attests, were followed by recitation of additional biblical passages meant to bolster listeners' belief that they beheld the Second Coming of Christ. These included Revelation 21:2–3, which describes "the holy city, new Jerusalem, coming down from God out of heaven, prepared as a bride adorned for her husband." The Friend wished for his listeners to associate this adorned bride with Jemima's body, raised up and anointed by the Spirit of God.

Although Universal Friends took care to avoid gendered pronouns when referring to the Comforter, critics and apostates like Brownell insistently referred to Jemima Wilkinson rather than the Public Universal Friend. Because it was highly uncommon and regarded as unseemly for a woman to speak in public in these years, "her" preaching was considered an act of insuperable arrogance. As Brownell writes:

> She exhorts in a pathetic Manner, with great Confidence
> and Boldness, and Confirmation of her being right, and all

others to be wrong; says, that she has an immediate Revelation for all she delivers; that she is the greatest Minister that
God has sent to the People this seventeen Hundred and odd
Years, and advancing herself to live as she exhorts others
to, fully in a State of Perfection, and no Liability of Error,
or Possibility of Defect in any Respect; and thus with many
great and exalted Expressions in Allusion to herself, (though
in a mystical Way) she utters and holds forth, which to many
serious, sincere, seeking people, it seems to have great effect,
for no Person would rationally think, that any Person in their
right Senses, would dare to hold forth and affirm such great
and exalted Things concerning themselves, and to have such
a great and marvelous Mission.

Although many besides Brownell assailed the Friend's arrogance, it was only through the strength of tremendous conviction
and righteousness that the Comforter was able to stand before audiences that sometimes contained as many leering cynics as repenting
sinners. Many who heard him were convinced by the display. Even
Brownell admitted that as a result of the Friend's somber sermons, he
was "awaken'd at Times to a serious Concern of my immortal State"
and encouraged to "seek some Way of Redress and Recovery" for the
sake of his salvation. He was not the only one so deeply affected:
Brownell asserts "many awakened ones" among the Friend's listeners
were "much taken in with her."

Brownell believed the Friend's followers were mostly "ignorant and illiterate People."[11] He reported that women in particular
were moved to join the Comforter. This came as no surprise, considering the Friend's assertions that both men and women should
stand to testify their faith and speak the prophecies they received in
meetings. The All-Friend's incipient feminism, which continued to
develop, staked out another important characteristic of his messianic
movement, one that marked those of his successors: each subsequent

American messiah would attract a predominantly female following, often through promises of equal rights among the faithful.

. . .

WHEREVER HE WENT, the Friend made himself disagreeable among well-to-do Quakers and old-light Congregationalists by chastising those who made their fortunes off the slave trade and selling rum to Native Americans.[12] This included a significant segment of the Rhode Island and Connecticut aristocracy. Drawing attention to these ill-gotten gains—and to the ministers who fattened their tithing hauls by them—did not endear the Friend to those in positions of power. But the Comforter's attempts to make inroads among families with the financial means to facilitate his operations were not conducted in vain: in Judge William Potter, a Rhode Island Supreme Court justice, the Friend had found a useful patron.

The Potters were a wealthy slave-owning family who lived on a commodious estate in South Kingston known by the Puritanical name of Little Rest. Judge Potter's daughter, Alice Hazard, was the first of the Potters to fall firmly under the influence of the Friend of Sinners. Others in the family soon followed. Their conversions were probably the result of the Friend's excoriating tirades against the evils of slavery: Little Rest had been built by exactly the kind of blood money the Friend deplored, and the family patriarch was bullied into inviting the Friend to share his dwelling by the fear of potential damnation the Friend assured him would result from his family's sinful legacy. After moving in, the Comforter declared South Kingston his headquarters, necessitating a fourteen-room addition to the Potter residence.

Association with such a notorious personage as the Public Universal Friend killed Potter's political career, as he well knew it would. Ezra Stiles, president of Yale and a founder of the College in the English Colony of Rhode Island and Providence Plantations (later Brown University), went to Little Rest to bring the judge to his senses. But Stiles was hardly the sort of person who could turn the Potters against their new Friend: he was a Congregational minister who arrived at Yale by currying the favor of New Englanders who'd grown rich off the slave trade. No better example of the hypocrisy the Friend deplored could be found in all New England. Stiles departed Little Rest dumbfounded by his lack of success. He nevertheless managed to do considerable long-term damage to the Friend's reputation: Stiles reported that the Friend had appointed twelve apostles and reconfirmed the rumor that the All-Friend claimed to be the Messiah. Of Alice Hazard, he wrote: "she says Jemima is the *son of G^d and the Messiah reappear^d in flesh.*"[13]

Stiles thought that Alice, and perhaps others in the family, were experiencing a fit of religious insanity. Meanwhile, the Friend consolidated his hold on the Potters. Penelope Hazard Potter and Alice Potter Hazard became lifelong adherents, and Penelope married another follower, Benjamin Brown Jr., whose four siblings were already Universal Friends. Judge Potter and his son Thomas likewise joined; as signs of their devotion, the former began freeing his slaves, and the latter married the disgraced Patience Wilkinson. Benedict Arnold Potter—later known only as Arnold Potter, having sensibly dropped his embarrassing first name—dropped out of Harvard to court the Friend's closest aide, Benjamin Brown's sister Sarah.

Shortly after settling at Little Rest, the Friend of Sinners began to issue prophecy that the end of days was much closer than anyone supposed: he predicted April 1, 1780, as the date of the apocalypse. Although this was proven incorrect on April 2, a remarkable omen soon followed: that May 19 was New England's infamous Dark Day, a date on which the sky dimmed to a shade of black across New England at noontime, possibly due to smoke from distant, unseen fires. The Friend seized on this bewildering natural event, claiming it was a sign of the apocalypse he'd predicted. The Dark Day was indeed a portentous coincidence, considering Jesus's prophecy—reported in Matthew 24, and delivered as part of the same speech in which he warned of the false prophets who would attempt to usurp his role—that a darkening of the sun, along with the moon and stars, would be among the first celestial signals of the apocalypse.

The Potters' daughter Susannah died on the Dark Day, lending extra solemnity to the Friend's pronouncement. Rumor later went out that the Comforter attempted to raise Susannah from the dead, although the veracity of these claims, like many about the Public Universal Friend, is thrown into question by the more obvious falsehoods alongside which they appear. The Friend did perform faith healings at this stage of his ministry, however, making a show of the laying on of hands during public meetings.[14] According to Abner Brownell, the Comforter blamed failed healings on a lack of faith on the part of the sick person— a convenient tactic later repeated by Father Divine and Jim Jones.

The Potter household remained the Comforter's headquarters for the next nine years. While based at Little Rest, the Friend enticed members away from the Kingston Friends meeting, including a former captain of the colonial militia named James Parker. Although he later became a troublesome apostate, Captain Parker was first one of the Friend's closest aides: Brownell alleged that it was Parker, along with a follower called Mehitable Smith, who absconded with his prophetic manuscript at the Friend's behest.

The Comforter's new headquarters made it easier for him to travel between incipient communities of Universal Friends that emerged across the region. In East Greenwich, Rhode Island, several families united to the Friend's cause and built their own meetinghouse. Similar strongholds emerged in New Bedford and New Milford, Connecticut, where Universal Friends erected another meetinghouse in 1784. Quaker congregations had not yielded in their view that the Friend's ministry was a preposterous heresy, and swiftly excommunicated any of their members caught attending one of the Friend's sermons. Rather than deter the Friend's advances, this defensive tactic only brought those who were punished—as well as their relatives—more securely into the Comforter's embrace.

Trotting between these communities of Universal Friendship, the Comforter continued to gain celebrity for the ostentatious way he chose to travel. The Friend had adopted the custom of riding as advance guard of his party. On one such occasion, the Comforter was thrown from his horse in the vicinity of a boy called Thomas Hathaway Jr., who rushed to assist the fallen rider. In gratitude, the Friend invited Thomas, then sixteen years old, to ride beside him at the head of his entourage whenever they passed through the region, as long as he observed the deference of never bringing his horse level with the Friend's. Thomas accepted, and through this happenstance, another important family became connected to the Universal Friends.

The Hathaway family bore the traces of social distress that tend to characterize those drawn into eccentric religious movements: they were traumatized by the war and in need of the Comforter's spiritual guidance. Thomas's mother, Deborah Gilbert Hathaway, was the daughter of a British colonel stationed in Nova Scotia. Her husband, Thomas Sr., was a wealthy shipbuilder who faced an obvious predicament when war broke out. With such clear connections to the Loyalists, Thomas Sr. decided to spend the war years in Canada, leaving his wife and children to fend for themselves. After returning from Nova Scotia, the elder Hathaway converted to his family's new religion in 1784, and became an important financial backer of the Friend's projects.[15]

Meanwhile, young Thomas Jr. had become one of the Friend's most steadfast companions. In a journal partially dictated by the Friend, who apparently realized that it would enter the historical record, the younger Hathaway wrote that "the great friend" drew crowds everywhere he went. Even the All-Friend's enemies were forced to admit his popularity: according to Brownell, some of the Comforter's sermons attracted thousands of listeners.[16]

The Friend's traveling ministry continued to yield adherents, including several who played pivotal roles in the Friend's developing plans to remove his followers to the frontier, away from the coastal cities he predicted would be destroyed for their wickedness. As had been the case from the beginning, women occupied crucial decision-making roles in the Friend's ministry. Among the lifelong devotees was Sarah Richards, who joined sometime in the middle of the decade. Following her husband's death in 1786, Richards became one of the Friend's most trusted advisers. After her conversion, Richards began to experience trances and prophetic dreams, and was one of several female followers who sometimes dressed in the gender-neutral style favored by the Comforter. Ruth Prichard, who became the movement's scribe and compiled its Death Book, became a lifelong follower after converting the same year.[17]

3. THE ALL-FRIEND IN THE CITY OF BROTHERLY LOVE

HAVING MADE A NAME for himself across central New England, the Universal Friend decided it was time to storm the ramparts of that great citadel of wayward Quakerdom: Philadelphia. Formerly the second largest city in the British Empire, the City of Brotherly Love was a bustling commercial metropolis and was still the political center of the thirteen newly independent states. After the All-Friend announced his intentions to evangelize in Pennsylvania, Thomas Hathaway Sr. hastened to sell his property, uproot his family, and join the missionary expedition into the seat of colonial power. Aside from Hathaway and the Comforter, the first southern missionary party included Judge Potter, Arnold Potter, Alice Hazard, Sarah Brown, and another follower named William Turpin.

There were few if any Universal Friends in Philadelphia at this time, but the Comforter's reputation preceded him. The missionaries at first had trouble finding accommodations, allegedly due to the "singular" costumes the women wore. Eventually the party found lodging in Elfreth's Alley, where they were hosted by a widow whose home was subsequently bombarded with bricks and stones.[1]

The Friend was shunned by Quaker meetinghouses on this first visit to Philadelphia in 1782, but obtained permission to preach in a Methodist church on Fourth Street. He drew such large crowds that some of the curious attendees could not gain entry. The marquis de Barbé-Marbois, a French diplomat residing in Philadelphia, managed to get into one of the October meetings. His recollections of the Friend demonstrate the reach of the evangelist's celebrity: "Jemima Wilkinson has just arrived here," he wrote. "Some religious denominations awaited her with apprehension, others with extreme impatience. Her story is so odd, her dogmas so new, that she has not failed to attract general attention." Taking note that a French noble and his companions were among the audience, the Friend implored his listeners, "Do these strangers believe that their presence in the house of the Lord flatters me? I disdain their honors, I scorn greatness and good fortune. Do not seek me, do not listen to me, unless you are touched by grace. Go away, no longer profane this temple, if you are still in the snares of the infernal angel."[2]

Barbé-Marbois was impressed with the Friend's "melancholy and thoughtful air," but like many he was more interested in the Comforter's physical appearance. "This soul sent from heaven," he wrote, "has chosen a rather beautiful body for its dwelling, and many living ladies would not be unwilling to inhabit that outer shell. . . . She has beautiful features, a fine mouth, and animated eyes. Her travels have tanned her a little." The marquis observed the All-Friend's hair in great detail, describing "her" graceful center part and shoulder-length locks, which she washed daily—a strange custom in those days—but never powdered. Naturally, the Frenchman was fascinated by the Friend's preference for shrouding his shapely body in masculine attire, which on this occasion was a smock that draped to the floor and offered "all imaginable modesty." Nor did the marquis fail to notice the Comforter's famous Quaker hat, which the preacher removed and, in his customary departure from Quaker etiquette, placed upon the pulpit where he preached.[3]

As with many others who reported on the Friend's activities, Barbé-Marbois seemed to think he was listening to a handsome woman with a preference for men's clothing, without realizing or acknowledging that the Friend no longer identified with the female sex. Even so, he marveled at the boldness of the Friend's activities, and at the liberality of the Philadelphians for tolerating them. "They would have burned her in Spain and Portugal," he declared, referring to the Catholic Inquisition. "Here, you can be sure that if she does not accomplish very much good, at any rate the perfect tolerance which they show her will do no harm."[4]

Among Philadelphia's more educated population, the Friend won fewer converts than he did in rural New England. The Comforter's folksy Yankee accent, unremarkable in Connecticut, became a liability in Pennsylvania. Nevertheless, Philadelphia produced enduring converts to the Universal Friends. Among the most important disciples were the Malin siblings: Rachel, Margaret, Enoch, and Elijah. Another was David Wagener, whose home in Worcester, a town just outside Philadelphia, would become the seat of the Friend's Pennsylvania mission.

Another adherent played an indirect role in helping to shape the Friend's evolving vision for establishing a New Jerusalem on the new nation's western frontier. This was Christopher Marshall, a man with pantheistic and mystic leanings. Marshall enjoyed debating the meanings of biblical prophecies with the Friend, and testing the preacher on the consistency of his teachings.[5] Scholars suppose that it was Marshall who acquainted the Friend with the beliefs and activities of the Ephrata community, another unusual religious sect then operating in Lancaster County, Pennsylvania.[6] The practices of the Ephratans, which included celibacy and apostolic communalism, would soon be incorporated into the Comforter's teachings.

Ephrata had been established in 1732 as an offshoot of the Society of the Woman in the Wilderness, a colony founded in 1697 by forty millenarian students of the Christian mystic Johann Jacob Zimmerman. After Zimmerman died on the eve of the group's departure for America from Germany, leadership fell to Johannes Kelpius, who led the sect of celibate mystics to settle along Wissahickon Creek near Philadelphia. The Woman in the Wilderness community took its name from Revelation 12, a passage of great importance to American messianic leaders. In that chapter of John's apocalyptic vision, there appears "a woman clothed with the sun, and the moon under her feet, and upon her head a crown of twelve stars." As the woman labors to give birth to a boy who will "rule all nations with a rod of iron," a "great red dragon" looks on, waiting to devour the child. But the babe is delivered up to heaven by divine intervention, and the woman flees into the wilderness, "where she hath a place prepared of God."

Like the Public Universal Friend, those at the Woman in the Wilderness colony were obsessed with the apocalypse described in the Book of Revelation. The mystic Christianity they practiced incorporated occult rituals derived from the European esoteric tradition, as well as theatrical solstice ceremonies replete with chants and bonfires. The community tabernacle possessed a telescope, which Kelpius used to interpret the heavens for signs of the coming millennium. Although the colony did not last very long, it injected a strong dose of European occult traditions into American folk religion. Community members wore "astrological amulets," conducted pagan healing rituals, and practiced alchemy. Kelpius sometimes cast horoscopes for visitors from Philadelphia who came to seek his advice.[7] Regarded as witchcraft in other times and contexts, the occult traditions observed in Wissahickon found a new home when a series of schisms branching outward from the original forty members produced the Ephrata commune, established by a Pietist mystic called Conrad Beissel. It was the Ephratan variety of occult lore that the Friend adapted to his own evolving teachings.

The Ephratans drew deeply from the writings of Jakob Böhme (1575–1624), a Pietist visionary whose ideas became the source of recurring theories about God's bisexual nature. Böhme's notion of a bigendered God was of interest to several American messianic societies that sought to establish gender equality, beginning with the Universal Friends. In Böhme's reading of Genesis, Adam possessed an androgynous, bigendered body in the golden age before the Fall. And since God had created prelapsarian man in His own image, it followed that He was both masculine and feminine. Beissel also believed that alchemical experiments could reveal the occult laws that governed transformations between matter and spirit. Following the recovery of this sacred knowledge, which was presumed to be lost in the Fall from grace, the Ephratans would lead the regeneration of the human race by restoring humankind's original bigendered form through some kind of "alchemical marriage" between the sexes. The crucial ingredients for the alchemical reaction, Beissel believed, were conserved sexual matter and spiritual energy. These would be accrued through the practice of celibate communism: Ephratans held all property in common and discouraged marriage and procreation. Those who had committed fully to the celibate life lived segregated by gender, and were venerated for being more spiritually advanced than the fornicating brethren. These ideas were not as fringe as modern readers might suppose, but derived from occult and Hermetic lore popularized by the Freemasons and Rosicrucian societies. Benjamin Franklin and George Washington were both acquainted with Ephratan mystical science, which was described to them by Beissel's successor, Peter Müller. Although they were pacifists, the Ephratans were humanitarians, and had hosted a military hospital for soldiers in Washington's army wounded at Brandywine in 1777.[8]

It is unknown whether the All-Friend ever became personally acquainted with Peter Müller. However, it was not long after the Friend's first visit with Christopher Marshall in Philadelphia that the All-Friend adopted the Ephratan practice of observing the Sabbath on Saturday rather than Sunday, and began preaching the virtues of celibacy.[9] Although he never formally required that his followers forsake all carnal contact, the Comforter thereafter desired sexual purity among those who called themselves Universal Friends, and considered his authority to approve or disapprove of marriages within his ranks to be absolute. By the time of the Friend's second visit to Philadelphia, his most devoted followers had already begun making plans to remove themselves from the sinful world: they wanted to live in a place like the Ephrata Cloister, where they might surround themselves with those who lived according to the Friend's commandments.

. . .

AFTER HIS FIRST VISIT to Philadelphia, the Comforter returned repeatedly to tend the flame of his reputation. The All-Friend had become a celebrity in the City of Brotherly Love, where news of his return in 1784 drew crowds as large as 700 listeners. Following a fortnight in the city, the evangelist retired to the Wagener estate, where he remained for a month before returning to New England in October via a preaching tour through New Jersey. Before departing, he summoned Thomas Hathaway to replace him in Worcester, so as not to leave the Pennsylvania converts without an intimate connection to the Public Universal Friend.[10]

Hathaway returned to New England when winter was over. James Parker went to Pennsylvania as the Friend's representative the following fall, but his tenure was not a success. The Universal Friends in the Philadelphia region became annoyed by his pretensions to sainthood in the new dispensation. Sarah Richards was next to preside over the Pennsylvania Universal Friends. Her appointment demonstrated the commitment to gender equality that distinguished the Society; both Richards and Ruth Prichard preached the Friend's message to prospective converts.[11] The Comforter enjoyed an expanding circle of devotees in southeastern Pennsylvania as a result of this evangelism.

Naturally, no one so eccentric as the Universal Friends went without periodic slander in the Philadelphia press. In 1787, salacious reporting on allegations of an attempted murder at the Wagener estate devolved into a smear campaign against the sect and provided the occasion for their affairs to be debated in print. Letters to the editor suggested the Universal Friends were indulging in sexual activities less benign than celibacy, including lesbianism.[12] Although this worried Sarah Richards, who considered it her duty to respond in writing, the Comforter sailed placidly above such worldly criticism, telling Richards, "I believe that the wicked will find some other Business to due before it is long Besides publishing me and them that Desire to due well in News Papers, Don't be troubled Dear Soul."[13]

But the Friend learned for himself how damaging the papers had been to his reputation when he returned to Pennsylvania in December 1787. Wary of the animosity aroused against him, the Comforter wisely remained in Montgomery County until May, when the Universal Friends dared once more to hold a public meeting in Philadelphia. Instead of curious freethinkers and excommunicated Quakers, the Friend now drew hostile crowds, stirred into opposition by negative publicity. After two days of preaching, the Friend retreated back to Worcester.

Meanwhile, the Friend's operatives in New England were engaged in preparations for their exit west. Like many others in New England, the Society of Universal Friends took an interest in the territories of western New York, which had been opened to American frontier settlement after Great Britain ceded the territory to the United States in the Treaty of Paris of 1783. Jemima's brother Jeptha was dispatched to scout the region in 1785 with the help of Seneca guides. The following year, the New Milford congregation of Universal Friends voted to establish a common fund to purchase land for a frontier settlement, where they would prepare a place for God: the New Jerusalem mentioned in Revelation 21.

Acquiring land in the newly opened territories was a thorny matter. Both the United States and Great Britain ignored the sovereignty of the Seneca Nation, but recognized that Native Americans still owned the land. A variety of other tangled claims, as well as uncertainty over the boundary between territories controlled by New York and Massachusetts, made land acquisition exceedingly complex. Into this confusing arrangement blundered James Parker. Eager to prove himself of worth to the Friend, Parker undertook the responsibility of finding a suitable locale for the New Jerusalem. Unfortunately, this was a disastrous delegation of authority that the Friend and others soon came to regret. After a series of bad deals with shady speculators, Parker had squandered the thousands of dollars entrusted to him by the New Milford believers for little more than 1,100 acres. But if the setback was disappointing, it did nothing to deter the Friend from proceeding with his plan to retreat into the wilderness. The apocalypse was nigh, and establishing an earthly kingdom worthy of being spared God's wrath was what the Comforter most desired.[14]

4. NEW JERUSALEM

B Y THE TIME the Friend finally departed for the New York frontier in March 1790, his colony was already well established by the
enterprising New England believers. Benjamin Brown had wintered
in Genesee County in 1787–88, but the majority of the New Milford
pioneers left Schenectady for the Genesee territory the following June.
On the final night of their journey west that spring, the party camped
on the east side of Seneca Lake. They heard falling water from their
campsite and, after traveling around the lake the next morning, found
the Outlet of Keuka Lake on the western shore. The site was pictur-
esque, and the waterfall offered an ideal location for a mill. Believing
the land to fall within the parcel that Parker purchased, the pioneers
put down roots. They cleared trees, burned them for potash, planted
wheat, and built a sawmill and a gristmill, as well as a number of log
dwellings. They called the settlement City Hill.

Although wood was plentiful, essential materials such as shingles,
nails, and glass had to be brought all the way from Utica. Building a
gristmill was a particular feat of determination: its grinding stones had
to be brought by sled in winter, then ferried across Seneca Lake on a
sailboat built by the intrepid Thomas Hathaway Jr.[1] When the Friend
arrived at City Hill, the village of 260 was the largest white settlement in the newly opened New York territories. More of the Friend's
adherents continued to move west, ultimately attracting several hundred pioneers to the region.[2] This might have been considered a success, but the rising population led to friction as approximately sixty

families crowded onto fewer than 1,200 acres. Those who contributed small fortunes to the communal scheme began to resent those who only gave what little they could. The promise they had made to live communally had not seemed so confining before Parker bungled the community's land deal. Poorer members of the Universal Friends had been promised subsistence acreage on communal lands, supplied by the wealthier congregants. Having sold what little they had and made the trek west, they trusted their fates to the Friend.

The Universal Friends eventually managed to increase their land holdings to more than 14,000 acres. Although expansion might have eased the crowding at City Hill, a rapid increase in the value of western lands injected toxic greed into the community. Now that the territory was worth more than thirty times the original investment, those who contributed to the initial communal fund fought to retain majority shares. William Potter, James Parker, and a few other Friends ended up with most of the land.[3]

The Friend was deeply unhappy with this, and acted to remove himself from the scene of so much greed. Parker's botched deals had already prompted some dispirited followers to strike out in search of land where they could get a clear title before the bargains were gone. In 1789, Thomas Hathaway Sr. and another wealthy follower, Benedict Robinson, had shrewdly partnered to purchase a pair of townships farther west. In exchange for reimbursement from the Friend's coffers, Hathaway and Robinson deeded land to the Universal Friend through the Friend's business agent, Sarah Richards, who then held the titles in her name.[4]

Thus it was that, halfway into the second decade of his ministry, the Comforter came to found the town of Jerusalem, New York, located on these lands. By 1795, the Friend controlled nearly 5,000 acres, and proceeded to parcel plots to loyal followers who came to Jerusalem from City Hill. Universal Friends who made the second westward procession to Jerusalem tended to be the poorest members of the Society.[5]

Once again, the settlers cleared ground, sowed crops, and erected a new settlement, which included a workshop, meetinghouse, barns, a shed, and numerous log cabins in which the Universal Friends dwelt until the construction of a sawmill alongside a nearby stream allowed them to begin building frame structures. Eventually they cleared pastures and began raising cattle and sheep. Maple sugar became one of the colony's cash crops. Later, the property included a cheese factory, a spinning and weaving shop, and a carriage house that sheltered the Friend's famous coach, ostentatiously adorned with the initials "U.F."[6]

More than fifty families settled on the land purchased by the All-Friend, who functioned as the spiritual and political head of their quasi-communal order. Although the Friend's enemies continued to allege that he lived off the toil of his followers, most of the labor done in Jerusalem was paid. The Comforter was by no means a freeloader, and proved he was not above hoeing, weeding, or basket weaving. The Friend additionally acted as nurse and healer to those who fell ill or injured; he learned to dress wounds and reset broken bones.

Communalism was only ever practiced in a loose way reminiscent of the Puritan social compacts, and the primary beneficiaries were the Friend and the coterie of a dozen or more celibate women who lived with him. Sarah Richards had died in 1793, but the Friend was joined at his residence by the Malin sisters, a freed slave named Chloe Towerhill, and Mary Bean, who took charge of the dairy that was eventually established in Jerusalem. Other followers, celibate and not, lived nearby in houses on the Friend's property.[7]

Jerusalem contained an unusually large proportion of female heads of household, likely because the gender imbalance among the Friend's followers meant that some dwellings in the community housed only women.[8] Many of those who visited the region commented on this trend with annoyance, and accused the Friend of alienating women from their husbands. Jerusalem also contained modest but meaningful racial diversity. Towerhill was not the only black member of the Society; a handful of others are mentioned in its records, indicating that the community practiced racial as well as gender egalitarianism, even if the number of nonwhite Universal Friends was never more than a few.[9]

. . .

IN JERUSALEM, the Universal Friends settled into a slow but inexorable decline. Far from the raucous crowds of Philadelphia and the seeking souls of war-torn New England, the Public Universal Friend had few opportunities to make new converts. And although not strictly enforced, celibacy remained in practice among the most faithful, meaning that few children were born into the sect. Members of the younger generation chafed at the austerity of their parents' religion, and at the humiliating punishments they witnessed the Comforter levy against his most loyal followers. The Friend of Sinners sometimes ordered those who transgressed his advice to wear bells that drew attention to their misdeeds. On one famous occasion, the Comforter allegedly forced Benedict Robinson to wear a Quaker bride's cap for three months after he married without the Friend's consent.[10]

As they grew older, and as the religious enthusiasm of the community waned into routinized farm work punctuated by Saturday Sabbath meetings, members of the sect defected. Even such stalwarts as Judge Potter, James Parker, and David Wagener abandoned the Comforter. After he and his father left the Society, a rebellious young Abraham Wagener was known to adorn his horses with jingle bells and drive a sleigh full of young women past the Jerusalem meetinghouse on Saturday mornings merely to annoy the Friend.[11]

Eliza Richards, Sarah's orphaned daughter, caused the Friend even greater irritation. Forbidden to marry Enoch Malin, an alcoholic ne'er-do-well of whom the Friend heartily disapproved, Eliza climbed out a window and eloped with him instead. On a horse that had belonged to her mother, Eliza rode with Enoch to meet James Parker. As a justice of the peace, Parker was authorized to pronounce them married. He did so to spite the Friend, whom he now considered his adversary.

Two years later, in 1798, Enoch and Eliza hatched a scheme to sue for ownership of the Friend's vast holdings in Jerusalem. Before she died in November 1793, Sarah Richards had her doctor draw up a will indicating that the property she held for the Friend would pass into the trusteeship of Rachel Malin. Because it was drafted by a physician instead of a lawyer, the will contained irregularities that allowed Enoch and Eliza to challenge its authenticity. With so much valuable land at stake, they succeeded in retaining Elisha Williams, a lawyer experienced in crooked frontier land schemes. The case dragged on for decades: Enoch, Eliza, and the Comforter all died before it was settled—but not before Enoch had turned a tidy profit by illegally selling some of the disputed land.

Other high-level defectors were determined to humiliate the Friend. Thomas Hathaway Jr. had split from the Society following his father's death. Judge Potter's son Arnold Potter likewise left the fold, and followed in his father's footsteps by becoming a judge in Ontario County. Each man felt he'd lost a family fortune to the Friend's ministry, and conspired to seek revenge. In September 1799, Parker issued a warrant for the Friend's arrest on charges of blasphemy. Thomas Hathaway Jr. volunteered to serve the warrant in person by apprehending the Friend as he rode to hold a meeting at City Hill. But the All-Friend proved the better horseman, and thwarted the plot by escaping. Enoch Malin was next to try apprehending the Comforter. He and a constable boldly attempted to storm the house at Jerusalem, but the Friend's loyal servants repelled their attack. A final, successful attempt required a posse of men to surround the Friend's house after midnight and break down the door with an ax. This time the Comforter was ill in bed, and in no condition to escape or resist. The invaders were satisfied by his promise to appear in court when his health was restored. The All-Friend lived up to his word, and used his sworn testimony to preach to those assembled in the courthouse. The case was dismissed when the jury determined that blasphemy was not an indictable offense.[12]

. . .

ALTHOUGH THE PUBLIC UNIVERSAL FRIEND had virtually
ended his public career with the retreat to Jerusalem, the settlement
remained open to visitors and became an early nineteenth-century
tourist attraction. One such visitor, François Alexandre Frédéric, duc
de la Rochefoucauld-Liancourt, immortalized the Comforter in his
popular travelogues after stopping to have a look at New Jerusalem on
his way to Niagara Falls in 1795.

When the duke's party arrived, the Friend was dressed in his usual
garb of ministerial robes and a white silk cravat. The Comforter first
offered the visitors a sermon, which gave Rochefoucauld the opportunity to observe the Friend's "fine teeth, and beautiful eyes," which made
"her" appear at least a decade younger than the reported forty years.
But the duke was bored by the Friend's "pedantic" sermon, which he
described as "an eternal repetition of the same topics—death, sin, and
repentance." Although he complimented the food to which his party
was treated, describing it as the best they'd tasted since leaving Philadelphia, the duke was perturbed by the Friend's manners: according
to his custom, the Comforter dined alone in his bedroom. When he
reappeared, the prophet had undergone a dramatic costume change
designed to impress the visitors. As the duke recalled:

> The all-friend had by this time exchanged her former dress
> for that of a fine Indian lady, which, however, was cut out
> in the same fashion as the former [robes]. Her hair and eye-
> brows had again been combed. She did not utter a syllable
> respecting our dinner; nor did she offer to make any apology
> for her absence. Constantly engaged in personating the part
> she has assumed, she descanted in a sanctimonious, mystic
> tone, on death, and on the happiness of having been an use-
> ful instrument to others in the way of their salvation. She
> afterwards gave us a rhapsody of prophecies to read, ascribed

to one Dr. Love, who was beheaded in Cromwell's time; wherein she clearly discerned, according to her accounts, the French revolution, the decline and downfall of popery, and the impending end of the world. Finding, however, that this conversation was but ill adapted to engage our attention, she cut short her harangue at once. We had indeed already seen more than enough to estimate the character of this bad actress, whose pretended sanctity only inspired us with contempt and disgust, and who is altogether incapable of imposing upon any person of common understanding, unless those of the most simple minds, or downright enthusiasts. Her speeches are so strongly contradicted by the tenor of her actions; her whole conduct; her expence, compared with that of other families within a circumference of fifty miles; her way of living, and her dress, form such a striking contrast with her harangues on the subject of condemning earthly enjoyments; and the extreme assiduity with which she is continually endeavoring to induce children, over whom she has any influence, to leave their parents, and form a part of her community; all those particulars so strongly militate against the doctrine of peace and universal love, which she is incessantly preaching, that we were all actually struck with abhorrence of her duplicity and hypocrisy, as soon as the first emotions of our curiosity subsided.[13]

The duke concluded that in spite of the Comforter's obvious flaws, there was a sufficient supply of "simple minded" men and women in the frontier region to keep the colony going indefinitely. Appearing in several contemporary periodicals, Rochefoucauld's damning account of his visit to Jerusalem was the most widely circulated biographical sketch of the Public Universal Friend. Along with David Hudson's slanderous biography, it transmitted a biased and dismissive view of the Friend and his accomplishments to posterity.

. . .

FINALLY, AFTER YEARS of suffering from dropsy and following a painful final illness, the Friend realized that he was on his deathbed in June of 1819. He had already preached his final sermon at Patience Wilkinson's funeral on April 19. Shortly before he died on Friday, July 1, in the forty-third year of his ministry, the Comforter told his people: "My friends I must soon depart—I am going—this night I leave you." The body the Friend had inhabited, formerly belonging to Jemima Wilkinson, was sixty-six years old when it died a second time.

Sabbath meeting was held as usual the next day, with 200 people in attendance. It was the closest the Friend came to a funeral, which was a vanity he expressly forbade. Later, a casket with an oval window allowed mourners to bid farewell to the Friend of Sinners. The coffin was interred in the cellar of the Friend's final residence, and later transferred to a secret grave, in compliance with the Friend's wishes.

Folktales about the Public Universal Friend circulated as late as 1936, when travel writer Carl Carmer profiled Jemima Wilkinson for the *New Yorker*. Carmer first heard about Wilkinson from a grandfather who grew up in Dryden. While still a young man, Carmer's grandfather got a job building houses on the property of some "strange folk" who, in his opinion, were not adequately feeding his work crew. When they voiced complaint to the man who had hired them, he told the carpenters that he would consult "the Friend" about how to resolve the problem. Another of those present understood what he meant, and reminded him that the Friend had died. No, the man told him, the Comforter had only "left time," and was still available for consultation. After going down to the lakefront and having what appeared to be an animated conversation with an invisible interlocutor, the man returned to explain that the Friend and God had decreed the carpenters would dine on cod and potatoes that evening.[14]

5. MOTHER ANN

BY THE TIME the body formerly belonging to Jemima Wilkinson was entombed in Jerusalem, another messiah had already come and gone from New England. Although her tenure was shorter than that of the Public Universal Friend, Ann Lee is the better remembered of the pair. She was also far less cagey about her declarations. According to her surviving followers, Ann Lee proclaimed herself the female vessel of the Christ spirit, and announced that her anointment as the female Christ marked the beginning of a new millennial dispensation. The concreteness of her claims left no room for doubt, which is partially why her legacy proved more enduring.

Ann Lee's adherents eventually called themselves the United Society of Believers in Christ's Second Appearing, but are more commonly known as the Shakers. Although she died in 1784, just a decade after her arrival in the United States, the devotion that Ann Lee inspired in her followers, and the shrewdness with which they executed their communal economic scheme, enabled them to carry on the movement long after her death.

Ann Lee was born in 1736 to a poor British family who consigned her to child labor in Manchester's factories, a relatively new phenomenon wrought by industrialization, and one to which the city's impoverished families were ashamed to resort. As a girl, Ann worked in Manchester textile mills and never learned to read or write.[1] Basing their accounts of her childhood on assiduously recorded but completely unverifiable lore, Shaker scribes described young Ann as a serious girl "subject to strong religious impressions and given to reverie and vision."[2] Official Shaker histories indicate that the girl had an intense aversion to carnal coupling, which she had no choice but to overhear in the family's tiny house on Toad Lane.[3] So strongly did her parents' sexual activity offend her conscience that Ann Lee chastised her mother for allowing herself to be defiled. The young woman's innate piety and spiritual tremors were supplemented by the Methodist revivals of the transatlantic Great Awakening; Ann Lee later told followers that she went in person to hear George Whitefield preach when he came to her native city.

Ann's mother was the more religious of her parents, but she died while her daughter was very young, leaving Ann in the care of a father she exasperated with her sensitivity to spiritual visions. The girl continued to toil away her childhood, trading cotton-sorting and work at the loom for fur-cutting in a hat manufactory, then taking a job as a hospital cook. Ending the exploitation of women and girls that Ann Lee witnessed in the factories remained a primary concern in her future career as a prophet—a priority second only to ending women's sexual exploitation in the home.

As Ann reached maturity, her father wished for her to marry. This suggestion horrified the budding mystic, but the patriarch ultimately prevailed. He had his daughter married against her wishes in 1762, to a blacksmith called Abraham Stanley.

To observe that Ann Lee hated married life is to put things mildly. Although she admitted her husband's initial devotion to her, Lee physically resisted and spiritually recoiled from intimate relations with him, particularly after enduring the trauma of three stillbirths and the death of her only child to survive infancy. Her spiritual anguish became so great that it drove Lee out of her private spiritual intuitions and into the arms of a small and embattled religious sect helmed by two tailors from Bolton called Jane and James Wardley, a husband-and-wife pair of prophets who had received divine news that the millennium was soon to begin. Shaker church history holds that when Ann entrusted Jane with her distress over carnal relations, the latter confided that she and James had a "spiritual marriage" in which they observed the practice of celibacy. This vow of purity, Jane told Ann, was responsible for the couple's refined spiritual status.[4]

The Wardleys were former Quakers who had been forced to leave the Society of Friends after they began to witness the workings of prophetic spirits in one another. The gift of spiritual visions awoke in them as a result of their involvement with the Shaking Quakers, one of the numerous sects to emerge in the wake of the Puritan Revolution. In eighteenth-century England, the terms "Shaker" and "Shaking Quaker" were used to refer derisively to any person or group whose religious enthusiasm found expression in bodily movements that were discomfiting for witnesses to behold, including ecstatic fits, trances, and "holy rolling." The century before, similar physical manifestations of religious fervor had earned members of the Society of Friends the initially pejorative name of Quakers.[5]

The Shaking Quakers traced their origins to France. Around 1706, a group of French prophets had begun to emigrate to London, where they settled among the Huguenots who had already fled France. These new arrivals were from the Cévennes region, where a clutch of mystics had begun to receive revelations about the coming millennium. The Cévenole prophets enticed nearby mountain villagers into millennial excitement that included trance visions, seizures, and shaking. After they aroused opposition from Louis XIV, who oversaw the persecution of French Protestants after revoking the Edict of Nantes in 1685, the king added the Cévenole mystics to the category of Protestants he royally encouraged to find somewhere else to worship.

By the time of the French prophets' emigration to England, London already contained a significant community of French émigrés: enough to require at least three churches. The French prophets wasted no time in proselytizing among their countrymen, but English tolerance was limited. The authorities began cracking down on religious enthusiasm among the French in an attempt to stifle the movement. This was only a partial success, as by this time the millennial prophecies had acquired native English adherents who began to evangelize in London and issue millennial prophecies all over England. In 1716, one among the English converts, Mary Keimer, sailed to Pennsylvania to herald the news.[6]

Keimer and others inspired by the French prophets were radically anticlerical, preached the corruption of all established churches, and encouraged laity to testify and prophesy regardless of gender or social status. They were, in short, yet another expression of populist discontent in England, and they emerged at a time when urbanization and industrialization were rapidly changing the English way of life. The new prophetic movements were popular enough to court opposition from the Quakers and Methodists, whose congregations were most at risk of losing members to outbreaks of millennial excitement.[7]

Jane and James Wardley emerged as leaders of one branch of the revived movement around 1747. This was the year they moved to Manchester, where enthusiastic meetings held in the homes of their followers eventually attracted the attention of Ann Lee, who joined the movement in 1758 while still deeply afflicted by a spiritual unrest that was compounded by the death of every child she bore. In the Wardley group, devotion and divine inspiration exceeded even the relaxed bounds of decorum observed by the Quakers and Methodists: the Shakers' inspired trembling and ecstatic convulsions, which were accompanied by emotional wailing, screeching, and "commotions," lasted late into the night.

The shouting and tramping offered a dramatic backdrop for the Shakers' renewed prophecies of the imminent Second Coming. So urgent was their need to spread the word that they barged into other churches to announce the errors of those assembled, and to pronounce themselves equipped with the only true faith—a tactic that radical Quakers had deployed in the seventeenth century.[8]

Manchester responded by ejecting the Shakers from its sanctuaries and imploring the authorities to put a stop to such rude behaviors. The constables were happy to comply, and they began arresting Shakers whenever the opportunity arose. Criminal records of these apprehensions reveal that Ann Lee had become a stout public defender of the faith and was not afraid to be arrested or jailed for expressing her views in ways obnoxious to anyone who did not share them.

According to latter-day Shaker accounts of these early years, it was after one such occasion that Ann Lee came into knowledge of the special mission that God had assigned her. About nine years after joining the sect in 1758, Lee developed prophetic powers that impressed even the Wardleys, who began to prioritize her gifts above their own. Her visions and revelations began to come with greater frequency. After a particularly inspired meeting in the Lee home, a mob dragged Ann away from her family and delivered her to a Manchester prison. The jailers were already acquainted with the prophet, and the warden resolved that it would be the last time she crossed his threshold alive. He locked her away for two weeks without a single meal, but was stunned to discover her alive when her cell was finally opened. Evidently, security was lax enough for one of Lee's devotees to steal into the jail and pour wine and milk through a narrow pipe stuck through the keyhole to her chamber. So dumbstruck were her jailers that Ann Lee strode out of the prison without further detention.

Emerging triumphant from the Manchester dungeon, Ann Lee announced to the Wardleys and the rest of her group that she experienced a new revelation in prison: the Deity had shown her a scene of the original transgression in the Garden of Eden, and communicated to her that carnal relations were the cause of humankind's degeneration. This was not all. Ann Lee, now calling herself "Ann the Word," disclosed that Jesus Christ had appeared in her vision and tasked her with the restoration of the apostolic church. As Shaker theology would later make clear, Jesus of Nazareth had made himself "a temple fit to receive the indwelling Spirit." By refusing further sexual relations, Ann the Word had likewise prepared a suitable dwelling for the Christ spirit, which she received in her Manchester cell. Not everyone was thrilled by this announcement. According to later Shaker hagiography,

Ann Lee testified that her own brother struck her in the face with a broomstick, leaving scars that remained visible for the rest of her life.[9]

In Manchester, opposition to the Shakers remained undiminished, and Ann Lee and her followers withdrew from public ministry by 1773 to concentrate on the revelations they were now receiving regularly from Ann the Word. As life in England became intolerable for the Shakers, the prophet at last received further instruction from God in 1774, directing her to establish the true Millennial Church in America. Accompanied by eight of her most devoted celibate attendants, Ann Lee set sail on the *Mariah* that August.[10] In Manchester, the sails of the remaining Shakers deflated, and the group eventually disbanded.

6. THE UNITED SOCIETY OF BELIEVERS IN CHRIST'S SECOND APPEARING

UPON ARRIVAL IN New York City in the summer of 1774, the nine Shakers dispersed to seek employment. John Hocknell, a former Methodist and the only Shaker with any funds to spare, went up the Hudson to locate a place for the faithful to resettle. He bought a piece of land near Niskeyuna and sent Ann's blacksmith brother William to guard it. Hocknell then went to England to collect his family before returning to New York in search of Ann Lee on Christmas Day, 1775.[1]

He found her working as a domestic servant, having narrowly escaped total destitution. In the interval, Abraham Stanley had nearly died, then deserted his wife as soon as she nursed him back to health. Hocknell rescued his spiritual leader, and the faithful convened in Niskeyuna in 1776, where they built a settlement of log cabins.[2] There they lived in relative peace and isolation for several years. Meanwhile, Ann Lee continued to receive revelations, and pronounced many prophecies in the wilderness.

In 1779, a New Light revival broke out in several towns along the Massachusetts–New York border. As the revival waxed and waned, travelers who had stopped in Niskeyuna and conversed with the Shakers spread reports of their beliefs among the New Lights at New Lebanon, New York. The New Light Baptist preacher Joseph Meacham was curious enough to visit the British sect the following year. New England's Dark Day, which occurred around the time of Meacham's visit to Ann Lee, once more offered convenient natural stagecraft to a messiah preaching the approaching apocalypse. After conversing at length with Lee and her compatriots, Meacham returned to New Lebanon and announced he'd met the female embodiment of Christ. A steady stream of visitors then began to arrive from New Lebanon, resulting in numerous converts.[3] This effortless success encouraged Ann Lee to inaugurate her public ministry in America and to expand her following as the basis of the Millennial Church.

Ann Lee's celebrity as a millennial prophet spread across the region, and it did not sit well with New York revolutionaries. The British had driven a wedge between New England and the other colonies by occupying New York City and controlling the Hudson. The area surrounding Niskeyuna was known to be a stronghold of Tory sympathies. Because they shunned violence and wanted nothing to do with the hostilities, the Shakers fell under the suspicion of colonial authorities: revolutionaries in Albany suspected the sect was part of an elaborate British spy plot. In July of 1780, David Darrow, John Hocknell, and Joseph Meacham were the first Shakers to be jailed for refusing to take up arms. Other arrests soon followed. By the end of the month, the apprehensions extended to female Shakers, whose pacifist ministry was accused of inducing quietism among prospective patriots. One of those arrested was Ann Lee, who was imprisoned at Poughkeepsie until December.[4]

Meanwhile, Shaker opponents grew in proportion to their converts. One of their most prominent critics, Valentine Rathbun, was a Believer who had already lost the faith by 1781, when he published a pamphlet excoriating Shaker doctrines. In addition to describing the Believers as a dangerous threat to the colonists' cause, Rathbun disclosed what he considered their most extravagant beliefs: they were celibate, wore their hair short and plain, required the confession of sins, engaged in strange and elaborate songs and dances, and declared themselves to be the true church of a new millennial dispensation. Moreover, Rathbun reported that the Shakers gathered at Niskeyuna held all property in common, and some among them made the preposterous declaration that they had achieved "perfection" from sin. Most disturbing of all, however, was their veneration of Ann Lee, whom the Shakers declared "Christ's wife" and associated with the "woman in the wilderness" of Revelation 12. Mother Ann, as she was known among the devoted, was the next chosen vessel of the Christ spirit and a manifestation of the female aspect of the bisexual Godhead, who had come to establish the regenerated Millennial Church in the new dispensation. She was, in other words, the Messiah.

. . .

AFTER THE PATRIOTS RELEASED Mother Ann from jail, visits to Niskeyuna increased as pilgrims arrived from farther afield to meet her. Feeling the presence of the Christ spirit within her, newcomers confessed their sins freely to Mother Ann. According to Shaker custom, the first step toward regeneration was unburdening the mind of past sins. The newly converted carried news back to their towns and villages that Christ had returned to America in the body of an Englishwoman.[5]

The war dispersed the new Shakers across eastern New York and Massachusetts. As believers grew in number, and as Niskeyuna became more burdened by the demands of hosting the pilgrims, Mother Ann and the other Shaker elders recognized the advantages of conducting a missionary tour. In spring of 1781, Ann Lee, now in her mid-forties, set out with her brother William and James Whittaker on a tour of New England that would last for more than two years. Occasionally joined by other Shakers of both sexes, they crisscrossed eastern New York, Rhode Island, Connecticut, and Massachusetts, "laboring" in private homes to teach Shaker beliefs to the newly converted and conducting a public ministry in towns across the region. Although their sojourns brought them within the orbit of the Public Universal Friend, the Comforter and Mother Ann never personally met.

The Shakers shared a number of traits with the Universal Friends. But whereas the Friend was often tentative and flexible about the application of celibacy and communal living, Mother Ann was rigid and resolute. The Shakers held fast to the prohibition on carnal relations, but the celibacy mandate was more than the prudish aversion to sex that many of Mother Ann's biographers alleged: like the Ephratans and other Pietist groups influenced by Jakob Böhme, Shakers believed that God was composed of coequal male and female aspects, and that humankind, made in God's image, was androgynous before being rent asunder by the defilement of original sin. The logical path to regeneration and spiritual purity was to emulate unfallen man by maintaining strict celibacy. Ann the Word was innocent of book learning, but she may have absorbed Böhme's ideas through more worldly English converts to Shakerism.[6] Regardless of where her beliefs originated, they persisted among her followers, who prayed to a bigendered "God, Our Mother and Father."

Shaker theology outlined a theory of history organized into four eras, each characterized by a different attitude toward human sexuality. The first age was given over to the hedonistic fulfillment of passion, and ended when the great flood of Genesis drowned nearly all of humankind. The second age was governed by Mosaic law, which articulated a moral code intended to circumscribe sexual practices, but which endorsed sex within marriage and permitted exploitation in the form of slavery, private property, and warfare. The life of Jesus Christ inaugurated the third era, and the apostolic church he founded observed celibacy, abolished private property, and practiced nonresistance. But the Church almost immediately fell into apostasy and continued to degenerate for centuries. The return of the Christ spirit in Ann Lee marked the beginning of the fourth stage of human history. The Shakers viewed it as their duty to restore the apostolic church and initiate the regeneration of mankind begun by Jesus Christ.[7] This required reinstating the practice of celibacy and nonresistance, and the abolition of private property. Only the true believers would be saved from the flames of the apocalypse.

During their tour of New England, the Shakers continued to generate converts in areas with significant New Light activity. But in many quarters, the Shaker missionaries discovered their teachings were dangerously unpopular. Numerous visits were cut short by mobs determined to drive Ann Lee and her associates out of town. The Shakers were beaten, clubbed, whipped, and threatened with death. Mother Ann was dragged from her bed more than once, and subjected to examination to determine if she was a man, or worse, a witch. Eventually the missionaries were physically removed from Massachusetts by a mob that chased them over the New York border, bringing a close to their perilous tour. The missionaries returned to Niskeyuna in September 1783, having successfully fortified the faith of Believers across the region. William Lee died in July of the following year, 1784. Ann Lee followed her brother to heaven on September 8.

The earthly vessel of the Christ spirit was dead once more, but Ann Lee's work upon the world was far from over. The Shakers referred to her spiritual presence in their midst and heeded the orders she issued through those chosen to act as her messengers. Sometimes Mother Ann manifested her will through a vision bestowed upon one or more of the faithful during a meeting. In this way, Ann Lee continued to have an impact on the development of the United Society of Believers in Christ's Second Appearing, as the Shakers came to call themselves. The sect went on to become the longest lasting communal order in American history.

Until the mid-nineteenth century, the United Society expanded under the inspired leadership of new Shaker elders. After a period of mourning that followed the deaths of the original Shaker pilgrims, the Society recommenced its missionary work under the leadership of Joseph Meacham, who became the leader of the Believers after Ann Lee's appointed successor, James Whittaker, unexpectedly joined the ranks of departed elders in 1787, at the age of 36. Over the course of the first half of the nineteenth century, the sect continued to grow, reaching a maximum population of around 6,000.

The proliferation occurred mainly during the years of Meacham's leadership, and continued until about 1803. Acting on a prophecy he claimed to have received from Mother Ann, Meacham oversaw the "gathering" of Shakers into a network of communal villages. After severing their ties to worldly concerns, converts to the United Society retreated from the world into a Shaker family. An initial gathering occurred in 1787 at New Lebanon, where a critical mass of Shaker converts from the New Light revival had made it the logical place to build the first Shaker meetinghouse two years prior.

Following their success in converting New Lights at New Lebanon and elsewhere, the Shaker elders dispatched missionaries to areas experiencing similar revivals. A missionary tour to New Hampshire during a revival there yielded about 200 Baptist converts and led to the gathering of Shaker communities in northern New England.[8] Similarly, after the Cane Ridge revival kicked off a bright-burning evangelical movement in Kentucky, the Shakers found many eager converts to the Millennial Church when they visited the region in 1805, even after the enthusiasm had largely burned out. This led to the gathering of the western Shaker villages in Kentucky and Ohio.

The social unit at each Shaker village was a "family" of celibate brethren, each led by male and female Shaker elders. At the movement's peak, eighteen such communities existed. Although each family operated independently, the Shakers at New Lebanon remained the most influential. As the intellectual and spiritual center of Shaker culture, New Lebanon was the official capital of Shakerdom.

The impressive growth of the United Society in the first decades of the nineteenth century signals a surprisingly successful conversion rate for such a severe religion: as with the Universal Friends, the Shaker celibacy requirement meant that very few children were ever born into the movement. "Gathered" members had already confessed their sins and committed to celibacy. Married couples in which both partners became true Believers were expected to live no differently from the other celibate brethren, and wives symbolically annulled their marriages by returning to their maiden names.[9] Although conversion of married couples later became rare, Shaker communism facilitated the gathering of converts by eliminating economic barriers to separation when only one spouse was a Believer. This was particularly the case for women who left their husbands due to dissatisfaction with married life, or who wished to avoid marital rape by never marrying in the first place. Although the Shakers were nearly equal parts male and female so long as Mother Ann was alive, the Society trended female as it aged. It was 64 percent women by 1880, and tilted past 70 percent female by the turn of the century. Widows and their children, as well as unmarried female siblings, often arrived together to the Shaker villages, seeking an economic arrangement that would not require submission to a male head of household. Shakers also appeared to take an interest in fostering female orphans rather than their male counterparts, likely due to the dearth of opportunities that such girls would face—a lack that would almost certainly confine them to the socially sanctioned "prostitution" of marriage.[10]

The Shakers owed the success of the family network in part to the industriousness of the communal villages they founded. In accordance with Mother Ann's oft-quoted maxim, "Hands to work, and heart to God"—and her legendary remark that there were "no slovens nor sluts in heaven"—Shaker villages became sites of sober diligence where constant occupation kept earthly temptations at bay. Each family functioned as a largely self-sufficient commune where the elders organized all production and consumption. Shaker industry began with agriculture, and later expanded into the craft workshops where the Shakers produced their famous furniture.

Shaker communalism was fruitful and inspired as much commentary as their ecstatic dance routines. Such dignitaries as the Marquis de Lafayette, the English sociologist Harriet Martineau, the Welsh industrialist and reformer Robert Owen, and the trailblazing Scottish feminist Frances "Fanny" Wright visited Shaker villages and reflected favorably upon the Shaker way of life in their writings. Thomas Jefferson was another earlier admirer. After being sent a copy of Shaker history, Jefferson supposedly wrote to the Shakers: "I have read it through three times, and I pronounce it the best Church History that ever was written, and if its exegesis of Christian principles is maintained and sustained by a practical life, it is destined eventually to overthrow all other religions."[11]

Nathaniel Hawthorne found literary inspiration in the Shakers. "The Canterbury Pilgrims" describes a chance encounter between a young Shaker couple and a party of refugees seeking shelter from the secular world in the Canterbury Shaker village, located in New Hampshire. Their paths cross by a well at nighttime, as the young Shaker couple defects from the Society in order to live as man and wife. The young couple listens to the stories of the refugees who come seeking shelter among the Believers: the first to speak is a poet who yearns for a place to practice his gift without starving to death. Next, a bankrupt merchant arrogantly declares his aspiration to manage the village's finances. Finally, a yeoman farmer—that idol of Thomas Jefferson— hopes to escape the penury of landless servitude after encountering financial ruin. All three desire what Hawthorne calls the "cold and passionate security" of Shaker society.

Hawthorne was not the only man of letters to take an interest in the Shakers. They appear in dozens of American stories and novels. In 1889, news of the United Society reached Leo Tolstoy in Russia, when the Shakers sent him a package containing their publications. Tolstoy studied the Shaker philosophy with keen interest, and was intrigued by the practice of celibacy. Following this introduction, the count struck up a correspondence with Shaker Elder Frederick Evans.[12]

The United Society's economic self-sufficiency offered an inspirational model for the numerous socialist and communistic experiments to be undertaken in the antebellum reform period. Robert Owen and Fanny Wright both established secular utopian communities inspired in part by the Shakers' principled, organized, and egalitarian approach to labor. Fanny Wright even appointed a former Shaker the overseer of Nashoba, the Tennessee plantation she attempted to run using freed slaves who would reimburse their manumission by working voluntarily in a community based on Owen's socialist experiment at New Harmony, Indiana. Later, the Oneida Community established by John Humphrey Noyes would succeed where Owen and Wright had failed by reintroducing a religious rather than strictly humanitarian motivation for communistic cooperation. Just as the Shakers thrived economically when they discovered a market for their handicrafts and furniture, the Oneida Perfectionists owed their fortunes to the patented manufacture of steel animal traps and later on, silverware. The Shaker example likewise encouraged numerous subsequent American messianic movements to build their followings as communal or communistic societies, and to live according to the principle of sexual equality. In every case, however, the longevity and stability of the Shakers proved to be the envy of the other reformers.

Shaker writers and historians displayed total confidence in the righteousness of their social experiment. As Shaker historians Anna White and Leila Taylor wrote in their 1905 history of the sect,

> Shakerism presents a system of faith and a mode of life,
> which, during the past century, has solved social and religious
> problems and successfully established practical brotherhoods
> of industry, besides freeing woman from inequality and injustice. To this there must be added that it has banished from its
> precincts monopoly, immorality, intemperance and crime, by
> creating a life of purity, social freedom and altruistic industry.[13]

If such elevated self-regard was a sin, it was one to which the Shakers gladly confessed. The movement faced a sharp decline in the years ahead, and White and Taylor seemed to feel that the world had not yet adequately recognized the ingenuity of the Millennial Church.

The Shakers entered the final phase of steep decline by 1892. Eventually the self-sufficiency of individual families would fail, leading to an intrusion of influence from the outside world when Shaker villages were forced to engage in worldly commerce. One by one, the societies began to close. As of this writing, only the Sabbathday Lake community remains, in New Gloucester, Maine. The last two Shakers live there.

7. THE ERA OF MANIFESTATIONS

S HAKER INFLUENCE ON THE development of nineteenth-century American socialism cannot be underestimated. However, it was the period of 1837 through the 1850s, long after Ann Lee's death, during which the Believers established their most enduring spiritual legacy. Described by Shaker historians as the "Era of Manifestations" or the period of "Mother Ann's Work" (and as the "New Era" by the Shakers), this decade was defined by an intense outpouring of spiritualist phenomena that would later be understood by Shakers and their secular counterparts as the inauguration of modern American spiritualism.

It all started when several teenage girls at the Watervliet community at Niskeyuna were discovered seized by a trancelike state in which they remained unresponsive to their surroundings. When they returned to consciousness, the girls reported spiritual visions, celestial travels, and conversations with angels. After making these initial events known to their brethren in the other families, the Believers at Watervliet found that they were not alone: the trance visions had spread across numerous Shaker villages. The Shakers attributed these remarkable events to the worldly will of Ann Lee, and concluded that she was not finished with her ministry.

Although 1837 marked a period of intensification in such phenomena, visions, prophecies, and spirit manifestations had been reported in Shaker villages ever since Mother Ann's bodily death in 1784. Shakers presupposed that the gift of prophecy was still active among them and did not question the gift when it manifested. In 1835, two years before the general outpouring began, a twelve-year-old girl in the South Union community experienced a vision of heaven in which she beheld Jesus, Ann Lee, and departed Shaker elders.[1]

The Shakers interpreted the resurgence of religious enthusiasm during this period as a sign of favor from the Deity. Writing decades later, Shaker Elder Frederick Evans described the Era of Manifestations as an "influx from the spiritual world, confirming the faith of so many disciples, and extending throughout all the eighteen societies."[2] Communications from angels sometimes accompanied the trances and trembling that punctuated the Shakers' characteristic whirling dances. On numerous occasions, Mother Ann and the Shaker elders appeared in order to issue new revelations to the faithful. During other visitations, they offered advice on workaday matters among family members and instructed the Believers in new rituals. Innovative dances from the period became codified into the Shaker repertoire.

Native Americans also visited the Shakers in spirit, often preceded by instruction from Mother Ann that the Shakers were to "take them in" to Shaker meeting, presumably so the Shakers could convert the Native American spirits. Sometimes Mother Ann or an angel acting on her behalf would distribute "spiritual" gifts to the Shakers during one of their ecstatic assemblies. These included invisible fruit baskets, "spiritual eyeglasses" used for seeing things invisible to the human eye, and other imagined items, such as musical instruments, that the Shakers enjoyed in their worship. Perhaps because they understood the potential ridicule that would ensue if they permitted outsiders to observe the Manifestations, the Shakers closed their meetings to non-Believers while they sorted out the meaning of the spirits' riotous work.

In an eerie but happier echo of Salem, many ardent Believers, particularly girls and young women, discovered that they could function as "instruments" through which the spirits of Mother Ann and the departed elders could literally speak their prophecies and wishes. Soon the instruments discovered that while they were entranced, other spirits besides the ghosts of Ann Lee and the elders could speak through them. As most historians of the American spiritualist movement acknowledge, the Shakers were the first to routinize the inspired practice of trance mediumship. Acclaimed trance medium Emma Hardinge described the Shakers as the "John Baptists" of what became known as modern American spiritualism. This quasireligious movement emerged in 1848 to sensationalize the nation with fantastic revelations from the unseen world, spirit visitations from departed American heroes and statesmen, and spectacular demonstrations of spirit presence and power made through trance mediums.[3]

The spiritualist era produced its own peculiar pair of American messiahs, both of whom were profoundly influenced by Ann Lee and the Shakers. Like Mother Ann and the Public Universal Friend, they were contemporaries who built celibate communal societies that enshrined the equality of the sexes. Unlike them, both were men, and they engaged in more direct competition for the title of American Messiah.

TWO

THE CHOSEN VESSEL

I have sought to fold the genius of Christianity, to fathom its divine import, and to embody its principle in the spirit and body of our own America.

—THOMAS LAKE HARRIS,
Brotherhood of the New Life

8. AMERICA'S BEST-KNOWN MYSTIC

I N 1850, A WOMAN by the fortuitous name of Eliza Ann Benedict left the town of Auburn, New York, with an urgent message. When she arrived in New York City, Benedict made arrangements to be received privately in the chambers of Rev. Thomas Lake Harris, the intended recipient. They made themselves comfortable.

The message she brought was not from anyone in Auburn, nor was it from any other mortal: as Harris looked on, Benedict allowed a trance to overtake her body. After regaining her calm, the trance medium channeled a spirit who identified himself as the apostle Paul. Through Eliza Benedict the spirit of Paul commanded Harris to go to Auburn, where the apostles had prepared important work for him to do. The reverend complied.

At the time of Benedict's visit, Thomas Lake Harris was fast becoming one of the most renowned spiritualist mediums in New York City—and that was saying something. By midcentury, spirit visitations like those that roiled the Shaker villages during the Era of Manifestations had become a regular occurrence in the secular world. What began as an earnest outburst of religious enthusiasm among Shaker girls had become a fad in cities and towns all over America. Calling themselves mediums rather than instruments, those who possessed an aptitude for channeling spirits from the beyond often parlayed their skill into a lucrative practice.

Reverend Harris would later specialize in channeling the departed souls of the English Romantics. Posthumous verse from Shelley, Blake, and Byron tumbled from the reverend's lips while he was entranced. These were duly recorded by the minister's assistant and publisher, Samuel Brittan. Although practically unknown today, Harris cut such a dramatic figure in New York society that William James declared him the best-known American mystic.[1]

As a boy, fate had dropped Harris into flames of the notorious "Burned-Over District" of central and western New York. For the first several decades of the nineteenth century, the region was the geographical center of the Second Great Awakening, a democratic revival movement that forever altered American religion, politics, and culture. Harris was not American by birth: he was born in Fenny Stratford, Buckinghamshire, on May 15, 1823. His parents, Thomas Harris and Annie Lake, emigrated to America in 1827 and settled in Utica, where they kept a general store. At the time of their emigration, Utica was emblematic of the American dream and its nineteenth-century narrative romance with westward expansion. It was a thriving industrial city, with a population that grew by 183 percent in the decade the Harris family arrived.[2]

Inauspiciously, Annie Lake expired just a few years after she and her husband relocated. Young Thomas was only nine, and the tragedy affected him deeply. Years later, Annie appeared to her son in night visions, surrounded by fairies. Her untimely demise and subsequent nocturnal visits held sway over Harris for the rest of his life: both Annie and the fairies periodically reappeared in the poetry he published under his own name. More important, Annie's virtues achieved mythic dimensions in her son's lively imagination; his memory of her formed the basis of the Divine Mother, a female deity Harris described as the female manifestation of the Godhead and empress of a fairyland called Lilistan.[3]

The elder Harris found himself another frontierswoman and married her without much delay. Thomas Sr. was a deacon in the church, and both he and his new wife were stern Calvinist Baptists who grudgingly found themselves in the middle of an evangelical revival.

Determined to deliver their boy from the devil's clutches, they put him to work at his father's store at the tender age of nine. This brought an abrupt end to Harris's formal education, but he proved a determined student, teaching himself from books by candlelight in the evenings. It was a scholarly habit he never lost: years later, latter-day followers of the bearded mystic marveled at his capacity to toil all through the night.

No matter his parents' caution, it was impossible to shield young Thomas from the religious unrest in Utica: roving ministers frequently held revivals in the region, and the movement was, by definition, evangelical. Universalism and Christian perfection, the revolutionary and democratic ideas associated with the Second Great Awakening, both made a strong impression on the boy. To satisfy his curiosity, teenage Harris visited a Baptist revival service, where he witnessed a genuine outpouring of the spirit that initiated his conversion to Universalism, a movement that overturned Calvinist doctrines of predestination by maintaining that all souls are eventually reconciled with God in heaven.[4] Universalism lacked the classist dimensions of the old Congregationalist churches, where wealthier families sat in the first pews as a mark of their high tithes and proximity to God.

While still an adolescent, Harris traded child labor for the work of a man; he began writing for area newspapers associated with the Universalist ministry and the antebellum social-reform movements it championed. He soon left home altogether, to study theology with Universalist clergy in the region. Harris recalled being a half-starved, homeless waif during this interval of apprenticeship—a vagabond who dressed in rags until a Universalist minister took him in.[5] The clergyman's wife left behind one of the few surviving accounts of the period, including a peerless description of Harris's literary talent: "His poetic utterances," she wrote, "were to me like views of sunrise and sunset, which we enjoy internally, but which we cannot remember."[6]

Harris became a Universalist minister in 1844 and acquired a parish in a small town outside Utica. There he met and married the first of his three wives, Mary Van Arnum. She would be dead by 1850, but not before giving birth to Harris's two sons.[7] The newlyweds moved to New York City, where Harris took the helm of a prestigious and relatively new congregation in December 1845. This was the Fourth Universalist Society on Elizabeth Street, one of the city churches most involved in social-reform activism. Among its members was Horace Greeley, publisher of the progressive *New-York Tribune*.

Harris quickly discovered that New York City was teeming with reform-minded clergy who believed, as he did, in the need for social transformation. As their egalitarian theology implied, the Universalists were a democratically minded folk. Not surprisingly, the denomination had grown rapidly in Jacksonian America and favored progressive political reforms, including abolition and women's rights.

Intellectual Universalists in Harris's New York congregation studied the works of Emanuel Swedenborg, a Swedish scientist, mystic, and royal mine inspector whose voluminous theological writings inspired the American Transcendentalists. Ralph Waldo Emerson called Swedenborg a "colossal soul" and compared the Swede to Shakespeare. Swedenborg found equally enthusiastic reception among religiously inclined labor reformers, particularly the American followers of French socialist Charles Fourier, whose ideas about "attractive" or associative labor found many adherents in the wake of the economic recession that followed the Panic of 1837. It was Charles Fourier, rather than Karl Marx, who set the agenda of socialist reform in antebellum America. Religious progressives who studied Fourier and Swedenborg believed that a nonsectarian, ecumenical Christian church rebuilt around Christian principles of social justice could be an instrument of radical social reform. Such a church might rescue the nation from its spiritual stagnation and the corresponding failure to live up to its democratic ideals. These notions appealed to the young Universalist from Utica.

Harris tended to elbow his way to the head of any group he joined. But for his first year in the city he did little to distinguish himself from other activist ministers. This changed in 1846, when Harris attended a clairvoyant trance lecture delivered by a celebrity of no uncertain notoriety. The clairvoyant was Andrew Jackson Davis, a self-taught philosopher who had acquired fame across New York for his oracular powers of clairvoyance. Harris became a regular at Davis's trance lectures, during which the visionary recounted the wisdom of departed souls he encountered in the Spirit Land—his term for the Universalist heaven to which he could transport his consciousness while entranced. In truth, Davis cobbled together his philosophy from the writings of Charles Fourier, Emanuel Swedenborg, and the socialist publisher Albert Brisbane, a friend of Horace Greeley's whose column in the *New-York Tribune* became a fountainhead for Fourier's ideas in America. As Davis's many detractors never tired of observing, his only miraculous talent was for plagiarism.

9. THE POUGHKEEPSIE SEER

COBBLERY WAS, in fact, what set Andrew Jackson Davis on the road to becoming a prophet. Born to an alcoholic roustabout and his illiterate wife, young Davis, who went by Jackson, lacked meaningful opportunities for self-advancement. His apprenticeship to a successful Poughkeepsie cobbler was the first event in a chain of consequences that led to celebrity status in New York City. In the mid-nineteenth century, cobblers trained in a guild that valued education and political engagement; the youngest apprentice was made to read the newspaper aloud while the older men worked. This was likely how young Jackson learned of a lecture in Poughkeepsie to be delivered by an acclaimed traveling mesmerist by the name of Stanley Grimes.

At the time, mesmerism enjoyed an improbable resurgence in popularity throughout the Americas. The technique was named for the German doctor Franz Anton Mesmer (1734–1815), who attempted to prove the principles of astrology with the scientific methods developed by his Enlightenment peers. Titled *The Influence of the Planets on the Human Body* (1765), Mesmer's medical dissertation hypothesized a causal relationship between planetary alignment and bodily function. Celestial movements, he explained, altered the forces of "universal gravitation" already at work between smaller individual bodies on planets such as Earth. By 1774, Mesmer had begun to experiment with ways of interfering with this force at the microcosmic level with patients at his practice in Vienna. On a human scale, the universal attractive force became known as "animal magnetism." The techniques by which Mesmer tried to manipulate it were various, and included an early form of hypnotism that carried his name.[1]

Viennese authorities disliked Mesmer's occult science, so by 1778, the doctor moved his practice to France. There he cultivated numerous patients for his exotic treatments, which often relied on the curative effects of music made on a glass harmonica he played himself. But Benjamin Franklin had also come to France, where his reputation as a man of science far exceeded that of Mesmer. At the invitation of Louis XVI, Franklin joined a committee of French scientists tasked with evaluating the scientific merit of animal magnetism. The committee expected that its ridicule of Mesmer's theories would end their adoption in enlightened France. Yet although Mesmer was embarrassed enough to slink away to Germany, not all of his students found the royal report sufficient reason to desist in their studies of magnetism.

Among Franklin's contemporaries, one of animal magnetism's cautious enthusiasts was the Marquis de Lafayette, who attempted to entrance a willing subject at the Niskeyuna Shaker village not long after Mother Ann Lee's death. Lafayette was a man of many liaisons; he acted as a conduit for correspondence between Mesmer and George Washington, whose various health ailments had spurred an interest in alternative medicine, including a primitive version of electric therapy.[2] But mesmerism's later success in America had less to do with Revolutionary War heroes than with a largely forgotten French noble. The Marquis de Puységur, one of Mesmer's pupils, pushed the study further toward the occult by hypothesizing that manipulations of the magnetic forces operating on a patient's body could induce a state of dreamlike clairvoyance. After learning of these developments, Mesmer distanced himself from the sleepwalking school of psychic perception, which allowed somnambulant "physicians" to diagnose maladies by gazing clairvoyantly into the interior of the human body. The new science flourished after it was carried to American shores in the nineteenth century, when Franklin was no longer available to disparage it.

Before he took up mesmerism, Stanley Grimes had already earned a reputation for his dazzling phrenological readings. When he returned to Poughkeepsie to demonstrate magnetic clairvoyance, young Andrew Jackson Davis was one of those who wished to put the new science to a very personal test. But Grimes was unable to magnetize the boy, in spite of Davis's predisposition to sleepwalking visions. Davis left the demonstration without confidence in Grimes, but remained curious. Not long after Grimes left town, a tailor by the name of William Livingstone decided to try his hand at mesmeric operation. He found Davis at the cobbler shop and asked if the boy would allow him to attempt another magnetism. Davis agreed to call on Mr. Livingstone at his residence, where he was easily magnetized on the tailor's first attempt.

Defying rumors of an improper relationship, Davis and Livingstone went on to build a lucrative clairvoyant medical practice in Pough-keepsie. But Davis soon realized his gift for diagnosis was greater than Livingstone's talent as a mesmeric operator. Before long, the seer scampered off to Connecticut to practice with a new magnetizer, a Universalist botanical doctor named Silas Smith Lyon. The two then made for New York City, where they settled in November 1845.

Reports of Davis's powers traveled mostly by word of mouth until Greeley's liberal *New-York Tribune* published a report on some of the "remarkable phenomena" Lyon solicited from his subject at their Vesey Street chambers. Among the curious investigators drawn in by this publicity was a man of "feminine mental characteristics" and, according to Davis's evaluation of his brain-auras, gemlike brilliance. This was Edgar Allan Poe, who would later satirize Davis in *Grantham's* magazine as "Martin Van Buren Mavis."[3] The writer had moved to New York from Philadelphia in 1844, and his literary renown placed him in the company of some of the finest intellects in the city. Poe was a curious but cautious skeptic of mesmerism. His 1845 *Broadway Journal* review of W. Newnham's book *Human Magnetism* dismissed the author's pretentious claims of magnetism's curative properties as "illogical throughout," but allowed that it might be beneficial as a powerful anesthetic for surgical amputations.[4] By the following year, Poe sardonically referred to mesmerism as one of the "matters which put to the severest test the credulity or, more properly, the faith of mankind."[5]

Davis's salons gradually found an elite audience: luminaries of the speculative branch of progressive clergy in New York City. Among them was Reverend George Bush, a die-hard Swedenborgian and respected professor at Union Theological Seminary. Using Davis as his reliable, if slightly illiterate medium, the spirit of Emanuel Swedenborg undertook an epistolary exchange with Professor Bush, who enjoyed the attention.[6] Although Bush later criticized Davis's descriptions of the celestial spheres as they increasingly diverged from the Swedenborgian texts from which they were obviously plagiarized, he became one of Davis's most influential early supporters. Bush's writings on Andrew Jackson Davis cast a veneer of respectability on the "Poughkeepsie Seer," whom Bush declared to be Swedenborg's heir.[7]

Another clergyman irritated Davis from the moment he laid eyes on him. In late 1846 or early 1847, not long before his trance lectures were published as *The Principles of Nature, Her Divine Revelations, and a Voice to Mankind*, Davis heard his new admirer exclaim, "When that Book is published, I shall lock up the Bible in the drawer under the desk, put the key in my pocket, and preach the angel-utterances of the New Philosophy!" Davis had noticed the man in attendance at a few of his lectures and was alarmed by such vehemence.

"The world must be awakened!" Davis recalled the furious young cleric shrieking, his fist clenched: "Religious organizations are trembling and tottering with age. Decay is certain! Shining and speaking through these lectures is the mighty spirit of a struggling Humanity. The spirit of Divine Love is misrepresented and crucified by modern churches of pride and power!" With an "oracularly luminous" glint in his eye, the minister trembled as he advocated for the overthrow of established churches. Davis recalled:

The extreme brilliancy of his eloquence, and the dazzlingly high-colored character of his most ordinary declamations, caused my spirit to shrink back as one would shut his eyes against the intrusion of too much light. . . . But I was destined to pass through a brief experience with this talented and vivacious person; as he was distinguished for the preaching of brilliant sermons and the writing of coquet poetry, I shall introduce him to the reader as 'the Poet' of this psychological drama.[8]

The zealous convert was Thomas Lake Harris. "The Poet," as Davis took to calling him, was not yet a literary celebrity, but he made himself known around New York's progressive reform circles. Davis tried to keep the ambitious minister at arm's length, but was careful not to alienate Harris: the well-connected minister might prove to be a useful apostle. Dr. Lyon did not fare as well. Once more chafing against the limitations of his operator, Davis suspended sessions with the doctor as soon as a benefactress gave him the $1,000 he required for printing his book and purchasing a new suit for his lecture tour.

Freed of the burden of workaday clairvoyant diagnosis, Davis accepted an invitation to summer in Vermont. On his return to the city in July, he stopped to visit Harris, by then preaching to a congregation in Troy. The Poet inquired about the New York reception of Davis's book, which had been advanced to newsrooms in anticipation of its August 1847 publication. Harris had read a disparaging review and readied a response, which he eagerly shared with Davis. His zealousness continued to perturb the Poughkeepsie Seer. So did the Poet's sudden announcement that he would surrender his pulpit and salary to evangelize Davis's teachings in the western region of the state. Alarmed, Davis assured Harris it would not be necessary to deplete his energies and jeopardize his frail health to advance ideas that were, in any case, invincible truths. But after finding the Poet intractable on this point, he tasked Harris with taking advance orders for the *Divine Revelations* from audiences in western New York.

Meanwhile, Davis's allies in the press and in New York reform circles mounted an impressive publicity campaign for the *Divine Revelations*. Its publication was nothing short of a sensation: as the *Tribune* observed, the *Revelations* received an unprecedented amount of pre-publication attention for a title by an American author, helping it sell nearly a thousand copies in just one week.[9] Spindly twenty-year-old Andrew Jackson Davis was a sensation, and Harris his most devoted acolyte.

. . .

DAVIS'S WORRIES ABOUT his roving disciple deepened after he received a letter from Harris that November. The Poet had become convinced Davis could foresee the future, and wrote him to request the most propitious itinerary for his evangelism after departing Cleveland. He confided that without Davis's divine foresight, he believed he would be martyred to the faith. Hoping to discourage Harris's belief in his omniscience, Davis sent Harris to out-of-the-way locations that would limit his public appearances and hinder his ability to draw large crowds.

When Harris reappeared in New York in March 1848, he was exhausted by his perambulations and disabused of the notion that the Poughkeepsie Seer could extend his clairvoyant powers to the future. Indeed, Davis's lack of foresight soon gave Harris the opportunity he needed to take his revenge. After Davis and his married benefactress were caught spending the night in the same chambers, Harris used the scandal to elbow Davis out of control of the reform newspaper that he had recently cofounded with Lyon, Samuel Brittan, and several other prominent New York reformers. The paper, named the *Univercoelum and Spirit Philosopher*, positioned itself on the cutting edge of the Universalist reform movements.

The *Univercoelum* had column inches to fill after Davis's departure, and the Poet stepped in to fill the gap. His byline began to appear in April 1848, as soon as Davis was gone. The first of Harris's features, "Progress in Cincinnati," detailed the Poet's experiences out West. Harris was pleased to report that Westerners had "outgrown" the "religious fanaticism" of the Second Great Awakening. In Ohio, men had shaken off the fetters of New England traditions, and set out to reform the churches, political parties, and civil-society organizations along more democratic lines. At the socialist Cincinnati Brotherhood community, Harris saw a practical application of the progressive humanism that excited the New York radicals. The Poet discerned a "Church of the Future" rising in the West, whose "creed shall be Truth" and whose sacraments would be the "good works" its members undertook to ensure "social [and] mental unity."[10] All that was lacking to bring about utopia, Harris believed, was more thorough education in the "science" of social reformers like Charles Fourier.

Decades before Henry George's *Progress and Poverty* (1879) catapulted the uniform land-tax to the forefront of the public consciousness, Harris endorsed Ohioan efforts to overthrow the "Land Monopoly."[11] He additionally observed that in Cincinnati, the "principle of distributive justice" implemented by reformers extended to racial justice.[12] Not only were African Americans welcomed into some reformed churches in Ohio; they were also admitted to some high schools.

Harris's fascination with frontier life resulted from his observation that western pioneers were, by necessity, predisposed to greater social commitment and cohesion than their eastern countrymen. On the frontier, the dream of establishing a millennial society in America— God's kingdom on Earth—was still alive. Harris was energized by the practice of what he called "high Spiritual Christianity"—his term for the no-nonsense, ecumenical Protestantism that arose in the western territories, which lacked the entrenched social hierarchies of the East. Likewise, the Poet admired the strength of the Odd Fellows and the Sons of Temperance in the region. He believed that these and other civic-minded brotherhoods, which were based on the kind of mutual affiliation Charles Fourier placed at the center of his labor-reform theories, had the potential to transform social relations. In the West, Harris found evidence that "the old parties, based on the obsolete formulas of the past, are beginning to pass away, and the motto 'Liberty, Equality, Fraternity,' ringing eloquent across the Atlantic, is rousing men to a warfare, whose weapons shall be moral power, and whose object shall be the regeneration of the race."[13]

This notion of a depraved human race in need of "regeneration" to a prior state of grace was one that would come to obsess numerous nineteenth-century reform movements. But long before it became the stated objective of Social Darwinists and eugenicists, bodily and spiritual "regeneration" was a cherished subject of esoteric Christian sects like the Ephrata commune and the Woman in the Wilderness colony—both of which practiced communalism and celibacy. Harris was now enthralled by the same ideas, and began to see himself at the spiritual forefront of the regeneration of the American body and soul.

It was a timely turn to more occult themes: by the end of the year, a new pseudoscience began to displace mesmerism at the cutting edge of American reform circles. Not long after Harris returned to New York City, modern American spiritualism swept across the nation like a prairie fire. The movement enjoyed immense popularity in New York, and Harris acted quickly to become one of its early figureheads. But like the Shaker Era of Manifestations, modern American spiritualism was a widespread and spontaneous outpouring of religious enthusiasm first initiated by adolescent girls.

10. THE FOX SISTERS

THE ORIGIN STORY of modern American spiritualism has become legend: in spring of 1848, the family of John and Margaret Fox began to hear strange knockings in a home they'd recently occupied in Hydesville, New York.[1] In sworn testimony related to the matter, Margaret stated that the rappings began the first night the family spent in the home. "It was not very loud," she testified, "yet it produced a jar of the bedsteads and chairs."[2] Unbeknownst to the Foxes, villagers already believed the dwelling to be haunted. Various prior tenants later swore out affidavits describing similar supernatural experiences in the Hydesville house.[3] By means of trial and error, the Fox children, Margaretta and Kate, aged fifteen and twelve, discovered the mysterious taps could be elicited with commands and queries.[4] Following a series of yes-or-no questions, the girls' mother learned that the knocks were communications from the spirit of a thirty-one-year-old traveling salesman who'd been murdered in the vicinity. Margaret Fox then summoned her neighbors to witness the dead man's communications. The spirit rapped out consistent answers to the questions put to him, and correctly tapped the age of a neighbor, Mrs. Redfield. By means of additional questions, the Foxes and their neighbors determined that the murder victim had his throat slit with a butcher knife in what was now John and Margaret's bedroom before being buried under the house in a ten-foot grave.

The next day the house overflowed with more than 300 people, forcing the questioners to proceed by committee. Other spirits joined the dead peddler. Witnesses swore that the spirits replied to questions in the Fox family's presence as well as when they were sent out, but that "after the confusion and excitement had subsided . . . the spirits seemed to select the two youngest girls" as their preferred "mediums."⁵ Efforts to dig up the dead man's grave on Saturday night were abandoned when the party struck water in the cellar.

If the Fox family was inconvenienced by these proceedings, they were also entertained. They asked the peddler's spirit to imitate sounds related to the murder, including the gurgling of his slit throat, the scraping of a body being dragged across the floor, and a noise "like that of pouring a quantity of clotted blood from a pail onto the floor."⁶ As the spirits became familiar with the family, more of them began to appear. Some employed dramatic means of communication, including writing on the floors of empty rooms and hurling wood blocks engraved with important messages through the windows of the Fox house.

The girls were eventually sent away from the excitement: Margaretta went to live with her brother David, and Kate was sent to Rochester to live with a sister, Leah Fish, a widow who taught music and took in lodgers. Even before Kate and Leah had gotten settled in a new home, they began to hear the spirit raps, along with the sound of more coagulated blood being poured on the floor. Kate and her niece Elizabeth, also twelve, felt cold hands upon them in bed. Soon after, Elizabeth found herself cured of a spinal problem, which the family credited to therapeutic calisthenics compelled by the spirits' ghostly touch. In subsequent disturbances, which Leah invited her Methodist neighbors to witness, books flew from shelves in the dark.

Hoping to be rid of the problem, the Foxes consented to an exorcism, but it proved a failure. Constantly harassed by spirit visitors, Leah summoned Isaac Post, a friend to the Fox family, to see if he might be able to help her calm the visiting souls. After she mentioned that back in Hydesville, David Fox had recited the alphabet so that the spirit could spell its name by rapping to indicate a desired letter,

Post suggested that the girls do the same with their invisible visitors in Rochester. Their method of communicating with the spirits became widely known as the "spiritual telegraph."

By autumn, additional mediums across the region had discovered their abilities to communicate with the dead. They inspired such a degree of public fascination—and in many cases, belief and trust—that spirit mediums were consulted for assistance with unsolved crimes. As was wont to occur, souls departed from the Earth erred as often as their terrestrial counterparts and repeatedly changed their minds. To turn back a rising tide of public doubt, the spirits sent a message through another young New York medium, Elizabeth Granger, indicating a date by which they desired to perform public demonstrations in Rochester. The Foxes received a similar message, instructing them: "You have a duty to perform. We want you to make this matter more public."[7]

The result of this command was a November 1849 demonstration of spirit communication held in Rochester's largest public venue, Corinthian Hall. Following an introductory lecture on November 14, committees of investigators subjected the Fox sisters to a battery of tests: they stood on glass and pillows, had their dresses cinched to their ankles, and disrobed for inspection by a "committee of Ladies" who searched for foreign instruments on their bodies. Members of the committee testified they could not determine any mechanism by which the Foxes might produce the raps themselves.[8]

The outcome of the Rochester demonstrations was a loquacious explosion of spirit communications and manifestations throughout New York state. The excitement soon spread across the entire country.[9] Skeptics and enthusiasts came together to "investigate" spiritualist phenomena, whose veracity was determined by putatively scientific tests. "Spirit circles" fanned out across the class and education spectrum: even Frederick Douglass, one of Rochester's leading intellectuals, was reported to have engaged in spirit investigation.[10]

The Fox sisters were quite busy by the New Year. That spring, the

North Family of Shakers invited the girls to Mt. Lebanon.[11] Before they had withdrawn from the Shaker villages at the conclusion of Mother Ann's Work, the influx of spirits who descended over the United Society of Believers promised that they had come to announce a new dispensation, and that more spirits would soon appear across the land. To the elders at Mt. Lebanon, the trend begun by the Fox sisters appeared to be the fulfillment of this prophecy.

The Foxes traveled to New York City in the spring of 1850. There they met with Andrew Jackson Davis, whom many spiritualists now revered as a prophet of the new spiritualist era.[12] The sisters and their mother resided for several weeks at the Barnum Hotel before being taken as guests in the homes of families who desired private consultations—often with the hope of contacting lost loved ones. One of these was Horace Greeley. During the three days he hosted the girls, Greeley undertook a private investigation of the strange sounds that followed the young women. After the Foxes returned to Rochester, he concluded:

> It would be the basest cowardice not to say that we are con-
> vinced beyond a doubt of their perfect integrity and good
> faith in the premises. Whatever may be the origin or cause
> of the 'rappings,' the ladies in whose presence they occur
> do not make them. We tested this thoroughly and to our
> satisfaction.[13]

While other New York papers delighted in ridiculing the credulity of spiritualists, Greeley's *Tribune* took a stance of cautious interest, much as it had done with regard to mesmeric healing.

In fact, spiritualism found its most skilled and ardent adherents among magnetic subjects. Those who had already developed talents of mesmeric clairvoyance or clairaudience realized they were uniquely susceptible to spirit influence, particularly while suspended in magnetic trance. The leap from mesmerism to spiritualism was not a large one for those who already believed in the existence of unseen forces at work in the world. Due to the remarkable impression that recent demonstrations of the telegraph had made on the minds of antebellum Americans, those who witnessed the first Hydesville rappings were disposed to compare them to jolts of electricity. As one report indicated:

> Persons sometimes feel a sensation of electricity passing over their limbs when they stand in the vicinity of those who get the sounds most freely, although the particular persons who seem to be the medium feel no sensation at all. In one or two instances we have seen a perceptible shock as if caused by a galvanic battery especially when the persons were under the influence of Magnetism.[14]

Spirit investigators believed that the simultaneous presence of spirits and electricity offered additional proof that matter and spirit were not separate things at all, but linked through a third invisible yet energetic medium. Departing from this hypothesis, spiritualists reasoned that mediumship most commonly arose among young females because women were "negatively" charged and passive. Males were considered "positively" charged and therefore less capable of receiving the influx. Rather than cast doubt on this theory, spiritualists interpreted the existence of male mediums as evidence that certain men possess a feminine disposition and a negative magnetic orientation.[15]

Visiting spirits often encouraged the association between electricity and spiritual science. One of the first celebrity spirits to appear in Rochester was none other than Benjamin Franklin, who politely demonstrated proof of his identity by "electerizing" the mortal body of one of his inquisitors.[16] Through constant appeals to the similarities between spirit communication and the science of electricity, the veneer of scientific inquiry with which phrenologists and mesmerists had coated their dubious work was made to adhere to spirit investigations. Many spiritualists considered contact with invisible "higher" realms to be a scientific achievement that signaled the progressive evolution of the species. For this reason, they paid great attention to the pleas the spirits often made to end slavery: when the spirits of Thomas Jefferson and George Washington manifested in séance parlors and on the trance lecture circuit, they tended to express regret for their participation in the slave economy, and advised that a more temperate and egalitarian society would ease the heavenward path of American Christians.

Spiritualism was an emphatically democratic movement that lacked organizational structures and institutions. The popular press, already a crucial mode of democratic intellectual exchange for abolitionists and temperance advocates, was the primary vehicle by which spiritualists received tidings from the spirit world. Most spiritualist newspapers took up these and other antebellum reform causes staunchly backed by the enlightened spirits, including homeopathy, variants of diet and dress reform, and women's rights. Trance lectures, during which a medium would channel a spirit who wished to speak at length before the public, became a popular form of entertainment. For the tens of thousands of Americans who attended them, it was likely the first time any had ever seen a woman permitted to stand at a public lectern.[17]

11. THE APOSTOLIC CIRCLE

THOMAS LAKE HARRIS had received the gift of higher communication by 1850, when he was paid a visit from a spirit who showed him a book closed with seven seals—an allusion to the seven seals that secure the scroll mentioned in the Revelation of Saint John. This scroll of secret knowledge, an important symbol of gnostic Christianity, was to remain shut until the Second Coming. During Harris's vision, the spirit visitor opened the sealed book, which contained "divine truth and wisdom" about the founding of a paradisiacal city: the New Jerusalem mentioned in the Book of Revelation. Immediately after this initial encounter, Harris's mediumistic abilities developed so quickly that when his wife, Mary Ann, died shortly after his vision, he personally witnessed her ascent to heaven.[1]

The spirits who chose Harris as their medium were often those of poets. His renown for channeling the English Romantic poets brought ridicule in the New York press and admiration within the spiritualist community. The reverend's star was rising fast, but Harris quickly tarnished his reputation by associating with one of the most outlandish circles of spirit mediums to emerge in the early days of the movement. This was a group first known as the Auburn Circle, named for the upstate village where Kate Fox had been sent after her family abandoned the haunted house in Hydesville.

After the Corinthian Hall demonstrations, Kate Fox continued the practice of spirit communication while residing with relatives in Auburn, where villagers had already cultivated a lively interest in mesmeric healing and magnetic clairvoyance. Not everyone in town was content to let a teenage girl be the center of attention. By summer of 1850, at least fifty mediums in Auburn had begun to develop talents in rapping, writing, and trance communication. Mediums emerged even within the town's most respected families. One Auburn medium surpassed all others: Eliza Ann Benedict achieved notoriety for channeling numerous biblical personae, including the Holy Spirit. Benedict's mediumship raised more than a few doubts in Auburn. Whereas the town's other spirit circles generally conferred with departed loved ones, unknown shades, and the occasional ghost of an American statesman, Benedict and her associates announced that their circle was chosen by God to transmit messages regarding the imminent return of the Messiah.

According to trance medium Emma Hardinge, who wrote the definitive history of the first ten years of spiritualist activity, the Auburn Circle's convictions resulted from the beliefs of several "bigoted" members of the group: these were former followers of William Miller, a Baptist preacher who'd led tens of thousands of upstate New Yorkers in an evangelical movement based on his dated prediction of the imminent Second Coming. After the appointed deadline came and went in 1844 without the return of Christ, the dissolution of the Millerite adventist movement became known as the Great Disappointment. Although a schism of ex-Millerites held fast to adventism and later gave rise to the Seventh-Day Adventist Church, thousands more sought other outlets for their religious energies. Many were drawn to spiritualism.

Millenarian excitement came to dominate the Auburn Circle when communications from the Holy Spirit were followed by visits from the spirits of Moses, Daniel, and Saints John and Paul.[2] Various spirits high in the Christian hierarchy dictated pamphlets through Eliza Benedict, whose followers dutifully published and distributed them. Benedict and her cohort believed that American Christians would heed the millennial tidings with joy and rally to support the divine mission the apostles outlined in their pamphlets. Instead, they earned the wrath typically

reserved for blasphemers, in addition to the scorn of most other spiritualists, who eschewed the Auburn Circle's elitism. According to Emma
Hardinge, the group's publications lacked credibility in part because
"the wisdom of Solomon appeared clothed in very bad grammar."[3]

The Apostolic Brotherhood, as the group took to calling itself,
failed to find many adherents from out of town. It did, however, attract
attention: news of spiritual contact with saints and other biblical dignitaries did not take long to reach New York City. They arrived in the
form of Mrs. Benedict herself. Apparently displeased with the poor
spelling abilities and deficient scriptural knowledge of the original
members of the Circle, the apostolic spirits dispatched Benedict to
Brooklyn in the fall of 1850, to inform the Rev. James L. Scott of
the Seventh-Day Baptist Church that the apostle Paul wished for him
to serve their cause. Through the obliging body of Eliza Benedict,
who sat to channel him in Scott's chambers, Saint Paul requested that
Scott return with her to Auburn to join the Brotherhood. The reverend
packed his bags and heeded the call.[4]

Before they left New York, Scott arranged for a private interview
between Paul's emissary and his friend Thomas Lake Harris. Clois-
tered in Harris's chambers, Mrs. Benedict once more channeled Saint
Paul, who now requested that Harris serve as one of the Brotherhood's
writing mediums.[5] Harris followed Scott to Auburn to rule jointly
over the Apostolic Circle as one of its principal "chosen vessels."[6] In
Auburn, Reverend Scott's presence would lend respectability to the
movement and help bring its millennial pronouncements into alignment with biblical prophecy; the Poet would reform their foundering
publication endeavors.

Following the installment of Reverends Harris and Scott as its
presiding mediums, the Auburn Brotherhood resumed publishing,
with noted improvements to its prose. The group had launched a periodical in February 1850 to publish the "Disclosures from the Interior
and Superior Care for Mortals," manifested through the Brotherhood's mediums. Adherents declared contents of the Brotherhood's

publications to be the thoughts of the "Lord supreme himself," speaking through whichever apostolic emissaries he pleased to send. After reforming the Brotherhood publications, Harris returned to New York, whence he dispatched additional communications from Saints John and Paul by post. The departed Romantics still clamored for the attention of Harris's pen, such that poems authored by the spirits of Shelley and Coleridge appeared alongside the apostolic "disclosures." Crowds of several hundred now came to hear apostolic pronouncements through Mrs. Benedict. Declared believers were as many as 200, and included some of Auburn's gentry. According to spirit investigator and historian Eliab Capron, the Apostolic Brotherhood was on track to become the largest religious denomination in the region.[7]

Benedict's ego grew in proportion to the increasingly grand responsibilities that the holy spirits assigned to her Apostolic Circle. The Brotherhood claimed authority over all Christianity, rejected earthly authorities and ecclesiastical institutions, and promised that cooperation with its leadership would ensure the arrival of the Messiah. Devoted members came to view themselves as the saints and harbingers of a new dispensation. The townsfolk of Auburn eventually decided they could no longer tolerate this aberrant turn in what had, until then, been a fad without any designs of social control.[8] Mounting tensions eased when Reverend Scott received a vision instructing the elect to depart for Mountain Cove, a remote site in Fayette County, Virginia, where they would begin building God's kingdom on Earth. There they would reestablish the apostolic church described in the Book of Acts, updated in accordance with the experiments in socialist utopian living that Reverend Harris had observed in Cincinnati. An initial set of pilgrims arrived in Virginia in October 1851.

. . .

WHEN THE FIRST 100 settlers arrived at the "holy mountain" in Virginia, they bought farms with their collective funds and began to build a community fit to welcome the Messiah. Most of the pilgrims, however, were middle-class villagers, and had little experience in agriculture. The settlement was helmed by Reverend Scott, who by this point had dispensed with the annoyance of communicating with Paul through Mrs. Benedict. Scott declared that "Heaven hath chosen an external agent" to continue the disclosures through "direct inspiration." This agent, of course, was himself.[9]

Not much is known about the Auburnites who made the journey to Virginia, but two things are certain: aside from being incompetent farmers, they were the most devoted and credulous of the Brotherhood's members. Nevertheless, cracks appeared in the communards' trust after just three months. Intelligence from on high was occasionally muddled or straightforwardly wrong; a series of bad decisions wrecked the finances of the nascent commune and put paradise behind on its mortgage payments. Worse yet was Scott's notorious abuse of the power he arrogated. Before long, the reverend stood accused by some members of the community of "licentiousness and adultery."[10] The apostles stoutly defended their earthly vessel, and Scott retained his leadership of the community. But subsequent arrivals from New York were dismayed by what they found in Virginia: a demoralized and nearly bankrupt farming collective run into the ground by bad luck and apostolic caprice.

By February, some among the disenchanted decided to quit the community en masse. Unfortunately for the fate of the experiment, the departing apostates included a wealthy follower who had not yet closed on the purchase of a farm adjacent to the community's lands. A few dozen faithful remained, but morale and expectations of virtuous communal living had cratered. The apostles intervened to send Scott back to New York for reinforcements. With Harris's help, he succeeded in securing funds to repurchase the lost territory. Flush with cash and confidence, heaven's agent returned to Mountain Cove to purge the community of dissenters through edicts of banishment.

Harris hurried to Virginia to help shore up the Brotherhood's faltering faith. He was joined by several families from the Auburn Circle who had apparently remained oblivious about the trouble down South. After they arrived in May 1852, the holy oracle revised its prior statements to proclaim that both "James L. Scott and Thomas L. Harris are styled vehicles of inspiration, provided for the transmission of truth from heaven to the external world."[11] The spirits foresaw that two mortals placed on equal footing might soon jostle for position, so they saw to it that "their minds were blended by supernatural influence, and thus made one adapted vehicle for transmission of truth absolute, and light, in confirmation and exposition of truth previously revealed from heaven to man."[12] This bizarre declaration was recorded by the oracles' scribes and dutifully transmitted to the remaining faithful at Auburn. The epistle blamed the community's trouble on untrue allegations made against the "chosen vehicles" by the "unsanctified" brethren evicted from the colony.[13]

Harris moved to reestablish control over the remaining members of the commune. "Harmonic worship," a practice indistinguishable from a group séance, was held on Tuesday, Thursday, and Sunday evenings in a Methodist church located on the communal lands. Clerks kept busy every day of the week, transcribing the prophecies of various spirits with whom the vessels communed while the faithful toiled in the fields. When winter came, the spirits called Harris to more temperate climes in New Orleans, where he took lodgings at the Veranda Hotel on St. Charles Avenue. There he received a celebrity welcome from Creole spiritualists in the city, which had become an important stop on the trance lecture circuit. The *New Orleans Daily Crescent* announced the Poet's evening séances, which were lucrative enough to pay his room and board until the season was over. In New Orleans, Harris also met the woman who would become his second wife, Emily Isabella Waters.[14]

The apostolic commune at Mountain Cove was ultimately a failure and an embarrassment to Scott and Harris: the impracticality of their methods emptied community coffers within about a year of Harris's arrival, forcing Harris and Scott to conclude the experiment by autumn of 1853. After an apostate published an exposé of the community in the *Spiritual Telegraph*, the Chosen Vessels were ridiculed for their hubris in the spiritualist press.

12. POET IN NEW YORK

AFTER THE COLLAPSE of the Virginia Eden, Harris cautiously returned to New York, where he devoted himself largely to his poetic work. He released his first collection of poetry, *The Epic of Starry Heaven*, in 1854, following a marathon trance-dictation of its 4,000 lines to Samuel Brittan over the course of November and December the previous year. The *Epic* was followed by *A Lyric of the Morning Land* (1854) and *A Lyric of the Golden Age* (1856).

Readers greeted the poems with mixed reviews, which partially rehabilitated Harris's reputation in New York's spiritualist press. Even Emma Hardinge, one of the most vicious critics of the Virginia debacle, admitted that "the disgrace which [Mountain Cove] entailed on the name of Spiritualism was temporarily obliterated by the brilliant evidences of spirit-power which Mr. Harris manifested in the improvisation of these wonderful poems."[1] Although Hardinge was horrified by Scott's and Harris's attempts to channel the apostles, she was more amenable to the Poet's clerical labor on behalf of the departed British bards who authored posthumous verse through him, including Byron, Keats, and Shelley.

Harris was plenty busy with English Romantics, but also moved to reinsert himself into New York reform societies. In the years that had elapsed since the Rochester rappings, spiritualism had divided the progressive left into two factions: some reformers, among them the elder Henry James, remained committed to the ideas of Fourier and Brisbane, and believed Swedenborg's ecumenical New Church offered the best way to put them into practice. These staid radicals considered spirit circles an embarrassing distraction from meaningful labor reform, which included the eventual abolition of slavery. Undeterred by naysayers, hardcore spiritualists meanwhile found all the confirmation they needed in the séance parlor, and worked vigorously to promote women's rights, dress reform, temperance, vegetarianism, and the numerous other pet causes championed by the cultural left flank of progressive politics in the antebellum period.

As a socialist trance medium, Harris did not fit comfortably in either camp. Wanting to have it both ways, Harris founded something he called "Christian Spiritualism." The name was meant to mollify members of the New Church who were open-minded regarding spiritual communication, but appalled by the excessive indulgences of New York City mediums. Harris drew a line to separate his God-fearing "Christian Spiritualism" from the "Infidel Spiritualism" that had overtaken the religious imagination of American progressives. Only a trained Christian minister, he argued, could prevent a spirit circle from succumbing to the opportunistic demons that beguiled those mediums who made willy-nilly contact with any spirit who came knocking. This was another attempt to restrict mediumship to a hierarchical, priestly class—a signature of the taste for authoritarianism Harris had acquired from the Apostolic Circle.

Harris eventually succeeded in forming the Church of the Good Shepherd, a congregation of New Church adherents who accepted his eccentric interpretation of Swedenborgian doctrine and so-called Christian Spiritualism. Services were held in Washington Square at the New York University chapel. Some members joined merely because they wished to belong to what they thought was an independent and progressive church; these included Horace Greeley and his wife, who continued to admire the Poet. Other converts to Christian Spiritualism had seen the occasional mesmeric trance or spirit possession go awry, and were convinced of the need for principled Christian stewardship and ministerial protection within an otherwise completely anarchic American spiritualism.

By 1857, Harris had literally risen to the top of the New York City spiritualist community: his name appeared first in the list of New York lecturers and trance speakers published by the *Spiritualist Register*.[2] Absolved of his Appalachian dalliance, Harris became a frequent lecturer at Dodworth's Hall on Twenty-Sixth and Fifth, the site of regular spiritualist meetings in New York. Harris also acted as a "test medium": an elite practitioner who was summoned to evaluate spirits whose identity or authenticity was in doubt. Mediums entrusted with this responsibility were generally those whose reputations were beyond reproach.

In 1857, Harris published *The Wisdom of Angels*, a text that described his personal development as a Christian spiritualist. As explained in the volume's prefatory remarks, Harris had learned to project his consciousness to other realms, as Swedenborg and Andrew Jackson Davis had done before him.[3] During one memorable projection, Harris telepathically transported himself to a meeting of spiritual dignitaries convened in a Greek amphitheater. There, Socrates called upon Harris to present the countervailing ideas then competing for supremacy in the minds of Western men. Harris replied that while sectarianism between churches existed, the American Christian denominations had more in common with one another than they did with their most serious opponent, a sort of pantheism he called "Divine Nature."[4]

A spirit rose to reply, identifying himself as a man who had lived in the pre-Christian era. He warned against the rise of priesthoods and pseudo-deities who "defiled" the nation with the superstitions that arose from the "sensuous perversion of religion"—a sickness he likened to the social malaise that afflicted Judea before Christ came to redeem his people.[5] Later on, Harris was privy to a conversation between the spirits of Plato, Socrates, Swedenborg, the Dutch microbiologist Antonie van Leeuwenhoek, and the ancient Greek painter Zeuxis. Swedenborg informed the others that mankind would continue its pagan worship of nature until they understood "the doctrine of degrees." The seer then unrolled a parchment to reveal a diagram that demonstrated the way in which the "hells" influenced the brains of men "immersed in Nature."

Swedenborg's diagram bore a striking resemblance to the science of phrenomagnetism developed by British physician Robert H. Collyer in the 1840s.[6] Collyer was clever enough to understand that as a deterministic science, phrenology disillusioned those who received unfavorable readings of their scalps. By contrast, mesmerism offered constructive medical diagnoses. Collyer's stroke of genius was to combine these two fields of expertise. His innovation, phrenomagnetism, held that the "magnetic" force theorized by mesmerists could be directed to various regions of the brain mapped by phrenologists, and thereby alter the personality characteristics and affective states of a given subject.[7]

Harris's adaptation of phrenomagnetism relied on the gender dichotomy popularized by spiritualists: while the right lobe of the brain was positively charged, energetic, active, and male, the left lobe was negative, passive, receptive, and female. To this Harris appended the mystic ideal of bigendered pre-Adamic man that had obsessed Rosicrucian alchemists, the Ephrata communists, and the Shakers. The angels revealed to Harris that during the edenic "Golden Age" of human civilization, bigendered humans were connected to the masculine part of the Godhead through the more passive and sensitive left chambers of the brain. Meanwhile, "because the lungs corresponded to understanding," humankind accessed the feminine aspect of the Godhead—which Harris and the Neoplatonist Gnostics called Sophia, or "divine wisdom"—through the lungs.[8] These teachings would soon form the basis of Harris's philosophy of internal respiration.

. . .

RED FLAGS WERE RAISED against Harris's suggestion, albeit ventriloquized by Socrates and Swedenborg, that modern spiritualism had fallen into the hands of Pharisees and priestlings who unwittingly served anti-Christian demons. The Poet's crusade against democratic spiritualism soured his friendship with his publisher Samuel Brittan, forcing him to publish *The Wisdom of Angels* with the New Church Publishing Association, a Swedenborgian publishing house.

In 1858, Harris published what would stand as the cornerstone of his subsequent life work. This was the first volume of his *Arcana of Christianity: An Unfolding of Celestial Sense in the Divine Word.* The text took its name from the *Arcana Cœlestia,* Swedenborg's voluminous annotations of the Bible. The *Arcana* was a tedious tome that detailed Harris's adventures in spiritual projection to the various planets in the solar system, whose inhabitants he interviewed. It was an absurdly pretentious text, but because it was serialized before publication, it did not take New York spiritualists by surprise. What stunned them was the *Song of Satan,* an epic poem that Harris appended to the hefty volume.

Emma Hardinge called the *Song of Satan* "an epic of so shocking and repulsive a character that even many of [Harris's] best friends were obliged to credit its inspiration to the source which the title so candidly claimed for it."[9] In the poem, Harris wrote that the Lord had summoned him to a "trial in the shape of a personal visitation from Infernal Spirits" in March of 1857.[10] Just as Christ had been tempted in the garden of Gethsemane, so was Harris tempted by the Lord: his spiritual body was projected into the hells, where a panoply of demons, bent on destroying Harris's "physical existence," each assumed the likeness of a formidable intellect. Among those impersonated by the evil "genii" were Henry VIII, Sir Thomas More, Milton, Shelley, and Wordsworth. One by one, they engaged Harris in "spiritual warfare"—a mortal combat of wit and logic.

Further commentary on this odd volume rests with scholars of such arcana. It suffices to observe that Harris got the reaction he wanted. Correctly foreseeing his simultaneous expulsion from New York's Swedenborgian and Spiritualist circles, Harris resigned the pulpit of the Church of the Good Shepherd in April 1859 and set sail for England on the fifth of May. From across the Atlantic, he dispatched an excuse for his hasty departure, explaining in an editorial for the *Herald of Light* that he had been summoned as the Lord's messenger to England, where the hells had made a frightful progression on Earth, requiring his skill in spiritual warfare to turn them back.[11]

In London, Harris lodged with Swedenborg's translator, Garth Wilkinson, and through him met numerous New Church disciples eager to learn more about the relation between Swedenborg's teachings and the influx of spirits swarming America's séance rooms. As his opponents in New York quickly surmised, Harris had traveled to Europe with the objective of converting the English New Church to Christian Spiritualism. The Poet enjoyed more success in Britain than he did in the United States, but his sermons in London managed to be both bland and abstruse; they lacked the fiery political radicalism of the New Church in England. Even after Harris discovered British receptivity to his ideas about social and spiritual regeneration, his audiences cooled and thinned.

Harris repaired to Bolton Abbey, in Yorkshire, to write in solitude. There the Poet developed the next stage of his spiritual teachings. Still concentrating on the legend of prelapsarian bisexuality, Harris began teaching that humans could achieve divinity by locating their lost spiritual counterparts of the other gender. To do so, they must first restore the lost connection to the Divine Feminine through the lungs. This could be accomplished through the practice of something Harris called "internal" respiration. The Poet tested his teachings on divine respiration in sermons given at Manchester, where they were received with genuine interest.

Meanwhile, the tide was already turning against Harris in London, as news from his American adversaries had begun to arrive by post. It was plain to leaders of the New York spiritualist movement that Harris only wished to set the minds of British investigators against the allegedly pagan and anti-Christian practices of American spiritualists, and dispose them toward his own divine authority. Charles

Partridge, Harris's former publisher, slammed the Poet in the pages of the *Spiritual Telegraph* in February of 1860. Partridge decried the authoritarian stance Harris was taking as antithetical to the spirit of free and scientific inquiry cherished by spiritualist investigators. Partridge additionally sought to destroy Harris's reputation by exposing the mercurial quality of his spiritual persuasion, recounting for readers the Poet's path through Calvinism, Universalism, Harmonialism, and Spiritualism—and subsequent denunciation of every faith he abandoned. He ridiculed Harris's failure to make up his mind about whether or not he was a Socialist—a critique the Poet took to heart.

13. THE BROTHERHOOD OF THE NEW LIFE

ALTHOUGH SPIRITUALISM LACKED well-defined institutions and churches, Partridge's editorial was tantamount to defrocking one of its renegade priests. Finding himself outflanked, Harris announced his separation from the New Church and retreated to Scotland at the invitation of a group of ardent believers who had come together in Edinburgh. This nucleus of Harris's followers had devised a name for themselves: The Brotherhood of the New Life. The brethren called themselves "pivotal men" whose adherence to Harris's teachings would make them instrumental to the regeneration of the race. The Poet liked their terminology, and soon revised to the singular: the "pivotal man" was to be Harris himself.

The Poet's spirit guides convinced him it would be folly to teach Christians the errors of sectarian backbiting while the hells were closing in on humanity. The work of regeneration had to begin immediately, and Harris needed to find a quiet and peaceful place to do it. At the spirits' suggestion, the pivotal man launched another communal endeavor, this time in the Hudson Valley. Like the Scottish society of internal breathers, it would be called the Brotherhood of the New Life.

The Brotherhood purchased a farm in Wassaic, New York, where Harris built a house for himself, his family, and a dozen of his most devoted disciples from both sides of the Atlantic.[1] One of the original communards, Jane Lee Waring, was a wealthy congregant from the Church of the Good Shepherd who put up some of the initial funds. Other members of the fledgling communal group included one of Harris's wealthy Southern converts, James Requa, who joined with his wife and children.[2]

Wassaic was another attempt to build John Winthrop's "city upon a hill" in America. The putative goal of the colony was to form "a nucleus for the quickening of the whole body of mankind, and of those especially who are destined to survive hereafter, to perpetuate a race of men in pure Godliness of life."[3] The new race would begin with those who located their spiritual counterparts and regenerated their bodies to immortality through divine respiration. To ensure the process of regeneration proceeded unhindered, Harris took the additional precaution of regularly "demagnetizing" himself, and instructed his followers to do the same.

Meanwhile, the nation teetered on the edge of civil war. Harris later claimed that he foretold "the prospective formation of the Southern Confederacy, and the fierce and bloody war for the dissolution of the Union" a decade before it occurred.[4] According to his business secretary and official biographer, Arthur Cuthbert, Harris considered slavery "the most monstrous outrage existing on this planet" and "felt in strong sympathy with the noble spirit that animated the Abolition Party, and even with that fiercer spirit that flamed up in the bosom of John Brown."[5] Nevertheless, the Brotherhood remained on the sidelines of the struggle: while the nation took up arms, Harris and his aspiring regenerates retired to their commune in upstate New York, where they pledged to do work of greater importance than any of the sacrifices being made for the abolitionist cause. What was the point of killing in the name of abolition, Harris asked, as long as everyone remained slaves to sin and to the exploitation of modern industrial capitalism?[6] This line of thinking was not exclusive to Harris or the Brotherhood: prominent Socialists like Horace Greeley, and many of the readers of his *New-York Tribune*, believed that emancipation would not be meaningful or adequate if freed slaves were forced into the crypto-slavery of indentured sharecropping, or the low-wage destitution of America's urban slums. The labor question had to be addressed first.

Recognizing this dilemma, spiritual regeneration at the Wassaic farm possessed a material corollary that would render slavery and wage exploitation obsolete. Together, the brethren would demonstrate an escape from the degrading alienation of capitalist society by returning—once more—to cooperative and associative modes of living modeled by the apostolic church.[7] The Brethren referred to the commune they founded as "The Use."[8] Harris taught that through equality in labor, the communards could reach a degree of convivial harmony that would restore their "spiritual senses"—capacities of seeing, hearing, and feeling that mankind had lost when human bodies were divided in the Fall. These senses would be sequentially opened by attaining the seven levels of divine respiration, which were enabled as the breather entered into complete harmony with the communism practiced at the Use.

Harris avoided detailing the mechanics of internal breath, preferring to allow religious psychology to determine who experienced it and who did not. But brothers and sisters of the New Life left behind numerous descriptions of their attainments of divine respiration. One sister likened her initial experience of divine breath as

> a river of water flowing through me, the current starting
> from the heart down one arm and through the neck and head
> on one side and down the other side to arm, then down body
> to leg and up and so on back to heart forming a circle. . . .
> I seem to breathe through the external part of my body taking in the air through the interface of the whole body. It is
> a different air from which I breathe in my lungs. My body
> at such times seems to be conscious of a changed air which
> surrounds us, but we are not in a fit condition to receive it at
> all times. I now at all times have a strange feeling as if I were

far away from those I am talking to or come in contact with;
it seems as if there was something in the atmosphere which
shuts me off from them. Nothing seems real; I do things
because I must, but am not in them.[9]

As Cuthbert wrote in his history of the Brotherhood, "All who
joined The Use, whether they made their home at its centre permanently or only temporarily, were in every instance more or less par-
takers in the same Life and Breath, and themselves experiencing,
in however inferior degree to Mr. Harris himself, similar organic
changes. . . . The Kingdom of God to them was not mere observation;
it was within them."[10] A letter written by Cuthbert's wife during the
Wassaic period confirms this impression. She wrote:

The Breath sustains us, not only in the discharge of laborious
daily duties, but enables us to watch for hours at night when
watching is needed. It removes disease and the tendency to
disease in the system, and makes the heart glad and peaceful
when it would naturally be sad and depressed. . . . Oh it is a
thing to be most devoutly desired, but not till you have sat
down and counted the cost. . . . The open breathers at Wassaic number 19; many have left and gone out into the world to
perform their different uses.[11]

Brethren who achieved advanced degrees of internal respiration
took special nicknames to denote their elite status: Requa and his wife
were known as Steadfast and Golden Rose, Mr. and Mrs. Buckner
were called Harmonious and Blossom, their daughter Arcadia was
Dimple, and Mr. and Mrs. Martin were dubbed Skillful and Sweet
Brier. A Mrs. Gallagher, of uncertain provenance, somehow ended up
with the name Tiny Funnyhorns. Harris and his secretary Jane Waring were known as Faithful and Lady Dovie.

14. SALEM-ON-ERIE

ITH THE 1861 ESTABLISHMENT of the first Brotherhood colony in Dutchess County, Harris began his tenure as the de facto
superintendent of one of the longest-lived and most successful communal societies in American history. Apocalyptic warnings served
their usual function of discouraging defection from the commune:
simultaneous to the community's founding, Harris announced that
the "Judgment of the Earth" was nigh, and that the "destruction of the
evil natural soul in mankind, and the birth of a new natural soul thru
germinal formation in the frame" were soon to begin.[1] At Wassaic, the
Brotherhood of the New Life took up the task of "germinating" new
souls by committing to celibacy at Harris's command.

As the Civil War raged, the Brotherhood prospered; it soon outgrew the Wassaic farm and relocated to a larger property in nearby
Amenia. There Harris founded and presided over a bank while his
followers toiled in a Brotherhood mill. Both ventures enjoyed moderate success, and Harris began to explore more expansive territory near
the shores of Lake Erie.[2] The society remained in Amenia until 1867,
when the Brotherhood, now numbering around seventy-five, began
the process of relocating once more. That October, Harris and his
closest disciples completed the purchase of just under 2,000 acres of
farmland between Brocton and Portland, adjacent villages in Chautauqua County.[3]

Brocton was little more than a village anchored by two churches,
nestled between a hemlock forest and the lakeshore, fifty miles west of

Buffalo. The Brotherhood land was level and arable, and the territory included the juncture of the Lake Shore and Allegheny Valley Railroads. After establishing themselves in the existing farmhouses and taking up their spades and plows, the brethren built a small village around the train depot located at the railroad crossing. Called Salem-on-Erie, the village came to include a hotel, grist mill, general store, and a seasonal produce market where the Brotherhood sold produce from its farms.[4] Harris developed additional plans to extract natural gas from the springs that plumed from the bottom of the lake, just fifty feet from his property.[5]

These businesses augmented the colony's agricultural activities, which included hay production, a nursery, and what became the Brotherhood's signature industry: the winery. The land purchase included some existing vineyards and a vintage initially operated as the Lake Erie and Missouri River Wine Company. Harris brought in a team of experts to advise the brethren on what sort of grapes might complement their existing crop. Within a few years, the Brotherhood's "medicinal" wines became known throughout New York.[6] In 1870, the Brotherhood erected a restaurant, wine shop, and bar near the Brocton train depot. Closer to home, the brethren built themselves a gymnasium, where they held band practices and hosted lectures. Music was a popular pastime at Brocton, as Harris believed sweet melodies could summon Queen Lily, his spiritual counterpart, into his presence.

Due to the relative success of their agricultural endeavors, as well as Harris's shrewd stock-market investment of his followers' liquidated assets, the brothers were able to snap up about a dozen additional small farms surrounding their lands in 1868. Their total land holdings, which included some speculation in Missouri real estate, had an estimated value in 1873 of approximately $200,000—a sum that caused curious reporters to question the colony's solvency.[7] Money, however, was never lacking: Some members of the Brotherhood possessed considerable financial resources. Although the poorer members sacrificed all they had to the community, its wealthier members usually did not;

they could do as they liked with their money, as long as they contributed enough to keep the enterprise afloat.

As news of the unusual endeavor at Brocton spread across New York, Harris emphasized to outsiders that he was no Communist, but the patriarch of a society that professed faith in paternalistic "imperial" socialism. The Brotherhood, he explained, "is simply an effort to demonstrate the ethical creed of the Gospel," adapted to account for the development of modern industries. Socialist "Use," Harris insisted, offered "the practical solution to the social problems of the age."[8] He referred to the labor unrest that had already begun to plague American cities at the start of the Gilded Age, and to the industrial monopolies that perverted American democracy and social relations.

Ambitions at Salem required more manpower than the brethren could supply, so Harris made missionary tours to the South, where he organized outposts of the Brotherhood and gathered new adherents.[9] The Poet then tapped his transatlantic networks to lure overseas believers to the New York hinterland. A significant number of Japanese immigrants also joined the Brocton commune, further diversifying a colony that already boasted international membership.[10] The Poet was pleased by the prestige of an international following, and persuaded himself that Shintoism was compatible with his teachings because it also taught the Divine Feminine.[11] The number of Japanese brethren numbered at least eleven within a year of the community's transference to Brocton; nine others had already returned to Japan to fight in the Boshin War.[12]

By 1873, population at Salem-on-Erie had surpassed one hundred. Families who joined as a unit were the community's backbone, but the Brotherhood had trouble retaining young blood: minors who joined with their parents typically abandoned the project when they came of age. Aside from the Requas and the Cuthberts, colonists included the Buckners, Freemans, Martins, and Brownells, all families from the Georgia outpost; a Shaker family of five called the Brewers; old standbys from the Church of the Good Shepherd called the Emersons;

chief viticulturist Dr. Hyde and his family of four from Missouri; the Moore family of five, also from Missouri; and a wealthy widow called Mary McConnell.[13] Of these, the Brownells were the last to come to Brocton, in April 1869. When they arrived, they found several dozen colonists tilling the fields, harvesting grapes, looking after the nursery, and minding the produce market in the village.

As is typical for communal societies practicing a form of microcosmic social transformation, the Brotherhood deemphasized familial bonds in favor of a group identity. Although Harris did not require families to separate, he encouraged new recruits to send their minors to live at the "Bird's Nest," the residence for children, at least until the ties of dependency were broken. Single young men lived together on a dairy farm known as "The Bower," while the rest of the brethren shared the cottages and farmhouses that dotted the landscape. Communal housing arrangements emphasized diversity: the Brownells lodged in the Garden House with Rosa Emerson, James Fowler, Dr. and Mrs. Gardner, a Boston teacher called Miss Grace Wilder, and two of the Japanese followers.[14] This sort of interracial, intergenerational, and communistic cohabitation was practically unheard-of anywhere else in the country.

Harris lived at Vine Cliff, one of the existing farms on the property. He decorated the estate with what became his typical extravagance: carpets, artworks, books, and flowers lent his chambers an air of studious sophistication. To enhance privacy, Harris successfully petitioned the municipality to abandon a road planned near the property, then tore down the farm's outbuildings to make way for ornamental gardens done in the style of an English manor. A small vineyard beside the house allowed Vine Cliff's residents to test grape varietals. Jane Waring took the lead in this endeavor, garnering praise and awards at regional grape fairs.[15]

At Vine Cliff, the Poet preferred to spend most of his time writing in his private study on the second floor, where he was attended by Japanese boys. When he left his cloister, it was to stroll the grounds in a long black cloak while stroking his beard and smoking a pipe, lost in thought. Although Harris allowed himself a dozen imported cigars every day, he forbade tobacco to those less advanced in the practice of internal respiration.[16] Waring was one of the few allowed to smoke. She liked to spend her days at Brocton experimenting with greenhouse cultivation and striding the grounds to oversee work crews while brazenly smoking a pipe.

Harris continued to advise celibacy to his followers, teaching them that propagation was an activity that stood between them and immortality. Meanwhile, he told outsiders that the colony's death rates declined as the number of celibates increased.[17] The Cuthberts and the Requas each had a son at Amenia, but the overall birthrate within the Brotherhood suggests that the brethren largely upheld the celibacy mandate. Harris did not entirely prohibit marriages, as long as he personally approved them. Unions like the one between Miss Wilder and Mr. Clark, who acted as the Brotherhood's sales representative for its wine business in New York, were sanctioned as matters of expedience, deemed necessary for those who might otherwise fall victim to more serious temptations by the devils who were always trying to thwart Harris's leadership.

Two marriages Harris wished to prevent were those of his sons. John, the elder son, was ill tempered, gluttonous, and deemed of insufficient Use. Harris accepted his marriage to a servant girl, but would not allow them to live together. Thomas Jr. was better liked than John, and had always enjoyed a broader radius of freedom. But Harris did not approve of his son's betrothed, and told the credulous girl that she had been selected as one of the transfers to a new Brotherhood colony in Cleveland. Flattered by the anointment, she hastened to discharge the mission that "Father" had given her. She discovered the lie when she got to Ohio, but the deceit was sufficient to dissuade her from returning to Brocton. After his fiancée jilted him for a man she met in New York City, Thomas Jr. abandoned Brocton and went west on his own.

By this point the Poet had practically dissolved his own marriage:

Emily Harris was not permitted to join the fun at Brocton. The Poet first packed Emily off to England, and later sent her back to family in New Orleans with instructions to reform her spiritual condition. Evidently, Emily had relapsed from the first degree of internal respiration: Harris curtly informed his wife that her spiritual condition was so low that demons were using her to threaten his life. Mrs. Harris, who would later be deemed insane, appeared to believe him. As she wrote an acquaintance in August 1867: "Faithful [Harris] has almost been destroyed through me because I could not hold my ground." When at last she was permitted to join him at Vine Cliff in 1869, the Poet kept "Lady Pink Ears" out of view, and few brethren even knew she was there. Harris wished to hide her obvious lunacy, lest it degrade his reputation.[18]

Salem-on-Erie was nominally governed by a nineteen-person council, but Harris devised ways to assert his predominance. Illness could be overcome with internal respiration, but as the pivotal man, Harris was obliged to take on the diseases contracted by his followers, including advanced tuberculosis. No matter how divinely he respired, the Poet's health was never particularly robust, and he blamed his frequent illnesses, and even his bad moods, on the infractions of disobedient brothers. As he had done to his wife, Harris told repeat offenders that demons were using their weak wills to introduce disorder and disease into the colony. In the nearby villages, he acquired a reputation for inventing humiliating punishments to test the faith of his followers. The sadism of these assignments ranged from routine stable mucking to the command that young Ernest Buckner, a disobedient child, stay the night in an abandoned house located on the Brotherhood property.

Damaging rumors began to circulate in 1869, when expelled members of the Brotherhood spread stories of child abuse and of Harris's improper conduct with women and girls. Harris and Waring found themselves accused, in print, of leading a sexually licentious colony of dubious spiritual elevation.[19] The allegations were unsubstantiated and eventually put to rest, but they caused the community to maintain a determined distance from its neighbors.[20] The aura of mystery surrounding its true purposes was enhanced by comings and goings of people of unusual pedigree for western New York. During a visit by Bishop Bugnion D'Erlach, an eccentric Swiss mystic who had been evangelizing Harris's teachings in Mauritius and Madagascar, the bishop announced to locals that he had achieved sufficiently divine respiration to see the fairies that frolicked at Brocton.[21] Even more curious were the British nobles who had integrated as members of the commune. Previously known to their friends in England as Lady Oliphant and Laurence, her son and a famous travel writer, the Oliphants were called Viola and Woodbine by the other brethren.

Harris had made the Oliphants' acquaintance during one of his English missions. He converted them both, then persuaded Lady Oliphant to join him at Amenia, where Laurence later joined her. The nobles' conversions drew scrutiny and notoriety to the Brotherhood. Concerned friends and London gossips wondered what could possibly have compelled Laurence Oliphant to abandon his promising political career for an obscure life of agricultural chores in America. Was Laurence insane? Was he madly in love with the rich and handsome Jane Waring, as some of her friends believed? Or did he sincerely hope Harris could cure him of the venereal diseases he had reputedly contracted during his London playboy days? Frustrating the chatterboxes back home, Laurence and Lady Oliphant professed only their sincere beliefs in letters to a small set of correspondents from whom they'd not yet cut ties.

Laurence Oliphant's letters to London revealed that his regeneration had begun with acts of penance in Amenia: there he rose at five and spent his mornings hoeing in the vineyards. He labored for ten hours a day, stopping only for an hour's rest at the noontime meal. "I am at present living a sort of hermit life," he wrote, "trying to get rid of the terrible old worldly magnetic poisons out of my system (which I have been imbibing all my life) without hurting or infecting my neighbors." He candidly revealed to old family friends, the Cowpers, that he lived in a shed, built his own furniture out of wine crates, and ate his meals alone out of a basket. Although forbidden to speak with his mother, Laurence beheld a "wonderful" change in her from afar. Harris and Waring steadfastly ignored him. But Oliphant remarked with wonder on his improved health and delighted in the way that manual labor allowed his mind to focus on "divine things," observing that "one of the objects of this severe physical exercise is to produce rest in the brain."[22]

Release from the responsibility of managing one's property was one of the first blessings awarded to initiates in the New Life. The Oliphants allowed themselves to be partially unburdened, but they preferred to make occasional infusions of cash rather than place their wealth entirely at Harris's disposal. Even so, their donations likely surpassed the life savings of most other aspirants to the New Life. One of Harris's posthumous detractors claimed that the Oliphants "enriched" the society with "several hundred thousand dollars of good English money."[23] This sum may be exaggerated, but the Oliphants likely tendered nearly $100,000 of the quarter-million-dollar initial investment in the Brocton property.[24]

In November 1867, Harris summoned Oliphant to Brocton, where he passed his first night on a spare mattress in a barn loft. At the Poet's command, he remained in relative seclusion and undertook water-hauling duty, which required him to spend two hours fetching water for the Brotherhood's horses after they were stabled for the evening. Oliphant apparently delighted in the menial labor that Harris assigned him at the Use, believing that he would be purged of the "worldliness" that afflicted him. He spent the winter of his trial year lugging firewood through the deep lakeside snow before going to work in the fields the following spring.

The aristocrat cut a comical figure on the farm, where his total ineptitude for manual labor and unfamiliarity with basic tools made him an object of amusement among the Irish field hands. In letters to Mrs. Cowper, who occasionally tried to tempt him back to London, Oliphant apologized for the "odor of stables" that adhered to his missives, in which he aggressively reinforced his delight in Harris's sadistic assignments. Rather than deter him from remaining with the Brotherhood, Oliphant told Mrs. Cowper that these tests only increased his desire to be of Use. "I kiss the rod," he told her, "that offers me this new evidence of my Father's love."[25]

Oliphant agreed to Harris's suggestion that he abandon Parliament and made arrangements to be substituted in the House of Commons. After cheerfully enduring months of humiliation, he was finally put in charge of overseeing the railway station bistro, where one of his duties was to board stopped trains and hawk sandwiches to hungry passengers. Lady Oliphant had also been put to work. She was a feeble fifty-six when she arrived in New York, and had never done a day of real work in her life. This omission was corrected at Salem-on-Erie, where she was ordered to be of Use in the community laundry. None of the other brethren perceived the Oliphants' treatment as extreme in any way: everyone had to endure some kind of trial to prove they were of Use.

In 1870, Harris allowed Oliphant to return to Europe as the *Times* war correspondent for the Franco-Prussian War, provided that he forward his salary to the Brotherhood. In Paris, Oliphant met Alice le Strange, another British expat of aristocratic lineage. They fell in love and hoped to marry. But Harris would only permit the union if Alice returned to Brocton for the standard initiation. Oliphant agreed to Harris's demand, and Alice succeeded in winning membership in the Brotherhood. The two were married in 1872 at St. George's in Westminster. After the newlyweds enjoyed a celibate honeymoon on the Continent, Alice was ordered to return to the lakeside colony.[26]

When Harris decided to divide the community and take part of the Brotherhood to Sonoma County in 1875, he instructed Lady Oliphant to remain at her washtub in Brocton. She and Alice lived together at the Vine Cliff commune until Harris summoned the younger Mrs. Oliphant to join him in the West. Alice did not last very long in California: after a short period, she left the Brotherhood estate, named Fountain Grove, and struck out on her own to educate the children of miners in the region. She longed to be reunited with her husband, and impatiently awaited his return.

15. CALIFORNIA IDYLL

WHEN HARRIS PURCHASED the first 400 acres of Fountain Grove in 1875, the Sonoma wine industry languished in recession. The West had been hit hard by the economic calamity that ensued after the Panic of 1873, scuttling the plans of speculators whose investments relied on European investments in American railroads. The rail connection from San Francisco to Santa Rosa had not been completed by the time the crisis struck, allowing Harris to buy land in Sonoma at bargain prices.

The Brotherhood spent its first several years in California occupied with construction and basic agriculture. The first colonists to arrive were Harris, Mrs. Requa and her son, and two Japanese converts named Kanaye and Arai. The pioneers lived together in a shack while a mansion of suitable grandeur was constructed on the property. When the house was completed, Harris sent for Waring and his wife. Other members went west at the Poet's request. The vineyards that put Fountain Grove on the map were not planted until 1880, when the price of grapes had recovered. The Brotherhood maintained a low profile in the meantime, quietly expanding into another 300 acres on the strength of its success as a dairy farm. By 1883, however, production had shifted almost entirely to the Brotherhood's medicinal wines.

Unlike at Brocton, where drudgery was carried out in the name of the Use, labor on the California winery could be pleasurable owing to the temperate climate and the natural beauty and fertility of the surrounding hills. The site was deemed more amenable to advancements in divine respiration, which opened the spiritual senses of most of the initiates. Harris was able to monitor each individual's progress toward regeneration by placing his hands upon the subject's "plexus," which functioned as the "great joy-nerve of the body." When a brother or sister entered fully into communal life, finding the "labor in joy and [the] joy in labor," the plexus "quivered for joy" and was "felt as a vibrating disk, with almost as many keys as there were chords in the solar fire." When this receptor of socialist joy was regularly stimulated, the worker felt connected to the universal plexus of all mankind, producing a feeling of solidarity that provided "frequent access of palpitant and exquisite delights."[1]

As the Brethren advanced in their practice of socialism and divine respiration, sightings of the "fay race," or fairies, became more commonplace. These were important events for the brothers and sisters at Fountain Grove, who described these sightings in their letters.[2] Harris taught that prior to the corruption of mankind that began in the Garden of Eden, the fays were able to live inside human bodies. The loss of internal respiration smothered the fays, but regenerated brothers and sisters made their bodies hospitable to their return. Because they were small enough to circulate through human blood vessels, hundreds of fays could coexist in a single human form.[3] One sister reported hearing "singing and laughing in my breasts." Her experience had begun with "a strange new feeling in the womb which lasted for a day or two; I was so very, very happy, but the joy was in my womb, not in my heart. There was no sexual excitement about it, but it was just the sweetest joy that ever came to me in all my life."[4]

Higher degrees of respiration led to the discovery of a brother's spiritual counterpart of the other gender. As the same sister wrote,

> In reading about the evolving of counterparts I could not
> realize in the least how it might be, until one morning I
> awoke with a strange and delightful sensation in my hands
> and arms, particularly in the arms. I cannot describe it; but

for the first time in my life my arms seemed to be full, <u>and</u> <u>as though they had always been empty before</u>; it seemed as though there was no swelling, but merely <u>as if every particle</u> <u>of matter was touched by another close to it</u>; it was not like anything else.[5]

Meanwhile, Harris continued to prophesy the coming apocalypse. He taught his followers that the human race was "inverted" by utter spiritual corruption, and that the apocalypse would sweep most humans off the face of the Earth. As early as January 1879, one of the brothers wrote that Harris warned the "Divine Event" was not long off.[6] The next year, Arthur Cuthbert wrote a Brocton brother that he saw no reason for the latter to bother making the trip to California: "The reason for this is that the end is very near, nay is, as it were, already in process; and while this is the case no one should change his pose."[7] But Harris had learned from the collapse of Millerite adventism, and never fell into the trap of giving a precise date for the chaotic "whirl" he said would destroy mankind when good and evil spirits descended and ascended from their respective spheres to battle for control of the terrestrial plane. The brethren at Fountain Grove believed the pressing of each vintage brought them nearer to the verge of the great "catastrophe."

· · ·

TOWNSFOLK IN SANTA ROSA did not discover the existence of a strange religious sect in their midst until 1879, following the publication of William Alfred Hinds's now-classic text, *American Communities* (1878), a historical survey of communistic societies in the United States. Hinds was a resident of the Oneida Perfectionist commune and had followed its leader, John Humphrey Noyes, in the study of socialist praxis in America. Oneida's reputation was already in tatters by 1879, when Noyes fled to Canada to avoid charges of sexual misconduct with adolescents—a practice that formed an important part of the communism of sexual relations among the Perfectionists. Hinds's slim volume was published in part to demonstrate that the Oneida Community was not a moral and historical aberration that would threaten the fabric of American society, but a conscientious and hardworking religious sect that issued from a longstanding American tradition of communal societies—one that stretched all the way back to the colonial era. His text describes the proliferation of Shaker villages, the establishment of the Harmony Society communes in Pennsylvania and Indiana, numerous Fourierist phalanxes, the Midwestern "Icarian" communes inspired by the work of Étienne Cabet, and several others. Hinds included a chapter on the Brotherhood of the New Life toward the end of his popular book.

Harris was equally well informed on American communal movements. He considered himself the natural successor to Ann Lee and repeatedly made entreaties for Shakers to join the Brotherhood. The Poet wrote to members of the United Society of Believers in Christ's Second Appearing to advertise his advancement "into broad realms, not to any extent traversed by your usual Shaker thought." Fountain Grove, Harris informed the Shakers, was an intermediary station en route to more glorious paradise, "where there we shall be neither male nor female, but counter-partial unity of the two-in-one. We shall be satisfied when we awake in the likeness of our Father-Mother."[8] Notwithstanding the presence of ex-Shakers in the Brotherhood, Harris's appeal failed to convince additional Shakers to convert en masse.

Harris also tried to attract members of the collapsing Oneida Community. "Our sympathies," he wrote Hinds, "are especially toward those who have devoted themselves, in a practical sense, to the substitution of 'altruism' for egoism, of mutuality for competition, in social life."[9] The property he "owned" at Fountain Grove, he told Hinds, was something he held in "trust from God, for his service in the race."[10] Harris knew that the Oneida Perfectionists valued education above almost all else. To impress Hinds, he alleged that Fountain Grove possessed the most voluminous library in the young state of California. He likened Fountain Grove to a "school" that prepared its students for "*a new era of human evolution*" that commenced with celibate communism.[11] Although they practiced complex marriage rather than regenerative celibacy, the Oneida Perfectionists also believed that a new evolution had begun in their nucleus of "Bible Communism," where babies were literally bred for superior spiritual qualities—a science they called "stirpiculture." Combining the positivist sociological adaptations of Darwinism that had begun to emerge by the late nineteenth century with the old Protestant project of social regeneration, Harris told Hinds that within the Brotherhood, "the race will take a new departure; that we approach a new beginning of human days and generations."[12] In the new era, he suggested, regenerated human society would be governed by patriarchal theocratic socialism.

Harris's private writings on private property indicate that his view on the matter had hardened over the postwar years, which were a tumultuous time for the labor movement. The Republican legislators who dominated the Reconstruction era favored business over labor, and allowed noncompetitive monopolies to emerge in booming industries like the railroads. Resentment ran high in the engine yards, particularly in the West, where railroad barons attempted to crush demands for higher wages by recruiting Asian immigrants to work construction jobs at lower rates than their white counterparts. In San Francisco, the postwar labor movement combined with anti-immigrant sentiment. The Workingmen's Party of California, founded in 1877 by labor organizer Denis Kearney, held massive rallies to protest the actions of their monopolist employers. They focused their ire on the railroad companies and their Chinese laborers. Observing the matter closely, Harris saw a "new aristocracy" emerging through the monopolies of the Gilded Age and singled out the Pacific Railway as one of the corporations "strangling" California. He lamented that oversupply in the western labor market was worsened by the fact that "[m]achinery is supplanting humanity." Accumulation of wealth by industrialists, he affirmed, was leading America to "national suicide and ruin."[13]

Harris believed that private ownership forces mankind into a "selfish and fatal individualism" that "makes him a miser, a voluptuary, a scorner, a misanthrope." When maintained to support a family, private property turns the family man into a "slave of the children of his loins." Harris called this wretched condition "familism," and listed it along with "sacerdotalism" as one of the supporting pillars of the "meretricious, cruel, and insincere" regime of capital, which "controls the people, the lands of the people, [and] the customs and the employments of the people."[14] The accumulation of wealth, Harris concluded, was immoral and anti-Christian, and was leading America straight into the clutches of demons. His sharpening views were influenced in part by a visit to Paris after the fall of the Commune. As Jane Waring later recalled for the Brethren back in California, she and Harris arrived in the city so soon after the defeat of the Commune that "the fires were still burning and the bloodstains were on the pavements and prisoners guarded by bayonets were marched through the streets at all hours, a fearful scene of human passions and contrast to which all our aims must lead to if we are faithful."[15]

. . .

AFTER ARRIVING IN CALIFORNIA, however, the Poet largely kept his views to himself. Once ensconced at Fountain Grove, Harris relied on more sophisticated vectors for massive social regeneration. The first of these was wine, which had become the Poet's passion.

The Brethren were already familiar with viticulture from their Salem years. In New York, wine had come to occupy a special place in the ideology of Brotherhood imperial socialism. As Marx explained in *Das Kapital*, a commodity contains a quantity of congealed labor that is theoretically reflected in its price. Wine, to the Brothers, was the ideal commodity on which to concentrate the energies of the Use:

the labor of many individuals flowed into the thousands of bottles that Fountain Grove produced annually and sold from its New York boutiques. In this way, the Brethren believed their wines would transmit the goodwill of mutual service to those who drank them.[16]

Harris claimed that the restorative properties of Fountain Grove wines resided in "living animates" that were "a million times smaller than bacteria," and that Brotherhood wines did not cause insobriety because they communicated to drinkers when it was time to stop consuming them. As he wrote to Sam Swan, who managed the New York wine shops where the Brotherhood sold most of its vintage, Fountain Grove wines were "charged with a potential intelligence by means of which, if there is a rational nerve in the organism that it can reach to make vibrations on, the spirit of the vinous intelligence itself will dictate when the organism for the time being is charged sufficiently." The Poet signed his letter "*In vino veritas.*"[17]

Harris did not rely on wine alone to disseminate the auras of New Life: although removed from the mundane tasks of farm labor, he toiled constantly over his writings. When inspired or pressed by the fays to complete a manuscript, he sometimes retired with Waring to Linn Lilla, a mountain residence that functioned as his private retreat. After coming down from the mountain, Harris would regale the other brothers and sisters with tales of his travels in the spirit lands and the knowledge he acquired from such luminaries as George Fox, the founder of the Quaker religion.[18]

Arai, one of the Japanese members, was put in charge of the printing press Harris installed at Fountain Grove, which he used to set private editions of the eighteen works Harris authored during the California period. The Poet attributed his prolific output to his uniquely dexterous command of the plexus, and claimed that by concentrating on his plexial disc, he received the divine consciousness directly into his body.[19] Although access to his work was restricted to those with personal connections to the Poet, the Brethren still considered Harris the Lord's chosen vessel and savior of the human race.[20]

16. PARADISE LOST

T HE RUIN OF Harris's California idyll was set in motion not long after Fountain Grove was established. The first crisis to befall the Brotherhood was underway by 1881. Laurence Oliphant was in Europe that year, working as a war correspondent in service to the Use. After learning his mother was ill with cancer, Oliphant went to Brocton to fetch her. He took the sick woman all the way to California, believing that the heightened spiritual atmosphere of divine respiration at Fountain Grove would cure her. But the Oliphants were not joyously received at Fountain Grove: Lady Oliphant's case was obviously hopeless, and Harris had no wish for a public trial of his powers. The betrayal cut deeply into the Oliphants' faith. Mother and son departed in haste, but not before Lady Oliphant noticed an Oliphant family ring on one of the Brethren's fingers. More than a decade prior, Harris had demanded that the Oliphants give up their jewelry in Brocton, which they presumed had been converted into communal resources for the common Use. Distraught and out of options, the pair removed to the home of a family friend who lived nearby, where Lady Oliphant succumbed to her illness. Bereaved and confused, Oliphant reunited with his wife but would not finally separate from Harris before returning to the East.[1]

The schism was already long in the making: By 1878, Oliphant had become convinced that Christ would imminently return to Palestine, and that Harris must relocate the Brotherhood to Zion or else be destroyed. Oliphant declared that he received this prophecy from his spirit counterpart, as well as from Harris's counterpart, the fairy called Queen Lily. Harris was outraged by this prophetic usurpation but did not take the ploy seriously. By 1881, Oliphant decided to act on his Palestine plan— and he did not intend to go alone. Arriving back in Brocton that year, he announced that the lakeside community was the true "pivotal center" of the Brotherhood and that he, not Harris, was the pivotal man. Laurence and Alice offered to take every willing member of the Brocton family to the Holy Land to fulfill the next phase of their work in the Use.

The Poet swiftly learned of this treachery, but there was little he could do from Fountain Grove to foil the plot against him. While Harris hurried to New York, Cuthbert wrote to his wife, who had sided with Oliphant, to chide her and the other defectors for their betrayal.[2] Harris arrived in Brocton to find that he had already been outflanked: all but a few had turned to Oliphant and shut their doors against him.

The feud ended with Harris transferring a "great quantity" of Brotherhood lands to Oliphant through an intermediary.[3] Those who remained loyal to Harris were aghast. As one Brother wrote to another:

> This is the most vile and wicked conspiracy, but all is set-
> tled . . . [Oliphant] has grabbed all the property, and when
> sold or sometime, will take them all to Palestine, where no
> doubt they will miserably perish.[4]

The schismatic brethren moved to Haifa in 1882, where they established what they considered the "true" branch of the Brotherhood in Palestine. Alice died in January 1886 as the result of a fever she contracted while visiting Lake Tiberias the previous December. She expired not long after Emily Harris, who breathed her last on October 1, 1885.[5] After his wife's death, Oliphant declared her his spiritual counterpart, but went on to marry Robert Owen's granddaughter Rosamund. Laurence died in Palestine six years later. The cause of his death was lung cancer, an irony Harris did not fail to notice.

. . .

THE DEFECTION of Harris's eastern kingdom was a serious blow to the Brotherhood. A worse scandal occurred in 1891. This was the publication of a salacious exposé in the *San Francisco Chronicle*, titled "Hypnotic Harris." Its author was a bluestocking veteran of the Boston reform circuit known as Alizire A. Chevallier, whom the paper described as a "woman suffragist, sociologist, spiritual scientist, philanthropist, nationalist, magazine writer and reformer."[6] Having learned of Harris through these channels, as well as Margaret Oliphant's recent biography of her cousin Laurence, Chevallier went to Fountain Grove, where she introduced herself and her mother as curious initiates in Brotherhood doctrine. Harris was sequestered at Linn Lilla when she arrived, but this proved no obstacle. The journalist quickly ingratiated herself with Lady Dovie, who satisfied her request to be taken to Harris's mountain retreat.

In her exposé, Chevallier described Fountain Grove as a place where the faithful toiled at their chores, leaving Waring and the other elect to enjoy the palatial manor without lowering themselves to manual labor. She alleged a racialized hierarchy operated at Fountain Grove, describing Harris's printer, Arai, as an "abject slave" forced to set and reset manuscripts to suit the Poet's mercurial tastes. And while Harris wore silk stockings and Waring traipsed the grounds in gowns and lace, Arai went about with holes in his socks. Imperial socialism, in Chevallier's view, was a sham.[7]

The reporter's dismay reached greater heights at Linn Lilla, where without so much as a handshake, Harris thrust his hands upon the suffragist's plexus to determine the status of her spiritual regeneration. Chevallier was later scandalized to behold Harris with his feet in Waring's lap, disgusted by Waring's unladylike habit of smoking a pipe, and shocked when Harris slipped into a convulsive mediumistic trance while seated near her on a sofa. She called the spectacle "a fine piece of acting," and claimed Harris drank down an entire glass of port after he came to, "spilling over his face and letting it drool down his whiskers."[8]

The exposé was most damning in its allegations of exotic sexual behaviors practiced at Fountain Grove. The Brethren were not celibate, Chevallier asserted, but engaged in promiscuous sex with the excuse that their spiritual counterpart was contained in a sex partner's body. The entire religion, she informed readers, was little more than an elaborate scheme by which Harris might indulge in polygamous affairs. After impressing the Brethren with her knowledge of their beliefs and rebuffing Harris's sexual advances, Chevallier claimed that the Poet invited her to establish a branch of the Use back East. But "on this subject," she wrote, "I gave him very little encouragement."[9]

After the article's publication, Harris declined to defend himself publicly, but in letters to his supporters, he wrote that Chevallier had tried to seduce him, and that "her mouth watered to the last."[10] The Poet's allies sallied forth to defend him in print. Thirty-one businesspeople and professionals of Santa Rosa signed a letter in Harris's defense and sent it to the *Chronicle*.[11] Waring's brother George wrote to defend the community against the claims of immorality at Fountain Grove, stating that he was "satisfied" with his sister's lifestyle and that he believed the group to be honest. There was no corroborating evidence for Chevallier's claims. The damage, however, was done. Chevallier came to be known as "Judas Iscariot" among the faithful.

With the reputation of the colony in tatters, Harris married Waring in Santa Rosa on February 27, 1892. Harris was sixty-eight; Waring was only four years his junior, and had been a member of the Brotherhood for three decades.[12] The Poet told the faithful that the marriage was merely a convenience that would allow the pair to travel Europe without causing further scandal. But the wedding had the reverse effect: papers across the country carried an announcement of the union, jeering at the absurdity of a celibate marriage. The newlyweds soon departed Fountain Grove, never to return.

Harris lived out the remainder of his days in exile from the Use, although he continued to advise the community's business operations from a distance. Without the Poet at its center, the Brotherhood lacked vitality and entered a permanent decline. Harris and Waring continued to visit with the faithful in England, and circulated between homes the couple owned in Canada, Florida, and New York City. Despite a long and slow slide into hostile senility, Harris continued writing and publishing his visions, verse, and revelations. He was no longer America's best-known mystic, only a bearded bard whose utopian society, which purported it held the solution to America's labor question, had been ruined by scurrilous rumors.

In April 1906, Arthur Cuthbert wrote his fellow Brethren in the New Life to inform them that early in the morning hours on March 23, 1906, Harris called for a glass of wine and his pipe and asked Waring to lay a hand on his plexus. She complied, upon which the Chosen Vessel let out a gasp, and died.[13]

THREE

THE GREAT COSMIC EGG

The accentuation of character called eccentricity of genius, is generally a normal departure from the artificial deformities of social etiquette with which the fashionable world labels its accepted associates.

—Cyrus Teed,
better known as Koresh,
The Immortal Manhood

The universe, as an alchemico-organic dynamo, is a perpetual, self-reconstructing and self-sustaining form and order. Its general form is that of the perfect egg or shell, with its central vitellus at or near the center of the sphere.

—Koresh,
The Flaming Sword

17. A MESSIANIC MEETING

ONE OF THOSE who had observed the unfolding scandal at Fountain Grove was the wily Dr. Cyrus Teed, who visited Thomas Lake Harris just days before his marriage to Jane Waring. Teed was in town from Chicago, where he led a messianic society called the Koreshan Unity. In the wake of Chevallier's exposé, reporters stalked the Santa Rosa estate, and the papers covered the messianic summit in anticipation of the announcement that Teed would assume control or partnership of the beleaguered winery.

Teed had just been made an honorary Shaker by the North Family at New Lebanon, and was fresh off a failed attempt to take control of the celibate Harmony Society at Economy, Pennsylvania. Newspapers across the country carried stories on his plans to unite the celibate communal societies of America under his messianic aegis. In Pittsburgh, reporters could barely veil their indignation at the idea that Teed had gone gold-digging in Economy, where locals had suddenly become fond and protective of the aging Harmonists. The situation in California was different: Teed had already established an outpost of the Koreshan Unity in San Francisco and long had an eye on the New Life estate. Thomas Lake Harris was an old mentor of Teed's, but the doctor decided the time had come for the student to trade roles with his teacher.

But first, Teed went on the offensive. In the January 2, 1892, edition of the Koreshan Unity's Chicago broadsheet, *The Flaming Sword*, Teed defended Harris against Chevallier's "malicious charge" by alleging that she, and not Teed, wished to sit in the "throne of command" at Fountain Grove.[1] Chevallier's "blind insinuations," Teed alleged, only demonstrated that she failed to comprehend the doctrine of the divine Two-in-One that Harris had been preaching for decades. He dismissed the testimony she collected from disgruntled former members of the Brotherhood as opportunistic fabrications.

Chevallier rebutted these assaults on her journalistic and personal integrity by writing to inform the *Flaming Sword* that although Harris had been "very kind" to her, he considered the Koreshan Unity "low and vulgar." The Koreshan master was accustomed to worse slander than this. But Chevallier's impertinence moved him to put his opinion of the Poet in print: Teed subordinated Harris to a lesser messianic role than his own, explaining to readers of the *Sword* that although the Poet was the "angel of the church of respiration," this was only one of the seven churches of the seven principles of organic life that would "remain imperfect until the theocrasis of the Son-of-man." By this Teed referred to his own "translation" into a bisexual deity, initially scheduled to occur in 1891, but later postponed to coincide with the Chicago World's Fair in 1893.[2] Teed thus arrived to Fountain Grove having proclaimed his superiority publicly—a tactic that had not proven effective for Laurence Oliphant. Harris received him nonetheless.

The *Chicago Daily Tribune* was keeping tabs on Teed's whereabouts, and got the first scoop on the meeting between the disgraced vintner and the Koreshan messiah. The *Tribune* was a reliable Koreshan adversary and immediately got ahead of the story by falsely reporting on February 25 that a "spiritual and temporal combination" had already taken place between the celibate sects. According to the *Tribune*, Teed would send badly needed reinforcements to Fountain Grove from his overcrowded communes in Chicago and San Francisco. The *Chronicle* corrected the record the next day, clarifying that although neither Teed nor Harris intended to share messianic authority, the Chicago messiah had come to propose "something of a partnership . . . the nucleus of a commercial and industrial system." This was Teed's Bureau of Equitable Commerce, a production exchange based on the anticapitalist economic system developed by Josiah Warren and Stephen Pearl Andrews, the co-founders of the defunct anarchist Modern Times community of Brentwood, Long Island. Lying through his gold teeth, Teed told the *Tribune* that he knew nothing about Harris until "quite recently" before the rendezvous at Fountain Grove. In fact, he had studied the Poet's work for more than half a decade, and had been planning to make a play for Harris's followers ever since he'd done the same to Stephen Pearl Andrews in 1885.[3]

Teed was a favorite object of tabloid derision in Chicago; since his arrival to the Windy City, allegations of wife stealing and polygamy in the Koreshan Unity had thwarted his attempts to expand there, and generated no small amount of negative publicity. Gossip on his California follies was sure to sell back home. In truth, the *Tribune*'s careless coverage might have been what caused the messianic negotiations to collapse: Teed left Fountain Grove without a firm commitment from Harris and returned to Ecclesia, the Koreshans' forty-three-member commune on Noe Street in San Francisco. But when a reporter from the *Chronicle* caught up with him, Teed claimed Harris endorsed his moves toward "centralization." Asked about his divinity, Teed told the paper he was "God Almighty as much as any regenerated man," and that he respected the Brethren at Fountain Grove: "I believe there are no purer people in America," he solemnly stated, "than the community over which Harris rules."[4] But the union Teed sought never came to pass: the winery burned down not long after the Harrises left for England, dealing a catastrophic blow to Fountain Grove's finances. Teed returned to Chicago, where the Koreshan Unity had already surpassed the Brotherhood as the most prominent messianic society in America.

18. KORESH, SHEPHERD OF GOD

TEED WAS NO ORDINARY OPPORTUNIST: by the time he visited Fountain Grove, he was already two decades into the project of
building a communal utopia organized around his messianic identity.
His assumed name, Koresh, was a transliteration of the Hebrew for
Cyrus, the name he was given at birth. Teed claimed that he was the
Cyrus foretold by the prophet Isaiah: the Shepherd of God who would
restore Jerusalem.[1]

Cyrus Reed Teed was born in Trout Creek, New York, in 1839. The
village was known as Teedsville to those who associated the hamlet with the relatively prominent Teed family, whose patriarch was
the local parson.[2] The same year as his birth, Teed's (alleged) distant
cousin Joseph Smith led a flock of followers to Nauvoo, Illinois, to
establish there the Mormon Zion.[3] Fifty-five years later, Teed would
shepherd his own following into the wilderness. Rather than west,
they would go south to establish the Koreshan New Jerusalem on the
last frontier east of the Mississippi: the untamed swamps of Florida's
subtropical Gulf Coast.

The Teed family relocated to Utica soon after Cyrus was born.
The dates and scene of his youth made him a very near contemporary
of Thomas Lake Harris, Teed's senior by just six years. But the age
gap made all the difference: their time in Utica was a near miss. And
although the Poet caught the tail end of the evangelical fervor that
roiled the region in the first decades of the century, Teed came of age
in Utica after the fires of the Burned-Over District had, for the most

part, burnt to embers. Following the Millerite Great Disappointment of 1844, which marked the bitter end of the Second Great Awakening, the new liberal churches turned their attention to temperance, abolition, and to a lesser extent, women's rights. All three movements were popular with progressive upstate evangelicals, and made a deeper impact on Teed and the Koreshan Unity than they did on Harris and his Brotherhood. The nineteenth-century women's movement was strongest in upstate New York, home to Susan B. Anthony, Elizabeth Cady Stanton, Amelia Bloomer, and many of the other radicals who organized and attended the 1848 Seneca Falls Convention. Rochester, a day's journey down the Erie Canal from Utica, was home to Frederick Douglass's *North Star* newspaper.

As with each American messiah to come before him, Teed never received much formal schooling. At the age of eleven, his parents sent the boy to work on the Erie Canal. He became what was known as a "hoggee"—canal lingo for the boys and young men who drove the oxen, mules, and horses that pulled the barges down the river. Child labor taught Teed unforgettable lessons in the cruel realities of capitalist exploitation, and contributed to his lifelong hatred of late-nineteenth-century laissez-faire market economics: as was customary, boys working the canal were paid a fraction of the salaries that men earned.[4]

Life on the towpath didn't allow for much leisure. But when barges stopped to exchange their cargo at ports of call, hoggee boys had the opportunity to explore the bustling industrial towns and cities that sprang up along the canal. Some barges carried travelers moving between Buffalo, Rochester, Syracuse, Utica, Albany, and from there down the Hudson to New York. Although it would soon be displaced by rail, the canal was still the region's principal conduit of east–west commerce and news. Working the barges in the early 1850s would have placed Teed in the company of the spirit rappers and trance mediums who crisscrossed the state throughout the decade—as well as abolitionists, socialists, feminists, labor reformers, and temperance activists.

Teed was on his way to a respectable middle-class life when the Civil War broke out in 1861. After a decade on the canal, he'd traded manual labor for a medical apprenticeship with his uncle Samuel, a physician. He married a second cousin, Fidelia "Delia" Rowe; she bore him a son named Arthur, who went on to become a landscape painter of minor renown and lived most of his life in Europe. When the Union Army issued a call for enlistees, Teed's unwavering abolitionist convictions compelled him to respond.[5] He entered the service as a corporal and served for about a year, when sunstroke forced him off the field. While hospitalized, he experienced paralysis in his leg and was subsequently discharged.[6]

After leaving the army, Teed continued his studies at New York Eclectic Medical College, which had been chartered the month before the official conclusion of the war.[7] Emerging in the mid-nineteenth century alongside mesmeric healing and water cure, eclectic medicine favored interventions that were less invasive than the brutal surgeries and debilitating bleedings that were still in vogue among conventional allopathic doctors. Folk remedies, including some derived from Germanic occult traditions connected with astrology and alchemy, found new favor in the offices of eclectic practitioners—only now, the herbal recipes used on family farms were enhanced with chemical compounds that often included poisonous metals such as lead, antimony, mercury, and arsenic.[8] After the war, growing skepticism about the effectiveness of mesmerism eventually led the state legislature to ban the practice in 1880. Eclectic medicine picked up the slack: mesmeric healers, including Andrew Jackson Davis, often re-trained as eclecticists.

Eclectic medicine was a natural choice for Teed, who had probably witnessed dozens of harrowing amputations in a Civil War army infirmary. He completed his studies by 1869, having specialized in electrotherapy. The newly minted doctor then returned to Utica, where he established a practice on familiar terrain.[9] Lacking the robust clientele of a traditional doctor, Teed busied himself in the "electro-alchemical laboratory" he maintained beside his home. There he conducted experiments with Faradic batteries and valuable metals like mercury and gold, which he claimed to be able to distinguish by taste.[10] As he later wrote, he toiled

> in the hope of discovering some occult or hidden principle
> or power which I believed lay at the foundation of a better
> control and regulation of the life forces than had ever yet
> been vouched to mortals, even in that profession in which, of
> all others, should have been acquired the direction of human
> destiny. I allude to the profession of medicine.[11]

In fact, he referred to alchemy—or as he termed it, "transmutation." Like other eclectic physicians, Teed viewed medicine and alchemy as coeval disciplines governed by the same universal laws. These relationships were sometimes hidden or "occult," but alchemists believed they could be uncovered through reason and scientific method. Alchemical treatises deriving from Hermetic mysticism and Rosicrucian lore taught the cosmic law of correspondences, which holds that everything in the universe functions by analogy. In this Western occult framework, the body and the maladies of its organs correspond to movements in the heavens, and plants can be read by an herbalist much as an astrologer reads the stars.[12] Ideas about individual practices of "reading" various expressions of the cosmos enjoyed a revival in the Romantic period, and occult esoterica influenced the works of Blake, Coleridge, Shelley, and the American Transcendentalists.[13]

Along with correspondences, students of Western esotericism believe in the transmutability of spirit into matter and vice versa. Teed's training in electrotherapy led him to innovate in this area, with his Faradic batteries. He hoped a successful transmutation of lead into gold would lead him to discover the universal cure for all disease.[14] Teed's experiments were highly specialized, but occult science was not limited to backwoods cranks and mad scientists: secret societies, including the Rosicrucians and the Freemasons, were superficially conversant in Western esotericism.

In the autumn of 1869, Dr. Teed experienced a breakthrough: observing one of his electrochemical reactions, he saw "golden radiations, and eagerly watched the transformation of forces to the molecules of golden dust as they fell in showers through the lucid electro-alchemical fluid."[15] Teed believed that through an electrochemical reaction, he'd turned matter into electricity and back into matter again. The result was pure gold—or so he thought.

Teed reasoned that a similar transmutation could effect regenerative processes in the human body. If the brain, as he believed, was the body's chemical battery, then it contained potential energies that might be used like a Faradic battery: with proper concentration, the brain might use this energy to effect physiological changes in the body. With this in mind, Teed concentrated his energies to his "innermost realm" until he felt a wave of relaxing vibration overtake his brain and then his body. After sinking into the "vibratory sea" of delight, Teed lost control of his body; he could no longer move or feel. Nor could he see or hear. When he attempted his power of speech, the doctor heard another voice speak through him: "Fear not, my Son, thou satisfactory offspring of my profoundest yearnings!" the voice majestically declared. "I have nurtured thee through countless embodiments. I have seen thee as thou hast wandered through the labyrinthine coilings of time's spiral transmigrations."[16] Teed realized he had been seized as the medium of a powerful spirit.

The "melodious accents" of the occupying spirit explained that over the eras, Teed's soul had repeatedly reincarnated in bodies that were brought low by disease or by violence. After each death, he was "clothed" in a new human vessel. Now that he had discovered the philosopher's stone, the voice confided, Teed would finally arrive at the "pinnacle of [his] celestial aspiration." The visual presence of the voice then revealed herself to Teed: "Offspring of Osiris and Isis," she commanded, "behold the revailing of thy Mother."[17] Teed regained his sight and saw before him a "gloriously regal" goddess emerge from an aura of purple and gold spheres beneath a diamond-studded rainbow. She carried Mercury's iconic caduceus and stood on a silver crescent. The goddess described herself as the "environment of that which thou hast become—the inherent psyche and pneuma of my own organic form."[18]

Her terminology was significant: *psyche* and *pneuma* refer to the gnostic doctrine of fallen souls. Gnostic Christians believe that salvation is awarded to those who seek the divine knowledge that humankind unlearned in the fall from heaven into a false world of illusion. The spark (*pneuma*) of this knowledge (*gnosis*) exists within each individual consciousness (*psyche*), and anyone who follows the intuitions of the *pneuma* can encounter moments of rapture during which they are illumined with occult *gnosis*. These intervals of rapture might be flashes of insight or ecstatic trances that last for days. Teed's illumination was a little of both.

Reaffirming the intuition that led him to uncover the secret of alchemical-organic transformations, the goddess told the doctor that she had come to "sacrifice" him on the "altar of all human hopes." Teed felt the union of their spirits in his body, and sensed the chasteness of the goddess's virginity. The bigendered spiritual union between Teed and the goddess would soon become a core tenet of the Koreshan belief system, and the underlying theological basis for the Koreshan practice of celibacy.

And then, just like that, she vanished—but only from sight. The goddess invisibly guaranteed Teed that she would be with him as he fulfilled his destiny to "redeem the race." She directed Teed to witness to the "surging mass of human woe," into which she vowed to descend alongside him as he worked for the salvation of humankind.[19] The divine illumination continued for three weeks, during which time the alchemist discovered additional occult knowledge that would form the pillars of Koreshan cosmogony.

The experience proved, to Teed's satisfaction, that when modern science is properly applied to occult theories of alchemy, the result could lead to spiritual transformation and bring about the next golden age of human civilization. Through deep and concentrated direction of his mental energies, Teed had enabled his feminine spiritual counterpart to materialize. As he wrote in his memoir:

> I had transformed myself to spiritous essence, and through
> it had made myself the quickener and vivifier of the supreme
> feminine potency, and had formulated the counterpartal
> energies, the pneuma and psyche, into the Majesty who, in
> all her radiant glory, had compassed me. While thus inher-
> ent and clothed upon with the femininity of my being, how
> vividly was awakened in my mind the passage of Scripture
> found in Jeremiah XXXI:22: "How long wilt thou go about,
> O thou backsliding daughter? for the Lord hath created a
> new thing in the earth, a woman shall compass a man."[20]

This verse, Jeremiah 31:22, was the same one that the Public Universal Friend cited in defense of his messianic authority. Teed more explicitly combined it with occult theories of spiritual and physical regeneration to a bigendered, pre-Adamic state.

Teed had already reasoned that the physical process of alchemy made it possible to regenerate the body by using the mind to interchange matter and spirit. By analogy, and with scriptural backing to boot, it now struck him that the same law of transmutation meant that a spirit could "translate" between itself into different bodies: for instance, from Enoch to Elijah to Jesus to himself. Alchemical transmutation thus offered a scientific explanation for the mysteries of metempsychosis and reincarnation, which formed the basis of Teed's messianic destiny.[21]

. . .

THE DOCTOR'S PUBLIC PRONOUNCEMENTS of his scientific discoveries caused the collapse of his medical practice in Utica. His business barely did better in Binghamton, where he moved in 1871, but it was there that Teed acquired his first loyal convert. This was Dr. Abiel W. K. Andrews, whom Teed fondly nicknamed "Abie." Andrews had served the Union in the Civil War; unlike Teed, he worked as a field surgeon, having earned his medical credentials at the University of Michigan.

Teed fast became a family friend to Andrews and his wife, Virginia. He was an avuncular figure to the couple's son, Allen, for whom he demonstrated his formidable talent at croquet. Teed stayed in touch with Abie after he left Binghamton for the northern Pennsylvania woodlands, where he sporadically practiced as a country doctor. When Delia's health took a turn for the worse, rendering her itinerant prophet–doctor of a husband incapable of caring for her on his own, she returned to Binghamton to live with her sister. Abie attended to Delia's illness and diagnosed her with Pott's disease, a form of tuberculosis that would eventually spread to her spine and kill her. Sympathetic Koreshan histories suggest that Delia was not angry with her husband for abandoning her, as might be supposed: although she initially doubted his reports of an angel who had declared him the savior of the race, she eventually came around and "fully accepted him as the messianic personality of the age, and strenuously resisted the suggestions of friends and enemies alike that Cyrus be committed to an asylum because of his extreme and radical convictions."[22]

Teed had begun to preach a stern, puritanical critique of the "prostituted" Christian churches, which in his view had become the servants of oppressive capitalist institutions. As he wrote one prospective regenerate, "Christianity so called—embracing Catholicism and Protestantism—is but the dead carcass of a once vital and active structure. It will rest supine till the birds of prey, the vultures and cormorants of what is falsely called liberalism have picked its bones of its fleshly covering leaving them to dry to bleach and decompose."[23] Amid such carnage and ruin, Teed would lead his followers in the regeneration of humankind.

19. THE NEW AGE

P RESSED TO PROVIDE for his teenage son and invalid wife, Teed relocated to Sandy Creek, New York, far from where his reputation might prevent him from establishing a successful practice. Nearby were a factory and sawmill that offered Teed a steady supply of injured workers who needed urgent treatment, no matter how strange the doctor.[1] Aside from his clinical work, Teed's efforts during this period were concentrated primarily on his writings. He corresponded frequently with Abie, as well as with a few potential converts. He familiarized himself with the teachings of Stephen Pearl Andrews and Andrew Jackson Davis, both of whom merit mention in an 1879 letter to Abie.[2] S. P. Andrews had written extensively on the subject of wage labor and how to get rid of it—a problem that would obsess Teed for the rest of his life. After the closure of the Modern Times community, S. P. Andrews organized a commune in New York known to his critics as the "brownstone utopia," and taught a system of comprehensive science he called "universology." This was, in effect, a modernized attempt at the sort of occult pansophy that inspired alchemists like Teed.[3] These theories cast a powerful spell over the country doctor, whose interest in Andrews propelled his desire to establish a communal society capable of removing its residents from the exploitative capitalist economy.

Teed made frequent trips back and forth to his parents' home in Moravia, where his first communal religious society formally affiliated on July 24, 1877. On that date, the eclectic physician and his five closest family members put their names to a document called the "Preliminary Covenant of Consolation." In the spirit of Matthew 22: 37–39, the signatories pledged to "contribute all we possess, including our services" to furthering God's kingdom on Earth, which "shall be called Vision of Peace (Yeru-Salem)." Lacking any property of his own, Teed was flexible on the subject of communism. His father, Jesse, made sure the covenant stipulated that he had donated the $50,000 property to Teed's religious "order," and retained the right to dispose of $5,000 of its start-up capital in any manner he wished.[4]

Within their little realm, the signatories agreed to "evert [*sic*] the sad consummation, the dissolution of the body," a process Teed also called bodily corruption. In the doctor's understanding, physical corruption was due to two things: "carnal desires" and capitalist exploitation. Teed justified communal living as an antidote to capitalist exchange, making the familiar appeal to apostolic communism as described in the Book of Acts. But he favored an esoteric biblical rationale for the celibate life: if Abraham's covenant was consecrated and maintained by circumcision of the male sex organ, the consecration of the New Covenant required another circumcision. This time, a circumcision of the heart would be observed by eliminating carnal desires through commitment to celibacy. "The carnal desires," he declared, "are the plants rooted in the will that germinate the spermatozoa in the man and the ova in the woman."[5] Sperm and egg cells, Teed explained, were incomplete, and were the first to physically degrade in the body. They were the cause of death, not life. Salvation through regeneration would be attained by mentally discouraging their production.

With ink dry on the covenant, Teed's next objective was to acquire additional converts. This was a goal best served by establishing a newspaper to record the progress of the new dispensation. In his prospectus for the *Herald of the New Covenant*, the doctor introduced the conceptual framework that would largely come to define his career as both theologian and social reformer: "True physical science," he wrote, "is the continent of the doctrines of immortality."

Teed forcefully distinguished his teachings from spiritualism and "any other ISM that denies the unity of fullness of the God-head in the Lord Jesus Christ." Teed attacked conventional mediumship from a Christian spiritualist standpoint, plagiarizing his readings of Thomas Lake Harris in the process: "Modern Spiritism," Teed averred, "is the channel through which the infernal regions are ejecting themselves to the surface."[6]

By November, the *Herald* was in print. "The object of this publication," Teed informed readers of the inaugural issue, "is to communicate the fact of the presence among men of the Prophet Elijah, or Elyah, the messenger of the New Covenant, and to point out the plan of preparation for the coming of the Lord, and to prepare his way before Him." This messenger was, of course, the good doctor himself. Privately, Teed viewed his role as equivalent to that of Jesus Christ, in a manner similar to the self-understanding of the Public Universal Friend and Mother Ann Lee: just as Jesus was the messenger of the end of the Judaic dispensation and the beginning of the Christian era, Teed's arrival signaled the end of the Christian dispensation and the dawn of a new age.[7]

Despite the energy put into its planning, the "consociation" at Moravia never got on its feet. Teed's parents tired of the scheme, and the eclectic doctor ended up back in Sandy Creek tending to accident victims from the sawmill. His communal fold of believers was reduced to the epistolary companionship of two loyal correspondents: Abie and Teed's sister Emma would remain staunch believers for the rest of their lives.

The Messenger returned to the drawing board. After discussing the matter in their letters, Abie and Teed decided to propose a merger between their movement, such as it was, and the prosperous Harmony Society at Economy, Pennsylvania. Andrews floated their proposal to Jacob Henrici and Jonathan Lenz, who had assumed trusteeship of the Harmonists after the death of the communal sect's founder, Father Rapp. The response was a firm no. Lenz politely observed that of all the propositions the Harmonists received, the pitch from the Moravian communists was the most attractive to date. But he regretted to report that the Harmonists did not receive the Lord's permission to unite with Teed. Instead, Lenz invited Andrews and any of his associates to visit Economy to see the workings of the Harmony Society up close. Teed and Andrews accepted the offer.[8]

Teed's study of the Harmonists convinced him that a successful utopian community required a specialized industry to sustain it. The Harmonists ran a distillery and textile factory, among other ventures. Likewise, it was a lucrative patent for animal traps that guaranteed the financial self-sufficiency of John Humphrey Noyes's Oneida Community. "I have been thinking over the matter seriously," Teed told Abie, "and from my experience in my more recent attempt to set forth publicly my gospel, I am satisfied that my first and preparatory work should be in the direction of effecting a small beginning in an industrial home."[9] Fortunately for Teed, his aging parents needed help with their mop factory. Putting the *Herald* on hiatus, he returned to Moravia determined to reinstitute apostolic communism, this time organized around the fabrication of mops.

Once more the Teed family household became the site of a communal society. This time it endured for nearly two years. Teed, Emma and her husband, their brother Oliver, and the Andrews family joined the commune. Next to enlist were members of what would become the core demographic among Teed's following: women attracted by what appeared to be a feasible way to leave their husbands. Teed believed that when the security of the "industrial home" was made known to those who needed it, he would surely "find some followers who could and would supply the pecuniary means for the advancement of the work."[10] Wealthy converts, he hoped, would help sustain the others until the commune perfected its model for self-sufficiency. This timeless strategy had already been employed with success by Thomas Lake Harris, and would be repeated by Father Divine and Jim Jones, Teed's successors in messianic socialism.

While the commune at Moravia lasted, Teed refined his doctrines, teaching that men and women were both "widowed" in their anatomy. The "defects" of each sex would be remedied when spiritual regenerates transformed themselves into sexually bigendered beings. Teed had a detailed explanation for how this could be accomplished: energies formerly expended in sexual intercourse could be redirected to charge the anthropostic battery (i.e., the brain). When fully charged, the brain would be powerful enough to cause a combustion in the conarium, a structure more commonly known as the pineal gland. The explosion would cause the production of gametes to cease entirely, allowing the body to regenerate to the bisexual completion of pre-Adamic man.

Teed believed that he would be the first to "translate" from the corrupt, mortal form to a bisexual, immortal body. But even the Messenger could not succeed on his own: spiritual translation was a collective endeavor. To burst his conarium, Teed required a critical mass of celibates to surround him, directing their conserved energies to his battery rather than their own. When he attained his deific bisexual form, Teed would destroy the depraved institutions of capitalist society, including the apostate churches that supported legalized prostitution in the form of marriage. After these obstacles to regeneration were eliminated once and for all, the entire human race would be brought under the rule of the New Order of celibate socialism and regenerated to bisexual immortality.[11]

All of this would occur quite soon, according to the astrological dimension of Teed's theories. The doctor taught that just as souls could dematerialize in bodies and repeat the life cycle, the universe likewise cycled through periods of decadence and regeneration. These cycles corresponded to 6,000-year intervals of Gold, Silver, Bronze, and Iron Ages, each of which roughly corresponded to a quarter of the Zodiac. The new dispensation had already begun with the birth of Cyrus the Shepherd, which heralded the dawn of the Age of Aquarius—a golden era of civilization marked by glorious advances in science. Because Aquarius and Pisces overlapped, the Aquarian Age would not fully ascend until the Piscatorial Age had concluded. Its end, Teed warned, would not be pretty: unlike the slow decay from gold to silver to bronze to iron, the passage from an Iron Age back to a Golden Age was never peaceful. The Civil War had already proven that.[12]

. . .

OVERTHROWING CAPITALISM with a communist mop factory proved impossible. Teed went to New York City to set up a distribution chain, but found that his wares were not in high demand.[13] Unlike the ingenious traps that made Oneida rich, the Teed family mops were hardly Aquarian in design. Business floundered.

Neither were the citizens of Moravia ready to tolerate the excesses of the Teed family's prodigal son. The village was not exactly inhospitable to unconventional ideas: it was located in an area already known to be a locus of uncommon of spiritualist activity.[14] But the cohabitation of married couples and runaway wives courted the same accusations of bigamy that had recently forced the Oneida Community to conclude its practice of complex marriage. Teed relocated once more, this time to Syracuse, where in spring of 1883 he set up a joint eclectic medical practice with his brother Oliver. The Institute for Progressive Medicine they opened on posh Onondaga Street catered to the city's wealthiest clients. An advertisement for the institute described it as "giving special attention to the treatment of Chronic Diseases."[15] This specialty entailed electrotherapeutic treatments for neurasthenia, a common catchall diagnosis for the psychosomatic malaise that afflicted the upper classes of late Victorian society.

Meanwhile, Teed and Abie tinkered with inventions. They hoped to emulate the successes of Harmony and Oneida with a product more valuable than mops, one that capitalized on their medical training and reputation. Patented as an "Electro-Therapeutic Apparatus," their invention was a booth in which a patient sat on a stool with her feet placed in a water bath. After being situated in the cabinet for privacy, the patient was outfitted with "a number of electrodes adapted to the various parts of the body," and softly electrocuted with currents of various strengths.[16] The device was never constructed.

Meanwhile, Teed doddered on with his eclectic medical practice, which soon landed him in more hot water. This time his name made the headlines:

A DOCTOR OBTAINING MONEY ON THE GROUND THAT HE IS THE NEW MESSIAH.[17]

So declared the front page of the *New York Times* on August 10, 1884. The activities of physicians in Syracuse were generally not of interest to the residents of Manhattan, but the story was strange enough to sell in the city. The *Times* had caught wind that Teed was not only defrauding "the best people in the city" of their money—he was angling to steal their women. Or so went the rumors. A Mrs. Charles Cobb alleged that Teed had extorted money from her and from her mother "under the plea that he is [the] 'Second Christ.'" Mrs. Cobb had been suffering from nervous prostration, a synonym for neurasthenia. After his consultation with her, Teed prescribed that Mrs. Cobb receive his electrical therapy at home, in bed.[18]

The details of Teed's theology had also become known to the *Times*, which reported: "when he is 46 he will be translated to heaven, whence he will return in 50 days to found a kingdom where all will be love. By love he means only a mind love of great purity and elevation. Those who follow him as the great exponent of this belief will live forever in this world." In the interest of selling the story, the paper ambiguously suggested Teed's community might have been created "after the order of the Oneida Community." But with no untoward sexual allegations forthcoming from Mrs. Cobb, the *Times* fell back on a scandalous rumor from Teed's time in Moravia: before coming to Syracuse, it was said Teed had "eloped with Mrs. Ella Wolsely [*sic*], whose husband keeps a livery stable in Moravia."[19] It was the first of many false accusations of bigamy that Teed would face over the next decades of his messianic career.

20. DR. TEED'S BENEFACTRESSES

THE SYRACUSE SCANDAL destroyed Teed's medical practice. Requiring another change of scenery, he decamped to New York City in the autumn of 1884.[1] Four of his followers, all of them female and none of them his wife, went along. They took an apartment in Manhattan, fell behind on the rent, and passed most of the season hungry and cold. Mrs. Sarah Patterson, one of those who followed Teed to New York, wrote to Abie begging that he take up a collection among the adherents who remained upstate.[2] Patterson and the other women depended financially on Teed, who had trouble drumming up another client base for his medical practice in New York.

Teed's mother and wife both died in October, but by springtime his luck began to change. An acquaintance introduced Teed to a Brooklyn society of intellectual ladies and gentlemen led by a Swedenborgian minister and a writing medium called Mrs. Peake. After sitting through the lecture the group had planned for the evening of his first visit, Teed so impressed the group with his questions that he soon took over the meeting. He held court until well past midnight, delighting his listeners with his convoluted science and acrobatic rhetoric. Teed's sparkling eyes, stylish beard, and dashing good looks made up for his short stature and threadbare clothes. He certainly made an impression: the session concluded with an invitation for Teed to return the next week, to speak on the subject of mediumship.

Teed was poor: he'd had to walk the eleven miles from his Manhattan lodgings to the meeting in Brooklyn. But for the first time, he'd found an audience receptive to his teachings. When he returned to deliver the lecture, Teed dazzled Mrs. Peake's society with his alchemical understanding of the human brain and its capacity to channel and materialize unseen spirit energies. It was a lexicon the group had never before heard applied to spiritual mediumship. Mrs. Peake had Teed's papers printed for the group's perusal, and at the following session, the spirits declared through her that the circle was forming the nucleus of the "Bridal Church," which would be "the beginning of the divine communital system, the inauguration of good will to men." The Messenger could barely contain his glee in letters to Abie, whose financial and moral support had sustained him for months.[3]

In March, Abie sent Teed several items relating to Thomas Lake Harris. Teed read them with interest and took care to outline the ways in which he intended to avoid the mutinies and obscurity to which Harris had fallen victim. First, Teed recognized that Harris's ambition to be the "Adam of the new race" was inhibited by his isolation. "He has been careful to seclude himself from the enmity of the world," Teed wrote. The Messenger would not be so shy:

> My desire is to do just what he tries to avoid. I look beyond my dissolution to the dematerialization of my church, not through hate but love. In my public effort I will exasperate those who will not believe, to the extent they will desire my destruction and will concentrate their hate upon and in me. Those who love me, will love me intensely. . . . Harris has simply turned his property over to divert from himself the wrath of the public. He does not come to ultimates. He feares [*sic*] the consequences. I shall walk undaunted into the fiery flame.[4]

Before the end of April, Teed had supplanted Mrs. Peake as the leader of the Brooklyn group. As his new Brooklyn followers spread word of his teachings, Teed's reputation as a lecturer on religious science landed him a weekly speaking engagement on Sunday afternoons at the Faith Healing Institute, a mind-cure establishment located on Fifty-Ninth Street, across from Central Park. The founder and presiding officer of the Institute, Anna J. Johnson, invited Teed to contribute to its journal, *Healing Voice*. Teed's contribution, and the first of his works he signed with his pseudonym, Koresh, appeared in the April 1885 issue. Having realized that the emerging mind-cure movement was comprised mostly of female disciples of Mary Baker Eddy, the founder of Christian Science, Teed used the article to announce that "the new kingdom [will] be formulated through the organic potency of the woman's brain," and foresaw that "Man must come to cognize the supremacy of the woman in this her own domain. When the woman's efficacy is understood by man, and he accords to her, her true position in the world, then and not till then shall we have in the earth the long promised kingdom, the so-called Millenium."[5] As a result of these proclamations of woman's rise to her rightful position, Teed began to keep a brisk calendar of appointments among members of the Faith Healing Institute and other allied mind-cure groups.

Dr. Teed's scientifico-biblical feminism brought his work to the attention of Cynthia Leonard, a New York suffragist and humanitarian who would soon become the first woman to run for mayor of New York.[6] Leonard had emancipated herself from a husband in Chicago and become deeply involved in antimonopoly activism and the women's movement, which at the time consisted of various groups affiliated with the suffrage, social eugenics, education, and dress-reform movements. Leonard hosted a weekly Science of Life Club in her home on East Ninth Street. The club's officers were all women, and meetings on the second and fourth Tuesdays of each month were closed to men. The group's stated objective was to "promote the scientific knowledge of reproduction" in order "to effect the improvement of the human race through a better understanding of hereditary transmission." In practice, this involved reading and discussing scientific papers on eugenics.[7] The club's male members included one of Teed's inspirations, Stephen

Pearl Andrews, who had begun to advocate for the free-love eugenicist practice of "stirpiculture" developed by John Humphrey Noyes at the Oneida Community, where children were bred for superior spiritual character.

The eugenicist ideology of Mrs. Leonard's group was not as alienated from Teed's messianic program as it might seem. "Reform Darwinists" like those in Leonard's club arose in response to conservative interpretations of Social Darwinism, which held that the state should not intervene to alleviate the squalor and misery of city slums. The poverty and hunger generated by the unfettered free market, these apologists claimed, were part of a natural process that would purge society of its weakest members and ultimately lead to the enhancement of the human race. Although they accepted the evolutionist narrative of Anglo-Saxon racial superiority that predominated at the time, eugenicist reformers like those in Leonard's society believed that without enlightened intervention, Anglo-Saxon civilization ran the risk of collapsing into the barbarity of ruthless competition, on the one hand, or falling under the rule of the uncouth and ignorant masses, on the other. Either would amount to the "race suicide" persistently feared by racist nativists as well as the Darwinists in the progressive reform community. As tensions between labor and capital reached calamitous heights throughout the 1870s, eugenicist reformers believed civilizational advancement could only be assured by drawing out the superior qualities of "the race" through improvements to education and social environment. The alternative was evolutionary regression, social division, and violent conflict.[8]

Because social reproduction was considered to be woman's domain, the study of eugenics thrived in late Victorian women's groups. Women reformers associated competition, selfishness, and sexual appetite with masculine Anglo-Saxon identity. They believed that if women were allowed to take a more active role in social planning, they could inculcate the positive traits associated with female Anglo-Saxon identity into the broader populace. These included cooperation, sacrifice, and sexual purity.[9] Eugenicists often adopted a Malthusian attitude toward overpopulation, and combined their desire to breed superior children with the assertion that it was better to have fewer of them in the first place. This required liberating women from unwanted pregnancies by encouraging sexual restraint, outlawing marital rape, and discarding the stigma of spinsterhood.

Although he wisely withheld any claim to messianic destiny, Teed found that his hodgepodge of celibacy, feminism, brain science, and communism appealed to Leonard's club: she offered Teed a standing engagement to speak at the club's Tuesday night meetings. The Messenger thrived before a receptive public: at his first engagement, Teed spoke for more than two hours without notes. He impressed everyone, including himself. As he wrote Abie, "There never has been such a power manifest before in any effort of mine. Mrs. Leonard completely broke up, and was moved to tears and great emotion."[10] Teed spoke to the group about organizing a College of Life where like-minded women and men could come together to study. Leonard endorsed the endeavor and promised that the club would support Teed however it could. S. P. Andrews, however, was troubled by the sudden celebrity of the interloping doctor. He had a right to be worried: it was Teed's intention to steal Andrews's followers and make them his own.

Through this network of progressive intellectuals, Teed became acquainted with his next landlady, a German woman named Mrs. Egli, who had become devoted to his teachings.[11] It was Egli who introduced Teed to an acquaintance of decisive importance. This was Elizabeth Thompson, a society matron who took an interest in patronizing freethinking New York scientists. Thompson was a woman of considerable influence: she was reputed to be the only woman entitled to take the floor of the US Congress, and had traveled to Washington to present Congress with Francis Bicknell Carpenter's *First Reading of the Emancipation Proclamation by President Lincoln*, a painting that still hangs over the west staircase in the US Senate. Thompson began bankrolling Teed's scientific writings almost as soon as she'd met him.

Like Teed, Thompson had acquired a reputation for eccentricity. She eschewed the fineries and indulgences of women in her class, dressed simply, and spent what she saved on more worthy causes. In so doing, she claimed to follow the example of Christ and the "undefiled religion spoken of in the epistle of James." Along with her belief in the need for systematic and methodical reform in American society, a fondness for the Transcendentalists' pantheism was what led to her patronage of the sciences. "To me," Thompson stated, "there can be no conflict between true religion and pure science. How can any one help seeing they are the two sides of the same shield?"[12] This was a woman after Teed's own heart.

The arrangements Thompson made with the thinkers she supported were a speculative form of patronage: Thompson offered a monthly allowance and tailored suits to writers, including Arthur Merton and S. P. Andrews, in exchange for the publication rights to their work. Whatever Teed told her in their initial meeting, she was so impressed that she moved from Stamford down to New York to study with him. Before long, Egli, Teed, and Thompson were housemates.

Thompson did something else that she did not ordinarily do: she offered to send letters of introduction on Teed's behalf to her friends in Washington. Teed told Abie that not even Albert Brisbane had succeeded so well with her, and that Thompson had promised to send his books to the counts and foreign ministers of Europe in order for his teachings "to come upon the world like a clap of thunder." Thompson believed Teed's work would shape the next 2,000 years of human civilization and form the basis of a new system of scientific government designed to enhance human evolution. She invited Teed to her estate in Stamford to hobnob with other progressive women, and guaranteed a monthly allowance of $50 until Easter, about nine months later. This was when she expected to have his manuscript in hand.[13]

But Teed was too busy to write. He remained at the helm of Mrs. Peake's circle, continued giving private lessons in physiology to Cynthia Leonard, preached to various spiritualist congregations, and was

contemplating a run for the state senate.[14] Thompson cut off her support in July 1886, after Teed failed to deliver a manuscript.[15] Mrs. Egli
had likewise withdrawn from her association with the doctor. Her
defection was more treasonous than Thompson's principled disappointment: Egli had taken up with three others—Anna Johnson, a
Rosicrucian called Ridell, and a Theosophist called Salter—to form
a group they called the Tetrarchy. Teed was boxed out. However, the
doctor wasn't disappointed for long: his indefatigable lecture schedule
was about to pay off.

21. TEED GOES MENTAL

A T ONE OF Teed's lectures on brain physiology, a middle-aged woman called Thankful Hale approached the speaker. She had been impressed by Teed's teachings, and offered him an all-expenses-paid trip to Chicago to speak before the mental science convention she was organizing over Labor Day weekend. He accepted without hesitation.

The mental science organization to which Hale belonged was the direct descendant of American mesmerism. It was one among a swath of organizations that came to be known as New Thought, each of which traced its origins to Phineas Parker Quimby, a clockmaker turned mesmerist who realized that his patients were curing themselves by the force of their own belief. Exploration of the power of autosuggestion led Quimby to develop his own theory of mental healing: doctors transmitted disease by instilling belief in illness to their patients; priests and ministers compounded the problem by associating the body with shame, sin, and suffering.[1] These could all be reversed by changing patterns of thought and belief.

One of Quimby's most transformed patients was Mrs. Mary Glover Patterson, an invalid widow who cured herself of crippling neuralgia using Quimby's mind-cure methods. Patterson became one of Quimby's most devoted pupils, and was one of those who carried Quimby's work forward after his death in 1866. As Mary Baker Eddy, she went on to found the Church of Christ, Scientist—more commonly known as Christian Science. Eddy was a jealous autocrat, and repeatedly dismissed the best pupils from her Massachusetts Metaphysical College, where students lived and studied under the same roof. One such threat to her preeminence, Emma Curtis Hopkins, went to Chicago after her expulsion, where she taught her own version of mind-cure metaphysics.

Another Chicago-area mind curist was Andrew J. Swarts, an ex-Methodist minister who studied with Eddy before turning away from her authoritarianism. Swarts was put off by Eddy's legendary hatred for mesmerism and spiritualism—his wife, Katie, was a well-known Chicago medium. The pair had partnered with several others to found Mental Science University, which had organized the September 1886 National Mental Science Association conference where Teed was scheduled to speak. When Teed arrived in Chicago for the convention, he discovered that it would not be necessary to create his own College of Life from scratch, as he'd planned to do in New York: he needed only to commandeer the Mental Science University. This, Teed realized, would be easily accomplished by taking advantage of the divisions within the eclectic mental science community.

The September conference was held in Chicago's Church of the Redeemer, which doubled as a candy factory. Teed wasted no time securing allies, and was somehow elected president of the Association on its second day. One of his first acts as president was to withhold the telegraph he was supposed to send to Mary Baker Eddy, containing news of a narrowly passed resolution stating that the Association recognized Eddy's contributions to mental science.

Teed's lecture, simply titled "The Brain," was scheduled for Sunday. It was the last day of the convention, and the new president was poised to upstage the preceding speakers. After several days of mind-cure testimonials and ambiguous theories of the mind's effect on the body and its illnesses, convention attendees were dumbstruck by the doctor's onslaught of terminology and diagrams, and by his detailed explanations of exactly which cerebral structures controlled the various parts of the body. While other mental science practitioners were self-starting reformers, ex-mesmerists, or part-time eugenicists with little to no education in physiology, Teed's eclectic medical expertise was unparalleled at the convention. His performance concluded with a successful faith healing of a woman who could barely walk. Katie Swarts closed out the convention later that day; like her husband, she was heckled during her talk. Teed's preeminence in the Association was assured.[2]

To consolidate his control over the Mental Science University, Teed moved to Chicago immediately. With the wind at his back, he announced the establishment of the Society Arch-Triumphant, a spiritually oriented group open to students of what he now called "Koreshan" science. The Society took its name from the fringe belief in the prophecy of a unified, antisectarian Church Triumphant that would be established in the millennial dispensation— it was another idea Teed absorbed from Emanuel Swedenborg via Thomas Lake Harris.[3] Among the Society's first members were Thankful Hale and Evelyn Bubbett. The latter had discovered Dr. Teed after attending the mental science convention with her sister; her devotion to Koreshan science lasted until her death in Florida decades later.

While attempting to goad Mary Baker Eddy into a public feud by slandering her as a "mercenary" agent of Satan whose "sophistical" teachings were responsible for thousands of unnecessary deaths, Teed adopted Eddy's methods. He conducted a purge of the Mental Science Association, first removing the Swartses and then ridiculing any remaining Christian Scientists out of its ranks.[4] Assured of the loyalty of those who were left, Teed rebranded the University as the College of Life, and purported to offer "advantages offered by no school of 'Christian Science,' 'Metaphysics,' 'Mental Healing,' or 'Mind Cure.'" Located at 103 State Street, the College of Life professed to teach the fundamentals of Koreshan Science, which it described as: "a complete system of *cult*, universal in its scope."[5]

After a lethally failed mind cure landed Teed in court in 1888, he expounded his mind-cure theories to a jury empaneled for the coroner's inquest. The Koreshan women who attended the inquest were heard to exclaim, "Wonderful! wonderful!" as Teed outlined his theories of mind cure, but the eclectic doctor failed to convince the jury of their relevance. Teed was indicted on charges of practicing without a license and arrested on the spot. After being set free on $300 bond paid by Koreshan Mary E. Daniels, Teed declared victory, calling his release from martyrdom a "glorious thing for the cause."[6] The Koreshan leader continued to list his credentials as a medical doctor on the College's promotional materials, but ceased practicing medicine altogether.

Students in the College of Life became adept in rehearsing the tenets of Koreshan belief, including the prophecy that the millennial year of 1891 would be marked by Teed's own "translation" to his immortal body. The total cost of a College of Life degree was $50, which included matriculation, diploma fees, and tuition for a course in each of the five branches of College study. These included gynecology, metaphysics, brain pathology, and the College's specialty: analogical biology and analogical physiology, disciplines that taught the "laws of universal form," according to which the human body, as microcosm, corresponded "analogically" to universal cosmic design. These classical occult subjects, now dressed in the raiment of modern science, were the College's main attraction.

The College was notably a female-centric space. Among the fourteen faculty members listed in an early course bulletin, thirteen were women. Before long, Teed realized that one of the College faculty members was endowed with a special role in the new dispensation. Annie G. Ordway, a middle-class housewife and ex-Theosophist, possessed the body into which Teed's spirit would pass after his spiritual translation. In recognition of her special status in the Unity, Teed gave her the name Victoria Gratia and designated her the president of the Society Arch-Triumphant. Although the Society was composed largely of women attracted to the freedoms of a sexually egalitarian celibate society, the elevation of one woman above the rest caused considerable friction and occasional attrition—including Teed's eventual expulsion of Thankful Hale at Victoria's behest.[7]

22. THE KORESHAN UNITY

D R. Teed continued to rail against the evils of capitalist "com-
petism," but bided his time before revealing his messianic destiny to
his students. Although he had already called himself Koresh in New
York, Teed delayed assuming the name in Chicago. It was not until
the year after his arrival, in April 1887, that Teed's messianic prophecies
became a subject of general knowledge. The *Chicago Tribune* reported
that Teed had not only positioned himself as a preeminent authority among the city's mind curists; he also was declaring himself the
reincarnation of Enoch, Noah, Abraham, Moses, Elijah, and Jesus.
In teachings he later unfolded to his followers, Teed explained that
his seven incarnations corresponded to the seven planets then known
to exist.[1] For his final four embodiments, which would occur after his
translation, Teed would prefer the body of a woman.

The *Tribune* also carried news of the first great discovery of the
Koreshan Age of Aquarius: Teed announced that the earth was a concave sphere, and that humanity lives on the inside. Ideology, and nothing more, had fooled modern scientists into believing the Copernican
model, which Teed confidently exposed as optical illusion. Light from
the sun and stars was refracted by the atmosphere, but astronomers,
Teed insisted, had failed to account for this refraction, which gave the
Earth's surface its illusory convexity.[2] The sun was located at the center of the Earth, which was lined with a seven-layered shell of iron,
lead, copper, silver, mercury, gold, and platinum. The number 7, which

reappeared as frequently in Koreshan cosmogony as it did in Theosophy, indexed the Hermetic doctrine of the spirit's ascent through seven progressive planetary spheres.[3] The Earth-egg, in this schema, was not coextensive with the universe, but was the solar center of yet another cosmos. Teed called his system the "cellular cosmogony." As with other theories promulgated by late-Victorian occultists, Koreshan universology compensated for its lack of empirical evidence with an attractive logic of symmetry and universal applicability. Rejecting the chaos that modern astronomers had discovered with their telescopes, Teed favored a geometric cosmos inside a cosmos inside a cosmos, ad infinitum. In every micro- and macrocosm, the same laws of nature applied by cosmic correspondence. This elegant cosmological system offered a placid and pleasing alternative to the collective anxiety caused by the fragmentations of modern life wrought by urban industrialization.

After the College of Life was up and running, Teed set up a printing house called the Guiding Star, which began to issue a Koreshan newspaper of the same name. He dispatched Koreshan emissaries, including "Professor" Royal O. Spear, to neighboring states to lecture on Koreshan science and distribute the *Guiding Star*. The amplified reach of Teed's teachings drew in his next important convert: occult enthusiast Henry Silverfriend was a prosperous dry-goods merchant in Kaukauna, Wisconsin. He converted to Koreshanity almost as soon as he'd heard of Cyrus Teed.[4] Silverfriend sold his stake in the family store, moved to Chicago, and donated the proceeds of his $1,900 share to the Koreshan Unity. Before this final transaction, Teed arranged for the Koreshan Unity to sell its printing press and equipment to Silverfriend, so that creditors could never lay claim to it. The press was Teed's most valuable tool for conversion and fund-raising.

By this time, Teed worked out an organizational structure for Koreshanity that would remain in place long after his death. The College of Life continued to function as the scientific and educational arm of the Koreshan Unity, while the Society Arch-Triumphant would be its vehicle for public outreach. Modeled on the "outer order" that the Shakers developed for those who embraced Ann Lee's divinity but had not yet committed to communist separatism, membership in the Society Arch-Triumphant cost only $2 in annual dues and guaranteed receipt of Koreshan publications. The elite inner circle of Koreshanity was the Church Arch-Triumphant, the communal and religious order at the core of the Unity. Its members lived communally in a six-flat apartment building on College Place. Initiates donated their worldly belongings to the Unity and forsook all former family ties. Ella Woolsey and Thankful Hale were among the first communal residents; joining them were two diehards from New York: Teed's sister Emma and the ailing Sarah Patterson. When Abie Andrews and his family finally joined Teed in Chicago, they too joined the communal order. They could not have been happy about what they saw when they arrived at the College Place commune: it was cold and crowded. The communards lacked money for heat and furniture because Teed burned through their communal funds at the Koreshan printing office and by paying down Unity debts.[5]

In spite of these hardships, the Unity slowly grew. Silverfriend pressed Teed to follow through with the Koreshan convention he proposed in the *Guiding Star*. It was held on October 8, 1888, at Chicago's Central Music Hall. Teed's stirring speech finally converted Abie's wife, Virginia, who had only reluctantly agreed to join her zealous husband in Chicago. Although Teed's remarks do not survive, Victoria's convention speech was so popular that the Koreshans deemed it necessary to preserve and publish it in pamphlet form. Titled "Woman's Restoration to Her Rightful Dominion," her remarks were meant to evoke comparisons to Lucretia Mott and Susan B. Anthony: "By some predisposed power," Victoria declared, "[woman] finds herself subject to a bondage, in some cases a willing slave, but, nevertheless, a slave to barbaric egotism from which modern culture and civilization are gradually but certainly enabling her to arise." The speech was squarely aimed at women who found Mental Science and Christian Science to be insufficiently supportive of women's rights. But it connected feminism to the labor question in a way only a few other radicals were willing to do: "The Messiah of the Christian age, or dispensation," Victoria continued, referring to Teed,

> came to lift the curse, not merely as pertaining to woman,
> but as also regarding man. . . . He came also to lift the curse
> of labor, and the activity and progress of the workingman's
> movement everywhere, present indications that the curse of
> labor or drudgery will also be removed.

Only when woman was relieved of the "prostituted desire" encoded into human relationships by the capitalist regime of ownership and control, Victoria declared, would she be relieved of the "indiscriminate and unsought-for multiplication of degraded progeny" wrought by "unrestrained lust." And when households ceased to be "multiplied beyond the reasonable possibility of proper support, culture, and refinement," woman would be "lifted to the standards of legitimate and essential use in these vital domains."[6] Proclamations such as these, contained in the first half of Victoria's speech, were red meat for women involved in the eugenicist flank of the late-Victorian social-reform movements from which Koreshanity emerged.

Victoria and Teed were both a hit at the convention, which scored an impressive forty additional recruits to the Society Arch-Triumphant. Attendance records for successive years indicate that the Society continued its modest growth over the course of the Unity's Chicago period, rising to fifty-eight regularly attending members by the second half of 1890 and as many as eighty-seven by April 1892. Recruiting moved at a much higher pace than ten per year, however: attrition was also high.[7] According to the *Chicago Daily Tribune*, as many as 100 Koreshans were crowding into Koreshan meetings by July of 1890.[8]

. . .

TEED HAD AT LAST established a successful communal society. But while the movements on which the Koreshan Unity was modeled tended to be "in this world but not of it," the Koreshan Unity functioned as one of many outlets for the urban unrest and bourgeois malaise in late-Victorian Chicago. All around them, the Koreshans saw the "surging mass of human woe" to whom the goddess had instructed Teed to minister. The concentration of wealth that gave the Gilded Age its name had generated misery and squalor among the overcrowded poor; among the rich, it begat alienation and nervous disorders.

American cities, and Chicago in particular, were hotbeds of labor unrest. The economic depression that began with the Panic of 1873 had lingered well into the next decade, encouraging ever greater numbers of workers and immigrants to turn to anarchism and communism. The railroad strikes of 1877, which destroyed millions in railroad assets, set the country on edge by raising expectations of additional armed clashes between labor and capital. It was not an anxiety soothed by the antiseptic balm of late-Victorian religion: lacking influence over the urban working classes, many of whom were Catholics deemed biologically and culturally unsuitable for assimilation by conservative eugenicists and nativist bigots, American Protestant churches threw their moral authority behind the businessmen who sang the praises of laissez-faire capitalism.[9] This was the corrupted liberal Protestantism that Teed trained in his crosshairs, alongside the more traditionally villainous and decadent Roman Catholic Church and its anti-Christian monarch, the pope.

Most Koreshans came from the distressed middle classes, who found themselves in the widening gap of vulnerability and uncertainty that yawned between the haves and the have-nots in Gilded Age America. Skilled tradesmen, the backbone of the middle class, were becoming casualties of industrialized mass production. And just as the scientific rationalization of labor had restricted workers' autonomy on the "scientifically managed" factory floor, the bureaucratization of clerical occupations was destroying the individuality of educated workers. Social

Darwinists and their allies in the Protestant churches maintained that all of this was progress, but this narrative was only convincing to the affluent. Instead of reviving a compromised Protestantism, the middle classes sought diversion in metaphysics and Eastern imports—including religious innovations like Theosophy and mind cure.

Unlike those fads—but like the Shakers and the Oneida Perfectionists—the Koreshan Unity had something material to offer: relief from the anxieties and tumultuous social transformations wrought by modern industrial capitalism. To the middle-class married women who made up the active core of its membership, the Unity offered an alternative to the drudgery of domestic servitude and the monotony of middle-class socialization: the regeneration of the race was a far higher calling than the reproduction of the labor force, and it resonated with progressive eugenic narratives for avoiding the race suicide balefully predicted by Malthusian materialists and Anglo-Saxon supremacists. To unmarried women, Koreshan communism offered an escape from the solitary and precarious journey into old age. The Unity validated the worth of women and workers as intellectual and moral agents by offering opportunities for education and political engagement.

The Koreshans welcomed anyone who agreed that women's emancipation and the overthrow of monopoly capitalism could not be achieved independently. Capitalist competition and women's subjugation were mutually reinforcing phenomena. But as Harris had done before him, Teed complemented his anticapitalist screeds with a message of millennial urgency: the end of the capitalist order was drawing nigh and would culminate with an apocalyptic confrontation between labor and capital. He referred to the inevitable conflict as the battle between Gog and Magog mentioned in the Book of Ezekiel.

Although mind cure was a favorite object of derision in the Chicago press, socialism was taken much more seriously. The papers regarded Teed's experiment in communism skeptically, but with a certain measure of respect: the Koreshans unwaveringly practiced what they preached. No one doubted their commitment to a communist lifestyle, and the community members appeared to be peaceful and happy in spite of their Spartan accommodations. In 1891, a group of Chicago Socialists even floated the idea of creating a community modeled after Dr. Teed's.[10] Later, in 1894, Teed spoke at a strike meeting of the American Railway Union alongside Eugene Debs, and a front-page *Washington Post* article even alleged the Koreshan master was the "Unknown" man who led rallies during Jacob Coxey's first-ever march on Washington—a nationwide Populist phenomenon better known as Coxey's Army.[11]

Coxey's Army was one of the many cohesive national movements to emerge from the unrest of the masses. Another was the Nationalist movement inspired by the socialist utopia depicted in Edward Bellamy's wildly popular novel *Looking Backward* (1888). Bellamy depicted a futuristic United States, where by the year 2000, army and industry had merged into an Industrial Army controlled by the state. The Industrial Army organized the production and distribution of all necessities. Except those exempted for careers in teaching and medicine, all citizens were conscripted into the army, which assigned each individual the role most suited to his or her abilities. Decisions about how best to deploy each citizen and benefit from his or her talents were made by a meritocratic elite. Bellamy's novel became a national sensation following its publication, and quickly led to the establishment of Bellamy-inspired Nationalist Clubs across the country. Adherents viewed Bellamy's Nationalist movement as an alternative to rule by rings of monopolies, on the one hand, or by the violent masses on the other.[12] Editorials in the *Flaming Sword* frequently praised Bellamy and his novel. Teed's only complaint was that the Nationalist system lacked "moral vitality."[13]

23. MESSIAH ON THE MOVE

T EED MOVED TO CAPITALIZE on Nationalist fervor by running
ads in Bellamy's Nationalist newspaper, *The New Nation*, and by
sending emissaries to the movement's strongholds. Royal Spear began
teaching Koreshan doctrine twice weekly at a boardinghouse on Post
Street in San Francisco, just off Union Square. Investigating the matter, the *San Francisco Chronicle* reported that Spear was evangelizing the
mind-cure science taught at the World's College of Life. The *Chronicle*
fixated on the gender imbalance of Koreshan recruits, describing the
audience as "three old men and a couple of young fellows" mixed into
a crowd of thirty to forty women.[1] Spear's outreach resulted in the
establishment of a Koreshan commune on Noe Street. Teed liked to
call it his "Golden Gate Hippocampus," although its official name was
Ecclesia.[2] Another branch opened in Denver.

The San Francisco colony quickly grew to rival the commune in
Chicago. Its recruitment of several wealthy women enabled the western outpost to take an enterprising lead in enacting Koreshan principles by founding the Koreshan Bureau of Equitable Commerce in
April 1890. The ultimate objective of the Bureau was to instigate the
transition to a moneyless society in which goods could be exchanged
according to a system of credit assigned on the basis of completed
tasks. Such a system had largely failed when Stephen Pearl Andrews
and Josiah Warren attempted to implement it at Modern Times, but
Teed believed the credit system could succeed if it were first established among a union of America's seven celibate communal societies.

In addition to advocating communism and women's liberation in its newsletter, *The Plowshare and the Pruning-Hook*, the Bureau organized a convention at San Francisco's Metropolitan Hall in 1891.[3] It was advertised in the *Chronicle* as an event to address "the great question of bread for the multitude, with a solution of the labor problem." The announcement promised the convention would also attend to the matter of obtaining "a people's railroad for the benefit of the people." This was a subject intended to appeal to California progressives stirred up by socialist reformers like Henry George, who vocally opposed the corrupt machinations of railroad barons like Sen. Leland Stanford.[4] In California, the Koreshans baited the public by distributing invitations that asked, "How can we settle the question of the transportation of freight and people across the continent and not be robbed by the railroad sharks?"[5] Teed and Victoria led a Chicago delegation to the San Francisco convention.[6]

During his speech at the convention, Teed adopted his usual apocalyptic pitch, proclaiming to the hundreds of prospective socialists: "The question for the people of to-day to consider is that of bread and butter. It must henceforth be a battle to the death between organized labor and organized capital."[7] This apocalyptic battle between Gog and Magog, thundered Koresh, was the threshold over which humanity must step to arrive at a future of peace and abundance. Teed's obstreperous remarks helped the Koreshans meet their objective for the evening: securing massive publicity for the launch of the Bureau's plans to initiate a "co-operative plan of distribution and collection in groceries and other household necessities" that would "do away with the middleman in commerce." The Ecclesians started selling memberships to their economic collective the very same night. The next day's *Chronicle* announced a "WAR ON CAPITAL," in its headline reporting on the event. But despite a crowd of several hundred in the Metropolitan Ballroom, the *Chronicle* dismissed the rally, stating that "few were there because they were really interested in the scheme, but the majority were there out of pure curiosity." Yet such was the reach of the Koreshans' intrigue that the Bureau's debut was reported a few days later in the *Los Angeles Times*, where its objectives were derided as "Impracticable Social Reforms" and unfavorably compared to the communal industries undertaken by the Mormons.[8]

Dismissiveness gave way to prurient fascination when Mary Mills, who had spoken at the convention, "deserted a hitherto happy family to join the converts of the pious pretender and charlatan, Cyrus R. Teed." Mills was a society matron who lived in a mansion on Van Ness Avenue, a wide boulevard then home to the city's elite. Her husband of thirty-three years, Dr. James Mills, was an eminent geologist and former student of Harvard scientist Louis Agassiz. Winning her conversion was a stunning victory for the Koreshan cause. Dr. Mills compared his wife's condition to that of "a fever that must run its course," suggesting that his fifty-five-year-old wife was suffering a bout of hysteria. The Harris–Oliphant scandal was still fresh in the minds of many San Franciscans, including Mr. Mills, who claimed that "Teed is working the old confidence game of Harris, who so successfully duped the Oliphants out of thousands of dollars, and after thirty years of proselytizing has become a millionaire."[9]

Eager to assemble evidence to support its portrayal of Teed as a wife-stealing home-wrecker bent on the corruption of women's morals, the *Chicago Daily Tribune* had dispatched a reporter to cover the unfolding scandal. But Mrs. Mills, fortified by a dose of Koreshan feminism, stoutly refuted her husband's claims of hysteria and religious mania. Mills understood the gravity of her actions: "I did not take this step in the belief that I would add to my present happiness," she admitted to the *Tribune*. Chafing against the demands of her position, Mills declared her separation from her family was "absolutely necessary if I wished to have a religious belief of my own . . . this state of celibacy is but a preparation for our future life, when the Christman will dwell upon the earth." She further explained that she and the Koreshans believed Teed to be "Elias," the second coming of Christ foretold in the Bible, and that "in two years he will be dematerialized, soon to reappear in the form of a man–woman, having the attributes of both sexes. He will live on earth and spiritually produce the sons of God, who will inherit the earth."[10] The papers printed her declarations with obvious glee.

Reporters had long jabbed at the Unity for being a predominantly female religion, suggesting that Koresh used his "magnetism" to prey on vulnerable women and break up marriages to obtain followers. But as Mrs. Mills indicated, women in the Koreshan Unity enjoyed a respect and equality not accorded to them in their domestic roles or in society at large. The Koreshan orchestra and drama troupe were coed. Women lectured on Koreshan science. And women held the majority of leadership positions in the Unity: a trio of female lieutenants known as the Triangle comprised a special rank of followers who made decisions in Teed's absence. The Koreshans operated a Women's Mission, printed a series of pamphlets for women, and supported Victoria Woodhull's candidacy for president of the United States. Henry Silverfriend's wife, Etta, was even hired to work on Woodhull's third presidential campaign in 1892.[11]

While newspapermen ridiculed the Koreshan assertions of the equality of the sexes, Teed slowly amassed a following of women inclined toward feminism and egalitarian socialism, but who refused to renounce organized religion in the manner prescribed by their Marxist contemporaries. In Chicago, at least one Koreshan woman entered the Church Arch-Triumphant to escape a physically abusive marriage.[12] Her story is known because her husband sued Teed for alienation of affection; most of the Koreshans' individual motives for joining the group are unknown, but it is likely that other women saw the female-dominated Unity as a safe place to escape similar abuse.

As 1891 came to an end, Teed revised the prophecy of his "translation," postponing the theocrasis for two years. Teed now claimed his translation would occur during the 1893 World's Fair in Chicago, coinciding with the battle of Gog and Magog which he foretold would erupt to destroy the city. Only the Koreshans would be saved—and they would achieve immortality.[13] Unfortunately, two of Teed's most loyal followers had already succumbed to mortal corruption: Abie Andrews and Sarah Patterson were both dead before the Fair.

Teed shuttled back and forth between Chicago and the San Francisco outpost until it seemed he might have a shot at uniting with the Harmonists, whose dying communal society still controlled assets believed to be worth hundreds of thousands, or perhaps even millions, of dollars. On its front page, the *Los Angeles Times* reported on Teed's promises to unite his network of cooperative communes using a six-track transcontinental railroad that would travel under the Rocky Mountains to reach the Pacific.[14] After visiting the Harmonists in October 1891, Teed informed reporters his trip had been a success, insinuating that the Harmonists finally accepted his second proposal to merge, and that he would send between 100 and 1,000 of his followers to Economy.[15] Henry Silverfriend and Teed's brother Oliver went to the Harmony Society to learn the community's trades, along with several other Koreshans. But the plan faltered by the end of the year: the Koreshans were denied membership as a result of Oliver's drinking and Teed's reputation as a philanderer.[16] Henrici denounced Teed's messianic pretensions when he learned of them, and the plot to commandeer the Society was finished.[17]

Undeterred, Teed carried on with his plan to unite the celibate communal societies then operating in America, revising expectations from seven communal orders down to six. He visited the Canterbury and New Lebanon Shakers that December, and made his highly publicized visit to Thomas Lake Harris in February. But all was not well in San Francisco: Royal Spear had quit the Bureau of Equitable Commerce over anxieties having to do with Teed's total lack of business acumen, and for his frustrating habit of justifying his frequent changes in plans by ambiguously stating, "Necessity compels me to make a change on the chessboard."[18] Spear and his wife remained believers in apostolic communism and lamented the Koreshans' failure in the city, claiming that the three-building compound on Noe Street was nothing but a home for elderly and invalid women who had nowhere else to turn.

After Fountain Grove proved impervious to Teed's attempts to seize control of its assets, something finally had to be done to accommodate the swelling ranks of Koreshans: Ecclesia was bursting with converts, but the Bureau of Equitable Commerce was an embarrassing failure. Beginning in the winter of 1891–92, Teed gradually ordered the San Francisco Koreshans to pack up their communal belongings and board a train to Chicago. Meanwhile, Teed told reporters that followers from Seattle, Los Angeles, and Portland would join those from San Francisco to make the journey east, among them a wealthy young heiress.[19] The College Avenue commune could never contain them all, but Teed and Victoria had found ideal properties for expansion: a mansion in the suburban neighborhood of Washington Heights would become the Koreshan headquarters, while an apartment building in the Normal Park neighborhood would house the majority of the Church Arch-Triumphant.[20]

The problem was that nobody wanted Koreshans for neighbors. A committee of vigilantes threatened Teed with tar and feathers, and the jilted husband of a Koreshan woman stirred Washington Heights into concerted action to thwart the communal relocation while he took Teed to court. In Normal Park, residents organized street protests and threatened to mob the Koreshan apartments. They had to be turned away by the police.[21] The ruckus made the front pages of newspapers across the country.

Trenchant opposition failed to intimidate the faithful, who in any case had little other choice: the rest of the San Franciscans had already arrived and crammed into the Koreshan commune. In May, Unity headquarters relocated from College Avenue to the Washington Heights manor, which the Koreshans renamed Beth Ophrah. The property encompassed eight structures, including a barn that became the new home of the Guiding Star Publishing House, which continued to issue *The Flaming Sword*.

Things didn't exactly improve after the Koreshans resettled. A suspicious device was found under the sidewalk in front of Beth Ophrah; a local chemist said it "resembled the bomb used by Anarchists a few years ago," in reference to the Haymarket blast.[22] An anonymous "Friend of Woman" also issued a specific death threat, which read: "TEED You will be shot and killed by me on sight. I am determined to rid this community of you dirty black s—of a b—. You will be shot the first time you show your face in a certain section of this city."[23] The author of the note presumably referred to Washington Heights. Teed once more appealed to the police for protection.[24]

The Koreshans tried to brush off these aggressions, but others could not be easily dismissed: Teed had to be bailed out of jail after being chased down the street in Washington Heights and arrested on charges of immoral intimacy with another man's wife. Although there is no evidence to suggest Teed ever broke his vow of celibacy, Victorian social mores meant that many observers could not interpret the Koreshans' communal living arrangements as anything but a brothel or a harem. In Normal Park, an assembly of more than 800 men gathered to hatch various schemes for persecuting their neighbors. As the calendar moved closer to the date of Teed's theocrasis, Koreshans began to suspect Teed's martyrdom would initiate the process. They prepared by sending all the Koreshan children away from Beth Ophrah, to the Normal Park apartments.[25]

. . .

THE WESTERN KORESHANS had barely gotten settled before Teed resumed his rounds of America's communal utopias. On June 26, Teed led a small party of Koreshans out of Chicago. After a sweltering train ride through Canada to Buffalo and points east, the weary travelers finally arrived at Mt. Lebanon, situated near the Massachusetts border. There they were received by the influential North Family of Shakers.

During his first visit to Canterbury and New Lebanon, Teed was encouraged by the Shakers' receptivity to his teachings, and decided the time was ripe to pitch them on unification. The North Family had made him a member of their outer order before he left in December, and two Shakers had come calling on the Koreshans at their Chicago headquarters in the interim. Teed was ready to seal the deal. He prepared for the return trip by exchanging letters with Elder Frederick Evans, who encouraged the visit, and by buttering up the United Society of Believers in the *Flaming Sword* by lavishing praise on Ann Lee.[26]

As they offered the Koreshans a tour of the strawberry patch, the dairy, the laundry, and the various manufactories at Mt. Lebanon, the Shakers put tough questions to their communist allies. The intelligence and sophistication of the Koreshan women impressed the forward-thinking North Family, as did the degree of equality Teed accorded them. Eldress Anna White invited the Koreshans to meet the entire Family, which was assembled for them later that evening. As Virginia Andrews wrote in her diary:

> This filled me with dread, and when we were led up to the meeting room from where the sisters and bros. were seated in a semicircle and we were appointed two chairs in front of the pulpit I wished I could melt away out of sight. Elder Evans came in with the brothers and I did not know but we were to have a fearful trial by questions but any fears were groundless. They asked us to tell of our persecutions and of the moving of our security. Victoria did the talking and told it all in a bright entertaining way.[27]

Always capable of rising to the occasion, Victoria calmly repudiated sensational stories the Shakers had read about Teed in the Syracuse papers. The meeting finished with the Koreshans joining the Shakers in song.

Apparently the visitors satisfied all of the Believers' remaining doubts: Teed and Victoria were both made honorary Shakers before their departure. After an emotional farewell, the Koreshans left New Lebanon on July 6, making a grand tour of New York, Boston, Marblehead, Roxbury, Cambridge, and Harvard. Victoria gave her blue-stocking lectures in each city along the whistle-stop tour. Upon return to Chicago, Teed had the Guiding Star Publishing House print a pamphlet containing Elder Evans's announcement of the Koreshans' ordainment as elders of a new order—as well as his recommendations that the Koreshans take up vegetarianism and agrarian communism. It was a sign of things to come.

24. ANOTHER NEW JERUSALEM

TEED WAS RESTLESS upon his return to Chicago. As the World's Fair approached, he faced the test that William Miller had failed in 1844, when the apocalypse Miller predicted failed to occur. After the Fair came and went without evidence of Teed's theocrasis, some Koreshans defected.[1] But the most faithful adhered to the Master. Of course, many had little other choice: they had given up their property, family, and professions to join the cause—and the Panic of 1893 had decimated the economy.

Teed's thoughts turned once more to New Jerusalem: it was a calling encoded in his name. He sought advice from Alesha Sivartha, a mystic devoted to the subject of Jerusalem, for recommendations on how to proceed with his calling. The two had been acquainted through their mutual alliance with Elizabeth Thompson, who had supported Sivartha when he was writing as Arthur Merton. Sivartha agreed with Shaker Frederick Evans, who advised the Unity to seek the placid shelter of agricultural isolation. But Sivartha suggested a more temperate climate for the holy city.[2] The notion appealed to Teed. After all, it would not be hard to convince the Unity to depart for southern climes: the Koreshans, like other Chicagoans hit hard by the deepening economic depression, had suffered through parts of the winter with no heat, and had even had their water cut off at Normal Park.[3]

Nor could the Unity forever withstand the onslaught of lawsuits and animosity it faced in Chicago. Teed had finally learned a lesson that the Shaker Elders, the Public Universal Friend, and Thomas Lake

Harris all knew much sooner in their careers: if it were to thrive, his New Jerusalem required distance from scrutiny and interference. This realization, combined with the inspiring tour Koreshans had taken of the marvelous White City erected for the World's Fair, led the Master to the conclusion that it was time to establish his own Koreshan metropolis.[4] So it was that in October 1893, Teed, Victoria, and Berthaldine Boomer went to Florida to investigate the potential purchase of Pine Island in Estero Bay.

Teed had received a tip on the Florida property from a real estate speculator he'd met at the World's Fair, and it jibed with stories he'd heard about Western Florida on cross-country railroad trips.[5] During these evangelism tours, Teed usually left Victoria in control of Beth Ophrah, and invited Bertie Boomer to accompany him instead. Boomer was one of Teed's most loyal companions, and her family was one of those that contributed hefty sums to the Koreshan coffers.

The Boomers had joined the Unity in 1888. Four years prior, they'd returned to their native city of Chicago from Pennsylvania, where they had begun to study the writings of Charles Taze Russell. Like Teed, Russell issued prophecies concerning the coming of Elijah the Prophet, whose appearance was a forerunner to the return of the Messiah. While residing in Pittsburgh, the Boomers attended some of Russell's lectures across the river in Allegheny, but they found his claims lacking in scientific rigor. Still seeking spiritual satisfaction, Bertie borrowed a stack of religious papers from her neighbor. Among them was the *Flaming Sword*. Ultimately, it was happenstance that brought her family into the fold: it wasn't until Bertie spied the Guiding Star Publishing House while riding the Cottage Grove Avenue streetcar that she decided to call upon the Koreshans. She came away with an armful of additional Koreshan literature, which she studied with her husband. They found it "too good to be true" and enlisted as members of the Society Arch-Triumphant.[6] Although they never joined the communal order in Chicago, Bertie became one of Teed's closest associates; he appointed her to the Planetary Court, a seven-woman advisory council that aided him in making important decisions. She later became one of the vertices of the Triangle.

When Boomer, Victoria, and Koresh finally got to Pine Island, they were disappointed to discover its owner wouldn't negotiate the price below $150,000—a sum far beyond what they could pay. But before leaving town, they deposited Koreshan literature in the train station at Punta Gorda. The pamphlets were later discovered by a German settler named Gustave Damkohler, another religious seeker attracted to Charles Taze Russell's Watch Tower Tract Society.[7] Not long after Teed and the advance guard arrived back in Chicago, the Koreshans received a letter from Damkohler asking them to return and settle on his land.[8]

The trio again departed for Florida, this time with Mary Mills in tow, to complete the Triangle. Upon arrival, the pioneers camped for several nights in an abandoned hotel they considered buying while they tracked down their latest convert. According to Koreshan lore, it was Damkohler who recognized Teed: tears sprang to his eyes as he cried, "Master, Master!" Koresh quickly brokered a deal with his eager new follower: Damkohler would sell the Koreshans 300 of his 320 acres for $200, as well as first right of refusal on the remaining 20 acres he set aside for himself and his son, Elwin. The property intended for the Unity was then transferred into Boomer's name.

Elwin navigated the Koreshan dignitaries down the coast to Estero in a sailboat called the *Guide*. The party landed on New Year's Day, 1894. That night, everyone crammed into Damkohler's tiny cabin on the banks of the Estero River: the Koreshan women slept sideways across the cabin's only bed, while Teed dozed in a cot fashioned from old sails in the attic. Damkohler and Elwin slept aboard the *Guide*. This was how they lived for the next few weeks, as Teed and the Damkohlers cleared the thick scrub from the land in preparation for the arrival of additional colonists. Meanwhile, the Triangle undertook the first of many experiments in creative comforts, and got acquainted with the snakes, rats, mosquitoes, and wild pigs that called Estero home. In the evenings, the party dined on fish, oysters, alligator, boar, and honey from Damkohler's beehives. The newcomers were delighted by the fruits that grew naturally in the region, including the mango trees Damkohler had planted near his cabin.[9]

Teed summoned a carefully selected advance work crew from Chicago, among them carpenters, farmers, and mechanics. They arrived in late January, at which point Teed left Victoria and Mary in charge of the budding commune while he and Boomer returned to Chicago to stoke excitement for the project. The leaders recruited twenty-four additional male volunteers, ranging from the adolescent to the geriatric, and put them on a train to Florida. Before leaving Florida, Teed had purchased a sloop named *Ada*, which ferried the settlers from the railroad terminus at Punta Gorda to Mound Key, an island in the Estero Bay. From there the passengers waited for high tide, when they could use rowboats to get around the sandbars and across the oyster beds that filled the bay. Until a stove was finally transported to the settlement, Victoria and Mary cooked over open fires for nearly thirty men, who slept in tents and hurried to construct cabins before the rainy season began. Lacking a sawmill, they built log cabins with thatched roofs that leaked throughout the winter.

New Jerusalem was certainly isolated: Fort Myers was located sixteen miles down a rugged and sandy road that made wagon travel nearly impossible. The Estero River functioned as the Koreshans' primary mode of travel, commerce, and communication. Until they were able to dig a well, the settlers relied on an open source that yielded water so sour it had to be cut with citrus juice. In the mornings, the Koreshan men went fishing in the holes along the river, catching the jewfish, sheepshead, perch, jack fish, and other native species that lay numb in the cool, early-morning water.[10]

In 1895, the Unity purchased machinery to set up its own sawmill on Estero Island. It enabled them to erect the grandest structures in the settlement, many of which remain standing; one of these was the Master's House, where Teed lived with Victoria and his sister Emma. Another of the large constructions was the dining hall and kitchen, which contained a 40-by-70-foot banquet room where the Koreshans could all eat together, hold Unity meetings, and hear their Master's lectures. An organ was later installed to accompany the Koreshans' large repertoire of songs.[11] Women's dormitories occupied the second and third floors of the building, which for a time was the tallest in Lee County. In the years after the colony's founding, Chicago Koreshans had continued to relocate to Estero, while Teed made missionary trips to Allegheny, Pennsylvania, to poach additional followers of Charles Taze Russell, who reportedly "flocked" to Florida in response.[12]

Land on the Florida frontier was relatively inexpensive, which allowed the Unity to buy Big Hickory and Little Hickory Islands, Mound Key, and Estero Island. The colony hit its peak population of about 200 people after Teed summoned the remaining Chicagoans to Estero in 1903. Against all odds—heat, hunger, mosquitoes, political adversaries, and the routine perils of remote Florida wilderness, let alone the fact that Teed was using city folk to start a citrus plantation on swampland covered in scrub pine and palmetto—the Estero colony succeeded in spite of its many opponents and detractors. The settlement grew to include dozens of buildings, including dormitories, a printing house, bakery, infirmary, laundry, concrete manufactory, general store, the Art Hall auditorium, and a grand residence for the Planetary Court. The Koreshans built sunken gardens and paved gravel paths through the wild landscape, making their settlement into an oasis fit to be called Jerusalem. The Unity's investment in citrus fruits prospered, and the cash crop largely sustained them.

Koreshan communism allowed plenty of time for educational and leisure activities. They wrote and performed plays in the Art Hall, listened to letters from traveling members read aloud at mealtimes, and frequently went to the beach to swim. The Koreshan orchestra performed for visitors from nearby Fort Myers.

. . .

ONE OF THE EXTRAVAGANT PROJECTS that Teed undertook in Florida was a definitive vindication of his hollow-earth theory. The project he launched, called the Koreshan Geodetic Survey, extended research that Teed and his associates had conducted at the Old Illinois Drainage Canal. In that experiment, Koreshan scientists suspended bright paper swatches from a bridge, then rowed several miles down the canal and dropped anchor. Teed knelt down in the boat, bringing his eye fifteen inches from the water's surface. The paper targets, as well as their reflections on the water, remained visible. Teed took this as definitive evidence that the Copernican model of a round Earth was false, but decided a more theatrical demonstration was in order.[13] The Koreshan Geodetic Survey, he believed, would expose surveys conducted by the US government as sham science.

Although he held government scientists in low regard, Teed went to Washington, DC, in late November 1896 to interest them in collaborating on the survey he planned to conduct on the Floridian coast. After failing to gain an audience with Henry Gannett, a prominent government geographer, he met instead with O. H. Tillman, one of Gannett's subordinates at the United States Coast and Geodetic Survey.[14] At the National Observatory, Teed met with Simon Newcomb, a navy mathematician, astronomer, and author of several nautical almanacs. None of them was keen on participating in Teed's quixotic study.

While Koresh was in Washington, his geodetic staff departed Chicago for Estero, with their equipment in tow. They established their base of operations on Naples Beach while the Master was in the capital. The survey commenced on January 2, 1897, after Teed returned to

Florida.[15] Chief "scientist" on the project was Ulysses Morrow, an editor from Allegheny, Pennsylvania, who before discovering Koreshan science had promulgated flat-earth theories in a paper called the *Herald of Glad Tidings*. After reading about the cellular cosmogony in the *Flaming Sword*, Morrow converted to Koreshanity and began incorporating Teed's theories into his works—without attribution.[16] Morrow and Teed named Bertie's son Lucius Boomer the assistant engineer, and the elder Boomers bankrolled the project.[17]

At Naples the survey crew began by observing the approach of various seafaring vessels, including their sloop *Ada*, and used a telescope to view the Sanibel Island lighthouse in the distance. Based on Teed's erroneous interpretation of Copernican theory, they calculated that the 94-foot-tall lighthouse would need to be higher than 560 feet to be seen over a convex horizon. But after years of publishing his calculations in the *Flaming Sword*, Teed already knew that his mathematical proofs were never enough to convince doubters: a demonstration of the Earth's concavity was the only way to persuade the world to adopt Koreshanity.

Over the course of four weeks, the Koreshan geodetic team deployed a device called a "rectilineator" they brought with them from Chicago. Comprised of three 12-foot mahogany segments that could be detached and reconnected, the rectilineator would allow the scientists to extend a line perpendicular to the force of gravity, beginning at a height of ten feet. Using a variety of instruments—including protractors, levels, triangles, rulers, compasses, plumb lines, and for some reason, thermometers—Koreshans painstakingly ensured all sections of the rectilineator were aligned before moving the rear section to the front. Because they feared their adversaries would tamper with the device, they guarded it around the clock.[18] The experiment took months to complete.

As expected, the "rectiline" eventually collided with the sea, demonstrating to the satisfaction of the Koreshans that the world was a hollow shell eight thousand miles in diameter, curving upward eight inches per mile. Teed and Morrow published the results of their expensive and time-consuming experiment in a book titled *The Cellular Cosmogony*, first released in 1898 and republished several times thereafter. Later editions appeared under the name of Koresh alone: Morrow's continued study of the geodetic calculations later uncovered inconsistencies that demolished his faith in the cellular cosmogony. After he brought the mathematical errors to the attention of Teed and others who'd worked on the survey, Morrow claimed, he was asked to leave the Unity.[19]

25. A TEST OF IMMORTALITY

CYRUS TEED ENJOYED several more years of evangelism, shuttling back and forth between various sites of Koreshan activity with the alacrity of a man half his age. Aside from the short-lived colony in Denver, small cells of Koreshans had formed in Los Angeles; Lynn, Massachusetts; Portland, Oregon; and across the greater Pittsburgh area. Adversaries and apostates in Chicago and Fort Myers periodically made trouble for the Unity in court and in the press, and Teed's enemies in Chicago continued to protest the Koreshan presence in Washington Heights until the mass exodus in 1903. He and the Koreshan orchestra were even once pelted with eggs during a public concert in Chicago.[1]

As their colony grew, the Koreshans saw the advantages of incorporating the settlement as a Florida town. This was easily accomplished in 1904. The move excited criticism from Philip Isaacs, the Koreshans' main opponent in the Fort Myers press, but it interested few others. Trouble emerged when Isaacs was elevated to chair of the Democratic Party in Lee County. Although the Koreshan men were registered Democrats, they'd annoyed the Party by supporting trust-busting Teddy Roosevelt when he appeared on the Republican ticket in 1904. Isaacs assembled a slate of candidates for the 1906 elections who vowed to strip the Koreshans of state funds to which they were entitled as a Florida town, and changed the rules of the party primary to exclude anyone who refused to sign a loyalty pledge to the Democrats. The Koreshans refused to sign without first striking out parts of the pledge that offended them. But they didn't stop there. To intimidate their political opponents, the Koreshans ran one of their own candidates, Ross Wallace, for county commissioner that year, and formed their own Progressive Liberty Party for that purpose. The PLP platform called for a uniform, standardized income and for immediate public seizure of all utilities; the party and its platform provoked Teed's enemies, who upped the ante by attempting to invalidate the Koreshans' voting rights.

The PLP had struck a chord by daring to oppose the corrupt machine politics of Lee County, and attracted enough disaffected Republicans, Democrats, and Socialists to become a force to be taken seriously. The feud between Teed and the Democrats intensified. Isaacs, now a judge, brought the weight of his office down on the Koreshan settlement while attempting to destroy Teed's reputation with salacious scandal-mongering. Teed began traveling with a posse of Koreshan bodyguards whenever he went to town in Fort Myers, but even this could not shield him completely. After the Master intervened to mediate a misunderstanding between Wallace and some of the Koreshans' Fort Myers adversaries, a hotelier by the name of Sellers slugged Koresh in the face. According to Koreshan history, the event triggered Teed's slow decline to bodily corruption.[2]

Teed began to suffer crippling nerve pain throughout his body. Although he continued to oversee affairs at the Koreshan outpost in Washington, DC, the Master periodically retired to the Koreshan beach house on Estero Island, where he convalesced in the company of Gustav Faber, former captain of the *Ada*. Faber gave Teed ice baths and administered electrotherapy treatments. Not so secretly, the Messiah was in agony. The Koreshans blamed their Master's affliction on his assailant, and began to murmur once more of martyrdom.

As he lay dying, Teed toiled over what became his final work: it was his attempt to join the cascade of literary responses to Edward Bellamy's *Looking Backward*. The result was a futurist dystopian war novel titled *The Great Red Dragon, or, The Flaming Devil of the Orient*. It was published in 1909, under a pseudonym Teed invented to disguise the novel's authorship from publishers.[3] In a foreword to the text, author "Lord Chester" accused publishing houses of declining the manuscript but ripping off its revolutionary ideas. Teed presumably referred to the 1908 publication of Jack London's *The Iron Heel*, a dystopian novel with a similar plot.

In fact, Teed lifted much of the action in *The Great Red Dragon* from a different novel: Ignatius Donnelly's 1890 bestseller, *Caesar's Column*. Donnelly was an ex-Populist Minnesota Congressman already famous for his pseudoscientific historiographies. He popularized the modern Atlantis myth and acquired additional notoriety for a book and lecture tour to promote the theory that Francis Bacon had authored the works attributed to William Shakespeare. *Caesar's Column* was a late-career work of speculative fiction. The novel depicted a semi-futuristic New York City where society was so corroded by the great "combinations" of monopolies that the poor had literally begun a process of evolutionary regression. Eventually, hordes of subhuman workers led by an international Brotherhood of Destruction rise up to overthrow the Oligarchy, a secret society of bankers and financiers who control the political and economic system. In a nod to the deterministic and eugenicist bent of American Progressives, Donnelly named the novel's titular character Caesar Lomellini after Cesare Lombroso, the Italian positivist criminologist. Because Caesar leads the New York masses to rebel in coordination with the degraded proletarians of Europe, Western civilization on both sides of the Atlantic is completely destroyed, forcing the novel's protagonists to escape in blimps to establish a new nucleus of Anglo-Saxon civilization in the mountains of central Africa. The novel expressed the darkest nightmares of middle-class eugenicists and the authoritarian Socialists galvanized by Bellamy's Nationalist movement.

Teed's novel adopted Donnelly's plot whole cloth, but situated the story in Chicago instead of New York. He explicitly identified the warring forces of labor and capital with Gog and Magog; as in Donnelly's novel, they utterly destroy American society. Teed retained the money-power conspiracy narrative favored by Donnelly, but rejected Donnelly's anti-Semitic tropes, which he considered anti-Christian. Instead, he adapted Donnelly's plot to include the yellow-scare narrative set forth in H. G. Wells's novel *The War in the Air* (1908), in which the United States is invaded by imperial Germany from the east and by the allied forces of Japan and China in the west. In Teed's *Great Red Dragon*, the war of Gog and Magog results in the mutual annihilation of armed capitalists and insurrectionary labor unions, paving the way for Sino-Japanese invasion. After years of studying their colonial masters, the narrator explains, the Asians had outwitted Western powers and beat them at their own imperial game. With their novels, Wells and Teed both responded to concerns raised by American imperialists and their critics, who sparred over the legitimacy and wisdom of the imperial adventures the United States had begun to launch in the Far East.

The title of Teed's novel referred to the beast of Revelation who chases the "woman clothed with the sun" into the wilderness. Teed first identified the woman in the wilderness as the goddess who appeared in his Utica revelation. He later associated her with Victoria Gratia, whose physical body would host his spirit after the theocrasis. *The Great Red Dragon* concludes with the emergence of a new imperial power, which arises out of Florida to vanquish the Sino-Japanese invaders with a fleet of airships powered by a newly invented dynamo. Ruled by an empress, the Florida colony claims victory and begins to export the regime of Imperial Socialism across the world.

Teed's novel was not a success and today is exceedingly rare—but a copy found its way into Jack London's personal library. The Koreshan master failed to publish the novel with a mainstream press during what remained of his lifetime. When he died, Teed was embittered by his literary flop. Compared with the success of Ignatius Donnelly and Edward Bellamy, he was a failure. Busy as he was with building New

Jerusalem and evangelizing the cause up and down the East Coast, the Master had failed to notice that political concerns and literary tastes were moving away from Gilded Age dystopianism and into a new era of imperial optimism.

.   .   .

THE MESSENGER'S BODY finally suspended animation three days before Christmas, 1908. Because the Master had always been murky on the matter, it was hard for the faithful to know whether or not Teed's translation had occurred. Some believed the theocrasis would simply entail the dissolution of Koresh's physical form "without corruption," after which his immortal body would pass from his spontaneously mummified corpse into the body of Victoria Gratia. Others thought Victoria was the Elisha who would be left behind by the Elijah, or Messenger, to complete the work of the new dispensation after Teed had theocratized. Another faction disagreed, and argued that Victoria's frame only offered a place for Teed's "immortal body" to wait until the time was right for the theocrasis. Victoria was left out of the debate: Teed had charged her with overseeing business affairs in Washington, DC, and the Koreshans at Estero did not immediately inform her of the news.

The faithful debated whether they should send Victoria a telegram. They did not wish to shock their empress, but neither did they believe she should learn of Teed's transformation from the newspapers. The message they sent said only: "Suspended Animation. Can you come?" Victoria later stated that she heard Teed's voice say "I have passed out" just before she opened the telegram.[4] The *New York Times* carried Teed's obituary on Christmas Day.

Most Koreshans were convinced the theocrasis had not occurred simultaneous to suspended animation, and that Teed had not yet translated his immortal body to its next destination. Where his soul had gone, nobody knew for sure. On Christmas the Koreshans remained remarkably composed. As a sister named Abby wrote to another: "On xmas morning everything moved on as usual. There were no Xmas demonstrations of any sort."[5] The day proceeded as any other until the Koreshans were all summoned to the dining hall for a meeting. "Brother George" wished everyone a merry Christmas, Sister Abby wrote:

> He then went on to tell the changes that had taken place in our Master, that his left arm was like glass [. . .] a new formation of an arm was visible and of the immense size of the face, and other parts of the body. The face looks just like an Egyptian God—Bro. Edgar our great Bible scholar was the next and he gave the Biblical explanation of everything that has transpired externally in the Master's body—Oh lots and lots was said but I cannot put down what was said.

Sister Abby, sixty-one, went on to describe Christmas 1908 as the happiest of her life, and believed the other Koreshans felt the same way. A procession of Koreshans went to the Estero Island beach house later that day, and marched

> up to Victoria's room where Master was nearly in the middle of the room in his bathtub nude to the waist. Before we started we were told of the Master's changed appearance and that it might be repulsive and it was wise that they thus prepared us, otherwise it might have made trouble. We all went up single file keeping to the right. The tub is a shallow one and so did not obstruct the view in the least. They have taken photographs so you will get a good idea from them of the very marvelous transformations, by no means good looking, oh no—some would call it hideous—not a trace of any of our Master's features are recognizable but a perfect likeness of Horus the great Egyptian god. A great, big, pugnacious

looking fellow—black as the blackest Egyptian. Still it was
not repulsive to the majority of us. I would like to look at it
over and over again. There was very little odor perceptible—
not like that of a corpse but I suppose a regular Egyptian
odor—to some it was very agreeable.[6]

This "transformation" had begun at two a.m. Christmas morning.
Teed's sister was one of those it repulsed: "When Sr. Emma first saw
it," Abby wrote, "she remarked in a commanding tone, 'That thing
ought to be put in the tomb.'" Others, however, likened the blackened,
swelling corpse to a chrysalis, inside of which the Master had begun
the work of regeneration. The various interpretations the Koreshans
made of the black carapace that had formed over Teed's body indicate
the authenticity of their religious belief in Teed's messianic teachings.
According to Sister Abby, some Koreshans drew a link back to Teed's
alchemical vision, in which the goddess called Teed by the name
Horus, son of Isis and Osiris: "Most of us call it 'Horus,'" she wrote,
"Sr. Esther always says 'it,' and many call it the 'Egyptian God.'"

After the chrysalis finally began to decompose, the Koreshans consented to the county coroner's command that they entomb their teacher's body. It was placed in a stone mausoleum designed for his sole
occupancy and engraved with the words "CYRUS, SHEPHERD, STONE OF
ISRAEL." Debates over the Master's theocrasis continued in the pages
of Koreshan letters and publications, and were further complicated
by the destruction of the tomb and the disappearance of the Master's
remains in a tropical storm in 1921.

. . .

THE FLORIDA COMMUNITY suffered from Teed's permanent
absence: factions had formed even before he suspended animation.
Teed had declared Victoria the Empress Pre-Eminent of the Koreshan
Unity in 1893, and the annual Koreshan Lunar Festival honored her

birthday. Some in the Unity considered her divine. Other Koreshans quietly tolerated Victoria's occasional abuses of power, and believed Teed had coronated her—on three separate occasions—to silence dissent from Koreshan women who envied her privilege and authority. Koreshan Thomas Gay had written to Teed complaining about Victoria's orders while the Master was ailing on Estero Island.[7] After Teed's death, Gay was one of several to proclaim himself the Elisha whom Teed prophesied would emerge to become the spiritual head of the new dispensation. He led a splinter faction called the Order of Theocracy out of Estero to Fort Myers, where they established another commune and ran the largest laundry business in town.

Victoria ultimately proved incapable of overcoming the divisions in the community. She eloped with a Koreshan dentist, C. Addison Graves, after which the Unity dropped her "like a hot potato."[8] According to Gustav Faber, Victoria and Graves were led astray by "the control of the nether world." This sinister power arrived in the colony in the shape of Brother Edgar Peissart, who had joined the Unity only a month before Teed's death. During his time with the Koreshans, Peissart passed himself off as a biblical scholar. In fact, Peissart was a particularly zealous religious seeker who had previously belonged to Charles Taze Russell's Watch Tower Society, a Mennonite sect called the River Brethren, and the House of David, an offshoot of the English messianic society established by Johanna Southcott in the early nineteenth century. Faber additionally claimed Peissart was an ex-medium who had come to the Unity from another Florida community called the Benjaminites, and that under his influence, Victoria Gratia, Addison Graves, and twenty-seven other Koreshans had attempted to open Teed's tomb to conduct a séance with the corpse. Alerted to the plot, others from the Unity prevented them from desecrating the Master's remains to perform this ritual. Peissart later joined a Florida group of Shakers before his final dramatic conversion to the Panacea Society, whose messianic leader—known as Octavia, Daughter of God—he attempted to displace.[9]

Neither factionalism nor the Master's death could kill the community entirely: the Unity lasted four more decades. It is rare for any communal religious society to achieve this sort of staying power, particularly after the loss of charismatic founding members. By the time the Unity finally collapsed, it had not outlasted the Shakers. But the Koreshans had accomplished, however briefly, a viable alternative to the alienation of secularized industrial urbanism, and a politico-spiritual antidote to the anodyne mainline Protestantism that increasingly served as a handmaiden to big business.

The Unity never built the grand temple or the city of 10 million that Teed had envisioned for the Floridian New Jerusalem. And it never achieved nationwide expansion. Instead the Koreshans began a slow decline after Teed's suspension, as the ranks of those who continued to await his theocrasis were slowly thinned by death and desertion. Koreshan children transitioned to careers in the secular world. Lucius Boomer, who as a boy had served as assistant engineer on the Koreshan Geodetic Survey, later became the manager of the Waldorf Astoria hotel chain, and through his New York society connections befriended presidents, film stars, and jazz musicians.

Others stayed to await the theocrasis, and the community trundled onward into the twentieth century. Only a few dozen Koreshans remained in 1941, when the last convert applied for membership. Hedwig Michel had learned of Koresh three decades after the Messenger's death. She was serving as headmistress of a boarding school in her native Germany when another teacher at the school, Peter Bender, introduced her to the cellular cosmogony in July 1939.[10] Bender was acquainted with a German couple called the Manleys, who had gone to Estero after a long-distance conversion to Koreshanity resulted in Harry Manley's conviction that he was the Elisha whose arrival Teed foretold. Michel was from a wealthy Jewish family, and escaped the Holocaust by leaving Germany to join the Koreshans at Bender's urging. She arrived to the United States in 1940 and made her way to Florida. After a year living with Bertie Boomer in Fort Myers,

Michel joined the Society Arch-Triumphant in December 1941, and finally signed a probationary agreement to join the Koreshan Unity on December 30, 1942. Although they knew she was a teacher by profession and trained as a journalist, the Unity hadn't much use for schoolteachers any longer, and business at the Guiding Star Publishing House had pretty much ceased. Michel started out as a maid, and was later promoted to manage the Koreshan Unity general store in March 1942. After ascending to the presidency of the Koreshan Unity in 1960, Michel donated the Koreshan territory to the Florida State Park Service, which promised to preserve the surviving structures. Today, many of the Unity's original buildings remain standing and open to visitors. Michel's lone grave sits between these monuments to one of America's most successful communistic societies.

The final lesson to be drawn from the career of Cyrus Teed and the Koreshan Unity cannot be measured in terms of years, membership, or economic productivity. Rather, Teed's ability to recruit followers into a system of practical messianic communism during a time of social and economic anxiety was a prelude to the even more spectacular endeavors of two of his successors in American messianism: Father Divine and Jim Jones.

FOUR

THE GLO-RAYS OF GOD

I AM canceling the human race and recreating in the cancellation of the human race, the angelic race. Then there will be no more human race, nor the Adamic nature that has existed in the bodies of the children of men, but the angelic nature, the Divine nature transmuted from the individual expressions of GOD to individuals in the form of man.

—FATHER DIVINE,
The Word of God Revealed
(as recorded by John Lamb)

26. DIVINE TRANSFORMATIONS

A S THE KORESHAN UNITY slowly died off, the movement from which it arose experienced a rebirth. It was mental science, and not Cyrus Teed, which underwent a translation at the turn of the century. As the Koreshans undertook their geodetic surveys and busied themselves with the arduous work incumbent on a colony of communists trying to survive in the untamed Florida swamp, mental science gradually shed its association with progressive social movements and embraced the ethos of liberal capitalism. At the turn of the century, the various competing schools of mental healing and mind cure that derived from mesmerism, phrenomagnetism, and Christian Science came together under the auspices of a very loosely affiliated movement known as New Thought. Under this ambiguous and inaccurate banner, New Thought teachers and institutions, including the Church of Divine Science and the Institute of Religious Science, maintained that the effects of positive psychology were not limited to achieving freedom from disease and sin: these and other gurus taught that amending thoughts and perceptions could literally alter reality. As the names of its affiliate organizations suggest, New Thought was part of a broader modernist trend in American religious culture, one that sought to bridge the gap between science and religion through the study of metaphysics.

As mind-cure metaphysics secularized along with American society, its evangelists increasingly preferred a vocabulary of private, personalized bliss and individualized material abundance over a collective project of evolutionary and social transformation. Generally speaking, New Thought teaches that when an individual realizes that he is an emanation of the divine Unity and makes an effort to "tap into" this Power or Source (or whatever), he can begin to access untold prosperity and abundance. By marrying the Western esoteric tradition with latent cultural gnosticism at the core of American folk religion, New Thought became—and, indeed, remains—the unofficial national religion of the United States.[1] Today's New Thought prophets are self-help gurus like Tony Robbins, who urges readers to "awaken the giant within," and Louise Hay, whose Hay House is a publishing juggernaut of New Thought and New Age literature. Perhaps more than anyone else in recent decades, Oprah Winfrey is responsible for popularizing New Thought among several generations of Americans who admire her.

New Thought was the ideology favored by Cyrus Teed's most notable successor in the American messianic tradition. But it was not the churn of exiles from Eddy's Massachusetts Metaphysical College or the glut of graduates from Emma Curtis Hopkins's Christian Science academies that produced the freshest New Thinker to emerge on the scene. He arose instead in Harlem during the Great Depression, where he became one of the most powerful and original religious leaders in United States history. Adored by tens of thousands and loathed by more than a few, he called himself Father Divine and was worshiped by his followers as God.

. . .

FATHER DIVINE BURST onto the national scene in 1931, after being convicted of disturbing the peace in the otherwise placid seaside town of Sayville, Long Island. Reverend Major Jealous Divine, as he then styled himself, was already well known throughout black neighborhoods of Brooklyn and Harlem as the founder of a weekly feast that took place at his sprawling Cape Cod on Macon Street in

Sayville, where he lived with twenty-odd devotees who simply called him "Father." Residents in the group home referred to these meals as Holy Communion, and they enjoyed them every day. Observance of the tradition was meant to evoke the primitive apostolic church, in which ritual communion was held daily.[2] On Sundays, Divine and his housemates threw open their doors to welcome anyone in need of a hot meal. In 1931, this included quite a few hungry souls and resulted in heavy traffic through the neighborhood. The cars were bad enough, but for some Sayville residents, the passengers were far worse: a motley crowd, mostly dark in hue, carpooled and bussed into Sayville from the city's poorest blocks, expecting a free meal and a few words of wisdom from the man who worked this weekly miracle of abundance. Sayville's forbearance eventually gave out, resulting in the black deity's arraignment and eventual conviction. Three days after sentencing Father Divine to a year in prison for little more than leading late-night hymns, Judge Lewis J. Smith of Nassau County dropped stone dead. Reached for comment in his cell at Riverhead jail, Father Divine's only comment was "I hated to do it." Celebrity status in Harlem, which later became God's principal residence, was guaranteed.

Father Divine went on to become a national sensation. During his lifetime, African Americans acknowledged Divine, often begrudgingly, as one of the most important civil rights leaders in America. In a 1949 article for *Phylon*, a journal for black affairs published by W.E.B. Du Bois, the prominent black sociologist Ira De Augustine Reid listed Father Divine's kingdom among the nine most important movements affecting the lives and culture of black Americans during the first half of the twentieth century. On this list, the Peace Mission appeared alongside Booker T. Washington's Tuskegee Idea, Du Bois's Niagara movement, Marcus Garvey's Universal Negro Improvement Association, and the transformative Great Migration to the industrial North.[3] One of the twentieth century's most lauded historians of American religion, William J. McLoughlin, characterized Divine as "one of the few black ministers [of his age] to preach something different from evangelical escapism."[4] Yet Divine's rise to stunning wealth and fame—and his decades of work on behalf of racial equality and workers' dignity—are not well recorded in the annals of the American civil rights movement. It would be fair to say that Father Divine's Peace Mission has, for the most part, been deleted from the history of black struggle in America for its tacky theology, its unappealing blend of communistic lifestyle and respectability politics, its disavowal of racial identity, and most of all, its iconoclastic leader: a squat, bald, dark-skinned man whose followers called him God and their Redeemer.

Divine was scrupulously circumspect about his origins and did whatever he could to frustrate his interrogators' attempts to determine his birthplace. He once claimed to have been "combusted" in New York, and sardonically informed one inquiring magistrate that he came from Providence.[5] This joke led at least one credulous journalist to report his admission of birth in Rhode Island. Court documents from his tangles with the law on Long Island identified God as George Baker Jr., the son of freedman sharecroppers in Georgia.[6] Some of Divine's Depression-era biographers told of how he abandoned a wife and children in the South to venture north as an itinerant minister. These various George Bakers probably existed, but there is no evidence that any of them reinvented himself as a millionaire black messiah.

Following an exhaustive public-records research, Divine's most recent biographer, the historian Jill Watts, concluded that the George Baker who became the Messiah was most likely born to a former slave and raised in Rockville, Maryland. The family was poor and lived in a crowded shack rented to them by Rockville's only black landlord. They shared their dwelling with other poor families—a common practice in Rockville's black ghetto, known to whites as "Monkey Run." The early experience of semicollective living had an important impact on George Jr.'s later career.[7]

George's 480-pound mother, Nancy, was too obese to seek employment out of the house, so her son was sent to work with his handyman father as soon as he was old enough to pitch in. This required the child to discontinue the rudimentary academic instruction that was available to black children in Rockville. However, hand-me-down Victorian textbooks cast off on black schools might have exercised early influence over the strict moral code Divine enforced in latter days: their emphasis on hard work and self-reliance would reappear in Father Divine's disdain for welfare relief and labor unions. Nancy Baker's obesity, which reached embarrassing celebrity dimensions when upon her death she was declared the largest woman in Montgomery County, likewise influenced Father Divine's teachings on personal responsibility and respectability. After his mother's death, George Jr. took off for Baltimore, where he found work as a groundskeeper. Nancy had raised her children in the Methodist Church, but once George Jr. was out on his own, he began to prefer the city's populist storefront churches. The religious enthusiasm of the self-ordained preachers who founded these churches was notoriously infectious. Baker soon fancied himself a minister. Before embarking on a preaching tour of the South in 1902, he honed his pedagogical skills by teaching Sunday school.[8]

After returning to Baltimore having saved but a single soul, Baker sought new spiritual influences for his ministry. Like many other Americans in the first decade of the twentieth century, he discovered New Thought. Baker developed a particular affinity for the work of Charles and Myrtle Fillmore, two former students of Emma Curtis Hopkins who went on to found the Unity School of Christianity.[9] From Unity School publications, Baker adopted several concepts that would later become articles of faith for followers of the Peace Mission. Fillmore taught that anyone—male or female, black or white—could enter into spiritual communication with the Divine Consciousness that others called God, and could attune his or her consciousness to its wisdom and thereby achieve a life of abundance. This was conventional New Thought fare. But like Ann Lee and Cyrus Teed, Fillmore taught his disciples to abstain from sex. The rationale for celibacy was a familiar one: sexual expenditure was physically depleting, and complicated the work of spiritual purification. But whereas Lee and Teed connected the corrupting influence of sex to spiritual stagnation and eventual perdition, Fillmore's spermatic economy held that sexual satisfaction competed with spiritual development in the marketplace of personal fulfillment.[10]

By examining the postmarks and addresses of the New Thought publications circulating at the turn of the century, Baker learned that New Thought was strongest in the West. He eventually scraped together the cash for a pilgrimage to Los Angeles. By this point in the nation's history, the City of Angels had become a locus of innovation in American religious culture. Baker was in town long enough to visit William Seymour's Azusa Street Revival, where he not only witnessed others speaking in tongues, but experienced the phenomenon himself.[11]

Back in Baltimore in 1906, Baker met an itinerant preacher called Samuel Morris, a tall and light-skinned black man from Allegheny, Pennsylvania. Morris had gone to Baltimore after discovering a Bible verse that changed his life. Located in 1 Corinthians, it read, "Know ye not that ye are the temple of God and the spirit of God dwelleth in you?" Morris believed the Good Book spoke directly to him, and set out for Baltimore to preach the good news: God had returned once more in a body. In Maryland he adopted the name Father Jehovia and quickly got used to being forcibly ejected from churches he visited. He had the obnoxious habit of rising in the middle of services to declare his divinity, or to express what many in the South considered an even more insane belief: Jehovia disavowed the existence of racial differences.

George Baker was in attendance for one of these performances. Whether out of pity or belief, he invited Jehovia back to the boardinghouse he shared with his landlady, Anna Snowden. Jehovia was a man of single purpose, and wasted no time converting the pair. A fourth adherent, John A. Hickerson, later joined them around 1908.[12] Snowden's house became a live-in church for disciples of God-in-the-body, and a template for Divine's Sayville project.

Baker's ardor for Jehovia's teachings earned him the leader's trust. Although adamant that he alone possessed the "Fathership" degree of God, Jehovia promoted Baker to the "Sonship" degree. These peculiar terms might have perplexed their associates in Baltimore, but they would not have confused a Koreshan. Cyrus Teed had used similar terminology in his attempt to convert his cousin Myron Baldwin, claiming that the "Sonship" degree of holiness was a concept derived from the original Greek text of Romans 8:23.[13] Like Teed, Jehovia associated the Sonship degree with the office of God's Messenger. It was no coincidence that Jehovia adopted Teed's obscure terminology: Morris resided in Allegheny City at a time when Teed enjoyed a small following there. Circulation of Koreshan publications in Pittsburgh had converted the Boomers, Ulysses Morrow, and numerous others; it is reasonable to suppose they also reached Samuel Morris. By the 1890s, Teed had also begun to preach in black churches. After delivering a sermon in a black congregation in Florida in December 1893, Teed was surprised by how enthusiastic his audience became over Koreshan teachings of sexual and economic equality: "They urgently request my presence again," he wrote to his sister, "The die is cast. The colored race is receptive to our doctrine, and understand it as no other people do except my own few. I am delighted at my reception by them!"[14]

The next year, in a Christmas Day lecture to the Koreshan Unity given on Hickory Island in 1894, Teed explained that Swedenborg believed that the black race would be the first to receive the "new circumcision" of the millennial order, and become the first members of the new angelic race.[15] Teed's scientific bent and eugenic leanings carried him to different conclusions: he believed that in Florida, the Koreshan Unity would be able to gather an integrated following "for the purpose of directing the amalgamation of present races for the perfection of a new race who will be the future chosen people of the Most High."[16] Teed considered himself the divinely appointed leader who might shepherd the "chosen portions of the race" to an island nation—probably Cuba—where they could begin the combination of the races.[17] He rehearsed the same idea in *The Great Red Dragon*, where a new, amalgamated "red" race in the Caribbean leads humanity in the regenerative process.

Although the Unity never acquired many black followers, Teed's experience witnessing racial struggle inspired him to theorize the ways in which racist exploitation might figure into the battle of Gog and Magog. He understood that the alleged "animal tendencies" of blacks were "greatly exaggerated" by their enslavers, who did not hesitate to quote the Bible to justify the abomination of chattel slavery—it was simply more evidence of the degeneracy of the Christian churches and their prostitution of the Word of God in the endless pursuit of lucre. Teed came to understand that the "race question necessarily involves the labor problem," and that the same industrialists who issued apologetics for slavery would foment racial animosity between blacks and whites to divide them and drive down wages.[18]

Teed's interpretations of Swedenborg and Greek scripture made such an idiosyncratic combination that the reappearance of his ideas and terminology in the sermons of an Allegheny lay minister suggest that Morris studied with the Koreshans, heard Cyrus Teed lecture, or read Koreshan publications. Jehovia additionally began to refer to his faithful disciple, George Baker, as "The Messenger" of his teachings. This, however, was where the appropriation stopped: the leap from racial amalgamation to the total disavowal of racial categories was one that Morris made on his own.

27. THE MESSENGER

ALTHOUGH HE FUNCTIONED as little more than Jehovia's fac-
totum, George Baker was so committed to his calling that he
completely cut ties with the past by registering under the false name
of Anderson Baker when the 1910 census officials came to Anna
Snowden's boardinghouse. But the holy household was not destined
to last much longer. Jehovia and Hickerson, who now called himself
the "Rev. St. Bishop, the Vine," came to loggerheads when the Vine
began to chafe at Jehovia's exclusive self-appointment to the Fathership degree. God revealed to the Vine that He dwelt not only in the
former Samuel Morris, but in every woman and man. This was an
assertion backed by the general drift of New Thought teachings. But
Jehovia vehemently disagreed and counted on the Messenger to settle the score. Rather than come down on either side, Baker instead
declared himself to be the receptacle of God's spirit, and in 1912 the
three man-gods parted ways.

Baker arrived in Georgia soon thereafter, for a second attempt at
Southern evangelism. The Messenger continued to promote Jehovia's
God-in-the-body idea, now inflected with New Thought nostrums
that contradicted the belief, prominent in Southern black churches,
that believers would only find relief from their sufferings in the after-
life. The Messenger preached a gospel of heaven on Earth—an abundance available to anyone who recognized his or her connection to the
Divine. He offered a literal taste of heaven in the banquets he held
wherever he was invited to speak. Although he refused to accept dona-

tions for his holy ministrations, the Messenger accepted contributions in kind—usually, the dishes that made up his communal feasts. He presided over these New Thought potluck spirituals by blessing the food and referring to the feasts as Holy Communion. With this filling doctrine of heaven in the here-and-now, Baker slowly amassed a small following.

Leading souls astray from their congregations was bound to cause trouble. In Savannah, local ministers managed to have the Messenger put on a chain gang. Rather than feel ashamed of his imprisonment, the Messenger regarded this persecution as a point of pride; he claimed divine responsibility when state prison inspectors were injured during the course of his sentence. In Valdosta, the Messenger's invitation to preach to another church was immediately rescinded when he took the lectern and began to discourse on the subject of the imminent arrival of a black messiah.

Valdosta was not as easily rid of Baker, who had complemented Jehovia's denial of race categories with a rejection of gender difference. These assertions of equality aroused the interest of more than a few women in the local churches. They invited him into their homes, where he preached the necessity of celibacy, following Matthew 22:30—a verse righteously cited by the Shakers, Universal Friends, and Koreshans. One of these ladies brought the Messenger to live with her, and several other women joined them. The Messenger organized the household as an egalitarian commune modeled after the examples set by Jehovia and the Shakers. But he went a step further: like the Public Universal Friend, the Messenger casually referred to himself and his followers as both masculine and feminine. There were not women and men, the Messenger explained to his eager listeners, but only "those who would call themselves women."[1]

Others in Valdosta called them women, too, and some called them their wives. When believers made their way into the Messenger's communal home, they took with them their household labor and sometimes, their income. Valdosta husbands afflicted by the mass conversion to celibate communism believed they were unjustly deprived of sexual attentions that were their inalienable right. The disgruntled men of Valdosta were sufficiently annoyed to have the Messenger arrested on charges that his insanity rose to the level of public nuisance. But when the police came to haul the Messenger away, those who formerly called themselves women tried to form a human shield around their leader. After this failed to deter his arrest, they stalked the police back to the Valdosta jail, where they publicly worshiped the Messenger as God. The jailed man, who refused to give a legal name, was booked as "John Doe, alias God."[2]

Imprisonment enhanced the preacher's reputation: news of the persecuted man's claims to divinity brought curious spiritual seekers to his jail cell. Some came to speak in tongues, but others were New Thought devotees who had read about the Messenger's teachings in the newspapers. To the surprise of the prison guards, some of these admirers were white. One of the visitors was J. B. Copeland, who defended God in court. Copeland structured his defense around the cross-examination of a local holiness minister who had testified against the Messenger's sanity. Numerous residents of the town, Copeland observed, participated in services where believers possessed by the Holy Spirit regularly spoke in tongues, yet they were never punished for insanity. The jury was unmoved by this defense, and fixated instead on abundant testimony that the Messenger held some sort of hypnotic control over the brood of women he'd led into the group home. Although jurors found the Messenger was doubtless of "unsound mind," they spared him confinement in the state asylum, provided he leave Valdosta without delay.

After a period of continued peregrinations across the South, preaching to largely apathetic audiences, the Messenger returned north, reaching New York City by 1915. One of the disciples to follow him there was Joseph Gabriel, a minister who'd had a small church of his own in Georgia. Gabriel had allowed Baker to preach to his congregation after witnessing the Messenger perform a miracle by traipsing across wet cement Gabriel had just poured, without leaving a single footprint.

In New York the Messenger initially herded his flock into a flat on Prince Street in SoHo. They later moved to a house on West Fortieth, not far from the Church of the Living God, located on Forty-First and Eighth.³ This was a congregation of yellow-turbaned, pink-hooded devotees of the Rev. St. Bishop, the Vine.⁴ After parting ways with Jehovia, Hickerson had gone to New York, where he preached an interpretation of Jehovia's 1 Corinthians revelation that extended godlike status to anyone who believed in his or her own divinity. The Messenger arrived just in time to watch as the doctrine of God-in-every-body descended into total chaos. It was an important lesson.

As the Vine's church collapsed, the Messenger and his set crossed over to Brooklyn, where they leased a flat on Myrtle Avenue. The Messenger paid rent by farming out the faithful as domestic workers and day laborers. Worship was held over a communal meal in the evening, after everyone had returned from work. The collective meal was a continuation of the tradition the Messenger had begun on the Southern circuit as a way to attract poor and hungry sharecroppers into his fold.

Residents of the Myrtle Avenue flat were a ragtag lot: there were divorcées, victims of domestic abuse, and previously unemployed housewives among them. But the Messenger had a canny way with the want ads, and a knack for finding jobs for the faithful. Members came and went, but the commune slowly grew: by 1919 they numbered nine in all. By economizing on shared food, lodging, and even clothing, the sect saved enough to purchase an ample home in the quiet town of Sayville on Long Island. Ironically, it was racism that allowed the community of celibate African Americans to integrate the all-white seaside town: a German American villager, angered by prejudice he experienced in Sayville during World War I, advertised his home for sale in the black newspapers the Messenger scanned for job listings, stating his preference for a "colored" buyer in order to spite his neighbors.

When Baker signed the deed to the eight-room house in Sayville, he did so as Major Jealous Devine. The homophony of "Devine" and "The Vine" was more than mere coincidence: before leaving New York, the Messenger had attempted to gather up members of the Vine's disintegrating congregation. Combined with the assumption of a name suggesting military rank, Devine hoped this elegant appellation would help him succeed in transplanting his employment-service commune to the suburbs. He adopted the honorific "Reverend" by way of explanation to middle-class neighbors in Sayville, who might otherwise have wondered why he lived with nearly a dozen adults who called him "Father." Devine later yielded to spelling conventions, altering his surname from Devine to "Divine." Aside from this thoughtful adjustment, he continued to use the same name on formal documents for the rest of his life.

Cosigning the deed with Divine was a believer called Peninnah, a hefty matron whom the others considered to be the Messenger's wife. She had been a member of Joseph Gabriel's church, but pledged allegiance to the Messenger after he cured her of crippling rheumatism. Peninnah was Divine's rock, a trusted and stalwart follower without whom he might not have managed. The followers referred to her as the "Mother" of their spiritual family, and to the Sayville house as their heaven on Earth. Early on, Divine taught them to refer to themselves as angels.

Using the same method adopted in Brooklyn, the Sayville community paid its bills by pooling resources. Later known as the "Divine Cooperative Plan," the arrangement included a strictly enforced code of ethics and conduct. As on Myrtle Avenue, Divine banned drinking and smoking, and expected followers to work and to donate all or most of what they earned back to the cooperative. In what became a signature of Divine society, use of the greeting "hello" was proscribed because its first syllable contained the name of "the other place." Since Divine banned cursing of any sort, the word "Peace" replaced "Hello" as salutation and became the watchword of the movement.[5]

In Sayville Divine played the part of the kindly preacher to neutralize any suspicions aroused by his unusual household. He made certain to be seen around town making large purchases for the commune, taking care to patronize local businesses.[6] He continued to advertise "reliable colored help" in Long Island newspapers, and became well known as a purveyor of trustworthy domestic employees.

The angels lived the rest of the decade in relative peace. Heaven was well appointed, its residents were cheerful neighbors, and Holy Communion praise seldom lasted past nine in the evening. In these, the quietest years of his career, Father Divine deepened his study of New Thought classics he borrowed from the Sayville public library. One of his favorite authors was Robert Collier, whose books taught readers the way to obtain material wealth from positive thought. Other texts beloved by Father Divine included Baird T. Spalding's *Life and Teaching of the Masters of the Far East* (1924), Bruce Barton's *The Man Nobody Knows* (1925), and Jiddu Krishnamurti's *The Kingdom of Happiness* (1927).[7] Divine's preaching included exegeses on these New Thought texts, and he often gave away copies of them for free.

Although speeches and teachings from the first decades of Divine's ministry do not survive, sermons taken down by Divine's secretaries in the 1930s are littered with New Thought dictums, such as his affirmation that "anger is destructive to the body."[8] Father Divine instructed his followers: "Positive thoughts will bring about positive conditions in your bodies, and negative thoughts will produce negative conditions in your bodies."[9] A more succinct rendering of New Thought ideology would be hard to find.

Ralph Waldo Trine, the immensely popular author of the New Thought classic *In Tune with the Infinite* (1897), had already linked positive thoughts to the creation of heaven on Earth. Trine wrote:

> The optimist, by his superior wisdom and insight, is making
> his own heaven, and in the degree that he makes his own
> heaven is he helping to make one for all the world beside.
> The pessimist, by virtue of his limitations, is making his own

hell, and in the degree that he makes his own hell is he helping to make one for all mankind.[10]

Trine defined the law of the universe as a "Spirit of Infinite Life
and Power that is [in] back of all, that animates all, that manifests
itself in and through all."[11] He explicitly equated this all-pervading
spirit with "God" and Emerson's "Over Soul." His metaphysical "law"
was a result of the same analogical reasoning that produced widespread belief in the unseen "ether" manipulated during a mesmeric
trance, and through which the spirits were capable of communicating via their chosen mediums. Father Divine combined Trine's New
Thought pantheism with the Theosophical concept of the I AM, telling his followers that he, as Father Divine, was "one with the substance and intelligence of every soul."[12] The insinuation was that he had
achieved unity with the Christ Consciousness, the Spirit of Infinite
Life and Power, and so on. Ergo, Father Divine was God in the flesh.

Christian Science castoffs made up a significant portion of Divine's
early following. African American communities were notoriously
underserved by hospitals; Christian Science and other mind-cure remedies stepped in to fill the gap in care, and were no less useful than
doing nothing at all. But whereas Mary Baker Eddy meant for her
abstruse prose to be treated as scripture by her followers, Divine jazzed
his way through sermons, inventing words, spinning yarns, and working his audience into an ecstatic fervor. One of the heuristics he used to
describe the objective of these passionate meetings, at which his angels
shouted and sang, was the New Thought idiom of sonic vibration:
Divine told followers they could "attune" their thoughts to the "Master
Mind" and "Universal Mind Substance" by being with him and following his example. Divine insisted that angels rise to confess all their sins
during Holy Communion feasts, instructing his followers that these
admissions were necessary to harmonize the redemption of their physical and spiritual bodies. Total harmonization offered salvation from
bodily death: as Divine told his angels, "I have come to take you out of

the grave."¹³ However, Divine wisely avoided performing public healings through the laying-on of hands. Instead, he encouraged his followers to heal themselves with righteous living and positive thinking.

Divine's New Thought rhapsodies became particularly risky and freewheeling when he told his followers that it would be possible to "transcend gravitation" through a total "sacrifice of every tendency of the mortal mind, beliefs, ideas and opinions, and by detaching yourself from all of mortality's convictions, comforts, opinions, and views."¹⁴ Transcending gravity, Father Divine explained, meant that when his followers were fully harmonized with his spirit, they would be able to transport themselves from place to place instantaneously—they might find themselves on a street in Europe the next morning, shaking hands with the French if Father so desired.

Having learned from the anarchy that caused the Vine's Manhattan congregation to implode, Divine centered his blend of New Thought pantheism and positive psychology around the authority of his own divinity: he was the only one who had fully attuned his mind to the Christ Consciousness. The angels never spoke of George Baker or even the Messenger: that person had been obliterated when he harmonized with the Universal Mind. This New Thought messianism brought curious students to Sayville, including a busload that arrived from the Colored Unity Center in Harlem. Unlike other New Thought gurus who made a handsome living from their teachings, Divine continued to refuse any remuneration for his instructive sermons. The source of the bounty on offer at Holy Communion banquets remained a mystery, and reinforced the idea that Father Divine possessed supernatural powers.

28. TROUBLE IN PARADISE

A S THE DECADE DREW TO A CLOSE, news of the little heaven on Long Island started getting around as angels evangelized to coworkers and friends. From a humble dozen in 1924, the group grew to more than forty converts over the next four years. Residents came and went, many of them leaving after Divine helped them get back on their feet. But weekend gatherings left little doubt that Father Divine's fame was traveling. The minister decided the time had come to put his Midas finger on the scales: he began publicizing his ministry in Harlem and Brooklyn, where devotees of Marcus Garvey and the Universal Negro Improvement Association had been left without a leader following Garvey's 1927 deportation. Garvey had prophesied the arrival of a black messiah, and Divine understood that with Garvey conveniently banished from New York, the role was available. Moreover, Garvey and the UNIA were the font from which many African Americans imbibed the New Thought philosophy of positive thinking and neo-Transcendental political quiescence.[1]

When curious slum dwellers learned the preacher offered free feasts on Sundays, many overcame whatever skepticism had initially held them back. Sayville soon became the terminus of a weekly pilgrimage for open-minded New Thought students, ex-UNIA members, spiritual seekers, and the merely poor and hungry. The result was exactly what Divine had in mind: his sect more than doubled by 1930, to approximately ninety followers. A third of them lived communally at 72 Macon Street; the others contributed to the Divine Cooperative Plan but maintained separate lodgings.[2]

No loafers were admitted to heaven. Father Divine expected all his angels to work, either at the well-paying jobs he lined up in hotels and private residences, or by helping with the staggering amount of cooking, cleaning, mending, and laundry that heaven required. In addition to prohibitions on drinking and cursing, complaining or voicing any other negative thoughts was strictly prohibited. There arose instead a refrain that later came to define Father Divine and his Peace Mission movement: "It Is Wonderful!" became the most frequent exclamation to cross an angel's lips.

Two of the most important strictures that Father Divine enforced among his followers were the ones meant to break the bonds of traditional family structures. Anyone desiring to become one of Father's angels was required to disavow his or her pre-angelic life, much as the young George Baker had done when he studied with Father Jehovia. This required the angels to sever kinship ties, even if that meant leaving behind wives, husbands, and children. As in the Shaker villages, married couples entering the mission jointly were expected to separate and to treat one another no differently from their other "brothers" and "sisters." To complete their separation from the world, many of Divine's followers ceased using their former names: those who accepted the Divine Cooperative Plan, adopted celibacy, and lived by Divine's moral code took on holy "angelic" names like Wonderful Wisdom, Pearly Gates, Universal Vocabulary, Sweet Determination, Beulah Land, Obedience Love, Message Bearer, Queen Esther, Willing Heart, Twilight Twilight, and Precious Jewel. Divine taught his followers that by shedding their personal identities, they made way for their total harmonization with God.[3] A more mundane but no less crucial step for separation from the world required followers to repay all the debts they incurred in their former lives before they started paying into Father's coffers. This included the return of stolen property and overdue library books, as well as sending belated payment for goods the sinners had dishonestly taken and consumed at former places of employment.

As the angelic family grew, its Holy Communion ritual occupied a central role in maintaining cohesion and enthusiasm among Divine's followers. Over lavish caloric intake, angels and visitors stood to testify regarding the ways Father Divine had changed their lives. Together, they praised the bounty of his blessings and sang special songs at the table, often led by Mother Divine. In Sayville, followers lined up at the scale each Sunday and Thursday so Father could be sure they weren't losing weight. Corpulence was opulence, and Divine did not want any of his followers to appear malnourished. In spite of the shame that surely occasioned his mother's funeral, which required the door of the Baker house to be cut away so that pallbearers could remove her custom-built coffin, Father and Mother Divine were both significantly overweight; the latter reportedly weighed north of 250 pounds.[4]

Father Divine's magnanimity appeared even more remarkable as the country slid into the Great Depression. His workers, having earned their reputations as hardworking, dutiful, and cheerful servants, retained their domestic positions and had an edge in hiring anywhere that Divine had established his reputation. When Major Divine learned that enterprising Harlemites were advertising round-trip bus tickets to his Sunday banquets, he began to hire his own transportation for prospective new recruits from the city. Crowds swelled on Sundays as the Depression deepened, requiring Sayville to send traffic police to organize the chaos that erupted on Macon Street. The angels orchestrated numerous seatings to accommodate their visitors, who waited in the yard for their turn at the holy table. Reporters dispatched to the scene marveled at the quantities of ham, chicken, stew, hominy, beans, coleslaw, spinach, and other soul food–inspired platters that emerged from the Divine kitchens, followed by "mountainous" bowls full of ice cream beside "cakes as big as automobile tires but higher." Twelve coffee percolators maintained a high level of energy. Recalling the early Sayville days, an angel called Sweet Notion reported that

"Every Sunday was like Christmas."⁵ Divine continued to bless each dish by placing a serving spoon or fork in it, and poured the coffee himself.

In addition to the Cadillac he drove, the minister's largesse fueled speculation about the possibly illicit sources of his wealth. By the late 1920s, the stereotype of the huckster black minister had become so familiar that it was the subject of parody and of cynicism in the black community: the rapid proliferation of black churches in New York during the first decades of the century had yielded a number of spiritual leaders who defrauded their congregants of what little savings they had. District Attorney Alexander G. Blue finally decided to launch an investigation of heaven after a former resident visited his office, claiming to have escaped the sexual advances that Father made among those who called themselves female. The fallen angel demanded that Blue help her recover the two years of wages that she said Divine owed her.

Blue dispatched two of his "dark-skinned operatives" to infiltrate heaven, each of them unaware of the other detective's presence. They returned without having observed a single misdeed. The failed investigation nevertheless made the newspapers. As detective Susan Hadley reported to her boss, Father Divine was not merely running a rescue mission: he was worshiped by his loyal followers as God.⁶ Sleepy Sayville was stirred by this revelation. Townspeople were embarrassed that such ludicrous blasphemy had been carried on right under their noses.

Along with heresy and financial intrigue, the increased presence of whites among Divine's charismatic worshipers raised alarm. Surely, the villagers surmised, Father's white followers were escapees from King's Park, a notorious insane asylum on the island's north shore. In fact, they were among the most educated and prosperous members of the sect, and tended to seek Divine not for relief from poverty, but for his spiritual teachings. White followers had begun to join the movement as early as 1926; their arrivals often demonstrated how far Father Divine's reputation had traveled. Among the earliest white converts was Heavenly Rest, who had learned of Father Divine in a Unity Church she attended in Boston.

Another of the early white followers was a middle-aged English mystic called Walter Clemow Lanyan, who began to spread tidings of God's second coming across the pond by conducting dozens of lectures on Father Divine throughout the UK and mainland Europe. Another white man became Father Divine's closest confidant. This was John Lamb, the alias taken by the former James Maynard Matthew, a Boston University graduate and successful car salesman. When Matthew joined the movement around 1930, he began to act as Divine's personal secretary.[7]

With the understanding that he was witnessing history, Lamb kept a diary of his experiences in Sayville in 1931–32. He attributed the sudden growth in the movement to several factors: the relative wealth of the United States, Lamb believed, was not enough to compensate for the lack of higher purpose in most Americans' lives. The Depression had removed the distractions of material luxury and left many Americans with no diversion from the "clouds of tyranny" gathering in Europe. "The philosophies of men," Lamb wrote, "were inadequate to cope with humanity's problems. Man had reached his extremity."[8]

The villagers of Sayville certainly had: no longer did the praise of Holy Communion conclude respectfully at nine p.m.: instead, the singing, shouting, clapping, and stomping now sometimes lasted into the morning hours. Calling heaven to complain never did any good: none of the angels could hear the telephone ringing over all the commotion.[9] Homeowners in Divine's immediate vicinity lay awake at night, fretting that their property would become worthless if the angels remained. After conspiring about how to end the ruckus, neighbors on Macon Street decided that Father Divine had to go.

Divine was well aware of the passions roused against him: he and his followers had doubled the black population in Sayville when they arrived in 1919. The KKK burned a cross in the town square four years later, and the minister and his followers encountered prejudicial hiring practices that made Divine's successful employment service all the more remarkable. Wishing to stave off further integration, a local businessman offered Divine property elsewhere on Long Island, totally free of charge, as long as the angels agreed to move there immediately. Father Divine demurred.

Police began to ticket cars parked illegally on Macon Street, but the amateurish blockade did little to thwart Father Divine. He responded by converting a large section of heaven's manicured lawn into a parking lot. More resourceful neighbors, suspicious of the source of Father's wealth, attempted to ensnare him in allegations of racketeering or mail fraud by sending him cash and checks. Divine wisely canceled the checks and returned the cash to senders whenever possible.

Tensions flared as Sayville's plans for evicting the black messiah backfired. Residents appointed a committee of concerned citizens to meet with the DA, who had not retired his interest in Divine's inexplicable wealth. The result was that in May 1931, the Suffolk County DA sent for another private investigator capable of infiltrating heaven. A mixed-race New York agent by the name of Rose Burrows heeded the call. To look the part of a prospective angel, she eschewed makeup and hid the voluptuous curves that served her well in undercover stings on illicit Harlem casinos and juke joints. Burrows turned up on heaven's doorstep wearing a dowdy housedress and carrying a secondhand purse. Her seamy assignments in the city had honed her powers of seduction. But after days of trying, Burrows's attempts to seduce Major Divine had failed.

The law sprang into action anyway: on May 8, Divine was arrested and taken to Suffolk County Court, which had indicted him on the charge of being a public nuisance. Mother Divine and a flock of angels appeared with Father in court, where the defendant was represented by Ellee J. Lovelace, a black lawyer who became a believer after Divine cured his debilitating arthritis. Divine pled not guilty and was released after Mother Divine produced $1,000 in cash from her purse to pay his bail on the spot. Divine's improbable wealth now helped him thwart his would-be captors.

Outrage over Divine's insouciance in the white community was now met with resentment in the black press, which began to call out the racist persecution. Tempers simmered over the summer as Divine's Sunday feasts, now drawing thousands each week, stretched late into the evening to accommodate the throngs.[10] Petitions demanding Divine's removal were presented to the relevant authorities. Some Sayville residents were less polite, dumping litter and garbage on the lawn at 72 Macon. This did little to hinder the banquets and nothing to calm the neighbors.

To those less credulous and threatened, Father Divine merely came off as a delusional braggart: he stated that "a [teacher] greater than Gandhi is here" and falsely claimed his bountiful system had ended panhandling in Manhattan.[11] One of his most unusual prophecies, recorded in John Lamb's diary on September 26, 1931, was similarly grandiose, although not often repeated: Divine told those gathered around him that he was preparing a "Vanishing City" for 10 million of his followers who, when they disappeared, would populate other planets. Catering to the occult inclinations of the group, Divine stated that there was no reason not to believe that Jesus was an extraterrestrial being: "Who can say," Divine implored his followers, "that HE was not a Martian or a Jupiterian, or is from some other planet where there is some superior form of conscious life."[12] Whether he knew it or not, Divine's extraterrestrial Christology echoed the interplanetary and celestial travels of Emanuel Swedenborg and Thomas Lake Harris.[13]

. . .

DURING ONE PARTICULARLY RAUCOUS Holy Communion on November 15, 1931, the police arrived to rearrest Divine and his followers en masse. According to John Lamb's recollection of events, Divine and his angels were in the middle of a "very spirited praise meeting" that lasted well into the night. Responding to complaints from neighbors, Officer Richard Tucker went to heaven with orders to silence the hosannas. But Michael St. John, Divine's holy bouncer, barred the officer's entry. In Lamb's account, which entered into Peace Mission mythology, "FATHER'S Will" held back the police for an hour longer. In fact, the officer who first responded to the disturbance had left for backup. Already past midnight, Tucker summoned Suffolk County DA Joseph Arata, who by this point was eager to demonstrate his worth to the citizens of Sayville. Arata arrived to Macon Street with reinforcements while the angels remained lost "in the midst of a great demonstration of the Spirit."[14]

As an angry mob brandishing makeshift weapons assembled on Macon Street, vowing to take matters into their own hands, Arata entered the house through the back door to have a word with Father Divine. He told the preacher that his angels had fifteen minutes to surrender to authorities or else be flushed out of heaven with fire hoses. Divine used ten of the fifteen minutes to gather his flock in silent prayer, and then led them outside and into the buses that were waiting to take them to the courthouse. Seventy-eight worshipers were booked, including Divine; fifteen of them were white.

Arraignment of the angels took all night; eventually, the rabble that followed the paddy wagons to the courthouse dispersed with fatigue. Two-thirds of the angels pleaded guilty and were fined $5 apiece. The remaining angels pled not guilty and were ordered to appear in court for trial the following Friday. Father Divine was slapped with the additional charge of maintaining a public nuisance. He paid his $1,500 bail in cash and was released, to the consternation of his neighbors.

At the trial, Ellee Lovelace was joined at the defense table by Arthur Madison, another black New York lawyer who had taken an interest in what he perceived as racial bias in the persecution of Father Divine and his followers. Madison would remain one of the evangelist's most trusted confidants, but would not recognize Divine's divinity until he'd spent a decade as his counsel.[15] After more than a dozen neighbors testified for the state, only four of the remaining defendants were found not guilty. The court postponed Father Divine's trial for public nuisance to a later date, but the outraged citizens of Sayville could abide no further compromise. A town meeting convened in the local high school to address the menace heaven posed to the community. Divine sent Madison to represent him at the November 21 meeting. The lawyer arrived with New York journalist Millard J. Bloomer and the New Thought writer Eugene Del Mar, both of whom supported the movement. Dozens of angels packed the meeting. After the committee related the citizens' firm request that Father Divine leave their town by January of the next year, John Lamb stood to enumerate Father Divine's good works. He then announced that if the citizens wished for the mission to move, Father Divine would comply. But nobody in Sayville believed this, and a committee of proprietors was appointed to find a legal path to be rid of the holy nuisance.

As racist Sayville was dragged through the headlines of Harlem newspapers, Father Divine's plight caught the attention of James C. Thomas, who offered Divine additional legal services. Like Arthur Madison, Thomas believed less in Father Divine than in racial equality. With his trial date approaching, Divine accepted Thomas as an addition to his legal team. As a former assistant US attorney, Thomas understood what Divine was up against in the Suffolk County courts, where he believed Father Divine would never get a fair hearing. Through Thomas's efforts, the case was rescheduled for that spring in Nassau County court, located in Mineola.

Meanwhile, polite society expressed dismay over the growing element of white followers collected by Father Divine's movement. One of them, Julia Arias, secured the movement some free publicity when her presence at the mission was revealed: Arias was a governess to the children of a Republican state politician, and had caused a minor scandal by disappearing without a trace.[16] Two of her New York society friends—JP Morgan's sister Louise Pierpont Morgan Satterly, and

Mrs. Henry Breckenridge, the wife of Charles Lindbergh's attorney—
took it upon themselves to determine the whereabouts of their miss-
ing friend. When they discovered that she had assumed the name of
Rebecca Branch and was residing at 72 Macon Street, they went to
Sayville determined to get her out. After the aristocrats realized they
could not persuade Rebecca Branch to abandon heaven, they used
their legal connections to have her confined to an asylum. Judge Dur-
yea, the justice who had been on duty for the late-night arraignments
in November, was the one who remanded Branch to the custody of
the psych ward at Central Islip State Hospital. Doctors decided that
although Branch clearly suffered from religious hysteria, this was not
adequate reason to have her detained.[17]

Divine's reputation spread throughout African American neighborhoods in the greater New York area as a result of media coverage
generated by similar stories of persecution directed against him and
his followers, who were financially independent and merely exercising
their First Amendment rights. As the periphery of believers expanded,
the Sayville contingent began to orchestrate Holy Communion banquets in Harlem, as well as in black neighborhoods in Queens and
New Jersey. By December, Divine was drawing such large audiences
to meetings in Harlem churches that he decided to schedule a rally at
Rockland Palace, a high-capacity venue that hosted some of Harlem's
famed drag balls.[18] Fully aware of the public-relations opportunity that
the event afforded, Father Divine ensured that half of the fifty angels
who joined him onstage at Rockland Palace were white.

By early 1932, Divine had acquired two new recruits who gave him
a stronger foothold in Harlem. One was Charles Calloway, who had
left a fruitful career in the railroad business in 1927 and began giving
large sums of money to Father Divine after attending meetings in Sayville. Calloway had converted some of his small fortune to real estate
holdings, which included several properties on 135th Street between
Seventh and Eighth Avenues. In March 1932, he invited Father Divine
to reside at an apartment house located on West 135th Street when-

The Public Universal Friend in his final years. (COURTESY OF THE YATES COUNTY HISTORY CENTER.)

The Whirling Gift.

ABOVE: Woodcut depicting Shakers seized by the "Whirling Gift" during the period of Mother Ann's Work. From *Two Years' Experience Among the Shakers* (1848) by David R. Lamson, a Shaker apostate. (COURTESY OF THE COMMUNAL SOCIETIES COLLECTION, HAMILTON COLLEGE.)

LEFT: Thomas Lake Harris. (COURTESY OF THE COMMUNAL SOCIETIES COLLECTION, HAMILTON COLLEGE.)

Eleanor Castle, Victoria Gratia, and Dr. Cyrus Teed staff the Koreshan Unity booth at the 1901 Pan American Exposition in Buffalo, New York. (STATE ARCHIVES OF FLORIDA.)

Cyrus R. Teed, also known as Koresh, stands beside a tarpon in Estero, Florida. (STATE ARCHIVES OF FLORIDA.)

Cast from the Koreshan Unity play *Women, Women, Women, Suffragettes, Yes*. Koreshan Unity Art Hall, Estero, Florida. (STATE ARCHIVES OF FLORIDA.)

A praise meeting in one of the Peace Mission's Harlem extensions. A portrait of Father Divine hangs in the background. (BETTMANN/GETTY IMAGES.)

Father Divine gazes toward the sky, perhaps aboard a chartered Peace Mission steamer.
(Carl Mydans/The LIFE Picture Collection/Getty Images.)

Father and Mother Divine are thronged by admirers as they arrive in Philadelphia, September 1939. (Bettmann/Getty Images.)

"Healing" at the end of services held at MLK Jr. High School, San Francisco, August 1972. (Photographs from Peoples Temple records; MSP 3800; California Historical Society; MSP 3800.04.0137.)

Blackboard in a schoolroom at Jonestown, Guyana, July 1977. (Photographs of Peoples Temple in the United States and Guyana; PC 010; California Historical Society; PC 010.07.0751.)

Jim Jones with a toucan, Jonestown, Guyana, circa 1974–78. (Photographs of Peoples Temple in the United States and Guyana; PC 010; California Historical Society; PC 010.08.0939.)

ever he came to Harlem. It was not long before Father Divine tired of the commute altogether and made Harlem his principal address. Later that year, he moved to a larger and more comfortable house at 67 West 130th Street. Calloway's home became known as the "Peace Mission" because he continued to allow some of Divine's angels to live there.

The second pivotal angel was Lina Brinson, a Harlem woman who made a small fortune with her fried-chicken restaurant. Like Calloway, Brinson had a nose for real estate; she also knew the neighborhood. In the summer of 1933, she leased an enormous, somewhat dilapidated building at 20 West 115th Street, containing meeting rooms, ample dormitories, a dining hall capable of feeding thousands daily, and a rooftop bungalow where Divine could locate his private office. There Brinson set up her own extension of the Peace Mission, holding meetings and serving meals for ten or fifteen cents apiece. Father Divine installed his offices there in November of that year, making 20 West 115th Street the new headquarters of his movement. Calloway closed his home in solidarity with this move to Brinson's building, and the Peace Mission name came with them.

The rapid move to such commodious new quarters was due to events that had transpired in the meantime. Father Divine's day in court had finally arrived on May 24, 1932. As it turned out, his legal team had erred in requesting a change of venue for the trial: the court assigned the case to Judge Lewis Smith, a conservative WASP and "dry judge" known for his zealous assignment of harsh Prohibition sentences.[19] The prosecution called a parade of dismayed homeowners before the court as Judge Smith listened with obvious sympathy.

The defense attempted to establish Father Divine's legitimacy as a faith leader; this proved an uphill battle in Judge Smith's courtroom. Styling himself a teacher with expertise in "Mental Science, New Thought, Psychology, Spiritual Science, etc." and boasting an entry in *Who's Who in America*, Eugene Del Mar was a key witness for the defense. Del Mar was a former banker and broker, student of New Thought celebrity Helen Wilmans, secretary of the New York Mental Science Temple, editor of *Mental Science* magazine, and author of several New Thought texts, including *Spiritual and Material Attraction* (1901), *Conquest of Disease* (1922), and *Man the Master* (1925). Presumably in his capacity as editor of *Mental Science*, Del Mar became acquainted with Father Divine after traveling to Long Island to investigate the rumors of Divine's extraordinary power to manifest abundance. By the time of the November 1931 incident, Del Mar partook of Holy Communion on a regular basis.

As one of Father Divine's educated white followers, Del Mar could not be easily dismissed as a lost soul or ignorant dupe. He nevertheless carried his own set of liabilities. After his name was published in the *New York Times* in connection with the Sayville fracas, Del Mar signed an affidavit testifying to some of the movement's more outlandish claims. Although he stressed that Father Divine's enemies knew nothing of his teachings and were motivated strictly by "color prejudice," some of Del Mar's laudatory statements were counterproductive to the defense.[20] He confirmed that Father Divine's followers considered their leader a deity endowed with "unusual powers." Many of the angels, he told Judge Smith, addressed Father Divine as God or believed him to be the second coming of the Messiah. He connected this belief to Father Divine's miraculous ability to feed the masses as Christ had done; Del Mar additionally confirmed that some of the angels had seen Father "multiply the food before their very eyes!"[21] As a New Thought enthusiast naturalized to the idea of mental healing, Del Mar did not believe it absurd to testify that some who came to Sayville experienced instantaneous healing, as he stated in his affidavit. But these were hardly suitable arguments for a courtroom ruled by a white Presbyterian judge.

Witnesses at the trial affirmed that Father Divine did not accept any donations or possess a bank account, inflaming Judge Smith's already cynical view of the case. The judge intervened in the proceedings to bully witnesses who refused to identify their race. After court adjourned for the day, Father Divine proceeded to nearby Union Baptist Temple Church, where thousands had gathered to hear him speak. God brushed off the day's litany of complaints against his movement and delivered a triumphant sermon, one that he thereafter considered his most important.* In a rousing speech, Divine promised the rejoicing crowd that the euphoria they felt was "but the reflection of a percent of a percent of a percent of the outer condition of the mind within! It is but the out picturing of a sketch of a reflection of a percent of a percent of a percent of the limitless blessings that I have in storehouse for the souls of the children of men!"[22] Divine explained that legal persecution was suffering he willingly chose to undergo for the sake of his followers, and that it would only strengthen them: "Every knock is a boost," he told the assembled angels, "every criticism is a praise, and every stumbling block is a stepping stone; it is a blessing! It is Wonderful!"[23]

In the sermon at Mineola, now a sacred Peace Mission text, Father Divine told his listeners that God was present in each of their five senses, and spoke of the Christ as "risen in your being! Your joints, and your sinews, your veins and your bones!"[24] He also introduced what became an occasional epithet for his followers by playing on the homophony of God's "glory":

> Therefore, I say unto you, let your light so shine now since you have seen the Light and since you have risen, for the Light has come and the Glory of God is risen upon you! The Glo-rays of God are risen upon you! And through the mighty Glo-rays of God, why, it has glorified His Great Name in the earth and manifested the Christ to the souls of the children of men. Aren't you glad! And the Glo-rays have made you a lump of radium! Aren't you glad![25]

---

* The Peace Mission distributed it as a printed pamphlet, and Miss Sybil Child gave one to the author when he visited Woodmont.

Divine made his participation in the American messianic tradition explicit by explaining to the "living radiums" in his audience that they emitted the light from the shining "city upon a hill" described in the Book of Matthew.[26] He promised that the light he possessed in his divine body would "light every man that cometh into the world! . . . Yea, I AM the Light of the world!"[27]

Divine's sermon so electrified his "lumps of radium" that he sailed back into court on a buoyant wave of support. But religious enthusiasm was not enough to save his case: after Judge Smith threw out the testimony of anyone not present for the November raid, the jury moved to convict. When Divine reappeared in court for sentencing on June 5, Judge Smith meted out the maximum penalty available under the law: a $500 fine and a year in prison. Three days later, Smith was dead of a heart attack—and Father Divine was one of the most famous men in New York City.

29. THE HARLEM KINGDOM

THE NEW CELEBRITY was released on bail two weeks later, and James Thomas eventually succeeded in having the Mineola verdict overturned. The angels celebrated Major Divine's release with a "Monster Glory to our Lord" rally held the following day at Rockland Palace. According to some reports, as many as 10,000 angels and curious onlookers smashed into the service, during which Father Divine declared that Judge Smith had died as a consequence of his own negative mindset.[1]

Father Divine began speaking with regularity in Harlem. To capitalize on his sudden fame, he held Holy Communion banquets all over New York City and northern New Jersey—sometimes several in a single day. These were the darkest years of the Great Depression, and thousands of poor city dwellers streamed into Communion banquets for a hot meal. Divine responded to demand by implementing his economic model across Harlem, buying or renting inexpensive properties where his followers could partake of the heavenly lifestyle afforded by the Divine Cooperative Plan. Those who donated their labor and possessions to the communal system became known as "consecrated" followers. The missions permitted nonbelievers and unconsecrated followers to reside in the new "extensions" of the Peace Mission as long as they observed the Divine code of conduct: brothers and sisters were housed separately; swearing, drinking, smoking, negative thoughts, and the identification of races remained strictly forbidden.

Aside from the dozens of low-cost restaurants and dining rooms that opened under Peace Mission auspices, Divine's angels became the proprietors of garages, florists, haberdasheries, hat shops, shoeshine parlors, and dozens of other businesses that operated in affiliation with the widening network of Peace Mission hostels and boardinghouses. Divine was soon believed to be the largest property holder in all of Harlem. In fact, he was careful to make certain that none of the group homes or businesses were ever deeded in his name. Instead, followers banded together to sign joint-tenancy agreements. Larger and more expensive properties often had more than seventy owners. The joint-ownership strategy made it impossible for adversaries to acquire entire Peace Mission properties through a lawsuit, and equally difficult for individual defectors to cause problems if they left the movement. It also allowed Divine to escape paying taxes.

The heavens were filled with angels of all sorts: Father Divine's followers were black and white, rich and poor, illiterate and educated. Some were doctors and engineers. Others were saved from the terrible fates that awaited them in penitentiaries and asylums. Beautiful young angels often aspired to be Sweets—the name Father Divine used to refer to the staff of dozens of personal secretaries who attended to the many clerical needs that arose from his desire to have each and every of his utterances taken down in shorthand and transcribed into records for eternity.

The ecstatic meetings at Rockland Palace continued to score converts, as the angels and curious newcomers shouted, stamped, and convulsed. The spirit that animated Azusa Street now haunted Father's joyous celebrations. But lest his listeners think he was just another Pentecostal or holiness preacher, Father Divine explicitly compared these uncontrollable outbursts of joy with the spirit that seized the Shakers. In a speech given at the Holy Communion table on Halloween 1932, he told the angels the story of Ann Lee's "revelations and inspirations" in prison—and of her relocation to New York, intending a favorable comparison to himself.[2]

Father Divine augmented his reputation for abundance by traversing New York City in luxury cars. Whether pulling up to the city courthouse or anchoring one of the Peace Mission's gigantic parades, Father and Mother favored a Rolls-Royce driven by a liveried chauffeur. Occasionally, Divine preferred an airplane. During one of his legendary Easter parades, in which thousands of angels marched in coordinated attire, Father Divine soared above Harlem in a plane piloted by Col. Hubert Julian, a Garveyite aviator known as the Black Eagle of Harlem. Julian had recently received an honor that most UNIA members in Harlem could only dream of: after parachuting into the coronation ceremony of Ethiopian emperor Haile Selassie as part of a flight show given by the Ethiopian Imperial Air Force—which consisted of only five planes—Julian received the honors of Ethiopian citizenship, the rank of colonel, and membership in the Ethiopian Order of Menelik.[3]

. . .

BY 1934, the Peace Mission had at least thirteen heavens in New York City and nearly fifty "extensions" across the country.[4] With a spiritual and real-estate empire on his hands, Divine increasingly relied on others in the movement to organize the group homes where his followers lived. One of his most trusted lieutenants gained fame and adoration in the movement second only to Father Divine. This was Faithful Mary, a former homeless and consumptive prostitute known around the Newark drunk tank as Viola Wilson.[5] Her hardscrabble life was one to which many in the movement could relate. She often told her life's story as public testimony of Divine's transformative power.

Faithful Mary was born in Dublin, Georgia, in 1892 to Dave and Dicey Rozier, an alcoholic Baptist minister and his wife.[6] Along with her fifteen siblings, Mary grew up in a crowded shack that offered little room for evading the shifting moods of Reverend Rozier, who beat his wife and children. Mary had enough of her drunkard father by age fourteen, when she ran away from home to work in the cotton fields. She married young, separated from her husband, and ended up a single teenage mother. Confused about what to do, Mary gave her child to an older married couple who offered to take him off her hands. She married again a few years later, but her husband fell ill and died.

Nearing thirty, widowed, and still poor, Mary joined the migration north after the Great War, arriving in Newark in 1920. Sometime thereafter, she received a recipe for a curative tincture for rheumatism in a dream. Mary prepared the tonic, found that it worked, and built a thriving business around its manufacture. After being ruined by a careless business partner, Mary then took a job as a matron on the Pennsylvania Railroad—an occupation that conducted her into a "fast crowd" fond of drink. Mary became an alcoholic, lost her job and every subsequent post she managed to obtain, and by 1928 had ended up, in her own words, a "hopeless vagabond." In Newark, she recalled in her memoir, "I was known as a notorious character."[7]

After learning that her sister was living "pillar to post," one of Mary's siblings, then residing in Buffalo, came to Newark to rescue her. Mary's sister got her cleaned up and took her to a Sanctified Church, where she absorbed the holiness doctrine of "second blessing," which refers to a moment of grace or transformation intended to set the believer on the path to Christian perfection. Mary's sanctification didn't stick, and when her sister returned to Buffalo, Mary went back to the bottle. Members of her former church were ashamed to look at her when they passed her carousing or lying about in the street. Awakening in a pool hall after a night of boozing, a light washed over Mary and convinced her that God had healed her. She ran down the street to the home of a woman she knew named Virgil. Mary called Virgil her friend, although she admitted she "used to give her a lot of trouble by standing in front of her house hollering and molesting her children." Upon hearing that God had saved Mary, Virgil asked, "What's up now, have you joined Divine?"[8]

This was how Faithful Mary learned about the Peace Mission extension at 65 Howard Street in Newark. She attended the very same evening, and departed with an entourage heading to Divine head-quarters in New York. Faithful Mary had a self-destructive streak, but she was also an innate entrepreneur. After witnessing God's good works in Harlem, Mary informed Major Divine of her desire to manage one of heaven's extensions. She quickly learned that God ran his earthly kingdom on a franchise model: by turning over all profits to the Peace Mission, enterprising angels earned the right to use the Divine name at their businesses. If they were local, Divine entrepreneurs might occasionally be blessed with the apparition of God himself. Divine did not supply mortgages or start-up cash for new extensions. Aspirants to these positions had to demonstrate their worth by saving the requisite funds themselves. Faithful Mary did so as fast as she could, and opened her first extension at 51 Bedford Street in Newark, where her astonishing transformation from gutter-drunk prostitute to celibate entrepreneur proved to be effective advertising for the growing movement.

Faithful Mary swiftly expanded her operations by negotiating the purchase of a former Turkish bathhouse in Harlem, which she began operating as a Divine heaven in January 1935. She then purchased the former Eastman Gaines School at 32 West 123rd Street, which became her Harlem headquarters. With Divine taking the credit for her transformation, Faithful Mary's example made him seem capable of working real miracles.

As more angels like Faithful Mary devoted their lives to the movement, heavens continued to open across the mid-Atlantic and then throughout the country. Divine's first biographer published a "partial list" of Peace Missions to appear across North America by 1936, counting 158 establishments in total: 47 of these were located in New York, 25 in California, 13 in New Jersey, 12 in Washington state, and the rest were scattered across the country. The extensions were easier to count than the number of Peace Mission followers. Father Divine claimed millions, but the most accurate count was likely the 50,000 that *Time* magazine estimated in 1937.[9]

Father Divine instructed his followers to purchase buildings with architectural significance whenever possible, and to restore them to their former grandeur. This resulted in the acquisition of numerous luxury hotels and derelict Victorian mansions. Divine stated that the Peace Mission's bargain purchase and occasionally lavish renovation of dilapidated buildings was the result of the regenerative power harnessed by followers who trained their minds on his mission and divinity. By transforming eyesores into spotless heavens, Divinites enacted the millennial promise of release from suffering that most other black churches relegated to an uncertain future date.[10] In many of the cities and neighborhoods where they appeared, Father Divine's Peace Mission businesses were effectively the first hotels and restaurants to accommodate both whites and blacks, precisely because they would not acknowledge that such categories existed. Only the twelve Southern heavens remained, most likely, without an integrated following.

. . .

PEACE MISSION ACTIVITY in poor urban neighborhoods across the country attracted the attention of the nation's most ambitious young black writers. One of the preeminent observers of the Harlem Renaissance, Langston Hughes, mentioned and quoted Father Divine in his poem, "Projection," placing him alongside other Harlem landmarks and icons, including Paul Robeson, the Savoy Ballroom, and the Abyssinia Baptist Church.

Richard Wright's first novel, *Lawd, Today!*, written during the early 1930s but unpublished during his lifetime, includes a discussion of Father Divine among friends in Chicago. The protagonist of the novel, named Jake, is Wright's satire of the black working-class male. Jake is lazy, hedonistic, violent, misogynist, gullible, prejudiced, and vain. He beats and deprives his wife, despises her religion, racks up debt, wastes what little spare money he has on gambling, and fritters away a debt-repayment loan on booze and whores. He is a caricature, but represents the kind of man from whom many of Divine's female angels might have fled when they joined the Peace Mission. Over breakfast at a greasy spoon between shifts at the post office, Jake and his friends Bob and Al discuss an extension of Father Divine's heaven that recently opened in Chicago. They half-seriously entertain the idea that Father Divine might just be God, merely for the poetic justice it would imply:

> "Yeah," said Al, warming to his subject. "All the folks hates us black people, so Gawd might have done made up His mind to show 'em that everybody's equal in His sight. So He might come down in a black skin, see? He come as a Jew the last time, and how come He won't come as a nigger now? You see, He'd fool all the white folks then."
>
> "Boy!" said Bob, "If that guy *was* Gawd, wouldn't the white folks just die!"
>
> They laughed.[11]

The passage in Wright's novel discloses one of the central supports of the angels' belief in Divine's messianic stature: if God first chose to dwell among a people dispossessed of their land and subject to the diktats of a sinful empire, it was logical for him to return as an African American in the twentieth century.

Nevertheless, Divine was an embarrassment to the black political class in Harlem. Newsman John Louis Clarke of the influential black paper *New York Amsterdam News* wrote that Father Divine's "highly publicized feeding of the multitude and his providing of 'heaven' where they may obtain cheap shelter are but acts in a clever scheme of bilking the ignorant and the gullible who make up the 'heavenly' roster."[12] Clarke's critique rehashed many of the claims usually raised against American messianic personae: he insinuated that Divine exercised an occult form of mind control; that Divine targeted "dim-witted" followers; and that these childlike innocents so desired a strong father figure that they would immediately attach themselves to another "cult leader" if anything ever happened to Father Divine.

Marcus Garvey became another of Father Divine's detractors. In exile, Garvey learned what he knew of Father Divine through articles, like Clarke's, that appeared in the black press. Perhaps believing that he was just another charlatan minister passing through Harlem, Garvey saw no reason to remark on Divine's doings until 1935. But after learning that many of his own former disciples were now celibate angels in thrall to a man they believed was a black messiah, Garvey seemed to realize that he might have done more to thwart the movement before it had picked up so much steam. He found himself in the difficult position of trying to halt the growth of the Peace Mission from overseas.[13]

Garvey admitted that he didn't know Divine personally, and made clear that he sympathized with the plight of anyone engaging in racial justice work in New York, where "misrepresentation" by the press was all but guaranteed. He assured readers that he would not be "destructively critical" of Divine because, as Garvey put it, "I never try to destroy any other Negro."[14] But he couldn't resist complaining of the "unrest" Divine was causing between blacks and whites: by this he referred to integration, something that Garvey's Back to Africa movement did not support.

Garvey was certainly no believer in Father Divine's abolition of racial categories, which directly contradicted Garvey's black transnationalism. Instead, he believed that Divine was of middling intelligence, and consequently, the stooge of a white conspiracy. He speculated that wealthy whites were funding the Peace Mission, which somehow amounted to a "big financial scheme" to extract labor and wealth from the followers. "Wherever American white people of a certain type get mixed up with any movement of Negro salvation or redemption," Garvey wrote, "you can mark it that crookedness is somewhere." The same accusation would later trouble Divine's self-appointed successor, Jim Jones, whose followers were predominantly black.

Garvey went further, stating that by stoking his followers' fanaticism, Divine was compounding the plight of the destitute and downtrodden by bringing them to the brink of insanity. Of the Peace Mission delegation sent to call on him in Jamaica, Garvey wrote: "they could surely be classified as mad men—men who had lost their mental balance." Garvey placed responsibility for Divine's actions on the shoulders of the rest of the black community, which had failed to kneecap the messianic pretender:

> Now, when any black man reaches that point of religious
> mania or fanaticism, it is time for the intelligent members of
> the race to call a halt; but I would not suggest that anything
> be done unkindly to Father Divine by attacking him through
> the Courts of State and Federal Officials as has already
> [been] attempted and which is the method of the jealous
> Negro in dealing with the other.[15]

The court actions to which Garvey referred represented a more serious flank of resistance to one of the Peace Mission's activities: the legal battles the movement constantly fought, which often derived from Divine's prohibition of all forms of insurance. For an angel to hold an insurance policy would imply less than complete faith in Divine's omnipotence and total control of his followers' destinies. This heavenly practice excited the litigious imagination of insurance company lawyers, whose employers were losing money to Father Divine. When a follower decided she or he was ready for the consecrated life, the surrender of all material assets included unnecessary life insurance policies. After all, of what possible use was life insurance to someone who was never going to die? The New Jersey insurance industry appeared to have been the instigator behind a 1932 effort to arraign Father Divine on charges of violating Section 72 of New Jersey's 1898 Crime Act, which made it a misdemeanor for anyone to impersonate Christ.[16] Divine was convicted and sentenced in absentia to thirty days in the lockup for violating the statute. New Jersey officials eventually withdrew the warrant for his arrest, likely because it wasn't worth the fuss of having hundreds of angels pour into the courtroom in protest.

The Divine insurance prohibition continued to cause problems for the movement. One of Father Divine's followers, a proprietor of the Father Divine Peace Mission Coal Company in Manhattan, was sued by the state for failing to take out legally mandated workers' compensation insurance. As they often did, hundreds of Father Divine's followers packed the courtroom to support their beleaguered brother, shouting "Peace" and "Father Divine is God!" until the judge threatened to expel them from the proceedings.[17] The case was initially settled with Arthur Madison promising that his client would buy the required coverage, but everyone ended up back in court, joined at the defense table by additional Divine companies, including Father Divine's Dress Shop and Father Divine Peace Mission Garage. All of the proprietors contended that they did not have employees, but "joint tenants" who worked as cooperative part-owners and received dividends in the form of shoes, clothes, lodging, and an allowance.[18]

30. PROMISED LANDS

IN 1932, A JAMAICAN MAN by the angelic name of Brother Alexander moved west to Los Angeles and took the good news of Father Divine with him. He established the first West Coast heaven on Compton Avenue, and the movement soon spread to San Francisco. As in New York, many recruits to the Peace Mission in Los Angeles were former Garveyites, including Hugh MacBeth and Carlotta Bass, the editors of the black newspaper *The California Eagle*.[1] Others came from the Utopian Society of America, which was headquartered in Los Angeles, or from the sundry New Thought–allied groups that flourished across the state.

In 1934, the LA angels began publishing *The Spoken Word: The Positive Magazine*, a periodical that became the mouthpiece of the nationwide movement, reaching a circulation of 10,000 before the end of its first year.[2] The *Spoken Word* reprinted Divine's sermons, sang the virtues of twin beds, lobbied for anti-lynching legislation, and reported on Peace Mission property acquisitions. In its first issue, the paper announced the angelic transformation of the Dunbar Hotel from a jazz joint to a "Beautiful Divine Kingdom." Until its sale to the Peace Mission, the Dunbar had been a fixture of black culture in Los Angeles, owing mainly to parties and jam sessions Duke Ellington hosted there. In addition to its 100 bedrooms, the building housed several Divine commercial establishments, including a candy store. A restaurant called the Divine Grill served meals for ten to fifteen cents and offered "other tangible evidences of God's presence." According to the *Spoken Word*, the hotel's transformation was part of Father Divine's project for "resur-recting" entire neighborhoods by clearing out their "dens of vice."[3]

The *Spoken Word* enthusiastically endorsed Upton Sinclair's guber-natorial bid, as well as Sinclair's End Poverty in California movement. EPIC candidates called for the government to seize abandoned facto-ries and tax-delinquent properties, and to use them to employ the poor and house the homeless. The *Spoken Word* advocated EPIC as a step on the road to universal implementation of the Divine Cooperative sys-tem. But while EPIC was compatible with the Divine plan, the Peace Mission bitterly opposed FDR's New Deal programs. Father Divine's official position was that government handouts constituted a sacrile-gious denial of his personal ability to provide abundance to all, and he forbade his angels from participating in any New Deal programs, including Social Security. Privately, he likely understood that poverty-alleviation programs cut into his recruitment abilities.

Los Angeles remained the seat of the western flank of the move-ment, with thirteen total extensions founded by 1937.[4] Additional West Coast outposts appeared in Oakland, Seattle, Denver, and numerous smaller western towns. The Dunbar became a locus of reunion among various smaller heavens across California, and a station from which buses departed for Divine's grand Harlem headquarters. Unlike their counterparts in the East, many western heavens were predominantly white in their initial years.

One of the most unusual Peace Mission extensions was located on Vendovi Island in Washington State. Vendovi was a 200-acre isle named after a Fijian chief held prisoner by US naval commander Charles Wilkes. After Wilkes captured Vendovi in 1833 to avenge the murder and alleged cannibalization of captured American sea-men, the chief became a trophy for Commander Wilkes to display. The two became companions of sorts, and Vendovi occasionally acted as Wilkes's master-at-arms in military parades. Vendovi had died by the time Wilkes was put in charge of an 1841 survey of American territories in the Puget Sound, but Wilkes remembered his captive fondly enough to name one of the territories after him. The island played host to a motley assortment of pioneer enterprises in succeeding years, including a sheep ranch and a fox-farming business called the Vendovi Island Fur Farms. Eventually it was leased to Henry A. Joerns and Ross Humble, two of Father Divine's white West Coast disciples.

Joerns was the publisher of the Seattle-based *Metaphysical News*. Launched in 1929 under the auspices of a group called the True Idea Association, the paper acted as a sort of clearinghouse for the various branches of Western esotericism holding functions in the Northwest. Its listings of "Truth Centers" throughout the region included Theosophical lodges, Rosicrucian societies, and Unity Churches, as well as New Thought discussion groups and courses taught by local gurus. After Joerns converted to Father Divine's Peace Mission, the *Metaphysical News* began reprinting Divine's sermons and excerpts from the diaries of John Lamb.[5] The paper became an important source of news for the Peace Mission in the Northwest. Joerns commissioned Humble, a young disciple of Emma Curtis Hopkins, to write a column for the *Metaphysical News*. Like Joerns, Humble was reasonably well educated, adrift from traditional American Protestantism, and swept up in the welter of metaphysical societies that flourished in the early twentieth century. The two soon decided to make Vendovi Island a West Coast retreat for Peace Mission urbanites. The colony would host temporary residents from throughout the predominantly white Northwest who wished to have a taste of the Peace Mission's integrated communal lifestyle.

The camp was never luxurious: the island lacked electricity and running water, and men and women slept in rustic dormitories. Year-round staff occupied cabins heated by woodstoves. Accomplishing the principal sacrament of the Peace Mission—the celebration of Holy Communion feasts—occupied most of the colonists' time: they harvested wild berries, trapped rabbits, raised goats, cultivated vegetables in the island's rich soil, and went clamming in the cove. Along with celibacy and positive thoughts, a culture of extreme thrift was crucial to the Vendovi mentality: from tanned goatskins the angels sewed blankets they sold in Bellingham whenever they went to the mainland for supplies. Ross Humble acted as Father Divine's surrogate on the island, elaborating on Divine's teachings at mealtimes and regaling Westerners with descriptions of the Peace Mission palaces back East. Communion banquets offered an occasion for renditions of Peace Mission songs accompanied by violin or mandolin. The colony was supported by followers in local towns, and often visited by delegations from Seattle, Everett, Bellingham, Vancouver, and elsewhere. Fishermen heard hymns as they sailed past the island at night. In the daylight, they could see the Peace Mission slogan "IT IS WONDERFUL!" spelled in clamshells on the shore.[6]

Father Divine promoted the island retreat as his "Peaceful Paradise of the Pacific," but never traveled there himself. Visitors and staff came from all over the country and indicated how far Divine's ministry had traveled by 1933: members of the twelve-person staff that summer hailed from Oakland, Newark, and Chicago, as well as smaller towns in Washington state. In 1935, Harlem angels organized a $40 per-person bus trip to carry twenty-three followers from New York all the way to the Peaceful Paradise of the Pacific. As one of the pilgrims wrote,

> When two or more apparently, get on the ferry boat and land here each individual seems to melt and lose an individual consciousness of being separate and apart and all are welded together in just One. The ordinary things that one considers even slightly important are never even thought of here. Everything seems to fade into insignificance except the Presence of Sweet Father.

The same visitor claimed the angels could hear Father Divine's voice through the sea breezes sawing in the trees.[7]

. . .

THE NATIONWIDE NETWORK of more than 100 Peace Mission extensions established by the mid-1930s was already quite an accomplishment—it was unthinkable before Father Divine attempted it.[8] "It Is Wonderful!" the angels crooned—but Divine was not content. Having demonstrated that his non-exploitative, egalitarian, and cooperative economic model was not only functional in modern society but a resounding success to boot, Divine set his sights even higher. He turned his gaze to the rural hinterlands of New York, particularly the fertile farmlands of the greater Hudson Valley. As the Great Depression wore on, forcing rural property owners to pull up stakes and sell, Divine seized the opportunity to advance the self-sufficiency of his heavenly empire by purchasing farms where his followers could begin to produce food for sale at a discount to his city cooperatives.

After sending Lina Brinson and Charles Calloway upstate as his scout and buying agent, Divine's moneybags began traveling upriver. The region selected for Divine colonization was a long and narrow stretch of rich soil nestled between the Wallkill and Hudson Rivers, just over the Hudson from Poughkeepsie. There, in quiet Ulster County, Divine established what became known as the Promised Land: a network of farms and rural cooperatives that he envisioned as the next phase in the expansion of his kingdom.

The first Peace Mission extension came to New Paltz on July 27, 1935, when an angel named Clara Buds purchased a modest 32-acre farm for $5,500.[9] Along with two other angels, Mother Divine went north to take charge of the farm and prepare it for her husband's benediction. Father Divine had meanwhile begun to evangelize the Promised Land to crowds assembled in Harlem. In August, the Divine Rolls-Royce led a caravan carrying 125 Harlem angels to the New Paltz farm for an inaugural celebration. The next month, another contingent of visitors steamed upriver to Poughkeepsie and proceeded by bus and car to the Divine estate.

Not long after the New Paltz purchase, the Divinites bought

another farm in nearby Marbletown. Transfer of the property brought increased scrutiny and attention to Peace Mission activities in the area. Known to locals as the Hasbrouck estate, the 140-acre farm was named after one of the most established Huguenot families in the region. Divine personally brokered the sale of the estate from Arthur Hasbrouck to a Harlem follower called Abraham Augustus for $11,000. The angels referred to the Hasbrouck estate as Stone Ridge Farm. It became Divine's favorite of the Ulster County properties: he preferred the Hasbrouck house whenever he stayed overnight in the Promised Land, and spoke there at least thirteen times in 1938. The house was a fine piece of historic architecture, but it was dear to Divine for more symbolic reasons: local lore held that Hasbrouck had served as a base of operations for members of the Ku Klux Klan, who used to assemble there before marauding the countryside or conducting one of their cross-burnings.[10] Perhaps in defiance of this legacy, the three white horses used on the farm were named Righteousness, Justice, and Truth, after three of the Peace Mission's core principles. The angels added several more farms to the Ulster collection in 1935 and 1936, including approximately 100 acres of property in and around the town of Saugerties, where the Peace Mission established a restaurant, hotel, candy shop, and gas station.

In nearby Kingston, four female angels purchased a fifty-room mansion that became the Peace Mission's upstate headquarters. One of the buyers was Heavenly Rest, the Bostonian who had been one of the fifteen whites arrested in the November 1931 incident at Sayville. Several of the wealthier angels relocated to the estate, including Florence Wuest Hunt, a middle-aged dairy heiress who had taken the name Mary Bird Tree. Another was an artist known in the movement as Glorious Illumination, who said she joined Peace Mission because she felt that modern life in the city was turning her into a machine. Observers of the moment suspected that, due to the opulence of the estate and Father Divine's frequent visits to his rapidly expanding Ulster County holdings, he might transfer the headquarters of the entire movement to Kingston.[11]

The Kingston property was managed by Miss Satisfied Love and her assistant, Miss Lamb. The optics of two black women presiding over a hotel that integrated its rooms by race but segregated the sexes by floor was not something that Kingstonians found easy to accept. Unlike the farms, the high visibility of the hotel made it a monumental demonstration of integrated, harmonious living in rural New York, and Father Divine wished to publicize his accomplishment. In August 1936, he chartered another steamer up the Hudson to ferry 1,877 of his followers, at least 50 of them white, to march in a parade through the village. According to reports, the angels merrily sang and "stomped" their way up to the Promised Land on the *City of Keansburg*, which departed Manhattan just after six a.m. and reached Kingston seven hours later. Dressed all in white, the angels filled the streets of the small town.[12] Father and Mother Divine were met by a blue Rolls that carried them in the parade, with pint-sized Major Divine perched on the folded convertible top. The Kingston angels offered the marchers one of the Peace Mission's ten-cent meals upon arrival at the mansion, which they reached by an ostentatiously circuitous route through the town.

Police had arrived in time to rain on the Divine parade. A local Legionnaire by the name of Harry Whitney had gotten "all burnt up" about a flag he'd seen waving at the parade, and called law enforcement to lodge a complaint. The responding officer demanded that the angels hand over the red, white, and blue banner, which stated simply: "PEACE, FATHER DIVINE IS GOD." The red-headed angel Whitney identified as the flag bearer said she didn't know where the banner was. But after threatening not to allow the Peace Mission steamer to depart until the banner was surrendered, the cops got their prize and informed reporters that Divine's flag would be destroyed. Divine's fame was such that the affair was deemed worthy of the front page in the next day's *New York Times*.[13] Reached for comment, one of Divine's lawyers replied to this absurd harassment by promising that Ulster County would soon be home to more than 2,000 Divine settlers; he estimated that 500 of the 1,877 on board the *City of Keansburg* would ultimately move to the Promised Land. It was not an exaggeration. Faithful Mary, who also attended the parade, had recently bought the Hotel Belmont in nearby High Falls, and was busy coordinating cooperative efforts among a number of other nearby businesses, including a department store, candy factory, bakery, gas station, and a dress shop run by Mother Divine, who had established her permanent residence in a cottage behind the Belmont.

Newspapers in nearly all-white Ulster County reflected the unease with which upstate New Yorkers greeted the Harlemites. In New Paltz, residents couched their racial animosity in claims that the Peace Mission's presence in the region would somehow injure enrollment at the local Normal School (later SUNY–New Paltz), and stoked the fear that the Divine colonies would hurt local businesses by favoring their New York "connections." Although some praised Father Divine for buying properties that cash-strapped families desperately needed to sell, even if at a sacrifice, others harassed the angels and anyone who did business with them. This included John Dellay, Divine's broad-minded but hard-nosed Ulster County real-estate dealer, whose children were bullied as "nigger lovers."[14]

It was Dellay who helped Divine conceal the identities of black buyers when exclusive properties came on the market. White Peace Mission members with unremarkable names served as fronts for these riskier purchases. Properties sometimes changed hands several times in the course of a week, and would end up owned by dark-complected angels before anyone knew what had happened. Divine resorted to one of these baroque plots in 1937 to acquire Greenkill Park, a country resort that had fallen on hard times. Although it closed not long after the Depression began, boxer Max Schmeling leased Greenkill Park as a training facility in 1932. Following a complicated series of maneuvers, twenty-seven Peace Mission angels purchased the estate as a joint tenancy.[15] To celebrate the acquisition, Father Divine donned a white summer suit to lead one of his steamboat excursions up the

Hudson, shepherding 1,750 followers to the resort. Its acquisition was, for many angels, yet another miracle. As the urban angels who came to Greenkill sang in one of the Peace Mission hymns to Father Divine's bounty, *"We have heaven right here in Greenkill. Take your eyes out of the sky. We have heaven right here in Greenkill. Live the life and you won't have to die!"*[16]

Although the Peace Mission buoyed the tax base in Ulster County, where many farms had been foreclosed or abandoned, economic arguments were no match for racial panic in some quarters. County officials employed a strategy local governments often used against black families who dared to move into white neighborhoods: outrageous reassessments of home values meant to jack up their tax obligations.[17] When Mother Divine tried to open a Peace Mission orphanage in Ulster County, the New Paltz Chamber of Commerce successfully quashed it. The letter the chamber's attorney read at a State Board of Social Welfare hearing in New York City declared that New Paltz residents found the Peace Mission's beliefs "repugnant" and that "The migration and transportation of a disproportionately large number of people into our midst without visible means of support, enchanted and hypnotized by a mortal who is financed in an unknown and mysterious manner, sustained by the most part with ignorant people of low intelligence, is shocking and obnoxious to our social order."[18]

Nonetheless, numerous other additions were made to the Promised Land over the years, such as the Divine Lodge, a former resort for Broadway actors, deep in the Catskill Mountains; and the Hope Farm managed by Simon Peter, a white physician who ironically had converted to the Peace Mission after burning down his practice for insurance money.[19] Ultimately, around 2,300 followers came to dwell in the Ulster County colonies. Their relocation took a considerable amount of courage: during the Great Depression, wealth in the hands of formerly poor blacks living in the lily-white Hudson Valley provoked animosity. A cross was burned outside Faithful Mary's hotel, and two more burned in the vicinity of Stone Ridge Farm in 1937, the same year that one of the Divine properties, a lodge east of New Paltz, mysteriously caught fire in the night, forcing angels to scramble down the drainpipes to flee the burning house in nightgowns. After hearing the news on the radio in Harlem, Father Divine rushed to the Promised Land in a maroon limousine to shepherd the homeless angels to safety. Greenkill Park, suggested as a possible future headquarters for the Harlem-based movement, burned in 1937.

Authorities never determined that the cause of any of the fires was arson, but the preponderance of razed buildings suggests that at least a few of the fires were deliberately set. Because Divine did not carry insurance, the movement lost approximately $25,000 the night of the New Paltz blaze. The story made the front page of the *New York Times*, which aired speculations that either the Klan or Divine himself had committed arson. The New Paltz sheriff declared the fire an accident.[20]

31. HEAVEN TREMBLES

THE ULSTER FIRES were significant setbacks, but Father Divine had other problems on his hands in 1937. God had been released from jail only the day before the New Paltz fire. In April 1937, Divine had been arrested in connection with a stabbing that occurred in Harlem. Paul Camora, a servant of the court, had gone to the Peace Mission extension on 115th Street to serve an order for Father Divine to return money given to him by a plaintiff, Jessie Birdsall, who claimed Major Jealous Divine owed her $2,000. Camora arrived with a friend, Harry Green, who was curious to see what heaven looked like on the inside. In his court testimony, Green claimed that when they entered, Father Divine had just finished a rousing sermon that concluded with a promise that his followers would live forever. Green estimated there were about 1,500 people present in the dining hall, and that, upon learning the latecomers intended to serve him a writ, Father Divine told the crowd to "go get him." This accusation was vigorously denied by Divine and his codefendants, Happy Boy Joy and Charles Calloway, as well as a reporter who witnessed the fracas. None admitted to seeing a weapon, but before escaping the building, Green had been stabbed in the stomach with an icepick. A warrant was issued for Father Divine's arrest in connection with the case, but the Harlem impresario had gone into hiding. After a manhunt uncovered him hiding behind a furnace at a Peace Mission extension in New Milford, Connecticut, Divine was booked on charges of felony assault. Divine and his codefendants appeared in court three times before they were finally cleared of charges. After prevailing in court, Father Divine presided over a ten-course victory dinner that lasted "from midnight to dawn."[1]

Divine had triumphed once more, but the embarrassing incident compounded two ongoing problems beleaguering the Peace Mission. The first was a case involving John Wuest Hunt, a follower who had taken the name John the Revelator. Hunt was the ne'er-do-well scion of a wealthy Cleveland family. (According to Faithful Mary, Hunt's grandfather had invented a lollipop known as the "all day sucker."[2]) He ran an ad agency in Los Angeles, frequented the red-light districts of Mexican border towns, and lived across the street from Lionel Barrymore in Beverly Hills, where he was known for throwing alcohol-drenched wife-swapping parties and projecting lewd films. Dissipation was not a cure for what ailed Hunt. After depression pushed him to the brink of suicide, Hunt sought help in various Los Angeles churches. He alighted on a Peace Mission extension, was struck by the faith and health of its members, and became one of the largest backers of Divine activity in the Los Angeles area. No longer home to swinger parties, his mansion began to resound with shouts and songs in praise of Father Divine.

Los Angeles was no stranger to charismatic religion. But the ruckus so outraged neighbors, including Barrymore, that the episode at Sayville was replayed, this time with John and his brother Warner, now called John the Baptist, arrested along with their secretary. The irony of this religious persecution could not have been lost on Lionel Barrymore, who, along with his siblings, had just starred in *Rasputin and the Empress*.

In Faithful Mary's account of events, Divine led John the Revelator to believe that he would receive powers equal to Divine's own if he were able to secure a $100,000 donation to the Peace Mission.[3] Whether or not this was the motive, Hunt became convinced by 1937 that he was Jesus Christ. Things only got worse from there. While visiting a Peace Mission extension in Denver, the Revelator was smitten by a seventeen-year-old angel called Delight Jewett. He invited Jewett for a joyride in his Packard along with several other angels. After some rousing Peace Mission hymns, Delight began speaking in tongues. Declaring her consecrated to the movement, the Revelator gave Delight the name Mary Dove.

The Revelator went back to Los Angeles with Delight, presumably with her parents' consent. In LA, he convinced the girl that she was the Virgin Mary and was destined to give birth to the Messiah in Hawaii. In the Revelator's prophecy, the birth was to be the result of immaculate conception, but he had sex with Delight anyway. The two did not return to Denver as expected, and instead drove to New York City. When Divine learned of their exploits, he admonished the Revelator for violating the celibacy rule, and ordered the holy lovers to separate dormitories.

Meanwhile, the elder Jewetts pursued Jesus and Mary to New York. During an audience with God, Lee Jewett backed off from the couple's demands that Delight return with them to Denver after Divine pacified him with the offer of a job managing a farm in the Promised Land. Elizabeth Jewett was not so easily pushed aside, and Divine relinquished the girl only after her mother began demanding payments for damages. Receiving none, the Jewetts sold their story to the *New York Evening Journal*, a Hearst paper, which dragged the whole affair into the headlines. A warrant went out for the Revelator's arrest, and the subsequent manhunt and Hunt's indictment on charges of violating the Mann Act continued to provide fodder for journalists. The New York press printed every strange detail of the case, including the investigators' discovery of a twenty-two-foot-long Duesenberg sedan that Hunt had custom-built for Father Divine at a Pasadena factory. The Revelator was eventually sentenced to three years in prison, but Father Divine managed to obtain the Duesenberg, an automobile associated with the fantastically wealthy. The Divine vehicle cost a whopping $28,000—enough to buy a fleet of Fords. The Revelator intended for the car to have a revolving throne in the rear, complete with a gilded halo that could be extended over Divine's head. Major Divine began to prefer the so-called throne car when traveling between Harlem and Ulster County, because its spacious interior allowed him to travel with an entire team of secretaries.[4]

. . .

FAITHFUL MARY WATCHED the Hunt trial unfold with morbid self-interest. Her stature in the movement was rivaled only by Hunt's; his removal solidified her position as second in command. This, however, was no longer a role that suited Faithful Mary. The papers reported that she and Divine had "quarreled" prior to the stabbing of Harry Green, an event that finally sundered the pair.[5] In Faithful Mary's account of events, Divine reproached her for criticizing his leadership and threatened to demote her to the kitchen of one of the Promised Land farms.

Faithful Mary's Harlem and High Falls empire hardly rivaled Divine's, but her sphere of influence had enlarged to such a degree that Divine's reprimand served only as provocation. While God was on the lam in Connecticut, Faithful Mary proclaimed the independence of her properties from the Peace Mission movement, declaring them now a part of her Universal Light movement. The name of the group gestured to the continued prevalence of New Thought themes among Divine's angels. However, Faithful Mary's movement did not hold universal appeal. Aside from Son Peter, a young man who grew up at 72 Macon and defected to become Faithful Mary's first lieutenant, the Universal Light movement failed to attract Peace Mission apostates. Mary had miscalculated the degree of Divine's difficulties: following his apprehension and release, Divine swiftly moved to crush her rebellion, commanding his angels to shun her businesses. They obeyed, and Faithful Mary found her High Falls establishments on the brink of ruin.

To get revenge, Faithful Mary and Son Peter joined forces with another fallen angel, who'd resumed using the name Verinda Brown. She had taken Divine to court and was seeking allies among the enemies of her enemy. Faithful Mary and Son Peter became star witnesses in Brown's lawsuit, offering testimony against Divine to Brown's attorneys; together they made the unlikely claim that angels in the Promised Land were going hungry and were being used as slave labor.

Verinda Brown and her husband, Thomas, had joined the Sayville commune in 1930, taking the names Rebecca Grace and Onward Universe. In the grievance she brought to court, Brown claimed she entrusted her life savings to Divine, which at the time had amounted to nearly a thousand dollars in cash and gold coins.[6] After Divine began lavishing his attention on other prospective recruits, Rebecca Grace took offense and left heaven. In October 1934, following a disagreement that resulted when Divine rebuked her for giving money to her husband instead of to him, she requested that the reverend return her investment in his mission. But Father Divine told Rebecca Grace—now back to plain old Verinda Brown—that this would be impossible: he had invested the money in real estate, presumably the first Sayville extensions. Brown left heaven without her savings—and initially, without her husband, who remained Onward Universe for a while longer.

The lawsuit that Brown filed against Divine dragged through the courts for years. At one point, Divine's debonair celebrity pilot brought the suit front-page coverage by attempting to broker a compromise. As the *New York Times* court reporter wrote:

> Colonel Julian, garbed in formal wing collar, ascot tie and spats and wearing a monocle dangling from his waistcoat, exhibited cash and warehouse receipts for a store of aged whisky. From confused accounts available after yesterday's denouement, it appeared that he had been urging the parties to settle the suit for several days, but had not succeeded in winning over Father Divine.[7]

Embarrassed by the publicity, Julian insisted that he was no angel: "I am not a follower of Father Divine," Julian told reporters, "But I am a Negro and I have seen the good things he has done. Any man who can make great numbers of people quit smoking and drinking and even make thieves return the things they have stolen, I am for. I am sick and tired of seeing the Negro race kicked around."[8] The Browns were willing to accept the offer of cash and whiskey, but Divine refused the compromise on principle. He was confident he would win the suit, as the plaintiffs' case appeared to rest on their allegation that Father Divine invested their money in real estate purchased under the names of "fictitious" persons: the angelic names of the Browns and their former correligionists.

As the lawsuit languished on the docket, Faithful Mary self-published a tell-all memoir of her time in the Peace Mission, alleging rampant homosexuality in Father Divine's kingdom, and claiming that Father Divine collaborated with the heads of individual extensions to cover up the deaths of more than 200 followers who had failed to attain everlasting life.[9] But by this time Faithful Mary posed little threat to Father Divine: her hotel in High Falls had to be sold, and she lost her Harlem properties one by one to cover her debts. Then Mary relapsed into drinking. By the end of 1937, the Universal Light movement was confined to a house on Fifth Avenue near 127th Street. The fallen angel finally begged Father's forgiveness, which he granted only after publicly humiliating the apostate: Divine required Faithful Mary to make a public confession at Rockland Palace on January 1 and 2, 1938, during which she repudiated her charges against the movement. She was absorbed back into a Newark branch of the Peace Mission, but her recovery was only temporary: Faithful Mary died from an overdose of sleeping pills after ending up poor, drunk, and destitute in Los Angeles.

32. RIGHTEOUS GOVERNMENT

ALTHOUGH 1937 WAS a rough year for Father Divine, he and his followers were still riding high on the demonstrations of political clout that had marked 1936. Several key organizers of the more politically radical missions in Los Angeles, including the editors of the *Spoken Word*, had moved to New York to be near Father Divine over the course of 1935. The *Spoken Word* soon ceased publication altogether when it was absorbed into the *New Day*, a long-running Peace Mission periodical based in New York that focused on Peace Mission acquisitions, Father Divine's sermons, and events attributed to his vengeful retribution against opponents. The exodus of leadership and resources from the California extensions helped ensure that the Peace Mission would die out faster on the West Coast, where there was considerable competition in the marketplace of transformative religious and political organizations. But it also had the effect of radicalizing Father Divine's political outlook as the more progressive angels from the West injected new energy into the Harlem headquarters.[1] The result was the Peace Mission's Righteous Government Platform, which the angels devised during their International Righteous Government Convention, held in New York from January 10 to 12, 1936.

Divine had already flirted with political power, most notably by pretending to be the kingmaker in New York's 1933 mayoral election. During the campaign, two candidates for the mayoralty, John O'Brien and Fiorello La Guardia, visited Divine in Harlem to court his support. La Guardia was cited as saying, "I say, Father Divine, no matter what you do, I will support you. I came in that spirit, and I came here tonight not to ask but to give, for I believe Father Divine, in what you say."[2] But Divine enjoyed the attention more than the idea of being wrong, so he demurred when it came time to issue an endorsement. The 1936 Righteous Government Platform marked Divine's debut as a policymaker with national ambitions. It announced that a "New Dispensation of GOD on earth" had already instituted new modes of "righteous government" among Divine's followers, who had banished injustice and untruth from their midst. The platform called upon secular governments to "legalize" the Divine way of life by guaranteeing equal rights and opportunities of employment, just as the Constitution demanded. Other planks in the platform called for an end to compulsory medical treatment for minors, including vaccinations; elimination of all laws requiring insurance; a cap on labor union dues; abolition of the death penalty; destruction of all weapons of assault and war; and the repeal of all racially discriminatory laws, including any that merely required citizens to identify themselves on the basis of race, creed, or color. Because Divine was aware that some would view the Righteous Government organizations as a front for Communist agitation, the Peace Mission held a "Peace Conference" on St. Nicholas Place the same month, during which Divine publicly disavowed Communist atheism.[3]

Weekly Righteous Government meetings occurred throughout the heavenly empire.[4] In August, West Coast devotees overcame the concerted opposition of LA ministers to hold a massive Righteous Government convention at the Hollywood Bowl. Faithful Mary reported that Republicans, Democrats, Socialists, and Communists were all represented at Righteous Government meetings, and that state-level office seekers continued to venture to Harlem to curry Divine favor. However, no major candidates in any of the parties adopted the platform.[5] This persuaded Divine to remain on the sidelines in the contest between FDR and Alf Landon, although he made it clear to his supporters that he disliked the New Deal.

Father Divine's opponents considered his political activities a baleful extension of his power into the secular realm. Many credulously repeated his claims to have millions of followers, and seemed genuinely concerned about the possibility that Righteous Government would be established on the strength of this following. Numerous concerned citizens wrote to FBI director J. Edgar Hoover to warn him of Divine's potential Communist affiliations, and to offer leads regarding any criminal investigation the FBI might be pursuing against the black messiah. But the credibility of many of these claims was marred by the proliferation of dubious accusations, such as the oft-repeated assertion that Divine was running houses of prostitution in the city and upstate. Aware of the campaigns raised against the movement, the Divinites also wrote to Hoover, telling him of the real-life miracles that Divine was working in American ghettos. They explained that Father instructed his followers to abhor crime and dishonesty, to pay all debts, and to make restitution for past misdeeds. Brother William Ross wrote to tell Hoover that Divine had saved him from a life of crime, and openly confessed to Hoover he believed Father Divine was the second coming of Jesus Christ.

Despite numerous entreaties to investigate Divine for various suspicions and alleged crimes—such as the swindling of his followers and collaboration with German spies—Hoover declined to investigate the Peace Mission.[6] He even refused a request from Sen. R. Louis Murphy of Iowa, who insisted that the FBI look into the case of three black women who deserted their families in Council Bluffs to join the Harlem heaven.[7] Hoover seemed to regard Divine as the leader of a benign cult that had, in fact, reduced the incidence of poverty, indigence, and crime in black ghettos. The Bureau's file on Father Divine nevertheless grew to hundreds of pages.

Some of the Peace Mission's most dogged opponents were members of the clergy and the academy. Elam Daniels, editor of the *Biblical Echo*, became a sworn enemy of Father Divine and lambasted him as the false Christ mentioned in Matthew 24:24.[8] Daniels went to New York to investigate the Peace Mission up close; he painted an unflattering portrait of Divine as a narcissistic mountebank: "When the little god is not charming them with his big words and beguiling oratory," Daniels wrote, "the time is spent in worshipping him."[9] Like many other evangelicals, Daniels was disgusted by Divine's messianic pretensions, and equally alarmed by the racial integration practiced in the Peace Mission.

Writing for the *Journal of Educational Psychology* in January 1937, F. Blair Mayne of New York University complained about the deleterious effects the Peace Mission had on youth, claiming that the separation of children from their natural parents "initiates a type of control and demands a type of behavior which is opposed to the laws of nature and the standards set up by society in general." This persistent complaint against the angels accused them of contributing to the perceived disintegration of "social control through the family."[10] This, of course, was one of Divine's stated goals, and a consistently recurring objective of American messianic movements that attempt to establish the kingdom of God on Earth, where all would live as one family.

. . .

BY THE LATE 1930S, the New Deal had alleviated some of the worst effects of the Depression, which blunted the appeal of Divine communalism. Although the Peace Mission never kept membership records, Divine and the secretaries who counted wads of cash nightly in the Harlem headquarters would have known that the movement had already entered a slow decline. Decadence was not apparent from outside the kingdom: Father Divine continued to expand his real-estate empire, which was the cornerstone of his integrationist crusade. The civil rights movement was still more than a decade away, and the Great Migration of African Americans north had, for the most part, only exchanged the scenery of racial oppression: black ghettos in cities across the industrial North sprang up to absorb the massive influx of transplants from the South. Squalid tenements owned by slumlords seldom obeyed city codes. Buildings were crowded, unsafe, and prone to fire. Residents were overcharged for rooms that often lacked indoor plumbing and adequate ventilation. Due to de facto segregation and racial discrimination, slumlords knew that African Americans would find it nearly impossible to find a rental outside of the ghettos. With a plentiful supply of tenants, Harlem landlords had no reason to compete with one another except in a race to the bottom. By contrast, Peace Mission dormitories were clean and orderly. The buildings were sometimes old and in varying states of repair, but they allowed Divine's followers to have a literal stake in the community where they lived.

Outside the city, integrated teams of angels carried forward the tradition begun in Sayville by using their hard-won communal wealth to acquire properties in exclusive white neighborhoods. Their efforts resulted in high-publicity friction that elevated the struggle to the pages of major American dailies. In Miami, angels handing out copies of the *New Day* were arrested, jailed, and threatened with lynching. This sort of racist opposition was obviously expected in the South. But as the people of New Paltz had demonstrated, in practical matters, the Mason-Dixon Line was usually a meaningless divide: when the Peace Mission attempted to integrate into wealthy, white neighborhoods, it provoked intransigent opposition.

Divine continued to split his time between Manhattan and Ulster County, often preferring to fly in private planes from Brooklyn's Floyd Bennett Field. One of Divine's angels, known as Flying Determination, eventually became his personal pilot. Flying Determination owned a red airplane, on which she'd painted "FATHER DIVINE, PEACE MISSION." Divine's employment of an African American aviatrix was remarkable for the way it demonstrated the Peace Mission's refusal to be encumbered by social restrictions imposed on the basis of race, class, and gender: Divine had black and white secretaries, employed male and female chauffeurs, and supplied a reliable client base for black men and women who wished to own their own businesses.

Late into the Depression, the Promised Land expanded to include ornate estates on the Hudson, including Elverhoj ("home of the

Elves"), an art colony in Milton, New York, that included a pier on the Hudson capable of docking Divine steamers. It was another purchase, however, that garnered the most attention from the media. Divine had acquired a 500-acre estate known as Krum Elbow; it was located directly across the Hudson from the Roosevelts' Hyde Park manor. The estate enjoyed more than a mile of river frontage; orchards and vineyards; and twenty-eight buildings, one of which was a three-story boathouse. Its owner, Howland Spencer, was an eccentric relative of the Roosevelt family. Like Divine, who bitterly inveighed against the "dole," Spencer was an opponent of FDR's New Deal programs. During Roosevelt's 1936 reelection campaign, Spencer took out ads in the local paper to impugn his neighbor's patriotism, accusing him of dictatorial self-aggrandizement. When Spencer found himself forced to unload some of his properties to cover his debts, he decided to sell Krum Elbow to the Peace Mission as a way to embarrass his presidential neighbor. Mary Bird Tree inspected the estate on behalf of the Peace Mission, while Spencer went in disguise to visit several Peace Mission farms. He liked what he saw—particularly the angelic rejection of public relief programs—and ended up selling the estate for less than it was worth. Twenty-one Divinites appeared on the deed, but about sixty went to reside there. Reached for comment on the sale, Roosevelt kindly stated, "I'm confident that the people in that 'heaven' in Ulster County will be good neighbors to us here in Dutchess County." Divine returned the compliment, saying, "I couldn't have a finer neighbor, could I?"[11]

Divine's plan was only halfway done. With neighborly overtures to the Roosevelts, he hoped to encourage the Democratic incumbent to support the federal anti-lynching legislation he and his followers had drafted and sent to Congress. To demonstrate his friendship with the president—and to get him on the record with regard to civil rights—Divine wrote to the president and Mrs. Roosevelt to ask their advice about whether he should buy the Vanderbilt estate, a historic property that abutted theirs. As the former governor of New York, President

Roosevelt was well apprised of Father Divine's doings before the two ever became neighbors. He understood that although Divine's electoral power was limited, he needed to tread carefully: the Democrats stood to lose at the ballot box if they were perceived as too ambitious on the matter of black civil rights. Although the president replied through a secretary, Eleanor Roosevelt personally wrote Father Divine to express admiration for the estate. She assured Divine that her family saw no inconvenience to his potential purchase of the property, but observed that her husband had hoped the estate would enter conservancy as a public arboretum, owing to the many rare species collected by its previous owners. Divine wrote to thank Mrs. Roosevelt, making no mention of the trees, and indicated he would try to acquire the property. After Divine published his correspondence with the Roosevelts, the *Poughkeepsie Star* endorsed his purchase of the estate. But its owner, the Newport socialite Margaret Van Alen, refused to sell her late uncle's estate to the Peace Mission. She deeded it to the national government for $1, stipulating her wish that it be made a national park.[12]

33. PHILADELPHIA

THINGS IN NEW YORK weren't meant to last. In spite of Father Divine's confidence, the courts eventually found in Verinda Brown's favor, ordering Divine to pay a judgment of more than $5,000. Father Divine appealed the ruling, but finally lost the case in 1942.[1] At this stage in his career, the money meant almost nothing: although he held no property or bank accounts in his own name, the Peace Mission controlled millions in assets. These were protected by the 1940 incorporation of several Peace Mission churches, including the Circle Mission Church and Palace Mission, Inc, which bundled Peace Mission properties into tax-exempt religious organizations. Divine made his chief angels the officers of the churches, which could not be sued for anything Father Divine had allegedly done to Brown or anyone else who came forward with a lawsuit. Dozens of angels would have lined up to pay the judgment on Father's behalf. But rather than weaken his followers' belief in his omnipotence, Divine cited the corruption of earthly authorities and refused to comply. To avoid arrest, Divine simply moved Peace Mission headquarters to a hotel acquired on Broad and Catharine Streets in Philadelphia.

Peninnah never made it to the City of Brotherly Love. After the establishment of the Ulster County colonies, Sister Penny spent most of her time upstate, far from the bustle of Manhattan. Her health had begun to fail as early as 1936: during that year and the next, heart trouble and kidney failure forced her hospitalization on two occasions; her second stay lasted for a period of months. Although her status was meant to be a secret, reporters discovered Mother Divine's where-abouts after her absence became conspicuous. Father Divine did not visit his wife in the hospital. Initially, he might have avoided her sick-bed because doing so would have drawn attention to her illness, as his movements were closely watched by New York reporters. But the most likely explanation is also the most perverse: if Father Divine truly believed that impurity of thought was the cause of illness and death, then Mother Divine was a backslider who was just as corrupted as numerous others whose deaths he had blamed on their own mental failings. Ironically, it was Faithful Mary who removed Mother Divine from the charity ward and paid her hospital tab. Mother Divine recov-ered, and was spotted at meetings in Kingston and High Falls as late as 1938. Her last known appearance was at a 1942 Holy Communion banquet in New York, during which she felt well enough to sing. But as of 1943, Peninnah Divine had completely disappeared.[2]

By the beginning of the Second World War, the Peace Mission was still operating in at least twenty-five states and numerous foreign countries. Father Divine did not let the war go to waste. Ever since the outbreak of hostilities, Divine championed the cause of Euro-pean Jews. He urged his old neighbor President Roosevelt to initi-ate the unification of the Americas into one massive nation-state as a deterrent against Axis invasion. The war had the additional effect of causing a conservative reformation of Peace Mission politics. This was due, in part, to the anti-cult movement of the 1940s, which arose in response to the fascist sympathies that some metaphysical groups harbored. After Guy and Edna Ballard's I AM movement drifted into open flirtation with fascism and sought alliance with the Silver Shirts, a Fascist brigade founded by the esotericist William Dudley Pelley, both groups found themselves ensnared in the FBI dragnet launched against far-right groups in the United States. A grand jury indicted twenty-four members of the I AM hierarchy for mail fraud, and the House Un-American Activities Committee targeted other esoteric organizations on the far left and far right.

Father Divine appeared to take note of the broad suppression of "cults" in the early 1940s. As an integrationist with an anti-statist socialist platform, Divine could hardly have been considered a fascist. Some continued to allege he was a Russian agent, or at the least, an enemy of American values. Father Divine sometimes used these accusations to embellish his own grandeur, claiming that it was he who aided the Communist Party and not the other way around. But the movement had never before been tested by the heightened scrutiny of wartime. Father Divine took the precautionary measure of adorning Peace Mission buildings and publications with American flags. He courted the FBI's sympathy by having John Lamb denounce a handful of his backsliding followers as Fascist sympathizers.[3] And although he had called for the elimination of all weapons of war in the Righteous Government Platform, Divine urged his followers to buy war bonds after the United States entered the fray. The Peace Mission was of course pacifist, but Divine allowed the US Coast Guard to house agents in the Divine Brigantine, a boardwalk hotel his followers had purchased on the Jersey Shore. As his angels volunteered for the civilian air-raid corps, Divine sent messages to Hitler, Mussolini, and Hirohito, to inform them of their disfavor with God. Later, after telegraphing a command that the Japanese emperor surrender unconditionally, Divine insinuated that the destruction of Hiroshima and Nagasaki was a result of his holy retribution.

. . .

SEVERAL OF THE WEST COAST EXTENSIONS had already closed by the time Father Divine relocated the Peace Mission from Harlem to Philadelphia, but the region yielded two consequential converts to the movement. These were Ruth Boaz and Edna Rose Ritchings. The latter adopted the name Sweet Angel when she pledged her faith in Father Divine, and her participation in the movement was destined to be great. Boaz, on the other hand, became one of the most public apostates of the movement.

Boaz joined the Peace Mission in Bellingham, Washington. She was, by her own description, a "hardened woman of the world" who had long wandered on the "seamy side of life."[4] Salvation arrived in the form of Father Divine's Peace Mission. Like Divine's many other female converts gone adrift in a society unforgiving of female transgression, Boaz and her mother sought Divine's protection and redemption. Penniless but filled with hope, they hitchhiked to New York to meet him. At this time, God still resided in Sayville, but the women met Divine at a Holy Communion banquet in Harlem. As often occurred when a prospective recruit was attending her first meeting, Ruth accepted a seat of honor next to Father. Her position displaced Christian Life, a former film actress and one of Father's favorite secretaries. Later that evening, Father whisked Boaz to a second banquet in Harlem, where she testified to her belief in his godlike power. The next day, Boaz confessed her errant ways to Father Divine, who listened without shock or alarm. "Mary was no virgin," Boaz claims he told her reassuringly, as they undressed to make love.[5]

After finally abandoning the Peace Mission during the first days of its decline in the early 1960s, Boaz published a tell-all article in *Ebony* magazine detailing her three decades in the movement, including the two years she purported to be Divine's mistress. Months before his death, she denounced Father Divine as a "charlatan," and described him as a mortal man "endowed with a malevolent spiritual force which he has used to capture the minds of sincere people and bend them to his will." Her words refer to the alleged powers with which witches controlled spirits in the eighteenth century, and that mesmerists and magnetists claimed to possess in the nineteenth. The charge would soon be known by the twentieth-century term popularized by Robert J. Lifton: "brainwashing." Boaz advanced another of the tropes that would become a hallmark of the anti-cult movement when it reappeared in the mid-1960s, claiming that the sect was "founded on ignorance, superstition, and fear" and made up of "an odd collection of neurotics, misfits, and fanatics held together by a fearful discipline and a mystical, unquestioning belief."[6] Her description is at odds with the fact that many of Divine's followers were educated professionals, and that a great deal of those who joined the movement acquired training in nursing and other stable careers. Although she admitted to arriving at Divine's door a desperate wastrel, Boaz claimed the Peace Mission "wrecked" her life by keeping her "spiritually and physically enslaved by this strange, enigmatic personality," and under his "total subjection" for "three unbelievable decades."

Edna Ritchings had a very different experience with the Peace Mission. After converting to the movement in her native Canada, Ritchings made the hegira to Philadelphia when she was just twenty-one.[7] There she became one of the Sweets, Father Divine's corps of secretaries, and took the name Sweet Angel. In 1946, Divine shocked longtime angels by announcing that he and Sweet Angel were married in Washington, DC. Peninnah Divine, he finally admitted, had laid down her body in Ulster County—but her spirit now resided in the beautiful blond Canadian.[8] As the reincarnation of Mother Divine, it was Edna Ritchings who would later take control of the movement after Father Divine made the "Ultimate Sacrifice" in September 1965.

. . .

THE PHILADELPHIA PERIOD of Divine's career was, in contrast with the Depression years, relatively calm. The 1942 judgment against him in New York state court meant that Divine could only visit the Empire State on Sundays, when it was illegal to serve a summons. Although he occasionally returned to the Ulster County Promised Land, Divine cited the court judgment as evidence that New York City had failed to appreciate the miracles he'd worked in Harlem.

The movement's funding arrangements remained unchanged after the consolidation into recognized churches, which allowed the Peace Mission to reabsorb considerable assets from the aging membership. Occasionally these large charitable gifts brought the movement back into the headlines; the most extravagant were literally front-page news. Upon her death at eighty-one in 1946, Mary Sheldon Lyon, known in the Peace Mission as Peace Dove, left half a million dollars to Palace Mission, Inc. and Palace Mission Church and Home—an amount worth more than $6 million in 2017 currency. Her brother received only $500 of Lyon's wealth as a "token of affection," while Patience Budd, a Divinite who cared for her during her geriatric illnesses, was awarded all of Lyon's household effects.[9]

With his range of motion restricted and old age setting in fast, Father Divine and the movement settled into a comfortable stasis. The Peace Mission continued to acquire new properties, although these purchases now focused on Victorian mansions in Philadelphia neighborhoods that were quickly becoming some of the nation's poorest urban enclaves. In 1948, Divine orchestrated the acquisition of the magnificent Lorraine Apartments, a Beaux-Arts apartment hotel on North Broad Street. Although Divine's offices remained at the Circle Mission on South Broad, the opulent Divine Lorraine became the symbol of the Peace Mission movement in its latter years. Angels from Peace Mission extensions all over the world—including Australia, Switzerland, the West Indies, and even the Panama Canal Zone—made pilgrimages to the hotel. Although the movement had already begun to decline in numbers and visibility, it retained an estimated $6 million in real-estate holdings in 1953.[10] That year, the Peace Mission acquired its crown jewel: the Woodmont estate in Gladwyne. Divine declared it the Mount of the House of the Lord, and permanently relocated his residence to Woodmont.

Scholars and critics of the movement agree that steep decline had set in by this time, when age forced Father Divine to curtail his travels. Although the *New York Times* reported as late as 1964 that the movement was "still amassing real estate," news of Father Divine was relegated to the back pages of the paper.[11] Relative national prosperity in the 1950s, combined with the movement's own celibacy diktat, ensured sharp attrition over the course of the decade. Increasingly, Father Divine delegated day-to-day management of the Peace Mission's empire of properties to Mother Divine and one of her rivals: Dorothy Darling, Divine's most trusted secretary. After 1960, just as the civil rights movement was entering its ascendancy, Father Divine's health forced him out of the public eye. Periods of serious illness related to diabetes led to stretches of secret hospitalizations, and he otherwise seldom left the stately grounds of Woodmont.

It was there, ensconced in his chambers at Woodmont, that Father Divine met one of his most consequential admirers: a winsome white minister from Indiana. This man, who helmed the first integrated congregation in Indianapolis, had come to see for himself the ways that Father Divine had managed to create an integrated movement, numbering tens of thousands of adherents who successfully lived according to the apostolic socialism described in the Book of Acts. The young reverend from Indiana came away deeply impressed by the Divine system of economic cooperation, and resolved to implement it in his own church. His name was Jim Jones, and his congregation, Peoples Temple, became the notorious legacy of messianic thought and deed in America.

FIVE

FALL OF THE SKY GOD

And you can call me an egomaniac, megalomaniac, or whatever you wish, with a messianic complex. I don't have any complex, honey. I happen to know I'm the Messiah. It's only a complex when you're confused. It's only a complex when you have some kind of neurotic compulsions and some kind of subliminal pressures. Honey, I don't have any conflict about it whatsoever. I'm not in conflict at all. I know as much as the light is showing up there through four squares, that I am God the Messiah. Now you take that in your pipe and smoke it, honey.

—Jim Jones,
FBI Tape Q1059–1

34. JIM JONES

B Y THE TIME Jim Jones went to Woodmont, most African Americans living in the urban Northeast had heard of Father Divine. The black Messiah's career was approaching its terrestrial conclusion, and no one could say he hadn't made a name for himself. Many of his followers could credibly state that Father Divine was their personal savior: his work lifted thousands out of poverty, rescued others from the clutches of addiction, and delivered still more from lives devoid of meaningful community. After his voluntary exile from Harlem and resettlement in Philadelphia, Divine at last acquired a measure of respect from the New York black religious establishment. Even Harlem congressman Adam Clayton Powell, a former critic of the Peace Mission, defended Father Divine in a 1951 article for *Ebony*, in which he asserted that Father Divine was certainly not a "cult leader." Powell stated that he had personally investigated Peace Mission finances and was satisfied that Divine was not running a con.

In 1953, reporter Sara Harris's salacious biography *Father Divine: Holy Husband* brought new attention to the movement after it had mostly receded from public view. At the time of its publication, Jim Jones was a student minister striving to integrate Somerset Methodist Church in Indianapolis. Harris's work got some publicity in the *Indianapolis Recorder*, a black weekly newspaper, when an Indianapolis church scheduled a talk related to the book in February 1954. Jim Jones, who by this point was a familiar face in the black community, might well have attended: he was an avid reader of the *Recorder* and a frequent visitor to the city's black congregations. The same year, Jones abandoned his post at Somerset, citing conflicts arising from his outspoken support of integration. He founded his own church in a small building on Hoyt and Randolph streets in Indianapolis, calling it Community Unity. The style of worship and preaching at Community Unity was the ecstatic "holy rolling" that characterized the low-income Pentecostal churches Jones preferred ever since his boyhood. Although American churches were sites of intransigent de facto segregation, Pentecostalism was a movement that cut across racial lines in America—it was popular among the poor and working classes in both black and white communities. As such, it was the ideal style and format for Jones to adopt if he were to succeed at integrating his flock.

Succeed he did. Jones made himself highly visible around the capital city. As the minister of a fledgling integrated church, Jones made ends meet by traversing Indianapolis on his bicycle, selling pint-sized South American monkeys door to door for $29 each. One of his customers was Edith Cordell, whose pet monkey had recently hanged himself. Cordell contacted Jones after seeing an ad the minister had placed in the *Indianapolis Star*. Jones sold her a monkey, then invited her to church the following Sunday. Cordell was curious enough to attend. What she found was a congregation unlike any other in Indianapolis: "It didn't make no difference what color you were," Edith's daughter-in-law June Cordell recalled decades later, "it was everybody welcome there in that church and he made it very plain from the platform."[1]

Although many first-time visitors were turned off by the integrated worship service, others admired Jones's project. For most congregants, the Pentecostal healing miracles Jones worked on a regular basis were the principal attraction. Cordell converted after Jones instructed her to sip water he drew from a baptismal sink at the front of the church. When she drank it, the water tasted sweet, like wine. More important, Cordell's painful arthritis instantly vanished after the blessed water crossed her lips. Far more dramatic were the tumor extractions

Jones performed in the church. For these miracles, the reverend or his wife would chaperone an afflicted congregant to the church bathroom, where they were told they would "pass" the cancerous mass at Jones's command. Jones would place the tumor in a paper bag and, after emerging victorious from the lavatory with the cured patient, hold it aloft for the rest of the congregation to see. It was a performance he continued well into the San Francisco years of his ministry, still two decades in the offing.[2]

As Jones's reputation spread, an elderly Pentecostal minister with a congregation on Laurel Street invited him to preach to his flock. Jones initially hoped to be named the next pastor at Laurel Street Tabernacle. But after he discovered the congregation was divided on the matter of integration, Jones forced the issue until he was finally asked to leave. He obliged, taking half of the largely white congregation with him.

Community Unity soon outgrew its original headquarters, and the congregants' tithes enabled Jones to move to a larger and more elegant house of worship. The building was a former synagogue purchased by Wings of Deliverance, a nonprofit Jones incorporated in 1955 to account for his church's many charitable businesses. There the congregation became more deeply involved in social activism, and Jones began to advocate socialism openly in his sermons. He started referring to the church as a "movement," and by early 1956, the congregation was known as Peoples Temple Full Gospel Church.[3]

Today Peoples Temple is best known not for what it was, nor where it came from, nor what it stood for. It is known instead for its horrific end: on November 18, 1978, more than 900 members of the Peoples Temple Agricultural Project in Jonestown, Guyana, died as the result of a mass murder–suicide following a fact-finding mission conducted by United States Rep. Leo Ryan, who was assassinated by a faction of Peoples Temple loyalists at Jones's command. The Jonestown Massacre, as it became known, was the largest loss of American civilian lives to occur on a single day until the terrorist attacks of September

11, 2001. The event remains a powerful cultural touchstone for those who remember watching the news of the slayings unfold on television. But the most enduring legacy of the tragedy is a macabre idiom whose origin has slowly been obscured by time. "Drinking the Kool-Aid," a phrase meant to refer to the method of suicidal annihilation used in Jonestown, has become a slogan used casually to describe willful self-deception, voluntary indoctrination, and blind obedience—particularly out of fealty to a group identity.

. . .

JIM JONES WAS A VISIONARY with stunning charisma, nearly boundless energy, and the intellectual resources of few other religious leaders of his generation. That he ended up a drug-addled paranoiac with grandiose delusions about his world-historical significance is one of the great tragedies not only of American religion, but also of American leftist politics. Although his biography has been narrated many times already, the story of Peoples Temple must begin with an understanding of its founder's origins.

Jones was raised in Lynn, Indiana, a Rockwellian small town anchored by a few factories, including one that made coffins.[4] He had been born to Lynetta and James Thurmond Jones in a nearby farming village called Crete. After the family farm fell victim to the Great Depression, the Joneses moved three miles to Lynn while Jimmy was still a toddler. There the family lived off the grudging charity of the elder Jones's siblings.

Jones had a lonely boyhood and was often left to his own devices. His father, known as Big Jim, was a veteran of the Great War who suffered permanent lung damage after breathing mustard gas on the western front. Big Jim was disabled not only by his war injuries but by a crippling mental illness that his embarrassed siblings passed off as alcoholism.[5] It fell to Lynetta to support the family by working whatever jobs she could get while her husband spent his days at the pool hall. In Lynn, Mrs. Jones acquired a reputation for her unconventional habits and her transgression of gender roles: she went to and from her factory jobs in workman's coveralls, smoked in public, and unlike most people in Lynn, she never went to church.

Jones would later attribute his concern for the poor and unfortunate to his mother's compassion for the hoboes and tramps who wandered along the train tracks running behind the family's house. But since neither parent was religious, a pious neighbor by the name of Myrtle Kennedy took it upon herself to introduce the boy to the Church of the Nazarene. Religion and the community ties it nourished spellbound the lonely boy. Soon little Jim was making the rounds of Lynn's various denominations, sometimes visiting services at more than one church on a given Sunday. He got to know the Quakers and the Methodists, but was most attracted to the dramatic theatrics of the Pentecostal churches, where the Holy Spirit caused congregants to writhe on the floor and speak in tongues. Years later in Guyana, Jones recalled that it was the "oneness" church—a rowdy Pentecostal congregation on the edge of town—that taught him to identify with those whom American society labeled as outcasts.[6]

Apocryphal tales of Jones's childhood often include a story that his mother told her son at a young age: during her pregnancy, she received a message in a dream informing her that she would give birth to the Messiah. This certainly might have affected the boy's choice of vocation, which defied his parents' disdain for organized religion: neighbors recalled that while other children were playing cowboys and Indians, young Jim made believe he was a minister in the makeshift chapel he constructed above the family garage, where he conducted mock baptisms for his playmates and officiated funerals for dead animals. A boyhood friend recalled stumbling upon Jimmy in the woods, standing on a stump to practice his sermons.[7]

Charming yarns of Jones's boyhood are inevitably mingled with darker recollections, such as the allegation that he tortured and killed neighborhood cats, and went through a phase of deep interest in Hitler and the Nazis.⁸ Later, at a high school pep rally, the boy known for hectoring his classmates about hell and damnation performed a mock mass funeral for members of the opposing team.⁹ However, speculations about Jones's childhood are best left to armchair psychologists; there are plenty of more reliable firsthand accounts from his well-documented adult life that are far more illuminating than unusual anecdotes from what seems to have been a rather ordinary prewar childhood.

Jones was too young to fight in the Second World War, but the global conflagration provided a dramatic backdrop for his incipient political consciousness. Death and destruction were the news of the day. The events that finally brought the war to its end—the atomic bombings of Hiroshima and Nagasaki—were indelible memories for Jones, who was fourteen when Truman decreed the fateful detonations. Jones remained preoccupied by the idea of nuclear holocaust well into adulthood: it was an obsession that determined the trajectory of Peoples Temple, guiding it first to California and then to South America.

Lynetta separated from Big Jim in 1945 and took Jimmy with her to Richmond, a small city near the Ohio border where she could more easily find factory work. Jones was already a familiar sight around town: toward the end of his Lynn years, he hitchhiked into Richmond to preach on street corners in one of the city's African American neighborhoods. As he finished high school in a new city, Jones wavered between the ministry and a medical career. To help his mother defray expenses, he took an after-school job as an orderly at Reid Memorial Hospital. There he met a nurse named Marceline Baldwin, who became his sweetheart and later, his wife. Jones had already acquired a habit for self-promotion by the time he met Marceline. He made much of having to pull himself up by his bootstraps, which was true enough. But he also told her that although he was the school's star basketball player, he'd quit the team in protest after hearing his coach use a racial slur for black opponents. It was a complete fabrication, but one that caused Marceline to admire the courage of her new boyfriend's convictions.¹⁰

Jones and Marceline married in the spring of 1949 in a dual ceremony that included Marceline's sister and her fiancé. The Baldwins were a civically engaged, churchgoing Methodist family; the double wedding filled their church to capacity, and the mayor and members of the Richmond city council attended. By this time, however, Jones had come to share his mother's skepticism regarding organized religion: frustrated by American Christians' complacency with segregation, Jones had begun to study Marxism. He privately became a confirmed atheist.

A few months after the wedding, Jones moved to Bloomington and enrolled at the University of Indiana.[11] College wasn't a good fit for a contrarian and self-satisfied outcast like Jim Jones. His roommate Ken Lemmons disliked Jones's hypochondriacal malingering, and moved out after Jones allegedly tried to stab a hatpin through the bottom of his bunk bed in the middle of the night. Like the stories of childhood animal torture and the time Jones fired shots at one of his few high school friends, Lemmons's recollection suggests that at an early age, a deep misanthropy underlay Jones's professed humanitarianism.[12]

After quitting her job in Richmond, Marceline moved to Bloomington to join her husband. She briefly enrolled in the university, but it was her nurse's salary on which the young couple depended.[13] Early in their marriage, Jones confessed to a distressed Marceline that he was a Maoist as well as an atheist.[14] In later accounts of this period, he claimed to have "sought out" other Communists on campus, and recalled that his attendance at a Paul Robeson event in Chicago resulted in an FBI investigation into his subversive activities, during which his mother was interrogated on the floor of the factory where she worked.[15] A lack of proof suggests these were retrospective fabrications, but Jones's college transcripts bear out an early interest in socialism. During his second year at IU, Jones enrolled in Russian, second-semester world politics, Psychology of Personality, History of American Social Welfare, and a sociology course called Society and the Individual. Although he dropped several of his classes and pulled

C's in the others, Jones's coursework indicates a social and political consciousness that was already on the way to a deep romance with left-wing political radicalism. He withdrew from college after the second semester in 1951, briefly returned to Indiana University to study pre-law, and eventually graduated in 1961 from Butler University, a college affiliated with the Disciples of Christ.

The newlyweds did not enjoy the privilege of a happy marriage, and seldom ever would. Among the papers found in Jonestown and classi-fied by the FBI was a note Jones wrote to Marceline nearly thirty years after their union: "How horrible it is to be God's wife," he admitted to his long-suffering mate, "but you do it magnificently."[16] From the earliest days of their marriage, Jones's desire for control would brook no uncertainty or questioning from his wife. In addition to occasional intimidation and psychosadism, Jones ridiculed his wife's Christian faith as childish and naïve. Even her fear annoyed him. Marceline worried the marriage might be headed for divorce. She pleaded with her husband to join her at church. Jones eventually consented.

This was, for Marceline and many others, a lethal decision: a visit to the Methodist church was what inspired Jones to reconsider the ministry as his chosen profession. On a bulletin board in the church hallway, Jones discovered the Methodist Social Creed, which had just been adopted in 1952. The declaration positioned Methodism as the most liberal of the mainline Protestant denominations, and persuaded Jones that organized religion was perhaps not as useless as he thought. The established churches were not inherently corrupt: they had only fallen into an apathy and lethargy that bordered on heretical neglect of Christ's teachings. If truly embraced, the principles outlined in the social creed would require Methodists to engage in community ser-vice, work to alleviate poverty, and foster love and caring in the com-munity. Upon reflection, Jones realized that "infiltrating" the ministry would be the most effective way for him to advance his Marxist con-victions: Christian charity and Pentecostal ardor could be combined to achieve radical social change through the solidarity and strong social bonds that existed in communities of faith.¹⁷ This was a powerfully transformative idea that later crystallized into one of Jones's favorite maxims: "The ends justify the means."

So it was that in 1952, Jones applied to be a student pastor at Somerset Methodist Church. In his first sermon, he espoused a philosophy of applying Christian values to everyday life, and concluded that Christianity was incompatible with discrimination and segregation. After Jones's political agitation caused a deliberate schism within Somerset, his integrationist faction separated from the Methodist denomination and became Somerset Christian Assembly, which then dissolved and re-formed as Community Unity before Jones finally settled on a name: Peoples Temple Full Gospel Church.

Marceline persisted at her husband's side in spite of her continued foreboding. Obviously he was unstable. But what he needed, she reasoned, was her firm support. Marceline found new purpose in helping to run the Temple's first care home for the elderly. Her nursing degree, combined with the help of her retired parents, produced the income on which the Jones family subsisted in the early years of her husband's ministry, when Jones's tiny church could not afford to pay him a salary.

Meanwhile, Jones burnished his reputation on the Pentecostal lecture circuit, hitting the road to preach in cities across the Midwest. Marceline was startled to watch the faithful stream toward her husband after the conclusion of a sermon, in awe of his oratory and his apparently miraculous clairvoyance. Jones was able to call out facts about audience members he knew or suspected would be in attendance, dazzling them by identifying past and present ailments and problems. At a church convention in Columbus, Indiana, an elderly evangelist told Jones he was blessed with a gift. In fact, it was a skill he had cultivated through years of observation and imitation.¹⁸ By studying other Pentecostal ministers, Jones learned the timing and art of speaking in tongues, and quickly mastered the role of the enthusiastic pastor who held paternal authority over other adults. He knew how to elicit the energy that would lead to spontaneous hollering, trembling, and seizure by the Holy Spirit. To accomplish his feats of clairvoyance, Jones collected information by talking to people at conventions and taking copious notes for use in later demonstrations. Pentecostal revivals were full of familiar faces.

Under Jones's leadership, Peoples Temple became the first integrated church in Indianapolis, a city that like many in the industrialized North was rapidly undergoing dramatic changes stemming from postwar white flight. Jones literally went out of his way to make black friends, canvassing African American neighborhoods to invite poor blacks into his church, and from his church into his home. As a parallel strategy, Jones took his integrated congregation for visits to black churches around Indianapolis. When invited back to preach, Jones would bring the Temple's "interracial-interdenominational" choir to sing backup for his thundering oratory.

The gospel choir proved to be a highly effective instrument for sheep-stealing, one that Jones favored throughout the Temple's early days. It was the best showcase of his principles in action: a visual demonstration of how he wished to transform what Martin Luther King Jr. would famously call "one of the most segregated hours . . . in Christian America."[19] Hyacinth Thrash, a twice-divorced middle-aged woman who lived with her sister, Zipporah Edwards, joined the church after the sisters saw Jones preaching on local television. Thrash was disillusioned with the churches she'd attended in Indianapolis, which like most black churches preached a life of patient forbearance. It had been a decade since she attended services. But after seeing Jones's choir on TV, she and her sister began attending the Temple. They remained members until its final day.[20]

As former Temple members later attested, Jones would use any tactic to poach adherents from any church, anywhere.[21] One of the larger hauls in the Indiana years consisted of a group of nearly twenty self-identified spiritualists. Even after the congregation expanded into a larger and more formal venue—the former synagogue on Tenth and Delaware—Pentecostal healing remained an integral part of the Temple's services, simply because it drew in so many new recruits. But as Jones shifted the Temple's outward focus onto crypto-socialist activism in the old Social Gospel style, he relied less and less on exhausting faith-healing claptrap. Eventually he confined his miracles to a special Thursday night service. Like Andrew Jackson Davis a century before, Jones had wearied of performing parlor tricks, and yearned to translate the spiritual attraction he held over his followers into a broad-based movement for social change.

Those who joined the church in the late 1950s and onward were explicitly signing up for an interracial congregation that was deeply involved in social justice work. Members tithed heavily to fund the Temple's social-service programs, and church socials became occasions for flaunting the Temple's integrated extended family to prospective new members and invited guests. Jones encouraged interracial friendships, work assignments, and living arrangements among his congregants. As a result of his work to alleviate poverty and racism, the young Reverend Jones was named to the "human relations honor roll" of the *Indianapolis Recorder.* It marked the beginning of his turbulent parapolitical career.

35. DIVINE ASPIRATIONS

L IKE MOST IN HIS PROFESSION, especially those involved in the black churches, Jones was aware of Father Divine. His knowledge, however, was based on hearsay and rumors that the Peace Mission was a "harem run by a demonically possessed immoral person," and therefore a fraudulent operation of little interest to him or to Peoples Temple.[1] He may have acquired this impression from Sara Harris.

Another book changed his mind. After an inspirational reading of Rufus Moseley's *Manifest Victory* (1941), Jones began to take a serious interest in Divine's activities. Moseley was a white Pentecostal minister of some renown on the Midwestern revival circuit Jones traversed. Moseley taught a mystical variant of Christian holiness doctrine that dovetailed with the God-in-the-body doctrine espoused by Divine, the Vine, and Father Jehovia. *Manifest Victory* reflected positively on Father Divine, with whom Moseley was personally acquainted. In the summer of 1956, Jones left Indianapolis, taking Marceline with him to Philadelphia, where they meant to investigate the Peace Mission for themselves.

At this point in his career, Jones theoretically disapproved of any religious group that indulged in excessive veneration of a living leader: it didn't seem very socialist. His doubts were further raised in Philadelphia. Upon arrival to a Peace Mission hotel, a concierge informed Jones that he and Marceline would not be allowed to occupy the same room. The couple decided to lodge elsewhere, and were so put off by this oddity that they nearly concluded their reconnaissance mission then and there. However, after spending time with the other congregations he intended to visit while in Pennsylvania, Jones decided to give the Peace Mission another chance. This broad-mindedness notwithstanding, Jones admitted to feeling "revulsion" as he entered the Circle Mission Church on Broad and Catharine. But the kindness of the angels slowly wore down his defenses. Although initially "nauseated" by their meek veneration of Father Divine, Jones wrote that he "could not help but see a peace and love that prevailed generally throughout the throng of enthusiastic worshipers. Every face was aglow with smiles and radiant friendliness."[2] After returning to Indianapolis, Jones took out ads in one of the city's black newspapers to advertise "2 free fellowship meals" in addition to the miracles he worked several times weekly.

Jones's visit to Peace Mission headquarters inspired him to return repeatedly over the coming years. Considering its distance from his flock in Indiana, this was no small task. Father Divine recognized the young minister's dedication by allowing Jones to preach to the angels in Philadelphia. In Divine's private office at Woodmont, the like-minded evangelists discussed the Divine Cooperative Plan, preoccupations with overpopulation, and racial discrimination. Re-creations of these meetings for a made-for-TV film depict Divine—played by James Earl Jones—as a sinister mastermind who makes ambiguously lurid recommendations for Jim Jones to take sexual advantage of his followers. Although Jones certainly went on to do just that, there is no conclusive evidence that Father Divine ever strayed from his celibate marriages to either of the two Mothers Divine.

Jones saw that in the Peace Mission, the angels had demonstrated that the collectivism practiced by the apostolic church could be successfully implemented in modern industrial society. In the extensions he visited, Jones observed a socialist society organized around love and humanistic values. The corrupting influence of consumerist capitalism had largely been driven out of the angels' daily lives. Although he continued to disagree with several Peace Mission precepts—namely the doctrine that Father Divine was God, as well as the angels' belief in their own immortality—Jones wrote that "there is so much good latent within this group that the presence of evil in the world would be completely subjected to God if the good of this movement was generally practiced and emphasized by all honest Christians."³ Although he never developed prohibitions as consistent as those enforced by the Koreshan Unity and the Peace Mission, Jones developed an antipathy for marriage and procreation that originated with his visit to the Peace Mission.

These attitudes were not the only things Jones borrowed from the Peace Mission. In "scores" of interviews they conducted with Peace Mission members over the years, Jones and Marceline heard testimony from former prostitutes, alcoholics, addicts, criminals, and vagabonds who had reformed their lives by following Father Divine's example. After witnessing the way that testimonials strengthened group identity and endowed the black messiah with mythological powers of retribution and saving grace, Jones made confessions of sin and declarations of salvation a central part of Peoples Temple meetings. Public testimonials of conversion experiences date at least to the Great Awakening, and their resuscitation in Jones's church would not have raised eyebrows were it not for the fact that parishioners were encouraged to credit Jones personally with their salvation, as the angels did with Father Divine. Temple members testified about cures bestowed on themselves and their loved ones, whom Jones rescued from alcoholism, drug dependency, and numerous other maladies. They attributed lucky breaks and fortuitous coincidences to Jones's ability to bless them with miracles.

Although these testimonials initially functioned as they did in the Peace Mission, Jones quickly became dissatisfied with encomium about his healing powers, which he knew were faked. He realized that in addition to their inspirational value, confessions could have a disciplinary function, much as they had for Faithful Mary. Unable to be placated by minor confessions of transgression, Jones created an "interrogation committee" tasked with ferreting out more serious misdeeds and confronting the offenders in "counseling" sessions. Other Peace Mission adoptions were more conspicuous and less adulterated: Jones began encouraging his parishioners to refer to him and Marceline as "Father" and "Mother"—a practice that endured to the Temple's final days. During sermons, Jones employed Divine terminology that had found its way from Cyrus Teed to George Baker via Father Jehovia: "I have come in the name of Jesus," he told his audience, "I have come in the fathership degree."[4] Jones even floated an endorsement of Divine celibacy, instructing followers to adopt orphans instead of procreating. Although the initial flirtation with celibacy was ended by Marceline's subsequent pregnancy, Jones later returned to celibacy—and abortion—as revolutionary tactics for controlling the costs of communal living and limiting the Temple's contribution to global overpopulation.

A more direct replication of Peace Mission tactics came in February 1960, when the Temple opened a free restaurant for the indigent of Indianapolis. Associate minister Archie Ijames and his wife, an African American couple attracted to the Temple for its social mission rather than its ecclesiastical trappings, took charge of the kitchen and managed to serve thousands of meals each month on a shoestring budget.[5] They bought discounted meat and produce and found free food at the railroad yard. Diners at the Temple cafeteria were mostly poor whites, city squatters, and the alcoholics who drifted through town on the railroad. The Temple's religious message was kept to a minimum in the Temple eatery, and no one indulged in illusions that the desperate men and women the restaurant served would one day become upstanding members of Peoples Temple.

Jones had also been impressed by Father Divine's apparent lack of interest in the scriptures. Although Divine sometimes mentioned specific verses from the Holy Writ, he was seldom seen with a Bible and much preferred to freestyle his way through public-speaking engagements. Readings from the ancient Word of God were hardly necessary when Divine was personally available to speak new pronouncements at Holy Communion banquets. Even when Divine was not physically present, and when he later became too infirm to dispense additional wisdom, the angels listened to recordings of his classic messages, as they still do today.

Jones admired the Divinite position with regard to the Scriptures, but immediately took Divine's views to new extremes. Jones began to disrespect the Holy Bible publicly at Temple services. The Good Book, he assured his congregants, was full of errors and lies. Jones would literally throw the Bible across the sanctuary for dramatic effect, and told his audience they need not be bound by the same tome used to justify slavery and colonization. Ironically, Jones justified this rough treatment of God's Word by citing the Bible itself. His favorite passage was from II Corinthians 3:6, which reads in part: "for the letter killeth, but the spirit giveth life."

When it came to weaning his Pentecostal congregation off their Bible thumping, Jones did not hesitate to call out black parishioners in particular. He told African American Bible clutchers they were collaborating in their own oppression. "The blacks amaze me the most," Jones chided. "They'll hold onto that black book. And King James was the first one that sent the Good Ship Jesus to Africa, to bring us back in slave chains."[6] This indictment of King James as the commissioner of both the vernacular Bible and the transatlantic slave trade is one that Jones repeated often during the historical segments of his sermons. Recruits from old-school black churches, as well as a good many of the white fundamentalists who spent their lives relying on the Bible for insight and comfort, were dismayed by Jones's cavalier behavior. Some left the church, but others were so committed to "Father" that they eventually accepted these difficult teachings. The Bible-tossing stunt became a standby in Peoples Temple services well into the 1970s, and the verse from Corinthians later adorned a Temple pamphlet.

Undermining the Bible by preaching its corruption by monarchists and colonizers allowed Jones to pick and choose the parts of the Scriptures that suited him. Aside from the story of Exodus, most of the Old Testament was useless to Jones. The New Testament, on the other hand, offered an authoritative foundation for the Temple's increasingly open embrace of socialism. Following in the tradition established by the Public Universal Friend, Ann Lee, Thomas Lake Harris, Cyrus Teed, Father Divine, and others, Jones often quoted the vague descriptions of the primitive church found in the Acts of the Apostles. Like his predecessors, Jones relished pointing out that before it was corrupted by Rome and other worldly powers that arrogated spiritual authority—be they kings or slaveholders—the first Christian church held all property in common. But unlike eighteenth- and nineteenth-century American messiahs, who either preceded or carefully avoided Marxism, Jones spoke favorably of international socialism.

. . .

DURING ONE OF HIS latter visits to Woodmont, Jones recognized that Divine's "ultimate sacrifice" was making its unmistakable approach. The time had come for Jones to make his move. According to an account Mother Divine published after Jones's death, the minister went to Woodmont in July 1958 to propose his leadership of the Peace Mission in the event that Father Divine decided to abandon his earthly body. Divine politely declined this bold request but appeared untroubled by it. To Mother Divine, however, it was a portentous warning that momentarily revealed Jones's egotistical duplicity.[7]

Jones continued visiting Woodmont as though nothing untoward had occurred. The Divines, by angelic custom, continued to welcome him. Nevertheless, Jones's behavior began to trouble Father Divine and his Spotless Virgin Bride. Jim and Marceline had begun adopting children in 1954; in 1958, they began adopting children of different racial backgrounds—including three Korean orphans and the first African American child to be adopted by whites in the state of Indiana. Around the same time, Marceline gave birth to Jones's naturally conceived son,

Stephan. Jones's integrated family was his way of responding to the "flower garden of integration" he observed in the Peace Mission.[8] He famously called his household a "rainbow family," and advertised it whenever he got the chance. The Divines were too shrewd not to realize that Jones wasn't going to take "no" for an answer.

In response to the young minister's obvious designs on their movement, Father and Mother Divine informally adopted a six-year-old Mexican American boy called Tommy Garcia. His mother, a skilled photographer named Georgia Garcia, had discovered the Peace Mission in Los Angeles and left her abusive husband in order to join Father Divine in Philadelphia. Although she took her two children with her, Georgia Garcia surrendered her offspring upon arrival to the Divine Lorraine and renounced all prior kinship relationships. While his sister was sent to a Peace Mission elsewhere in Philadelphia, to be raised communally among the brothers and sisters, Tommy was whisked off to Woodmont, outfitted with a new suit, and placed in the care of a valet called Happy Love, who chaperoned the boy to school and oversaw his daily routines. Father Divine, already aged and somewhat infirm, began to take a vital interest in Tommy and enjoyed playing the role of a father figure in a more traditional sense. The Divine intent was for Tommy to inherit the spiritual leadership of the Peace Mission. The boy's Mexican American ancestry was an important feature in this scheme: since World War II, Father Divine had advocated the union of all nations in the Americas. With a black American patriarch, a white Canadian matriarch, and an heir of Mexican lineage, the Divines had put the theory into practice within their own regal nuclear family—albeit within an organization that forbade any recognition of family ties or racial distinctions.

36. THE MINISTER WANDERS

AFTER THE CUBAN REVOLUTION OF 1959, Jones became impatient with Father Divine's longevity. Tired of waiting around to inherit the Peace Mission, he decided to establish his own socialist Promised Land in Indiana. In public, Jones continued to state that it was his goal to counter godless Communism with Christian communalism. If the people, including his people, desired the fairness and justice of collective living, Jones declared, then it would be better to satisfy those desires with a wholesome, American version of that life.

With this stated goal, Jones left for Cuba in 1960. His plan was to recruit forty Cuban families to return with him to Indiana, where they would operate farms purchased by Peoples Temple—a scheme obviously copied from Divine's Ulster County kingdom. While in Cuba, Jones focused his recruiting efforts on blacks: he believed Afro-Cubans would wish to escape the Castro regime, making it easier to persuade them to move to infamously racist Indiana, where the modern Ku Klux Klan had established its headquarters.[1] Jones abandoned the plan after failing to convince more than a single Cuban to join him.

Following his return to Indiana, Jones retrained his sights on reforming Indianapolis through more conventional political means. He had begun courting politicians as early as 1956, when he placed ads in the *Indianapolis Recorder* to endorse black candidates for office.[2] It was not until four years later, however, that Jones finally obtained political office for himself. In 1960, the newly elected mayor of Indianapolis created the position of human rights commissioner and appointed Jones to the post. The salary for the position was only $7,000 per year; it was clearly not meant to be considered a full-time job, but that was how Jones treated it.[3] He quickly transformed a PR sinecure into a high-visibility integration campaign by using his position to bully and embarrass discriminatory businesses. Jones enjoyed remarkable success in the role, considering he only held it for seven months: he publicly shamed five Indianapolis restaurants that were refusing to serve black patrons, forcing them to change their policies, and helped to desegregate the Riverside Amusement Park.[4] Jones also used his post as an excuse to speak before the local branches of the NAACP and the Urban League—two potential sources of new recruits.

Assisting the new commissioner in his human rights campaign was Ross Case, a Disciples in Christ minister who had learned of Jones and his congregation from a Peoples Temple member attending the same spiritual camp meeting as Case and his wife. Case had integrated his home congregation, and was so impressed by the Temple's incipient practice of Christian communalism that he moved to Indianapolis to become an associate minister in August 1961. In addition to taking the burden off Jones by picking up the slack on home visits to Temple members, Case brought intellectual rigor to the Temple; an important effect of his presence was to tame Jones's increasingly open talk of communism back down into discussions of "communalism" and "apostolic socialism." Without this counterweight and incrementalism, Jones might not have succeeded in expanding the congregation in the way that he did.

Case became the fourth associate minister Jones appointed to share his duties at the church, joining Archie Ijames, Russell Winberg, and Jack Beam. Although Peoples Temple was notable for its predominantly female leadership in its final years, Jones was cautious about diversifying the staff along gender lines in Indiana. As the parson's wife, Marceline occupied a powerful position in the church's administration. And as soon as she joined, Patty Cartmell became one of Jones's closest advisers. But both women's roles were informal.

It was just as well that Jones counted on a reliable staff of associate ministers: in autumn of 1961, Father was on the verge of a nervous breakdown provoked by the demands of his active congregation, his humanitarian work, and the deluge of hate mail and threatening phone calls he received as a result of his integration campaign. Although some of the letters and calls were genuine—as suggested by the fact that Marceline was once spat on in public with her black son—Jones inflated the persecution and threats to galvanize his followers' resentment of racist whites. Jones also invited some of the controversy himself: under the auspices of the Human Rights Commission, Jones struck up an epistolary exchange with Dan Burros, a lieutenant of the American Nazi Party, ostensibly to convince Burros of his errors. The Nazi replied courteously, thanking Jones for his "good intentions" and congratulating him for having the good sense to understand his enemies. On Nazi Party stationery, Burros declined Jones's invitation to debate, observing that their positions were irreconcilable, and that Jones's integration work would "mean the end of the White Race." Jones forwarded the letter to the *Indianapolis Times*. It was excellent publicity.[5]

. . .

AS JONES TOOK ON ever more responsibilities in the effort to fashion himself into a pioneering leader at the vanguard of the civil rights movement, real physical exhaustion collided with his old habit of malingering. At Temple events, Jones suffered dramatic fainting spells, sometimes clutching his chest as he crashed to the floor. Marceline was often capable of reviving her husband from these spells with shots of "vitamin B12"—which no doubt contained a serious dose of speed. As his collapses grew more frequent, Jones's advisers finally convinced him to see a doctor, who diagnosed him with an ulcer and commanded the minister to take a leave of absence.

Reverend Jones resigned as the mayor's human rights commissioner and agreed to take time away from Peoples Temple, scheduling a family vacation to Hawaii. He traveled there by way of Guyana, a remote British colony he wished to explore as a possible site for relocation of his entire movement. Influenced by the spiritualists the Temple had recruited in Indiana, and by the clairvoyant healer Edgar Cayce, Jones had begun to hear prophecy from supernatural beings he called "the messengers."[6] Their most urgent communication concerned the imminent commencement of nuclear war with a strike on nearby Chicago. After sharing the prophecy with his associate ministers, Jones became convinced of the need to relocate Peoples Temple to safety.

Not long after Jones left Guyana for Hawaii, *Esquire* magazine published a story titled "Nine Places to Hide"—a list of geographic sites most insulated from the dangers of nuclear war.[7] Five of the nine sites were in the Americas: Eureka, California; Guadalajara, Mexico; Belo Horizonte, Brazil; Mendoza, Argentina; and Chile's Central Valley. Jones decided to try Brazil first, and returned via Cuba, where he claimed to have met Fidel Castro.[8] The sojourn to Brazil ended up lasting two years. Jones and his family construed their stay as an extended mission trip, which was paid for by the Temple. Yet although the Joneses befriended another American missionary family and joined in their service to the poor, evangelism was not what most interested Jones in South America. Chaperoned by a Brazilian woman, he explored the local variants of Spiritism and candomblé, an Afro-Brazilian syncretic religion. Bonnie Malmin, the daughter of the missionary couple the Joneses befriended in Brazil, recalled that Jones began to speak to her about reincarnation. He told Bonnie that in a past life, she had been his and Marceline's daughter. As for his own past, Jones claimed to be the reincarnation of Ikhnaton, the heretical Egyptian monotheist. He later reincarnated as the Buddha, Jesus, and Lenin.[9]

In 1963, Jones moved his family from Belo Horizonte to Rio, where he taught in a local school. By this time, Jones's parishioners were begging him to come back. In Father's absence, associate minister Russell Winberg was running the church into the ground: he and his wife had steered the congregation firmly back into a conservative Pentecostal format. The lack of healings bored some members and the reintroduction of the Bible alienated others. Social services declined and discussion of apostolic communism vanished. Winberg was simply not as captivating as Father Jones. As the Temple hemorrhaged membership and money, Ijames and other stalwarts pleaded with the Joneses to return. The church finances weren't all they were concerned about: Temple members had endured the Cuban Missile Crisis while their spiritual leader resided in a nuclear safe zone.

Jones heeded the call to save the church he'd founded, but the Temple's days in Indianapolis were numbered. Ross Case and Jack Beam had already gone separately to California to evaluate the possibility of relocating Peoples Temple to the safe zone near Eureka. While the Beams settled in the East Bay, Case had gone north to Ukiah, a small city a few hours north of San Francisco. Although well south of Eureka, Ukiah was far enough from any targets to be spared the worst of the fallout. It was also where Case managed to find a job. As the seat of Mendocino County, Ukiah was home to government entities where Temple members would be able to procure employment.

Case had left Indiana in June 1963, as Temple leadership collapsed into infighting in Jones's absence. As he placed physical and psychological distance between himself and Peoples Temple, Case began to doubt his involvement. After Jones returned to the States, he adopted the habit of equating his will with God's commandments when giving instructions to his associate ministers. This did not sit well with Case, whose religious education had taught him to respect Christ above all else—certainly above other mortals. Case still considered Jones a prophet, but he was disconcerted by the reverend's authoritarianism and pretensions to quasi-divinity. Case and his wife drifted from the Temple. Although Case and Jones later decided to put their differences behind them and reunite in December 1964, the reconciliation did not last long. Once again Case had become worried that Jones was attempting to usurp the role of Christ in the minds and hearts of his followers.[10] And he was right.

In support of his belief that Jones had received a special mission from God, Temple member Harold Cordell wrote Case to itemize Jones's many accurate prophecies, including the "liberation" of Temple member Eva Pugh through the death of her husband, Jim, who was a hardy forty-eight years old at the time of his unexpected death. According to Cordell, Jones had also correctly prophesied President Kennedy's assassination, the "crisis in Hanoi," and an Eastern Airlines plane crash. With this track record, the nuclear detonation that Jones predicted would occur at 3:09 on the sixteenth of an unnamed month and year would certainly come to pass.[11] Cordell continued, "James Jones is certainly a deliverer and the same Anointed Spirit or Christ spirit that we know resided in Jesus. I feel by seeing him acting as by God and hearing him teach and oppose the ungodliness of pseudo-religions today that he is one of the greatest prophets and messengers that have ever appeared on this earth."[12] Disgusted by this grandiosity, Case finally broke with Jones in February of 1965. By the time a caravan of 140 Temple faithful arrived to Redwood Valley from Indiana that summer, the former associate minister was considered a traitor.

Enthusiasm for the move to California had taken on fresh urgency after the messengers revealed to Jones that a nuclear strike on the United States would take place in July of 1967. In the two years that remained, the Temple needed to establish its new home in a safe zone and lay aside provisions for the coming nuclear winter. The exodus from Indiana broke up some families and caused strain in others, when unwilling members had to choose between joining the migration to California or remaining separated from their loved ones by thousands of miles.

After trekking across the country, Peoples Temple settled in Redwood Valley, just north of Ukiah. By most accounts, these were the golden years of Peoples Temple and the promise it held for transforming American society. In California, Jones gathered about himself the devoted core of his following. Those who went west were true believers in integrated apostolic socialism: they were men and women who quit their jobs, sold their homes, left their relatives behind, and in some cases, abandoned their spouses and children to follow their leader to the edge of the continent.

Some made the journey because they could not bear to be parted from their relatives. Others were completely devoted to Father above all else, and believed as Patty Cartmell did: as she liked to say, Jones was "the only God you'll ever see." Although the meaning of this phrase would change over time to encompass literal deification, it originally meant that unlike the invisible, distant Creator—the falsified, fairy-tale deity Jones called the Sky God—Temple members, and Jones in particular, embodied Christ's godliness by resurrecting the lifestyle of the apostolic church. It was another variation on the Perfectionist theology that endowed John Humphrey Noyes with a semi-deified stature at the communist Oneida colony in nineteenth-century New York. Later, Jones would put a finer point on Cartmell's turn of phrase: he began to call himself "God Socialism" within a few years of his arrival in California.

37. CALIFORNIA MYSTICS

A COMBINATION OF STRATEGY and felicitous accident led Peoples Temple to resettle near another communal religious society. Jones, Beam, and church stalwart Joe Phillips, whose son Jones had supposedly healed of a heart defect, went to Ukiah for a reconnaissance mission after Case's defection. In the restaurant of the Palace Hotel in downtown Ukiah, they overheard a group of men and women talking at the next table. After eavesdropping on their conversation, Jones introduced himself, and learned that his new friends were the Board of Elders of Christ's Church of the Golden Rule.

As the Temple aspired to be, CCGR was a religiously oriented communal society that possessed considerable assets. These included the Ridgewood Ranch in Willets, an estate just north of Ukiah renowned for its thoroughbreds: it was the home and final resting place of the famed racehorse Seabiscuit. No doubt, the church's valuable land was part of what appealed to Jones: it was no Peace Mission, but the 16,000-acre ranch had plenty of room and available structures to house the Temple contingent scheduled to arrive that summer. In fact, Ridgewood Ranch was but a faint shadow of what had quite recently been a real-estate empire. Christ's Church of the Golden Rule boasted an impressive if checkered record of accomplishment since its founding. Jones quickly discovered that its history was a playbook from which he and the Temple had much to learn.

Christ's Church of the Golden Rule was incorporated in the winter of 1943–44 by members of Mankind United, a quasireligious pacifist society founded by Arthur L. Bell, an ex-Christian Scientist and belated Bellamyite Nationalist born in 1900. Bell claimed to possess special knowledge accumulated by fifteen years of private study in something called the International Institute of Universal Research and Administration. This was a secret school founded with the combined wealth of a league of humanitarians who preferred to be known only as "The Sponsors." The institution they started was dedicated to determining how human relationships and society might be reordered to reflect Christ's Golden Rule. In practice, this involved organizing something called the Universal Service Corporation—a vaguely Christianized variant of Bellamy's Industrial Army, in which members would live communally, as in the apostolic church.[1] Bell, who used twenty other aliases, was chosen to be one of the Sponsors' evangelist disciples, known as the Vigilantes. He was the only Vigilante to come forward publicly.[2]

The Sponsors were sworn enemies of the Hidden Rulers, a cabal of global elite who were busy masterminding an international conspiracy to use financial markets to enslave the vast majority of the human race by gradually depriving them of education and prohibiting the practice of Christianity. When these two impediments to slavery were finally removed, the Hidden Rulers would confine their subjects to fixed castes and force them to live out their days in underground cities not unlike those depicted in Fritz Lang's 1927 film *Metropolis*.

In the midst of the Great Depression, Bell had little trouble finding men and women with time on their hands and an interest in crafting a new world order. He gathered most of his followers from the various occult and metaphysical societies that proliferated in California in the early twentieth century, many of which were affiliated with far-right or far-left politics. At the movement's peak, Bell could regularly draw audiences of several hundred people almost anywhere he went in California.[3] Dozens of branches of Mankind United, called "bureaus," cropped up in cities across California and Oregon. Bell resided in San Francisco, and although Mankind United spread up and down the

Pacific Coast, the San Francisco Bay remained the center of its activities. Greater Los Angeles, home to twenty-five bureaus, was another area of dense concentration. In Southern California, the central node of Mankind United activity was the Faith-Grace Bureau, founded by a follower of Father Divine named Mrs. Bess Delight Comfort.[4] Styling himself the Voice of the Right Idea, Bell was able to visit many of the bureaus personally, often claiming to use the "power of mind" to effect his "translevitation" between them. In fact, he used body doubles, which allowed him to preside over three or four bureaus simultaneously. For added mystique, Bell allowed rumors to circulate that he was the second coming of Edward Bellamy.[5]

As Jim Jones would later do, Bell imparted an air of conspiracy and intrigue to Mankind United that endowed the bureaus with a grandiose sense of their importance. As one former bureau manager stated:

> Bell always kept us in a state of suspense. We never knew
> why we did most of the things we did. If we ever questioned
> any of his orders, he would inform us 'You don't know why
> this is to be done, but you will see. Trust me and the Spon-
> sors, there is a purpose. You'll see later that this is necessary.'
> So we did it. [. . .] Big things were in the making, and we
> were a part of them. . . . He always kept us occupied . . .
> always kept us busy, so busy that we couldn't think and place
> things in perspective.[6]

Members of Mankind United often had little to do besides evangelizing the cause. They distributed handbills outside their meetings and in neighborhoods surrounding the venues where Bell was scheduled to speak. Their handouts often bore the provocative phrase, "We are not cattle—nor need we be slaughtered merely because of the contempt of our political rulers." Members focused their recruitment efforts on those who had been ruined by the Great Depression and felt acutely the vulnerability of the individual worker in industrial society. They placed particular emphasis on elders, and condemned capitalism for discarding seniors as useless burdens. For this reason, Mankind United attracted thousands who had previously been involved in organizing on behalf of the Townsend Plan and Upton Sinclair's EPIC campaigns.

Christ's Church of the Golden Rule functioned essentially as the communal "inner order" of Mankind United: membership required the donation of all worldly possessions to the commonwealth and obedience to the Universal Service Corporation. "Student ministers" were expected to relocate to one of the church's communes, also known as "Laboratories for Abundant Living." Those who went communal were expected to cut all ties with the outside world, but their example was meant to serve as a demonstration to the world that "practical Christianity"—that is, apostolic socialism—could be obtained in the twentieth century.

Although Bell moved between several lavishly furnished residencies, life on the communes was austere. Many were overcrowded. This was especially true of the "seminary" building located on Silver Avenue in San Francisco, where student ministers for the forty-eight Bay Area CCGR "church projects" lived.[7] "Project" was the euphemism used to designate the communal businesses that made up the CCGR empire. In the Laboratories for Abundant Living, smoking and drinking were banned, vegetarianism was in vogue, and the student ministers often worked at their "projects" for twelve hours daily. The wages of communism were room and board. The $3,000 universal salaries promised by the Sponsors remained hypothetical; communards instead received a $5 monthly allowance.

Bell was an encouraging, but stern taskmaster. As he told student ministers: "This is a crusade, not a Sunday School picnic." But communal life brought church members a notion of belonging and a feeling of security not available anywhere else in the outside world—not even in their families. The elective family of CCGR was much stronger: members lived together, worked together, ate together, studied together, and shared the belief that they were working to bring about a better tomorrow. At its peak, there were at least 850 communal members.[8]

Christ's Church of the Golden Rule was eventually attacked by the state of California: the state attempted to oust Bell as the sole trustee and appoint a receiver to administer the sale of church properties in order to restitute damages claimed by disaffected members. To pay its legal fees, CCGR began a slow retreat, abandoning its southern empire and retrenching in the Bay Area and points north. Bell stepped down from leadership of the movement in 1951, and the church continued to decline until it was confined to a few rural projects in Northern California. The final prophecy issued by the Voice of the Right Idea was that those who remained faithful to the Universal Service Corporation would be "translated" to another planetary system where they would achieve immortality in perfected bodies and live in a world that corresponded to the one imagined by Christ.[9]

When Jones chanced upon CCGR in 1965, the movement was badly in need of new blood. It was a remarkable stroke of luck: just as Jones had given up on commandeering the resources of the Peace Mission, a landed communal society safely within the nuclear safe zone seemed to be ripe for a takeover. Located just twenty minutes north of Ukiah in Willits, California, CCGR was an important early ally to Jones and his people, some of whom found housing in Willits. After learning that other congregations had declined to rent their facilities to Peoples Temple due to their alleged racial prejudices against Jones's integrated congregation, CCGR invited Jones to use their community schoolhouse for Temple meetings. There the Temple held two meetings every Sunday, separated by a midday communal feast. It was an arrangement that lasted approximately three years.

As had occurred earlier with the Peace Mission, Jones envied the solidarity and group morale instilled by the communal lifestyle he observed at the CCGR ranch in Willits. He began to adapt CCGR traditions into Peoples Temple rituals, and emphasized the two groups' common goals in preparation for a second run at a merger with a more established communal church. Imitating Mankind United, Peoples Temple dabbled in vegetarianism and venerated its elders. During the period in which the Temple held its meetings in the CCGR school-house, Jones lifted freely from Mankind United lore in his sermons. His terminology was slightly adjusted: Jones's "messengers," for example, came to resemble the Sponsors and Vigilantes. Garry Lambrev, among the first of the California recruits to Peoples Temple, recalled:

> Jim would talk about the messengers a lot in the early days. When I talk about early days they're basically the first three years I was there: '66, '67, '68. Later he made few if any references to them, at least in public. And he would say, you know, "I'm a channel of the divine, but I'm in a chain of command in which I'm the recipient of orders just as you're the recipient of my orders. And for things to go well, we have to understand and to listen, and understand and obey. And my orders cover a whole lot more territory than your orders do, and I've got a lot more responsibility on me, but I'm still a servant and I depend on the messengers."[10]

As usual, Jones was speaking the language of those he wished to convert. Allusions to the messengers and to an occult chain of command were intended to convince members of CCGR who attended Temple meetings that he was another of the Vigilantes.

Jones realized that vintage metaphysics and mysticism held crossover appeal for California spiritual seekers like Lambrev, as well as members of CCGR. Metaphysics had remained a serious subject of study in Christ's Church of the Golden Rule. In the mid-1960s, when Peoples Temple arrived to California, some of those at Ridgewood Ranch were engaged in deep study of the writings of Edgar Cayce, considered the fountainhead of modern New Age thought by scholars of the occult.[11] Jones recognized an affinity with Cayce. Like Andrew Jackson Davis, Cayce had begun as a clairvoyant faith healer. He later cemented his reputation as a prophet of the New Age with his writings on reincarnation. Lambrev, a bibliophile who studied history at Stanford, recalls that in addition to *California Cult*, a study of Mankind United and CCGR published in 1958, Jones borrowed his copy of *There Is a River*, a biography of Edgar Cayce written by a patient Cayce had diagnosed and cured. On its first page, *There Is a River* compares Cayce to Franz Anton Mesmer's disciple Marquis de Puységur—and to Andrew Jackson Davis.[12] With this discovery, Jones found additional key referents for the persona he crafted in the early days of his California ministry, installing Cayce and Bell beneath Father Divine, who ranked just below Mao, Lenin, and Christ. From then on, it was natural for Jones to speak often and publicly about reincarnation, which soon occupied an integral part of the Temple belief system. As he had done in Brazil, Jones revealed his past reincarnations as the Buddha, Jesus, and Lenin. This time, he made the revelation to his entire congregation.

Jones realized that many of those drawn to Peoples Temple by his swerve toward interfaith mysticism had gifts of spiritual intuition that complemented his own. Lambrev was among them: he recalls how on at least one occasion, Jones enlisted him in identifying the past life of another parishioner. On the way into a service, Jones pulled Lambrev aside and told him that the Messengers had disclosed that Lambrev knew the identity of a woman Jones had seen in a vision, speaking to an assembly of people. Lambrev pictured the woman Jones described and instantly knew who she was: Harriet Tubman. Later during the service, Jones asked one of the Midwestern stalwarts, the gruff widow Eva Pugh, to rise. With the congregation looking on, Jones told Pugh that the Messengers had revealed that she was the reincarnation of Harriet Tubman. Pugh was greatly pleased. Occasions like these fortified parishioners' sense that Jones indeed had some kind of spiritual gift.[13] Whether meant as encomium—or in the case of unflattering past lives, as reproach—the identification of Temple members' past lives had the effect of reinforcing Jones's message that his followers were a spiritual elect. With so many reincarnated dignitaries in their midst, how could they believe otherwise?

Looking back, Lambrev sees that Jones adopted Eastern ideas like reincarnation as part of "the sort of Theosophical merging into New Age" that was occurring in the late 1960s in California. Jones's New Age ramblings also resumed the spiritual Darwinism of Thomas Lake Harris, John Humphrey Noyes, and Cyrus Teed. He identified his clairvoyant powers with a superior stage of evolution he had gained, and to which he sought to elevate his followers. Echoing Father Divine, Jones told his followers that his evolved consciousness allowed him privileged access to what he alternately called the "Universal Mind Principle," "Universal Mind Substance," "the Infinite Mind," "the Hundredfold Consciousness"—or for short, "The Consciousness" and "The Principle."[14] Because Jones equated Universal Mind Principle (etc.) with apostolic socialism, his claim to be a chosen medium for its expression on Earth led back to the Temple doctrine of Jones's super-human stature. In this context, the extreme sacrifices that Jones made for "the cause" were understood by rank-and-file members as proof that he was the living manifestation of apostolic socialism. Or as Jones took to saying, "I am God Socialism."

Jones combined proclamations of his tangible divinity with polemic against the violent "Sky God" described in the Bible. The notion of an all-knowing, benevolent, and ultimately good God, Jones taught, was a vain superstition peddled by Christian ministers anxious to distract their listeners from the obvious contradictions contained in the Bible, and thereby uphold the status quo. Jones rejected orthodox Christian theodicy arguments, which hold that evils present in the world operate according to parts of God's plan that are inscrutable to mortals. According to God Socialism, this was an old canard favored by white racists, colonialists, and capitalist oppressors who wished to keep the poor and downtrodden in line. As Jones explained, the irascible and vindictive Sky God of the Old Testament was an impostor who ruled a fallen world that for centuries had degenerated into a perversely cruel and exploitative economic system known as modern capitalism. In this framework, Jones positioned himself as the enlightened gnostic in a world betrayed by a priestly class that preferred to worship wealth and illusion.

Most of the poor and socially marginalized people Jones drew into Peoples Temple required little convincing that they lived in a fallen world. Jones had only to point to the injustices and humiliations that the vast majority of his congregants had experienced directly: intergenerational poverty, racial discrimination, sexism, homophobia, and drug addictions induced by social exclusion and spiritual despair. Many of the Temple elders were born in the Jim Crow South before their families migrated to find jobs in Indianapolis and the other Northern cities Jones canvassed. They had suffered privation, witnessed lynchings, and were denied education and political enfranchisement. To these injustices was added the threat of civilizational annihilation by nuclear weapons, merely because greedy capitalists could not bring themselves to live in the same world as Communism.

Rather than reserve enlightened and deific existence only for himself, Jones articulated a nuanced and empowering deo-morphic theology that included anyone who lived according to the principle of apostolic socialism. As he told his congregants in 1974, "I'm Daddy God, and you're my baby gods, and I want you to be just like me."[15] In Jones's codifying system of evolutionary atheistic-socialist supernaturalism, the Kingdom of God was coextensive with the practice of apostolic socialism. In the religious imagination of Peoples Temple, a celestial heaven existed no more than the Sky God. Like Father Divine and his angels, Jones and members of Peoples Temple believed that it was possible to live in heaven upon Earth. By enacting apostolic socialism in Redwood Valley, Peoples Temple would create the conditions for a collective deified existence.

Vilification of the Sky God did not mean that Jones had no use for Him. It was the inscrutable Sky God, after all, who had required the Jews to wander in the desert for forty years. For Temple members raised in the black church, Exodus remained a powerful explanatory parable for the black diaspora and its attending injustices. While he rejected other passages in the Bible as lies, this story was upheld as containing a measure of truth. Jones repeatedly returned to the Exodus story in his public ministry as a way to encourage the downtrodden to join his flock in Redwood Valley. Their time of wandering, he promised, would be over when they joined the Temple: Daddy God had established a new Promised Land. Although initially used metaphorically to refer to the Temple's bucolic socialist retreat in Mendocino County, it was not long before talk of the Promised Land took a more literal turn.

After the prophesied apocalypse of July 1967 failed to occur, Jones remained genuinely worried about nuclear holocaust. He claimed to be stockpiling supplies in a cave where the Temple might survive the chaos that would ensue upon attack. By the late 1960s, Jones had found a new outlet for his paranoia, one that would eventually doom the Temple community: he was convinced the US government was monitoring his deeds, that the CCGR schoolhouse was bugged with microphones, and that the FBI and CIA were plotting to put a stop to his socialist experiment.

By October of 1967, God Socialism had appointed a select committee of trusted Temple members to explore the possibility of relocating Peoples Temple beyond American borders, in the event the authorities cracked down on his church, as they had done with the Black Panthers and other radical groups. The all-male group included Phillips and Lambrev, and was tasked with exploring the idea of moving Peoples Temple to the Soviet Union.[16] Phillips and Lambrev expressed doubts about the Soviet record on human rights and the difficulty of learning Russian, angering Jones. The plan went nowhere. Although discussions of an eventual move to the USSR never fully faded from the inner circles of Peoples Temple, Jones was soon persuaded that another country would make a better host for the movement. The Republic of Guyana, which Jones had visited in the early 1960s, had gained independence from the British and installed a Socialist government. Unlike the Soviet Union, Guyana was a multiethnic postcolonial nation whose residents spoke English. It was a perfect fit.

38. NEW DIRECTIONS

I N 1968, the elders of CCGR decided that Jones had violated their most sacrosanct rule. His self-appointment as chief interpreter of metaphysical laws and the truths of the world's great religions had stolen away some of CCGR's membership, and his arrogance had rankled the rest. The elders informed Jones he needed to find somewhere else to hold Temple services.[1]

Expulsion from Ridgewood Ranch only reinforced Jones's notion that he was an outsider whose command of his own spiritual gifts was threatening to more entrenched religious systems. Despite the spin he put on it, the rift with CCGR was highly inconvenient, and the loss of the Temple's closest allies in Mendocino County had the potential to demoralize his flock. In moments of duress such as this one, Jones relied on prophetic revelations to chart a new course. When these occurred in public, Jones's receipt of uncanny insights often took on the spectacle of nineteenth-century mesmeric clairvoyance and trance mediumship. As Lambrev recalls:

> The Sunday just after we'd been expelled from Christ's
> Church of the Golden Rule [in mid-1968], we had a meet-
> ing out in the open air, and Jim almost at some point went
> into what I recognize mainly as trance. He was just com-
> plete trance. And he started speaking, and it was as if all the
> vedas, all the great teachings of all the great religions, com-
> piled into one: he just put them all together, explained them,

and put them out so beautifully. And it wasn't anything casually memorized. It was something absolutely awesome and
inspiring.[2]

Survivors of Peoples Temple tend to agree with Lambrev that in
spite of what he later became, Jones had a remarkable instinct for recognizing both the humanity and vulnerability of those he met, and a
corresponding ability to tell them exactly what they needed to hear
at precisely the right time. Many who came to hear him preach in
this period saw and felt the gift, and Jones's reputation soon spread
throughout Northern California.

As a result, what began as a church composed primarily of traditional family units soon came to include many stray singles attracted
to a community based on social equality and civic engagement. Word
was getting around Bay Area progressive and radical circles that a
minister with an interracial, intergenerational gospel choir and congregation had settled in Redwood Valley, that he was hip to Eastern spiritual teachings, and that he'd exchanged Bible thumping
for meaningful social action. It was a rumor that attracted idealistic
youth from liberal and activist families who felt out of place in the
mainline churches. Some, like Christine Lucientes, were recruited to
the Temple straight out of the high school and adult education classes
that Jones taught when he first moved to Redwood Valley: like almost
everyone else in the church, Jones balanced a full-time job with his
demanding schedule of church activities. Other new recruits, like the
Stanford-educated lawyer Tim Stoen, came across the Temple somewhat haphazardly. Stoen was an idealistic young attorney who hired
Temple members to refurbish his offices after he moved to Ukiah to
become an assistant county DA. He soon became a Temple diehard
and Jones's chief legal counsel. A third category of recruits was composed of troubled youth like Debbie Layton, a problem child whose
parents allowed her to join the Temple after a British boarding school
failed to set her straight. Layton's brother, Larry, had joined Peoples

Temple along with his wife, Carolyn. Both were young teachers in the area school system.

The followers were not all liberal ex-Christians. In California, the Temple's Social Gospel reboot attracted Buddhists, New Age pantheists, atheist progressives, and a handful of Jews.[3] They were drawn in by the combination of Jones's undeniable charisma and the Temple's collective derring-do: rural Redwood Valley was a far cry from San Francisco, and most Ukiah natives had barely interacted with African Americans. Integrating "Redneck Valley" was no small task, and the Temple undertook it with style and vigor. Although the Civil Rights Act had been passed in 1965, the nation was still rigidly segregated by de facto barriers erected by poverty and racial discrimination. The Watts riots had occurred the summer of the Temple's move, Michigan governor George Romney and President Lyndon Johnson ordered the National Guard and the US Army to quell racial unrest in Detroit in the summer of 1967, and Bobby Kennedy and Martin Luther King Jr. were assassinated the next year. To many nonwhite Americans, the gains of the civil rights movement had begun to seem illusory. In defiance of the cultural inertia on the matter of racial equality, Jones ordered his rapidly growing congregation to be purposeful about integrating even when carpooling.

As the community grew, recalcitrant Temple members from Indiana pulled up stakes and sojourned west. Others from Mendocino County, Sacramento, the Bay Area, and the Central Valley had learned of Jones's healing powers and set out for Redwood Valley in search of last-ditch cures for cancer, heart disease, and other serious ailments. Jones earned a particularly strong reputation for rehabilitating drug and alcohol addicts. The Temple method was a simple recipe of cold-turkey suffering overseen by no-nonsense Midwesterners, supplemented by exhausting manual labor. It often worked.

Whenever he was credited with saving a life, Jones was seldom content to bask in praise. He quickly turned the miracle into a recruitment pitch by paraphrasing the words of Jesus from the Gospel of Luke, recently popularized by John F. Kennedy: "To whom much is given," Jones thundered from the pulpit, "much is required." What was required, of course, depended on the family assets of the person who'd been cured. With this speech, Jones converted entire families to Temple fellowship. This was the case for the family of Temple survivor Yulanda Williams: her father, a minister, suffered from a heart condition and was told by his doctors to stop working. After a healing conducted by Reverend Jones, the ailing minister believed he'd been cured. Jones also attempted to work his more conventional healing methods on Williams's sister, who was addicted to drugs. The family joined the Temple and donated property to the church as a gesture of gratitude.[4]

As he had been doing since Indianapolis, Jones faked many of the miracles he performed by having loyalist church members come to church disguised as cripples or enfeebled cancer patients whom he then proceeded to "heal." Espionage conducted by Patty Cartmell and other trusted disciples allowed Jones to reveal uncanny "insight" into the private lives of individual congregants during a healing. Throughout the healing segment of the services, Jones would don his famous dark glasses to facilitate his "trance." In fact, the glasses hid the source of his clairvoyance: looking down to read from the notecards that Cartmell and his other spies supplied. The dark glasses later became Jones's signature trait in the 1970s, when he used them to disguise the fact that he spent many if not all of his waking hours high on amphetamines.

Although they later learned that many of the healings were deceitful, several former Temple members remain convinced that some of Father's miracles and uncanny insights were the result of a genuine spiritual talent Jones possessed. Writing in 2010, Peoples Temple survivor Laura Johnston Kohl asserted that Jones had some kind of clairvoyant power.[5] She believes that although the pace of healings was exaggerated by Jones's chicken-gizzard cancer extractions, about 10 percent of the healings were genuine. However, Kohl added, as Jones became more and more exhausted—and more strung out—the healings and clairvoyance relied increasingly on forgery.[6]

. . .

UNTIL 1968, news of Peoples Temple spread mostly by word of mouth. It was not until the assassination of Martin Luther King Jr.—which Jones claimed to have prophesied—that the Temple began to focus its outreach on poor urban neighborhoods in San Francisco. After giving a stirring speech at a memorial service for King at a black church in San Francisco, Jones began cultivating relationships with the city's black ministers and their congregations. As part of these "exchanges," Jones would bring members of his congregation, including the interracial choir, down from Redwood Valley to worship in San Francisco. Ostensibly a display of interracial solidarity, the visitations were part of a strategic recruitment effort. Before departing, Temple members would collect contact information from prospective recruits, and later write to extend personalized invitations to services in Redwood Valley. It was a reliable and effective tactic for sheep-stealing that Jones had already practiced in Indianapolis. In Redwood Valley, city visitors marveled at the integrated community Jones had assembled in redneck country, and were impressed by the Temple's brand-new redwood church. The building was constructed around the existing Temple swimming pool. Visitors were told that Jones had ordered the pool be dug on Temple property so that members could avoid the racist harassment to which they were sometimes subjected at area lakes.

Californians who joined the church often did so because of this visible commitment to integration. For Kohl, who came to Redwood Valley as a young woman in 1970, it was the trauma of watching five of her political heroes gunned down over the course of the 1960s that pushed her into the family embrace of Peoples Temple. In Jones, she found a leader she believed was comparable to her dead heroes: the Kennedys, Medgar Evers, Malcolm X, and Dr. King. Kohl was afraid that without structure and organization to her life, she might destroy herself. She recalls:

> I came into Peoples Temple because I'd tried some other
> ways of making a change in society. I was trying to figure out
> a way not to be a victim of a society and a country that was
> just bullying people and had become lawless. So you know,
> I tried Woodstock to see if I could get stoned. . . . I tried for
> about six months living and working with the Black Panthers
> in Connecticut. And that didn't work out very well for me.
> And at that point I moved West and first got involved with
> Peoples Temple.[7]

Kohl had heard about Jones from a like-minded friend after moving to San Francisco to be near her sister. By this point, Jones was a minor celebrity in Bay Area progressive circles. He increasingly sought billing as a civil rights leader intimately connected to some of the era's other heroes of the Left: Dennis Banks, César Chávez, Angela Davis, and the West Coast Black Panthers. In Jones, Kohl believed, she had found a leader who could protect her from her own listlessness, and redirect her energies into the movement he was building for a better world. As she remembers:

> We were at the very cutting edge of the way we wanted
> society to evolve. So we wanted to be totally integrated and
> we wanted to have people of every socio-economic level,
> every racial background, everything, all included under one
> roof . . . we were trying to be role models of a society or a
> culture that was totally inclusive and not discriminatory

based on education or race or socioeconomic level. We all
joined with that in mind.[8]

Leslie Wagner-Wilson was another Californian whose family
became involved with Peoples Temple in the late 1960s. Her mother
had learned about the Temple's free services for troubled youth, and its
record for getting people off drugs. Because Leslie's sister, Michelle,
had a drug problem, their mother brought the girls to services in Redwood Valley. It was like a revelation: the interracial congregation and
choir were black, white, Mexican, and Native American. Blended
families filed in to fill the pews, and to top it all off, Marceline Jones
gave a stirring rendition of the Temple hymn "Black Baby," a song that
recognized the struggles black children would face throughout their
lives. The service lasted until past one o'clock in the morning. All of it
was like nothing Wagner-Wilson had ever seen growing up in the Sacramento Valley. As she recalled, "It was the first time I heard of blacks
having a life before slavery, and it amazed me when Jim talked about
my people as if he were not only deeply knowledgeable, but sympathetic. After all, he said, he was Native American, and his people had
suffered inhuman treatment."[9] In winter of 1970, Wagner-Wilson's
family moved permanently to Redwood Valley. Jones took to calling
Wagner-Wilson his "little Angela Davis": she was to be a new foot
soldier in the socialist mission of the Temple, which Jones increasingly
identified with global Third World discourse and the plight of freedom
fighters in Algeria, Tanzania, Kenya, Vietnam, and Cuba.

39. GOING COMMUNAL

B Y 1970, PEOPLES TEMPLE had doubled in size over five years, and counted about 300 committed activists.[1] Temple members still resided in private homes organized around family units. But since his arrival to California, Jones had begun to take steps to deconstruct the nuclear families in his congregation. He desired for his people to identify as a single common family without regard to the artificial boundaries of race, class, gender, education, and profession. Temple households took in troubled foster children and wards of the court from all over the state, thanks in part to the employment of several Temple members in Mendocino County social service agencies. Among them were Kohl and Sharon Amos, a California recruit who quickly rose up the ranks to become one of Jones's closest advisers.

Struggling with Governor Reagan's slashing cuts to social services, county agencies were glad to unload children in their custody on a church that offered a loving, integrated community. The Temple facilitated the exchange of children, whether fostered or sired, from one group home to another. Shuffling kids between various guardians and homes was sometimes rationalized as a practice intended to allow everyone to find the best living arrangement possible within the Temple's extended family. But Jones's objective was to undermine and then delegitimize the nuclear family, particularly in the minds of the next generation of Temple leaders. In addition to these innovations in childrearing, Jones showered praise on Temple members who remained single by choice as more dedicated to the cause. Although he went out of his way to sanction interracial marriages, Jones discouraged most other marital unions as counterrevolutionary and bourgeois. Having made clear his disdain for possessive marriage relations, Jones began to take many sexual partners besides his wife.

It was around this time that Jones began to expound semi-publicly on the race theory that he would use to unite the collective consciousness of his extended Temple family: he began to identify himself and all those who genuinely worked to separate themselves from bourgeois capitalist society as "niggers." Some Temple members might be viewed by outsiders as white, Jones admitted, but they were not "honkeys." This was the derogatory term that the Temple reserved for white racists and capitalists. Jones began to tell a version of his family history that included a confrontation with his putatively racist father. Determined to humiliate Big Jim as a hypocrite, Jones claimed to have conducted genealogical research that revealed, in his typically vulgar words, "a nigger in the woodpile." Although Jones theorized that practically everyone in America had nonwhite ancestry, a dark complexion like his made the Jones family connection to miscegenation more apparent. Sometimes the story would change slightly, to include Lynetta's claims of Cherokee ancestry, but the intent remained the same. Jones wished to be accepted the way he saw himself: entitled to claim solidarity with the suffering of the oppressed.[2]

This exercise in race craft allowed Jones to divide the peoples of the world into a binary system wherein racial phenotype was not indicative of ethnicity. It was another tactic Jones borrowed from Father Divine, who rejected racial categories and instead divided the world's peoples into an angelic race and less-than-angelic others. Jones adapted the same powerful we–they mentality to his more forthrightly radical and racially charged political agenda. He encouraged Temple members to identify themselves as niggers, while "honkey" became a paramount slur against outsiders perceived to be racists. It was a label also used to criticize Temple backsliders and defectors considered to have betrayed the cause with counterrevolutionary activity.

The ultimate honkeys were the CIA, FBI, and police henchmen whom Jones depicted as mercenary agents of a greedy white power structure: they thrived on exploiting blacks and all the other oppressed people Jones classified as niggers. "They beat up enough people, these rookies from Mississippi," Jones told his people during a 1974 sermon in Los Angeles, "that's where a lot of these white under-policemen come [from]. Not the chiefs and the commanders and supervisors, but a lot of these rednecks running these streets, they come directly from Alabama and Georgia and Mississippi."[3] It was an accusation that rang true to many of the African Americans in the Temple, especially those who hailed from the South.

During the early Nixon years, Jones had also begun to predict the installation of a right-wing police state in the United States. The coming regime, he prophesied, would round up African Americans and the poor, in order to confine them to concentration camps. The assassinations of King and RFK in 1968, the 1969 murder of Fred Hampton, and the 1973 CIA-backed coup in Chile lent credibility to his otherwise fringe theories about a covert fascist plot against democratic efforts to build a more just society.

.   .   .

AS THE CHURCH began to expand rapidly following Jones's outreach in San Francisco, it naturally evolved into its next phase of transformation: the establishment of Temple communes unrelated to nuclear family units. The church had already acquired expertise in administering group homes: in addition to its communitarian approach to parenting, Peoples Temple had established several eldercare residences in Redwood Valley by the late 1960s. Marceline Jones obtained a post as inspector of eldercare facilities for the state of California. Under her guidance and with the shrewd and practical management of frugal, hardworking Midwesterners like Rheaviana Beam, Peoples Temple care homes for the elderly and disabled were kept in impeccable condition and brought significant revenue to the Temple's coffers.[4]

As more college-aged students joined the Temple or aged in place, the church organized additional group homes for students at Santa Rosa Junior College. Students living in these communes included some of the most militant leftists in the Temple, hand-selected for college education by Temple staff. Jones fostered some of their revolutionary ardor by encouraging the Temple youth group to study Marx and Mao rather than the Bible, and by forcing adolescents to undergo what some former members described as paramilitary training—outdoor drills meant to prepare them for post-nuclear survival.[5]

Resident communes for unmarried members came next. Houses and apartments for rent were scarce in Mendocino County, especially if African Americans were among the soliciting tenants. Moreover, it made economic sense for Temple members to split household expenses many ways in order to have more money left over for advancing the cause. This was particularly the case as the Temple began to employ more and more of its congregants in various church-owned businesses. Communes were self-governing, but Temple secretaries and accountants managed their finances. Some were comprised of seniors who fared far better by pooling Social Security resources, while others resembled intergenerational, multiracial families. San Francisco communal sensibilities emerged in those communes made up of young activists. Most of these were packed to the gills, and operated with extreme frugality.[6]

"Going communal" became a badge of honor among Temple members who proudly identified as zealots. Those who worked full-time outside the church—at the welfare office, the state hospital, the nearby Masonite factory, or the school system—joined communes and turned over their paychecks to the Temple. Their salaries subsidized the expenses of Temple members who worked without pay writing church publications, conducting round-the-clock security on Jones's parsonage, or helping to organize the Temple's numerous charitable activities. Increasingly, after-hours unpaid labor became standard among the zealots: members were expected to work demanding jobs for the Temple in addition to their professions as nurses, teachers, and factory laborers. Among the zealots, sixteen-hour days were the norm and all-nighters became routine.[7]

As Kohl wrote of these years in her memoir, Temple members took extra precautions with their health to compensate for their lack of rest: they consumed high doses of vitamin E, practiced deep breathing, ate soybeans to adjust to a post-nuclear-war diet, took cold showers every day, and drank Dr Pepper for some obscure health-related reason that Jones never fully explained. They slept on their right sides, because Jones told them it put less pressure on their hearts. As the cold showers suggest, celibacy had once more become in vogue—it was essential for keeping the peace in the crowded youth communes.

As the church became larger and ever more diverse, Jones created a Board of Elders—a name lifted from CCGR terminology—to act as his personal counsel. Around 1970, the board was replaced with a body Jones called the Planning Commission, named after the Soviet governing body. The PC, in Temple parlance, began with a few dozen members and later expanded to more than 100 as Jones acculturated greater numbers of his flock to its unorthodox methods of public group criticism, during which members accused of counterrevolutionary activity were berated and humiliated. Members of the PC putatively advised Jones on matters related to the Temple's future directions; in the early 1970s, this included the Temple's decision to expand its Los Angeles and San Francisco ministries to include satellite churches in those cities.

In reality, most decisions remained with Jones. Rather than an advisory council, the PC was a mechanism for social control: Jones created alliances and divisions within the PC to test the loyalties of individual members. Because they were privy to information that could jeopardize the Temple's reputation, it became standard practice for PC members to sign false confessions of sexual deviance, child abuse, murder, and conspiracy to kill the president. Some were instructed to put their names to blank paper. Temple notaries signed, sealed, and filed the confessions. If members were ill at ease with signing fraudulent documents, Jones and Temple leaders assured them that the ends justified the strangely paranoid means. Today, several archival boxes of false confessions survive in the records of the California Historical Society.

During meetings that lasted into the early-morning hours, Jones forced members of the PC to divulge every last detail of their personal and sexual lives. They also shared information about other Temple members collected during in-person "visitations" conducted by a specially appointed committee. Ostensibly an outreach program that provided Temple leadership with the opportunity to schedule extra counseling or services to struggling members, the Visitations Committee engaged in espionage, such as snooping in members' medicine cabinets while conducting home counseling visits. Jones would use whatever information his visitors gleaned in callouts during Temple services, to demonstrate his clairvoyant omniscience. His preferred subject was sex.

Midweek "family meetings" in the Temple were open only to members because Jones publicly shamed errant Temple members from the pulpit, and summoned delinquents before the congregation for a thorough dressing-down. Initially these meetings preserved the format of confessional testimonials begun in Indianapolis in imitation of Father Divine. In Redwood Valley, they became known to some members as "catharsis sessions"—so called after a method of brutal mutual criticism practiced by Synanon, another Northern California commune that specialized in curing drug and alcohol addiction. Jones had likely studied Synanon for insight into how to tame the numerous drug addicts in his church into submitting to a life of clear-headed radicalism. Members of Synanon shaved their heads, lived communally, and played something called "The Game": a structured form of character-building verbal assault that recalled the nineteenth-century Oneida Community's practice of mutual criticism. Like Oneida and

Peoples Temple, Synanon was preoccupied with controlling its members' procreation. Whereas Oneidans practiced male continence and members of Synanon underwent sterilization, Jones was a fair-weather proponent of celibacy, and often required pregnant Temple women to get abortions.

Closed-door meetings eventually came to include harsh corporal punishment, meted out in the name of protecting the cause. Because Jones had developed a distrust of American law enforcement and a damning critique of its role in perpetuating misery in the lives of black Americans, he insisted that his parishioners not report punishable offenses to the police.

Instead of denouncing its members to the relevant authorities, the Temple dealt with infractions, even those as serious as child molestation, by dispensing its own strict justice. Stocky Jack Beam and Ruby Carroll were usually those who administered beatings, first with a belt and later with a rubber hose or a paddle known as the Board of Education. When family meetings finally concluded, often after midnight, the PC would adjourn to a member's house or to the room above the Temple offices on East Road to exchange gossip and experience additional catharsis.

40. PEOPLES TEMPLE HITS THE ROAD

I T WAS IN THE SUMMER of 1971 that Peoples Temple began its legendary evangelism tours. With membership blossoming in San Francisco and Los Angeles, where the Temple held biweekly meetings in rented facilities, the church invested in a fleet of thirteen decommissioned tour buses so that zealots from Redwood Valley could fill seats in city meetings over the weekends. The Temple also began to embark on missionary trips to more distant cities, including Seattle. Services drew several hundred people in each city.[1]

Jones often exhausted himself by visiting all three of the major Temple sites in a single weekend. The journey took him from Redwood Valley to San Francisco to Los Angeles and back within seventy-two hours.[2] But Jones didn't travel alone: for zealots on the communes in Redwood Valley, marathon weekend worship added to the strain of a normalized routine of sixteen-hour days. By Monday morning, they were exhausted. Teachers complained that Temple schoolchildren dragged to LA and back often fell asleep at their desks; adult members staggered through the first day back at work. Fortunately, there were enough zealots at the Ukiah Masonite factory and at the county welfare office to allow Temple members to cover for one another while taking turns napping on the job. Jones, however, seldom rested. Although he forbade the use of drugs, Jones increasingly relied on a stash of uppers and downers to regulate his schedule.

The baker's dozen of Greyhound buses enabled Peoples Temple to expand its outreach program on a national scale over the summer months. In the weeks leading up to an evangelism tour, Jones dispatched an advance crew to scout suitable locales for him to preach along the way. These crews arranged sleeping accommodations for the busloads of Temple members who joined Jones on the road. They slept in church fellowship halls, at private homes, on campgrounds, and when they had to, in their buses and on the pavement. Arriving ahead of the others to cities across the South, Midwest, and Northeast, the advance crew would leaflet black neighborhoods, panhandle for donations, and advertise the upcoming visit of a spiritual healer and his interracial congregation and choir. The formula proved as successful as Jones's sheep-stealing in San Francisco, and garnered members from the various cities the Temple visited, including New Orleans; Houston; Washington, DC; Brooklyn; Detroit; Cleveland; and Chicago.[3]

Continuing to style himself a leader in the vein of the assassinated heroes of the 1960s, Jones took his corps of uniformed bodyguards with him on these journeys. On at least one occasion in Houston, he used a body double to act as a decoy for potential assassins. Jones's obsessive precautions were, on the one hand, accoutrements for his self-fashioned cult of personality: he and his aides would go on to stage several assassination attempts over the course of the decade. But Jones also suffered from pathological paranoia induced by his addiction to amphetamines. Most Temple members remained unaware that Jones's eyes were frantic and bloodshot behind his signature shades; others knew of their pastor's substance abuse because they helped steal his meds from their hospital jobs. Like Marceline, they accepted his hypocritical dependence with that familiar revolutionary rationale: the ends justify the means.

Naturally, one of the first cities scheduled for a visitation by the Peoples Temple caravan was Philadelphia, where the Peace Mission movement was left bereft of its patriarch. Father Divine had finally sacrificed his earthly body in September 1965, after which time Mother Divine assumed control of the still formidable domains of the Divine kingdom. It was not an easy transition. Mother Divine was acutely aware that many followers, including Woodmont fixtures like Dorothy Darling and St. Mary Bloom, remained skeptical of her claim to authority. Divine's longest-serving secretaries and most devoted followers had all known Peninnah Divine, and resisted the idea that she had chosen to migrate into a white body. After Father Divine's death, deputies devoted to the second Mother Divine helped her purge those perceived to be insufficiently loyal from the ranks of the Palace Mission, Inc., one of the Peace Mission's incorporated churches. Palace Mission owned Woodmont, as well as many of the older New York City properties. Rumors circulated that Mother Divine was evicting older angels from the Peace Mission's New York holdings and quietly arranging the sale of the buildings with the help of two white henchmen. Dorothy Darling and St. Mary Bloom were sent packing from Woodmont, forced to relocate to the Circle Mission Church on Broad and Catharine. According to Tommy Garcia, the Circle Mission Church became semi-estranged from the Palace Mission, where Mother Divine concentrated her allies.[4] It was Garcia who delivered another blow to Mother's plans for the Mission's future: the year after Father Divine took leave of his body, Garcia abandoned Woodmont. The sixteen-year-old ran away to LA, leaving the former Edna Ritchings in sole control of the aging movement.

Jones had contacted Mother Divine to offer his "services" to the Peace Mission immediately after learning of Father Divine's departure from his mortal frame, and invited her to come to Redwood Valley in the event of a cataclysmic nuclear war. She declined, and for a while suffered little interference from Jones or his confreres: they were busy building their own Promised Land in California. But after acquiring his pack of Greyhound buses, Jones's top priority was leading a Temple delegation to visit the Peace Mission in July of 1971. Privately, Mother Divine remained highly suspicious of the interloping minister and his rainbow family. She nonetheless directed the angels to make room for the Temple contingent at the Divine Lorraine and Divine Tracy hotels in Philadelphia. Objections arose almost instantly upon their guests' arrival: the angels reported back to Mother Divine that Jones's people were taking down the names of Divinites who expressed interest in the Temple care homes out West.

Jones had a special treat in store for the Temple members who'd schlepped across the country: on July 23, they boarded the Temple buses and went up the Main Line to Woodmont, where Jones called to pay his respects. Many in the Temple delegation had never before seen such opulence. Perched atop a wooded ridge at the end of a long lane, the imitation French Gothic manor resembled a castle. A manicured lawn and formal gardens sloped down the hill toward the drive by which the Greyhounds accessed the estate. As implemented at the Mount of the House of the Lord, the Divine economic program hardly resembled the participatory rural communalism of Redwood Valley, where Jones was always circulating in an effort to be seen getting his hands dirty while lending a hand to Temple members. In the eyes of Temple socialists, Mother Divine and the corps of Rosebuds living in luxury at Woodmont were no better than capitalists who lived for free off the sweat of workers.

Just as Marcus Garvey had stated decades before, Jones told his followers that the urban religious communalism of the Peace Mission was little more than an elaborate fraud. Worse still was the inference Jones knew his followers would draw after he had socialized them to view all social injustices and personal disappointments through the lens of institutional racism: a white woman lorded over Woodmont, and her absurd lifestyle was paid for entirely by an army of mostly black laborers. Behind her back, Jones made Mother Divine out to be a highfalutin honkey who led the Peace Mission straight into apostasy after Father Divine's final sacrifice. The kingdom was in desperate need of his reform.

After his people had filed through the Shrine to Life, a mausoleum that holds the remains of Father Divine's terrestrial body, Jones was momentarily left alone with Mother Divine in Woodmont's most sacred space. It was there that Jones informed Mother

Divine that just as her spirit had exited the body of Peninnah Divine to inhabit a younger and lighter-skinned woman, the spirit of Father Divine had taken up residence in his stocky white frame. Gobsmacked at such a bold pronouncement, Mother Divine merely informed Jones he was wrong. But if she thought that Jones could be so easily dissuaded, it was Mother Divine who was mistaken. As she recalled seven years later:

> For the several days they remained in Philadelphia, the mili-
> tant attitude of Jones and the leaders of the group became
> increasingly obvious. His distaste for the government, the
> establishment and the prosperity of the followers in general
> began to be expressed in casual then more deliberate remarks
> he made to MOTHER DIVINE and others.[5]

The Divine matriarch was determined not to let Jones get the best of her. Although by now convinced that Jones bore ill will, she allowed him and his people to continue their stay. This was another error. On the final evening of their visit, Jones and his followers packed the Crystal Ballroom of the Divine Lorraine hotel for a Holy Communion banquet meant to celebrate their shared veneration of Father Divine. Jones was seated at a place of honor next to Mother Divine. The attending angels conducted the banquet with the Peace Mission's typically elegant flair: ice sculptures in the shape of swans adorned one of tables.[6]

Tensions in the room were already running high when Temple members rose to interrupt the angels' stream of praise and testimony to Father Divine's abundance. One after the next, they stood to testify to Jones's power in their lives: his ability to get them off drugs, out of the streets, and into a community of inspired meaning where everyone shared in the work that had to be done to make apostolic socialism a reality. At the head of the table, beside the empty place set for Father, Mother Divine seethed. Finally, Jones rose to announce that Father

Divine's spirit had come to reside in him. The Temple members, inter-mingled among the angels, leapt to their feet and shouted praise to Father Jones.

Holy Communion came to a halt as a murmur of disbelief washed over those assembled. Furious, Mother Divine commanded Jones and his people to gather their belongings and leave the Divine Lorraine immediately. As Mother Divine's burliest angels escorted members of Peoples Temple from the building, the matriarch told her disturbed followers that Jones had finally revealed himself as "the other fellow"— Peace Mission argot for the devil.

Back aboard the Temple buses, Jones confided to his people that while he was alone with her in the Shrine to Life, Mother Divine had acknowledged his sexual prowess, begged him to make love to her, and began removing her clothes. Jones's followers were already accustomed to their pastor's sexual bluster: Jones not only acknowl-edged that he had affairs with a great many of the Temple members, but openly discussed his use of sex as a mode of revolutionary dis-cipline for church members he believed had become selfish, with-holding, or bourgeois. He exhorted Temple members of both sexes to proclaim what a valiant and accomplished lover he was in family meetings. Mother Divine, Jones explained, was not insensible to his superior sexual abilities, and became irate when he refused to com-ply with her demands that he make love to her over Father Divine's dead body.[7]

After returning to California, Temple members who'd accompa-nied Jones on the trip to Pennsylvania conducted a letter-writing cam-paign to members of the Peace Mission whose names and addresses they'd collected in Philadelphia. They sent leaflets advertising Jones's own "Mount of the House of the Lord" in California to every Peace Mission extension they could locate. The objective was to persuade the angels that they were being conned: the letters unfavorably compared Mother Divine to a slave mistress, repeated Jones's assertion that she had made a heretical sexual offering in Father Divine's mausoleum, and invited members of the Peace Mission to join the true God in California. Yet as Mother Divine later asserted, Jones had not reckoned with the fact that Father retained his power over his followers even after he had abandoned his body: the Temple received few replies to its direct mail campaign.

But Jones was not finished. The next June, Daddy God sent several nearly empty Peoples Temple buses across the country to Philadelphia. Temple zealots assigned to this special mission stormed into the Peace Mission's Philadelphia hotels unannounced, handing out leaflets and announcing their invitation to live in one of the Temple's Redwood Valley communes or retirement homes. As the angels attempted to expel the invaders from their hotels, the confrontation escalated. Finally, after being drenched with water and forcibly ejected from the heavens, members of Peoples Temple got back on their buses, circled the block, and used a megaphone to announce a three-p.m. departure that Sunday for anyone who wished to make the journey west.

A dozen Divinites accepted the invitation. The recruits included eleven female angels: Ever Rejoicing, Love Magdalene Joy, Mary Love Black, Joy Sunshine, Valor St. John, Love Life Lowe, Meekness Faith, Heavenly Love, Virgin Humble, Rose of Sharon, and Purity Lamb. Simon Peter was the only male defector.[8] Because he occupied a position of prestige and authority in the Peace Mission as one of Father Divine's most loyal and trusted recruits, as well as one of the key architects of the Ulster County Promised Land, his defection deeply wounded Mother Divine.

Most of the Peace Mission recruits were old and certain to add additional financial burden to the Temple. Ever Rejoicing, née Amanda Poindexter, was ninety by the time she joined Jim Jones. The elderly women were nevertheless a boost to morale in Redwood Valley: because many had never traveled far beyond Philadelphia, they were overwhelmed by the natural beauty of Mendocino County and pleased with the Temple's clean and orderly accommodations for seniors. Everyone saw to it that the women were treated like queens. Jones tended to pay solicitous attention to elderly black women in the church, often posing for pictures while planting kisses on their cheeks. The "Peace Mission ladies" were lodged together in a comfortable home vacated by the Cartmell family, who had gone to staff the newly acquired San Francisco headquarters. The majority of the new recruits, including one who weighed at least five hundred pounds, died off quickly, but they are still fondly remembered by surviving members of the Temple.[9]

Jones believed he could offset the costs of taking on a dozen aged angels by acquiring their Peace Mission assets. After years of studying the Peace Mission and several personal audiences with Father Divine, who took a genuine interest in sharing the details of the Divine Cooperative Plan with his would-be protégé, Jones could not have been unaware that his new followers' assets would be tied up in complicated joint-tenancy arrangements. Nevertheless, he believed Temple attorneys Tim Stoen and Eugene Chaikin could somehow crack Divine's otherwise foolproof system and score a significant financial windfall. After the dozen angels arrived in California, Chaikin and Stoen immediately set to work attempting to recover the property of their new charges. No amount was too petty to pursue: Chaikin intervened on behalf of Joy Sunshine to recover the remainder of a $2,142 mortgage loan, owed her by another angel, Smile Love.[10] Chaikin also represented Valor St. John, on whose behalf he inquired about the tenancy-in-common stake she owned in a Peace Mission mansion on Madison Avenue in New York City.[11]

The property from the Peace Mission never amounted to much. In any case, it paled in comparison to the Temple's monthly income in the early and mid-1970s: after Jones cultivated booming followings in Los Angles and San Francisco, the Temple was raking in as much as $30,000 in weekly donations. Meanwhile, financial advisers in the church leadership hierarchy helped ensure that Temple communes and businesses were run with austere thrift. Top aides Debbie Layton and Terri Buford helped Jones squirrel away the profits in overseas bank accounts in Switzerland and Panama.[12] God Socialism was convinced that his capitalist adversaries would eventually try to destroy him, beginning with the Temple's finances. He wished to be economically prepared to escape from the United States—a flight he considered inevitable.

41. BACKLASH

J ONES'S CERTAINTY THAT Peoples Temple would eventually be harassed out of the country was due in part to his drug-induced paranoia. But Temple activities had aroused legitimate suspicions. In autumn 1972, Jones and the Temple were the subject of a series of sarcastic articles in the *San Francisco Examiner*—the first concerted attempt to besmirch the pastor's reputation. The writer, religion columnist Lester Kinsolving, was an Episcopal priest with a bee in his bonnet—at least when it came to religious con men. After hearing rumors of miracles in Redwood Valley, Kinsolving contacted the *Ukiah Daily Journal* to get the scoop on Jones, whose allies at the paper promptly informed the preacher of Kinsolving's snooping. Jones sensed trouble, but compounded it by overplaying his hand: Kinsolving surmised the Temple must have something to hide when his office received a hand delivery of dozens of unbidden letters from Temple members praising the words and deeds of Pastor Jones and defending the presence of armed guards at Redwood Valley services as their dutiful fulfillment of a local sheriff's request—a statement Kinsolving easily exposed as a lie by calling the sheriff's department.[1]

The skeptical priest went north to observe Temple services and evaluate the man who was said by the Temple's own legal representative to have raised dozens from the dead.[2] After he witnessed armed guards patrolling the church grounds, Kinsolving ferreted out details on the church's curious finances and learned that a Ukiah Baptist minister had requested a formal investigation of the Temple. The

Examiner approved an eight-article exposé on Jim Jones and Peoples Temple.

But Kinsolving had underestimated Jim Jones. After two of his acidic reports appeared in the *Examiner,* Jones ran a counteroffensive: he directed the Temple's letter office to deluge the paper with indignant correspondence, and ferried busloads of followers to San Francisco for a peaceful picketing of the *Examiner*'s offices. In this first high-profile test of public opinion in San Francisco, Jones and his surrogates did what they always did whenever the church came under fire: they inventoried the Temple's undeniably good works and implied that its critics were bigots. Who could oppose an organization that opened eldercare homes, took in dozens of foster children, cured and employed former drug addicts, and established a forty-acre ranch for the developmentally disabled? Only racists who hated the Temple's integrated following.

Bowing to pressure from the Temple and its allies in San Francisco, the *Examiner* killed the four articles that had not yet been published— including those in which Kinsolving detailed allegations of physical abuse, the forced signing of false confessions, and Jones's claim to be the reincarnation of Jesus Christ. The final bombshell article was to be called "Sex, Socialism, and Child Torture with Reverend Jim Jones."[3] But Jones had quashed the exposé, and the triumph went straight to his head.

The media attention resulted, somewhat unexpectedly, in the recruitment of two men who were rapidly welcomed into the Temple's inner circles: Mike Prokes, a TV news personality from Modesto, read Kinsolving's articles, performed an independent investigation, and soon became a member of Peoples Temple, as well as its principal spokesman. Prokes issued a formal rebuttal to Kinsolving's series on San Francisco radio. Tim Carter had a more typical Temple background: he was an aimless Vietnam veteran disillusioned by American wars. Carter and his sister were thoroughly vetted before they were permitted entry to the San Francisco temple, as had by then become standard practice: Jones insisted that his followers weed out honkies and potential spies by conducting a thorough interrogation of new visitors. The Carters passed the test, and were welcomed into services to be "niggerized."[4]

. . .

IN SPITE OF his road tripping across America, Jones still lacked a national reputation. But as California churned with the energy of radical left politics, the Temple began to emerge as a power broker between the New Left and the Democratic establishment. Jones positioned himself as a man of the cloth who was willing to sacrifice his time and reputation on behalf of the poor and downtrodden. Truly, Temple PR suggested, here was a Christian minister who followed the example of Christ, and who was ready to say what other preachers would not: America's problems with poverty, drug addiction, urban violence, and homelessness were all generated by capitalism.

To prove the American military-industrial complex was inherently evil, Jones invited torture victims of Augusto Pinochet's regime in Chile to speak to his congregation and elicit sympathy for victims of the CIA's numerous plots to aid right-wing governments. Black activists from the South were brought to the Temple to regale its members with news from the struggle against fascist segregationists. And when members of the press were jailed for disclosing confidential information or for refusing to name their sources, the Temple sallied forth with donations and scholarships to promote press freedom. At one of his grandstanding press-freedom events, held on behalf of the Fresno Four in 1976, Jones surrounded himself with California political heavyweights: even Gov. Jerry Brown attended. Jones's breathtaking cynicism and hypocrisy did not go unnoticed by San Francisco reporters, who all knew about the quashed *Examiner* articles.

The presence of Jerry Brown and Lt. Gov. Mervyn Dymally at a Peoples Temple benefit gala in 1976 offers an indication of how quickly

Jones rose to prominence in San Francisco. After his failed raid on the Peace Mission, Jones concentrated on replicating Divine's model of urban communalism by relocating his center of operations from Redwood Valley to San Francisco. The transition had begun with the acquisition of a cavernous Masonic Temple on Geary Boulevard in 1972, just down the block from a Black Muslim cultural center. After its renovation, the massive structure served as Jones's primary residence. Its large auditorium became the site of regular weekly services and a hub for the Temple's city-outreach programs. The same year, the Temple purchased a former Christian Science church in Los Angeles, as well as an adjacent apartment complex for housing LA communal members. Both congregations flourished. In the poor black neighborhoods where its city outposts were located, Temple nurses and doctors offered free medical checkups, physical therapy, drug counseling, eye exams, and preventative screenings for health conditions that predominantly afflicted the poor.

Gradually Jones shifted the entirety of the Temple's communal movement to the new urban front in what he increasingly regarded as a cultural war against the poor and minorities. Temple offices did not relocate to San Francisco until November 1976, by which point nearly the entire Redwood Valley communal movement had been transplanted to a network of communes in San Francisco.[5] The most successful of the city communes was a household in Potrero Hill run by Joyce Shaw and Bob Houston, who fostered up to a dozen children at a time. Elders jammed into a communal apartment hotel in the Tenderloin district—a far grittier version of the Divine Lorraine. Laura Johnston Kohl estimates that, using the loose definition of "commune" as a group home for Temple members who weren't related, there were easily twenty Peoples Temple communes in San Francisco. This included the Geary Boulevard headquarters, where a warren of rooms above the sanctuary and a few trailers parked in a back lot housed a surprisingly large number of young singles.[6]

The Fillmore District was not selected at random as the site of

the new Temple headquarters: it was a black neighborhood in turmoil after having been identified as a target for "redevelopment"
by the San Francisco Redevelopment Agency, whose longtime
head, Justin Herman, was vilified as a "white devil" in the black
community.[7]

Although the fight over redevelopment was pretty much over—
President Richard Nixon had eliminated funding that SFRA needed
to continue it—Jones believed the Fillmore was where the action
was. Certainly, it was an area in dire need of the Temple's free health
screenings and legal aid. While Temple members immersed themselves in community service, Jones quickly ingratiated himself in the
city's Democratic political class.

George Moscone was one of the principal beneficiaries of the Temple's political clout. Moscone faced a close race in the November 1975
mayoral election against John Barbagelata—to date, the last Republican to be elected to the San Francisco Board of Supervisors. Barbagelata and Dianne Feinstein, the moderate Democrat in the race, split
the city's centrist votes and sent the November election into a December runoff. Moscone was faced with an uphill climb: the city's conser-
vatives and opponents of the countercultural movements of the early
1970s coalesced around Barbagelata, who blamed left-wing politics for
the city's crime and drug problems. With the mistaken understanding
that Jim Jones controlled at least as many as 2,000 votes in the city,
Moscone personally appealed to Jones for support in the lead-up to the
runoff.[8] Jones was pleased to be needed. At his command, the Temple
swung into action, sending hundreds of volunteers to help get out the
vote, in part by driving poor and elderly minority voters to the polls.
Moscone prevailed by fewer than 5,000 votes in the runoff, and Barbagelata went to his grave convinced that Jones had somehow rigged
the election.

Moscone promised Temple attorney Eugene Chaikin that Jones
and four other Temple members would be considered for appointments in his administration.[9] But after the election, Moscone turned

a cold shoulder to Jim Jones. Joe Freitas, who had also benefitted from Jones's electioneering, appointed Tim Stoen to a junior position in the DA's office. But this did almost nothing to satisfy Jones, whose staff continued to nag the mayor for additional appointments throughout the spring. To mollify Jones, Moscone wrote to congratulate him and to "add my personal endorsement to your unique and novel ecumenical experiment with the Nation of Islam on May 23rd in Los Angeles." He referred to a joint meeting between Peoples Temple and the Nation, to be held on that day. Lieutenant Governor Dymally had agreed to participate in the endeavor. A native of Trinidad and Tobago, Dymally was one of the state's most high-profile black politicians, along with LA mayor Tom Bradley and California assemblyman Willie Brown. Both Dymally and Brown were crucial allies of Peoples Temple during its San Francisco period, and Dymally would later offer support to the Jonestown Agricultural Project through his Caribbean connections to Guyanese prime minister Forbes Burnham. Jones would even afford Dymally a rare visit to Jonestown in December 1976.

With a political appointment from city hall not immediately forthcoming, Jones made repeated efforts to ingratiate himself with Jimmy and Rosalynn Carter. During the 1976 presidential campaign, Peoples Temple helped pack a political rally when Rosalynn Carter made an appearance in San Francisco. The intergenerational, interracial crowd that Jones was able to field on a moment's notice was just what the campaign needed. In exchange for the favor, Jones extracted a private meeting with Mrs. Carter in the garden restaurant of a posh Nob Hill hotel. The Carter campaign apparently remained convinced of Jones's power in a crucial state: when vice-presidential nominee Walter Mondale stopped in San Francisco International Airport while on the campaign trail, Jones was one of a handful of local leaders invited to board his plane.[10]

During Carter's first months in office, Peoples Temple PR man Mike Prokes wrote to California senator Alan Cranston requesting that Jones be named ambassador to Guyana. This was a ludicrous conflict of interests, considering that in December 1973, Jones's church had arranged for the lease of 2,500 acres of Guyanese jungle. There, a full day's journey by boat from the Guyanese capital of Georgetown, Peoples Temple had begun building a settlement where they might be left to practice racially integrated apostolic socialism without fear of reprisal from racist cops, fickle politicians, and journalistic saboteurs—and of course, free from the risk of nuclear war and concentration camps that Jones continued to prophesy. The moderate socialist government of Prime Minister Burnham had agreed to a hundred-year lease on land for the Temple settlement, which Burnham thought might shore up Guyana's hold over the territory. From Burnham's point of view, any immigrants at all were badly needed: ever since he had taken a hard left turn and declared Guyana a cooperative socialist republic in 1970—in part to fend off a challenge from the more radical ex-PM Cheddi Jagan—emigration out of Guyana dramatically accelerated.[11] The relocation of an avowedly socialist, interracial American church mission was not only good PR for Burnham's government; it would deter military incursion by the Venezuelans and bring economic development to the impoverished northwest region of the country.

Jones and Mike Prokes continued to needle Moscone's office throughout 1976. Although the mayor delayed in offering Jones a political appointment, Moscone occasionally appeared at Temple meetings—as did assemblyman Willie Brown, San Francisco supervisor Harvey Milk, *Sun-Reporter* publisher Dr. Carlton Goodlett, actress Jane Fonda, activist Angela Davis, and other luminaries of the left in California. When in September 1976 Jones's followers threw a dinner to honor the legacy of Dr. Martin Luther King Jr. and unsurprisingly named Jim Jones the guest of honor, Moscone, Dymally, Brown, Freitas, Davis, and Goodlett all attended, as did former Black Panther Eldridge Cleaver and the celebrated leftist defense attorney Charles Garry.

Moscone finally appointed Jones to the Human Rights Commission toward the end of 1976. But when he arrived for the swearing-in ceremony, Jones informed the mayor that he would not take the position after all. Moscone correctly inferred that Jones was holding out for an appointment with more influence. They compromised on an appointment to the Housing Commission. While serving as housing commissioner, Jones made a name for himself as a defender of oppressed communities. But it was not a post he held for long.[12]

. . .

JONES BELIEVED THAT 1976 had marked the year of the Temple's ascendancy. He had proved himself a power broker in one of the most politically cutthroat cities in America. He was connected, however ephemerally, to the president's wife. The Temple was still bringing in tens of thousands of dollars in weekly donations, and Jones continued to draw crowds across the country. It was exhausting work.

As a result, Jones fell even deeper into a dependency on amphetamines. His behavior whipped between violent extremes. Punishments in PC meetings had taken a dark turn in 1975, and grew increasingly severe as the stakes of potential embarrassments were raised along with Jones's political profile. Members recalled beatings and sexual humiliation: some were forced to undress or engage in public sex acts to prove they were not racist, selfish, or bourgeois. Even before December 1973, when Jones got busted by the LA vice squad for lewd conduct in the men's room at a theater known for gay cruising, he was obsessed with preaching about the preponderance of repressed homosexuals in the Temple, and the corresponding need for him to have sex with male as well as female Temple members as part of his liberational ministerial duties. Peoples Temple did not condemn homosexuality—several high-profile members were gay—but Jones used it as a way to emasculate and control male followers he claimed were in denial of their same-sex attraction, as well as to satisfy his own urges. Stoen was able to get Jones off the hook with the LA vice squad and even managed to have the case files sealed. But after his arrest, Jones's advances on male members of the church became more frequent, as did his public disclosures of which male members he'd needed to penetrate in order to teach them to accept their homosexuality. As with his female conquests, these men were usually white.

It was Jones's obsession with sex, and with manipulating the sex lives of those in his inner circle, that had caused the first serious defections from Peoples Temple in 1973. A group of college students calling themselves the Eight Revolutionaries defected en masse, leaving behind an eleven-page handwritten manifesto complaining about Jones's fixation on "sex, sex, sex" at the expense of radical politics. More offensive to Jones's self-image was the accusation that he had allowed an incipient classism to evolve within the Temple, where aides and full-time Temple staff considered themselves above the rank and file.[13] The most serious charge, however, insinuated racism abetted by Jones himself. "You said that the revolutionary focal point at present is in the black people," the eight undersigned wrote. "Yet, where is the black leadership, where is the black staff and black attitude?" Nowhere to be found, they observed. Unable to track them down or bring them back, Jones could not hide the defections from his church. He began to refer to the defectors as the "so-called Eight Revolutionaries," and accused the students who dared to criticize his revolutionary techniques of violent radicalism. In family meetings, he portrayed them as a Weathermen-like cell that had betrayed the Temple's pacifism by plotting to kill people with explosives.

By 1976, a number of other high-level defections had begun to fuel Jones's paranoia about a widespread conspiracy to destroy Peoples Temple. Added to the familiar cast of villains—honkeys, racist cops, the elitist press, the Eight Revolutionaries, the FBI, and the CIA—were estranged loyalists who posed a far more tangible threat to the Temple: they understood its finances, and had heard and seen too many damaging things. Although most defectors wished only to escape the church, Jones threatened them with retribution if they ever publicly opposed him or the Temple. Jones told defectors to move 1,000 miles away if they wanted to be left alone, and sent loyalist thugs to harass those who defected without going into hiding.

Jones's mounting paranoia was not limited to defectors. On tour, Jones began to speak with increasing urgency of the need for African Americans in the cities he visited to join the Temple in order to escape confinement in concentration camps. Jones had adapted this bullet point from the King Alfred Plan, a widely discussed conspiracy theory that derived from the 1967 bestselling novel by John A. Williams, *The Man Who Cried I Am*. Jones referred to the King Alfred Plan on many occasions in recorded sermons, but made no mention of its fictional provenance. Instead, it became a set piece in his dim representation of the life that awaited those who refused to see the writing on the wall: the honkeys were planning to eliminate them.

In a 1976 sermon in Philadelphia, Jones compared the plight of American blacks to that of Jews before the Holocaust, likening American institutional racism and the recently uncovered Tuskegee Experiment to the medical experiments the Nazis conducted on Jewish prisoners. "Yesterday," he told his listeners:

> the Academy of Science demanded, the world's scientists demanded, the US scientists demanded [at] the world science convention that they be allowed to teach that the black people are an inferior race. I got the newspaper here. Don't you know what they're getting ready to do? That's what they did with the Jews, before they murdered seven million of them. Now I know some of you say, I got my Bible, it'll take me through. The Jews—some of you walkin' out [*people exit in disgust*]—the Jews were *chosen* people. That's what their Bible said. But seven million of them were exterminated in gas ovens. Buried alive, burned alive. Shot in *Christian* churches.
> [...]
> [You] say, it won't happen here. Have you been reading about our [poor/black] young women, 12 and 11, that have

been eugenically, they call it eugenically, given therapy so
they can't have babies? Meaning that they've been *sterilized*?
Did you read last year of the three hundred and some—the
seven hundred and so men that were given syphilis, black,
and not even given a penicillin shot when it could have cured
them, and hundreds of them died, many of them went crazy?
Treated just like a guinea pig? Worked on like a rat, by the
United States Department of Health?

This Philadelphia sermon demonstrated Jones's fine-tuned rhetorical strategy of knitting together various obsessive harangues into a convincing worldview predicated on racialized capitalist oppression. Jones even advanced a conspiracy theory that attributed Patty Hearst's 1974 kidnapping by the Symbionese Liberation Army to fascist *agents provocateurs* who hoped to cause a backlash against black Americans. Echoing Cyrus Teed and Arthur L. Bell, Jones explained that the Hearst kidnapping was part of a capitalist plot to cause a war between poor whites and blacks, in order to eliminate the relative surplus labor:

Why do you think they're having this happen across this
nation? Boston, white people supposed to be set afire by black
people. White people shot on the street, supposedly by a black
cult, or black political group. They want the poor to start a
war amongst themselves. Because with this mass production,
they don't *need* poor workers anymore. The cotton fields don't
need cotton pickers, because they've got mechanized cotton
pickers. So they want to do away with a lot of the poor people,
and there's no better way to do away with them than to start
a *race* war between blacks and poor whites, and that will kill
them off, just like they killed them off in Vietnam, for a long
time. They killed us all off in Vietnam. Thirty-seven percent
of our people that died over there were black, yet only 10%
of the population is supposed to be black. [You] say, I didn't

come here to hear about that—No. You came here thinking this was another church, some of you. You thought you'd be lied to, just like your preachers lied to you. *I've* come to save you. I've come to save you, *not* from *sin*, but from the *sinners*, the honkies that have sinned against you![14]

Jones went so far as to claim that white reactionaries were dressing up in blackface to commit crimes in order to hasten the racist dictatorship that would inevitably be installed when Americans demanded a restoration of law and order. He assured listeners that by joining Peoples Temple, they placed themselves among a special elect who saw through the lies of the capitalist media, the racist school systems, Uncle Tom preachers, and the bourgeois media. Only his truth could save them.

Jones's claims in members-only meetings far exceeded those he made in public: he convinced some of his following that top aides had assembled an atomic bomb in Mexico. Among his most trusted inner circle, Jones had also begun to test the waters for possible "last stand" measures, to be taken in the event that the Temple found itself faced with destruction by the fascists. Jones had every right to be concerned about racist police tactics, the racist and classist criminal justice system, and the extralegal smear campaigns and FBI-led persecution of leftists in the United States. But the idea that the Temple had become a target of state repression was one of Jones's paranoid devising: it resulted from his constant efforts to portray himself as a subversive leader of the civil rights and New Left movements, an activist on par with Angela Davis, Bobby Seale, Dennis Banks, and César Chávez. Although Jones was on friendly terms with Davis and Banks, who were among those to publicly defend him when the Temple later did come under siege, it was Jones who sought to benefit from the association.

Jones first floated the proposition of mass suicide with an experiment conducted among a small set of advisers while holding a meeting on the stage of the auditorium of Benjamin Franklin Junior High School on New Year's Day, 1974—not long after the Eight Revolutionaries defections in autumn 1973. During the meeting, Jones offered his exhausted inner circle permission to indulge in a rare treat: a glass of wine supposedly pressed from Temple grapes. Later in the evening, after everyone had partaken of the wine, Jones told them it was poisoned. After watching how they reacted, Jones reassured his advisers it was only a drill, but that members of Peoples Temple must be prepared to die defending their faith in apostolic socialism.

Over succeeding years, Jones conditioned wider circles of Temple faithful to accept the possible necessity of dying for the cause. Black Panther Huey Newton, who had relatives in the Temple, inadvertently gave Jones a convenient slogan for this drastic measure with the title of his 1973 memoir, *Revolutionary Suicide*. Jones had preached against suicide for decades, teaching that anyone who killed himself would regress back to zero on the evolutionary ladder of reincarnations, forcing him to endure countless lives of suffering before being given the opportunity to live in heaven on Earth once more. Newton's concept of revolutionary suicide originally meant sacrificing one's life while fighting for justice. In Jones's adaptation, the phrase was stretched to include dying like the Jews at Masada, who had committed mass suicide rather than surrender to pagan Roman invaders. Unlike reactionary suicide, revolutionary suicide would confer a special spiritual status on those who died in the name of the cause.

. . .

THE FINAL YEARS OF Peoples Temple history left behind a chaotic record of missteps, scandal, overreaction, panic, and tragedy. Few could have predicted that just two years after having tea with Mrs. Carter, Jones and nearly a thousand of his followers would be dead. But the Temple's year of ascendency had the effect of training a spotlight on Jones and his shady affairs—and what it exposed wasn't pretty.

To make matters worse, practically everything Jones did in response to criticism only brought more problems.

Expecting heightened scrutiny as his public stature increased, Jones stepped up security at the Temple: its double doors remained locked during members-only meetings. Temple guards frisked visitors to open services before they were cleared for entry, and Jones seldom went anywhere without his posse of uniformed bodyguards. Combined with Jones's uncloaked political ambitions, these absurd and paranoid theatrics excited the San Francisco press. But whereas Jones had previously managed to choke investigations by the *Examiner* and curry favor with Herb Caen, the *Chronicle* reporter assigned to cover the Temple, it was a lightweight lifestyle magazine that managed to bring him down.

Stymied by editors at the *Chronicle*, who were wary of Jones's political power, reporter Marshall Kilduff pitched an exposé of Peoples Temple to *New West*, a monthly devoted to breezier fare than investigations of potentially corrupt churches. Although *New West* initially declined the pitch, a change to the top of the masthead led the magazine to reconsider. Kilduff teamed up with Phil Tracy, a former *Village Voice* reporter who had only recently arrived in San Francisco, where he acted as contributing editor to *New West*. The duo met and profiled a dozen defectors from Peoples Temple. Among them were Al and Jeannie Mills, former Temple stalwarts known in the church as Elmer and Deanna Mertle. The Millses had filed suit against the Temple, alleging Jones had swindled them of all their property and that their teenage daughter Linda was severely beaten at a Temple family meeting following accusations the teenager was violating the celibacy rule by engaging in lesbian trysts with a school friend. Also going public was Grace Stoen, who was suing Jones for custody of her child John Victor. Jones claimed he was the boy's father, citing an affidavit Tim Stoen had signed, requesting that Jones impregnate his wife. Four of the Eight Revolutionaries resurfaced with additional testimony.

All of the defectors had damning things to say. They readily confirmed that Temple services open to the public, especially those to which political allies were invited, were nothing more than "orchestrated events" designed to flatter guests and to impress them with the Temple's good deeds. By contrast, Kilduff and Tracy wrote, daily life in the church was "a mixture of Spartan regimentation, fear, and self-imposed humiliation."[5] Other revelations were far more unsavory, such as the claims that up to 100 members might be paddled during a single disciplinary session, and that Temple members were made to fight boxing matches as a form of punishment. Asked for comment, some of Jones's allies didn't help his case. Regarding Jones's electioneering skills, Willie Brown told the reporters, "In a tight race like the ones that George [Moscone] or [District Attorney Joseph] Freitas or [Sheriff Richard] Hongisto had, forget it without Jones."[6] Such a statement might have sounded impressive in a smoke-filled back room. It did not look good in print.

Reports of a break-in at *New West*—later determined to be the result of an employee who'd locked himself out of the office—heightened expectations surrounding the article's publication. San Franciscans following the unfolding story assumed that Jones ordered the burglary. But the Temple denied involvement, and in any case, Kilduff and Tracy's finished copy survived the alleged burglary. The night before its publication, the magazine's editor read Jones the essay over the telephone. It was an incendiary piece.

After the infamous article hit newsstands, Jones could not immediately be reached for comment: fearing surveillance and investigation by the FBI, CIA, and IRS, as well as a protracted legal battle over the paternity and custody of John Victor Stoen, Jones had fled to the Promised Land in Guyana. Although Marceline and other advisers believed he would stay in South America only until the scandal had blown over, Jones never returned to the United States. He resigned his position on the Housing Commission by radio patch.

Jones's flight set the countdown to the destruction of Peoples Temple, which he had secretly been planning for years. "Father" had already begun to accelerate the migration to the Promised Land in April 1977, when lawsuits began to batter the movement. Stung by his San Francisco downfall, Jones was determined not to be without his adoring children. He ordered his aides to arrange a mass migration of more than a thousand people to a colony that was never intended to become home to the entire congregation. Jones stated that the mass migration was necessary because he could no longer protect the Temple from American fascism. But by this point, Jones had other ideas for how to protect the legacy of Peoples Temple and ensure his place in history.

42. JONESTOWN

DOZENS OF BOOKS written by Peoples Temple opponents, loyalist survivors, reporters assigned to document the embattled church's tribulations, and historians who have pored over the FBI's RYMUR (RYan MURder) files have made it clear that there will probably never be agreement on some of the most fundamental aspects of what happened in Jonestown after Jones arrived. The community was deliberately located beyond the purview of the American news media, law enforcement, and families of Temple members. Most witnesses to the settlement's daily activities perished there in November 1978. With regard to the American messianic tradition, the most salient detail is this: from the day he departed American soil, Jim Jones never preached another sermon. Some of the elders in Jonestown continued to view Jones as a deity and the Temple as a religious body. But most now regarded Peoples Temple as a radical political organization, and considered Jones to be one of history's great socialist leaders.[1] He had finally cast off what Temple survivor Kathy Barbour called the "cloak" of religion, which she and many other members had seen through since the early days in Redwood Valley.[2]

As with previous Promised Lands, the Guyana settlement was founded on grand ambitions. Relocation had been discussed among the PC and top advisers at least since Jones proposed a study on the possibility of relocating the Temple to the USSR in the late 1960s. After considering Brazil, Cuba, the Soviet Union, Tanzania, and Uganda, the PC gave Guyana's multiethnic Socialist republic its top recommendation. After Jones negotiated a lease with the Guyanese government in December 1973, the Temple began sending troubled and restless youth to Guyana, where their energies were put to use constructing a settlement for Temple members who'd finally had enough of American fascism. In Jonestown, they would build a classless society where elders would be valued, people of all races would form one large family, and women would exercise equal rights and responsibilities to men. After its arrival in California, Temple membership had become predominantly female, and Temple leadership evolved in response. By the end of its days in Jonestown, the Temple's day-to-day operations were supervised by women close to Jones: lawyer Harriet Tropp, Jones's occasional sex partners Maria Katsaris and Terri Buford, his longtime mistress Carolyn Layton, her sister Annie Moore, and diehard zealot Sharon Amos were among those who ascended to Jones's right hand over the course of the 1970s.

The Jonestown settlement developed slowly for its first two years. But because the project placed a faithful bet on the abilities of young men who'd been written off as past and future wards of the court and prison systems, it became another tool in the Temple's political PR kit. The initial settlers enjoyed modest successes as they experimented with slash-and-burn agriculture in the middle of the jungle, and slowly erected the town pavilion, outhouses, kitchen, and dormitories. By most accounts, those who went to Jonestown before the summer of 1977 enjoyed life in the jungle in spite of the grueling manual labor: it was rewarding work, and allowed those who had previously sparred with Jones to keep out of his way. As late as Lieutenant Governor Dymally's visit to Jonestown in late 1976, the settlement was so impressive that Dymally later wrote to Mayor Moscone to urge him to visit. He told the mayor:

> It was an experience that I will never forget. There they
> were, young and old, black and white, all working together
> to build a new community in the heart of the jungle. In that

virgin forest, the members of the Temple are raising cattle
and pigs, and planting cassava (a tropical food similar to the
yam). They are building homes, repairing tractors and heavy
machinery, and building roads.

What was more inspiring was the support, commitment
and high morale of the people there.

It is a project that all Californians can be proud of and
I hope some day your busy schedule will permit you to visit
Jonestown as I did.[3]

By the time the *New West* exposé appeared, Jonestown was lurch-
ing toward its chimerical goal of economic self-sufficiency. Everything
changed when Jones arrived that August, followed by wave after wave
of pilgrims the colony was not prepared to absorb. By 1978, the commune was bursting with new arrivals: cottages simply could not be
built fast enough to shelter the continual stream of newcomers, who
crammed by the dozen into structures meant to house only four.

Jonestown accommodations were meant to reflect the Temple's
socialist values. Babies were raised communally in a nursery named
after Cuffy, a Guyanese freedom fighter. Children lived separately
from their parents in a communal children's home. Elders crowded
into dorms for seniors, some containing triple bunks. Married couples required permission for cohabitation, and were allowed to occupy
double beds in the lofts of some cottages pending approval of the Relationships Committee, which arranged and approved couplings and
pregnancies.

Despite the crowding, Temple members kept arriving not only
because Jones told them to but because the news from Guyana was
always rosy. "I am still waiting for you," teenage Patricia Houston
wrote her mother, Phyllis: "Jonestown is too beautiful to show in pictures, write on letters, etc. You have to be here and get the beautiful feeling of being where you are free. I am glad that Dad [Jones]
has provided this place for us."[4] In fact, letters from Jonestown were

censored and filled with generic praise of Jonestown's beauty. Some appeared to be dictated by an authority figure, with phrases repeated across the communications of numerous colonists—this was particularly the case regarding assurances that the colonists had enough to eat. But other letters contained heartfelt appreciation of the inspiring and enriching lives the communards were leading, now that they were free to practice apostolic socialism with less interference from the US government. Jonestown was not merely the prison camp that some escapees and survivors later claimed it was. Seniors who'd passed their whole lives without access to education were learning to read in the Jonestown schoolhouse. According to Tim Carter, Jonestown had eliminated illiteracy in the Temple. Nurses at the Jonestown clinic provided free services to the local Guyanese and Amerindians. Children were being brought up to value fairness and equality.

To the members of Concerned Relatives, an advocacy group comprised of worried family and friends of Temple members in Guyana, none of the Temple's PR was convincing. The group was a loose affiliation of Temple relatives and defectors who wished to rescue friends and loved ones from Jonestown, where they correctly suspected that some people were being held against their will. The Stoens and the Millses were the backbone of Concerned Relatives, along with Steven Katsaris, whose daughter Maria had been one of Jones's many sexual interests in Redwood Valley, and was now one of Jones's top aides in Jonestown. Concerned Relatives began its campaign by lobbying local officials and members of Congress for an investigation of the Temple. Although emissaries from the Guyanese government and American consulate had visited the Jonestown settlement and determined that there was no cause for alarm and no sign of confinement, Concerned Relatives did not desist. They used Guyanese and American courts to try to force Jones to hand over John Victor Stoen, and demanded that the Temple allow the parents of minors in Jonestown to see their children. And they encouraged the Social Security Administration, the IRS, and the US Post Office to investigate Peoples Temple.

After his arrival in Jonestown, Jones kept the community in a constant state of alarm. His paranoia became infectious as he employed thought-control techniques on the isolated communards. Chief among Jones's strategies was to have his voice occupy more and more of his followers' collective consciousness: when he wasn't holding all-night family meetings in the Jonestown pavilion, Jones literally broadcast his thoughts over the community loudspeakers, so that workers could hear him as they toiled at their various agricultural tasks. Even when he lay in a drug-induced stupor, tape-recorded reruns of Jones's rants were broadcast across the settlement.

Many began to suspect the obvious: Jones was losing it. Top advisers recommended that Jones moderate his conduct, but in Jonestown, cooler heads seldom managed to prevail: the extremists Jones had promoted to leadership positions—Sharon Amos, Carolyn Layton, Annie Moore, and Johnny Brown Jones—usually carried the day. There were at least a few dozen Temple members—and as many as several hundred—who wished to die defending socialism as much as Jones did. The crucial difference was that Jones and his top brass kept almost everyone else in the dark about the community's failures to break even, its untouched overseas millions, and the exaggerations Jones made regarding purported threats against the community. His twisted presentation of the American news—in which he falsely claimed Nazis were holding rallies in San Francisco and Los Angeles and that race riots had broken out across America—were meant to give the impression that there was no going back to California, because there was no worthwhile life to which the communards might return. The United States, he repeatedly related, was welcoming the onset of a fascist dictatorship.

Slowly Jones and his aides conditioned hundreds to believe they actually were locked in a struggle for their collective survival. Whenever the Temple was dealt a legal setback or forced to contend with the fallout of a defection, Jones manufactured a state of emergency in Jonestown, connecting the latest tribulation with a vast right-wing conspiracy against the Temple. During the infamous "Six Day Siege" of September 1977, the communards lost a week of work in the fields when Jones forced them to secure the perimeter of the settlement around the clock, using machetes and other agricultural tools as weapons to ward off the mercenary invaders Jones alleged were encircling the village. Marceline Jones, who was in San Francisco at the time, credulously sent word of the siege to Jones's allies, resulting in patched-in radio communications from the likes of Angela Davis and Huey Newton, who urged the revolutionaries to stand strong.

In fact, the entire "attack" was staged by Jones, his aides, and the Jonestown security detail, who crept into the bush and fired their weapons to simulate an ambush. After the siege concluded, emergency drills and meetings increased in frequency and eventually became known by the code name "White Nights," regardless of the time of day they occurred. During White Nights, Jones often spoke about the possible necessity of dying for the cause and invited others to do the same. The communards repeatedly upheld the decision to commit revolutionary suicide, if necessary. But whenever the community "voted" in favor of depriving fascist conspirators the pleasure of killing them in an invasion, Jones and others berated those opposed to suicide as lacking in revolutionary principles. At a White Night in February 1978, the communards were told the time had come to drink what was said to be poisoned punch. It was only another test. The results pleased Jones but worried many in Jonestown, who saw they would have no choice about whether to participate if and when the time came: armed guards supervised the entire process. Many in Jonestown also knew that anyone who demonstrated mutinous tendencies—including attorney Gene Chaikin—was given a grilled cheese sandwich laced with Thorazine, an antipsychotic drug. When not confined to Jonestown's clinic, drugged colonists staggered around the settlement as an example to others. A sensory-deprivation cell dug into the ground menaced as another potential punishment. Tactics in Jonestown evinced an eerily modern return to the stockades and scarlet letters of the Puritan theocracy.

. . .

THROUGHOUT 1978, morale and finances deteriorated as the Temple's legal troubles multiplied. Jones instructed an educated follower named Edith Roller to begin teaching Russian in the Jonestown schoolhouse, and resuscitated hope in the idea that the Temple might relocate to Russia if the going got tough in Guyana. Led by Sharon Amos, Temple staff in Georgetown were in fact conducting serious negotiations with the Soviet embassy, where personnel had expressed cautious interest in having a delegation from Jonestown visit the USSR. The potential embarrassment a mass relocation would cause the United States was too delicious not to consider. These contacts resulted in an October 1978 visit from Soviet consul Feodor Timofeyev to the Temple commune, where he was feted with unprecedented enthusiasm in Jonestown. As Jones became increasingly desperate and paranoid that autumn, Amos ratcheted up the pressure on the Russians. But she was an inexperienced diplomat, and her grating impatience put the Russians off the idea.

A conspiracy against Jim Jones did, of course, exist: it was the plot openly waged by Concerned Relatives, who continued to gain valuable allies as a result of Jones's erratic conduct. Following high-level defections from Jonestown, particularly those of Yulanda Williams and Debbie Layton in spring of 1978, Concerned Relatives could point to affidavits sworn out by apostates as proof that they were not exaggerating the danger Jones posed to his people. Layton's sworn testimony addressed the cruel and abusive treatment of residents in Jonestown, and alleged that Jones was mentally unwell.

Although Williams was released voluntarily on the condition that she keep her mouth shut, Debbie Layton's unexpected defection caused a protracted White Night in Jonestown. Her escape inspired Terri

Buford to defect later that year. These were crushing blows to Jones, who told his followers he literally died (and presumably expended valuable energy resurrecting himself) when Layton abandoned them. Terri Buford and Debbie Layton had both been involved sexually with Jones; both had knowledge of the Temple's shady finances; and Layton had personally overseen some of the church's cloak-and-dagger overseas banking.[5] Layton's affidavit also alleged preparations for mass suicide in Jonestown; it got her a temporary passport and a ticket out of Guyana. After returning to the States, Layton submitted the same allegations to the US State Department and to members of Congress. Leo Ryan, a California congressman with constituents in Jonestown, took notice.

Custody battles and legal troubles came to a head when Ryan scheduled a visit to the Guyana settlement. Jones initially planned to forbid the congressman access to Jonestown, but his lawyers eventually persuaded him that transparency was in the Temple's best interest. After a tense two-day visit that included interviews with Temple members whom Concerned Relatives believed were held against their will, a party of fifteen defectors departed Jonestown with Leo Ryan, his aides, and the press corps that joined them. Jones ordered an attack on Ryan's party as they boarded two planes on the remote airstrip at Port Kaituma, seven miles from Jonestown. Ryan was killed in the attack, along with three newsmen and one Temple defector. The congressman's aide, Jackie Speier, who now serves Ryan's former district in Congress, was shot and left for dead—as were several of the others.

When he received confirmation that the congressman had been assassinated, Jones called the final White Night. There was no other option, Jones told his people. Russia would not take them, and it was pointless to abandon the cause now that the assassination had occurred: the CIA or the Guyanese Defense Forces would soon arrive to kill them all and send their children back to fascist America. It was better to die for the cause. Whereas Newton's theory of revolutionary suicide would have required the Temple to defend itself to the death, Jones told his people it was more honorable to choose the time and method of their demise. Together, they would make an unforgettable statement that it was better to die for socialism than live another day under fascism.

So it was that on November 18, 1978, nearly everyone in Jonestown died as a result of cyanide poisoning. The children were the first to "step over": Jonestown nurses summoned the mothers of babies and small children to carry them to the front of the pavilion, where a cocktail of Flavor Aid, cyanide, and tranquilizers was squirted into their mouths with syringes. Most of the adults drank the potion voluntarily, but survivors of the massacre say they may have had little choice: just as had occurred during the rehearsals, armed guards enforced the act. Jones was one of the few who did not consume the poisoned elixir. He died of a gunshot wound to the head.

The Jonestown Massacre, as it is sometimes known, marked the end—for now—of a two-hundred-year tradition of American messianic communalism.

EPILOGUE

THE AMERICAN DISPOSITION toward communalist religions changed radically on November 18, 1978. Although the Jonestown murder-suicides took place in a small Socialist country on another continent, the inescapable and indelible imagery of the tragedy—in which Americans saw hundreds of bloated bodies strewn around the Jonestown pavilion—brought an end to what had been a relatively tolerant attitude toward idiosyncratic religious movements in the United States throughout the 1970s. The Jonestown tragedy reinvigorated an otherwise flagging trend known today as the anti-cult movement (ACM). This "movement" had its roots in the traditionalist response to countercultural activity in the 1960s, and is part of a longer cycle of cult/anti-cult activity in American culture, including the seventeenth-century witchcraft panic, the nineteenth-century anti-Masonic movement, and the anti-cult movement of the 1940s.

Although the "revolutionary" suicide of Peoples Temple was a uniquely grotesque and terrifying event, the decision to die at Jonestown was consistent with aspects of Temple political ideology and what might be called its theology. However, the media and the vast majority of the American public turned not to religious scholars for explanation and understanding but to self-promoting psychologists and other "experts" affiliated with the anti-cult movement. They did so because ACM activists cast themselves as so many Cassandras who had been sounding the alarm for the entire decade that Peoples Temple amassed the majority of its followers.

The truly American response to the Jonestown tragedy was characterized by a strong entrepreneurial current: a cottage industry of professionals, ranging from academic psychologists to rebranded bounty hunters calling themselves "deprogrammers," emerged to steer Americans out of the clutches of putatively demented cult leaders. Professional deprogrammers, the term used for those who claimed to specialize in undoing the effects of brainwashing, went on *Donahue* and testified before congressional committees about the continuing dangers of cults hidden in the midst of Reagan's America. The cult menace remained a national obsession until it was finally eclipsed by the emergence of global jihadism early in the twenty-first century. As a result, any group engaged in that very American activity of critique, separation, purification, and regeneration became subject to social sanction and government scrutiny.

The anti-cult obsession had deadly consequences for the Branch Davidians, a messianic society led by Vernon Howell, a prophet who had taken the name David Koresh. Responding to allegations that the Davidians possessed illegal firearms and engaged in aberrant sexual practices, the Bureau of Alcohol, Tobacco, and Firearms sent more than seventy armed agents and two Blackhawk helicopters with a warrant to search the Davidians' complex of buildings at Mount Carmel outside Waco, Texas, in February 1993. Following a violent confrontation and the subsequent fifty-one-day siege of the property by the FBI, Attorney General Janet Reno concluded the standoff by authorizing the bureau's plan to assault the cornered Davidians. The attacks ended up killing four agents and at least seventy-four of the Davidians, most of whom died in a fire that razed the building where they were under siege. Ironically, the use of force was publicly justified by constant appeals to the horror of Jonestown, which stoked fears that the Davidians would commit mass suicide rather than surrender. There was no evidence that the Davidians ever intended to do so—but in any case, they were murdered before anyone could know for sure. Their classification as members of a "cult" made the killings acceptable, if not inevitable, in the eyes of many Americans.[1]

. . .

EVADING THE "CULT" LABEL is imperative for any minority religion that hopes to avoid a violent and tragic end. In the twenty-first century, a new messianic religion has so far managed it. Concentrated in Silicon Valley, the latest amalgamation of old American messianic tropes has gathered under a techno-futurist, New Age banner emblazoned with the word "Singularity." Although the Singularity refers to an event, specifically a moment of technological rapture, it is, like all American messianic religions, more of a mindset than a coherent belief system. Adherents to the movement are growing in number, and their plans for redesigning life as we know it have become increasingly grandiose. Fortunately for these devotees, the Singularity movement has largely evaded perception as a cult-like organization. It has done so by avoiding, for the most part, the dangers of conflating human salvation with the destiny of a single individual, and by reconciling American messianic thought with its old adversary: capitalism.

Adherents to the movement are students of the work of Ray Kurzweil, a septuagenarian futurist and entrepreneur. Kurzweil believes that within his lifetime, a historical achievement known as the Singularity will allow humankind to ascend to the next level of evolutionary existence: its inseparable union with artificial intelligence. In fact, the Singularity will render the distinction between human and artificial intelligence largely irrelevant, as they will become increasingly imbricated and difficult, if not impossible, to distinguish. In Kurzweil's view, intractable problems like climate change, resource scarcity, sickness, and even death will be eliminated by the Singularity, not least because it will liberate humankind from the organic prison of carbon-based bodies.

In his book *The Age of Spiritual Machines* (1999), Kurzweil claims that humans will "become software." As a consequence, he writes, "there won't be mortality by the end of the twenty-first century."[2] Kurzweil likes to describe the advances enabled by the Singularity as a logarithmic upturn on the evolutionary curve. He believes that his work is hastening the evolutionary development of the human species into something that can no longer be called strictly human. Like Thomas Lake Harris and Cyrus Teed, he sees a new race evolving to supplant the old "corruptible," decadent, miserable humanity. His evolutionary, deo-morphic theology is not unlike theirs; nor is plugging into the Singularity all that dissimilar from the attunement to Abundance extolled by Father Divine, or the mission to become as gods on Earth under the holy regime of apostolic socialism. But unlike his predecessors in American messianic thought, Kurzweil believes that capitalism is not the engine of damnation, but of salvation.

. . .

ENTHUSIASTS OF THE SINGULARITY believe the unfettered free market, particularly the one in Silicon Valley, will bring about the quantum rapture they eagerly await. Opponents of the movement decry its uncritical embrace of AI as naïve boosterism for corporate prerogatives. I decided to look into things myself.

In August 2017, I jumped security and made it into the Singularity University Global Summit at the San Francisco Hilton. It was no easy task: the convention is very well staffed, and black-suited convention employees kept an eye out for convention registration badges at the doorway to every ballroom lecture hall and breakout-session dining room. The enormous badges, proudly emblazoned with the name of each attendee and that of his or her employer, were to be worn from a lanyard printed with the phrase "Be Exponential." The absence of one around my neck was noted in glances directed at my midsection. I'd already been bounced from the expo hall once, and my ploy to acquire a press pass, recommended by a friend who'd crashed the party the year before, had failed. The Global Summit isn't a secret, invitation-only convention. But admission is priced north of $2,000, so I couldn't afford to be exponential. As indicated by the badges I studied as I wandered between sessions, large multinational corporations like Deloitte and Procter & Gamble send midlevel executives to the summit to do reconnaissance on technological innovations in established and emerging markets.

The steep entry fee is part of the high-gloss veneer of selectivity favored by the organization. Most attendees believe their presence at the summit confers a special stature on their intellect and an illustrious destiny on whatever entrepreneurial endeavor has brought them there. Alumni of Singularity University receive "enhanced" clearance, which provides access to private lunches and sessions where the most elite futurists gather to discuss questions related to the future of human civilization. Attendees were overwhelmingly young, male, and poorly shaven.

I spent the afternoon in Hilton Grand Ballrooms A and B, where plenary talks were held. There I listened as innovators and "disruptors" were invited one after the next to take the stage and share with those assembled whatever TED-talk platitudes they'd rehearsed in hotel bathroom mirrors the night before. As a resident of San Francisco, I was accustomed to their techno-futurist cheerleading and unaffected by the customary flattery of libertarian entrepreneurialism steeped in Objectivist self-regard: a "small group of people," one speaker informed the audience, was now capable of doing things that no nation-state can do. The obvious inference was that some of those people were in the building.

As the afternoon wore on, I heard about RNA sequencing and was instructed that "as a species we have changed the ways we think about the world around us." I learned that through interplanetary colonization, explorers might acquire resources from other planets, such as a small quantity of helium 3, which could meet all human energy needs on Earth. I was told that we should make every person "the CEO of his own health." And I listened as one speaker claimed that there was one thing that no one fights over, and that it was oxygen. What if energy or food, the speaker asked, were to become the "next oxygen?"—the abundance would lead to world peace. I glanced at the Shell employee seated beside me, to see if he, too, had registered the unintended irony. He had not.

The hyperpositivism on display in Kurzweil's writings was everywhere to be seen at the Singularity University Global Summit. But so were the trappings of American messianic discourse. While seated in those hotel ballrooms, lit by the blue glow of smartphones and the massive projections of each speaker's PowerPoint presentation, I was able to experience something that years of research on religious enthusiasm could never conjure: I got to feel what it was like to be surrounded by true believers in a cause that was only valued by an in-crowd, an ascendant elect. Circulating among them, I sensed the presence of that spirit that presides whenever so many ardent believers come together in its name. I could feel the souls uplifted. And yet my afternoon ended with a bruising fall from that levitation.

During one of the final keynote addresses, Will Weisman, a high-ranking dignitary from Singularity University, sat to interview a woman about her company, which uses blockchain technology to simplify the process of paying royalties to recording artists. Her clients included the heartthrob singer-songwriter John Legend, who had recently been visiting prisons to perform for the downtrodden and forgotten. "It's so nice to see the social impact being woven into what you're doing and the people you're working with," Weisman told the blockchain entrepreneur. "And it would be amazing to get some of those folks here and have them drink some of the Singularity Kool-Aid—although I'm sure you're passing that on!" She assured him that she was.

. . .

NEEDLESS TO SAY, Weisman was unaware that jokes about drinking the Kool-Aid are supposed to be made by an organization's detractors—not its adherents or evangelists. Apparently, nobody in the audience knew this either: a ripple of polite laughter washed over the auditorium. The tone-deafness of making a Kool-Aid joke in San Francisco was lost on everyone present. Forty years on, the lives of hundreds of activists who died hoping to make the world a better place were trivialized into a meme divorced from its referent and clumsily deployed to wrap up an interview at a corporate conference.

What seldom emerges in conversations with techno-futurists is the realization that there is already enough material abundance on Earth to keep everyone alive and happy. Only greed comes between basic resources and the hungry, sick, and homeless people who need them. That conversations about limitless abundance would occur in one of the richest cities in human history is hardly surprising. But the fact that more than 7,000 people go to sleep on that city's pavements each night is a problem that cannot be solved by quantum computing, algorithms, or mobile apps—to say nothing of multinational banks, fancy consulting firms, and fossil-fuel companies. It is an abuse of power that exploits the weak and vulnerable in the interest of making a profit. Correcting such a miscarriage of justice requires not technological disruption, but the compassion of a human heart.

The American messianic impulse is based on a fundamentally irrefutable truth first observed by the Puritans: the injustices of capitalist culture cannot be reformed from within. They are symptoms of the system's health, not its disease. As Peoples Temple survivor Bryan Kravitz reminded me four decades after Jim Jones issued his last warning about the fascist conspiracy to confine African Americans to concentration camps, private corporations run prisons whose inmates are disproportionately gathered from the sort of poor black and brown communities where Jones concentrated his outreach. Jones's prophecy was correct, but for one detail: Americans did not require a fascist regime to jail more than 2 million people. It was a conspiracy conducted in the open, with the support of presidents of both major political parties and the broad approval of most American evangelicals.

America's messianic societies were not perfect: in their quest to tame the vices of hypertrophied American individualism, some of America's messiahs engaged in forms of repression and control that most would consider authoritarian, if not abusive. Particularly in its final years, Peoples Temple exploited human tendencies for religious zealotry and set them to work toward a violent extremism that previous messianic societies lacked.

By and large, however, American messianic experiments in apostolic socialism appealed to converts' highest ideals: they stood for equal access to jobs and education, gender parity, racial justice, and more dignified human labor. By joining together in communal bonds of solidarity, adherents often staked everything they had—all their material wealth, as well as their affective energies—on the survival of the group. These sects were strange to outsiders—as strange, perhaps, as the apostolic communes were to the pagans of the Roman Empire. That they appear irrelevant to American historians, aberrant to contemporary evangelicals, and abhorrent to the average consumerist is a signature of the victory capitalism has achieved over the American religious imagination, and a sign of how far American Christians have strayed from the values their Messiah held most dear.

ACKNOWLEDGMENTS

THE AUTHOR WISHES TO THANK Aaron Joseph, Ruth Halvey, Lindsay Owens, Jim Rutman, Katie Henderson Adams, Gina Iaquinta, Christian Goodwillie, Mark Tillson, Frances Kaplan, Lyn Millner, Carolyn Funk, A. P. Rung, Albert Plenty, Namwali Serpell, Shannon Garrison, Nikil Saval, Catherine Flynn, Garry Lambrev, Laura Johnston Kohl, Kathy Barbour, Bryan Kravitz, Yulanda Williams, Kristin Bedford, E. Black, Tommy and Lori Garcia, Fielding McGehee III, Rebecca Moore, Jill Watts, Joanie Rubin, Margarita Guillory, Bob Paquette, Elizabeth Bernhardt, the late Michael Predmore, Quincie Hamby, Bill Gwynn, Anne Peery, Zach Zaitlin, and the librarians and archivists at Hamilton College, the University of Rochester, Syracuse University, Columbia University, the San Francisco Public Library, the California Historical Society, and the State Library and Archives of Florida.

Research and writing were supported by the Walter Brumm Special Collections fellowship fund at Hamilton College Libraries; the Faber Residència d'Arts, Ciències i Humanitats in Olot, Catalonia; and by a postdoctoral fellowship at the University of Rochester Humanities Center.

The office of the Hon. Nancy Pelosi assisted with a Freedom of Information Act Request.

NOTES

Names of archives, special collections, public records, and periodicals are abbreviated throughout the notes. These abbreviations are identified in the bibliography.

INTRODUCTION

1. The story of the Walla Walla Kingdom of Heaven is drawn from Russell Blankenship, *And There Were Men* (New York: Alfred Knopf, 1942).
2. William McLoughlin, *Revivals, Awakenings, and Reform: An Essay on Religion and Social Change in America, 1607–1977*, Chicago: University of Chicago Press, 1978).
3. Harold Bloom, *The American Religion: The Emergence of the Post-Christian Nation* (New York: Simon & Schuster, 1992).

CHAPTER 1: THE PERSON FORMERLY KNOWN AS JEMIMA WILKINSON

1. David Hudson reports her year of birth as 1751; c.f. David Hudson, *Memoir of Jemima Wilkinson, A Preacheress of the Eighteenth Century; Containing an Authentic Narrative of Her Life and Character and of the Rise, Progress and Conclusion of Her Ministry.* [1821] (Bath, NY: R. L. Underhill & Co., 1844), 10.
2. Herbert A. Wisbey, *Pioneer Prophetess: Jemima Wilkinson, the Publick Universal Friend* (Ithaca: Cornell University Press, 1964), 5. Unless otherwise noted, citations of Wisbey refer to this biography.
3. Ibid., 2–3.

4. Ibid., 143–44.
5. Hudson, 11; E. W. Vanderhoof, *Historical Sketches of Western New York* (Buffalo: Matthews-Northrup, 1907), 107.
6. Wisbey, 4–5.
7. Paul B. Moyer, *The Public Universal Friend: Jemima Wilkinson and Religious Enthusiasm in Revolutionary America* (Ithaca: Cornell University Press, 2015), 15ff.
8. The Friend recounted this episode years later to James Emlen and others. Recorded in James Emlen's journal, October 8 [1794], quoted in Edwin B. Bronner, "Quakers Labor with Jemima Wilkinson," *Quaker History* 58.1 (Spring 1969): 43–44.
9. Mrs. Walter A. Hendricks and Arnold J. Potter. "The Universal Friend: Jemima Wilkinson," *New York History* 23.2 (April 1942): 160. Moyer, 11. Wisbey reports that there was no mention of typhus or Columbus fever in regional newspapers in either 1775 or 1776.
10. Quoted in Wisbey, 11.
11. Quoted in Ibid., 12–13. Spelling and capitalization per original.
12. I follow Paul B. Moyer in using male pronouns when referring to the Friend's identity as a prophet. As Moyer writes, "Using the feminine

pronouns [as many of the Friend's contemporaries did] implicitly denies a belief devoutly held by [the] Society of Universal Friends and their leader: that Jemima Wilkinson had been transformed into a heaven-sent masculine spirit." Moyer, 9, 100.

CHAPTER 2: THE UNIVERSAL FRIENDS

1. François-Alexandre-Frédéric Rochefoucauld-Liancourt, "Anecdotes of Jemima Wilkinson," *Travels in North America. The Monthly Visitor and New Family Magazine* (January 1801), 26.
2. Wisbey, 15.
3. Charles Lowell Marlin, "Jemima Wilkinson: Errant Quaker Divine," *Quaker History* 52.2 (Autumn 1963): 91.
4. See Abner Brownell, *Enthusiastical Errors, Transpired and Detected, by Abner Brownell, in a Letter to His Father, Benjamin Brownell* (New London: 1783), 21.
5. Quoted in Hendricks and Potter, 160.
6. Joscelyn Godwin, *Upstate Cauldron: Eccentric Spiritual Movements in Early New York State.* (Albany: SUNY Press, 2015), 32.
7. Wisbey, 32.
8. Ibid., 72.
9. Brownell, 4.
10. Ibid., 8.
11. Ibid., 6, 7–8.
12. Everett Webber, *Escape to Utopia: The Communal Movement in America* (New York: Hastings House, 1959), 78–79.
13. Quoted in Wisbey, 44.
14. Ezra Stiles wrote about her healing efforts in his diary. See Wisbey, 49.
15. Mrs. William Hathaway, *A Narrative of Thomas Hathaway and His Family, Formerly of New Bedford, Massachusetts, with Incidents in the Life of Jemima Wilkinson and the Times in Which They Lived* (New Bedford, MA: E. Anthony & Sons, 1869), 31.
16. Brownell reported that a meeting in New London attracted "more than three thousand People." Quoted in Moyer, 28.
17. Wisbey, 62–63.

CHAPTER 3: THE ALL-FRIEND IN THE CITY OF BROTHERLY LOVE

1. Moyer, 83.
2. François, Marquis de Barbé-Marbois. *Our Revolutionary Forefathers: The Letters of François, Marquis de Barbé-Marbois During His Residence in the United States as Secretary of the French Legation, 1779–1785.* Trans. Eugene Parker Case (New York: Duffield & Co., 1929), 162–63, 165.
3. Ibid., 163–64.
4. Ibid., 166.
5. Letter from Christopher Marshall to "Friend," January 28, 1789, [JWP].
6. Marshall maintained an epistolary relationship with Peter Müller, the spiritual leader of the Ephrata community. Moyer, 117.
7. Catherine Albanese explains that the Woman in the Wilderness colony brought Hermeticism, Rosicrucianism, Kabbalism, Pietism, and the influential mysticism of Jakob Böhme together in one sect. See Albanese, *A Republic of Mind & Spirit: A Cultural History of American Metaphysical Religion* (New Haven, CT: Yale University Press, 2007), 79.
8. Ibid., 79–81.
9. Mitch Horowitz, *Occult America: The Secret History of How Mysticism Shaped Our Nation* (New York: Bantam, 2009), 20.
10. Wisbey, 84, 87.
11. Moyer, 49.
12. Moyer, 110.
13. Quoted in Wisbey, 91.
14. Moyer, 120–27.

CHAPTER 4: NEW JERUSALEM

1. Hathaway, 14–15.
2. Moyer, 3.
3. Ibid., 120–26.
4. Ibid., 135.
5. Ibid., 135–138.
6. Wisbey, 159.
7. Ibid., 124–26.
8. Moyer, 145.
9. Moyer, 35.
10. Ibid., 152.
11. Wisbey, 153.
12. Wisbey, 142–52.
13. Rouchefocauld-Liancourt, 30–31.
14. Carl Carmer, "The Woman Who Died Twice," *The New Yorker*, May 9, 1936, 45–50.

CHAPTER 5: MOTHER ANN

1. This might account for why her father's name was sometimes spelled "Lees."
2. Anna White and Leila S. Taylor, *Shakerism: Its Meaning and Message* (Columbus, OH: Fred J. Heer, 1905), 15.
3. Ibid. and Henri Desroche, *The American Shakers: From Neo-Christianity to Presocialism*, trans. John K. Sacavol (Amherst: University of Massachusetts Press, 1971), 44.
4. Desroche, 47–49.
5. Stephen J. Stein. *The Shaker Experience in America* (New Haven: Yale, 1992), 3.
6. Desroche, 16–21.
7. Ibid., 37.
8. Stein, 5.
9. Raymond Lee Muncy, *Sex and Marriage in Utopian Communities. 19th-Century America* (Bloomington, IN: Indiana University Press, 1973), 17; Clara Endicott Sears, *Gleanings from Old Shaker Journals* (Harvard, MA: Fruitlands Museum, 1944), 25.
10. Ann Lee's niece Nancy would later marry John Hocknell's son, Richard, and leave the movement. Desroche, 50.

CHAPTER 6: THE UNITED SOCIETY OF BELIEVERS IN CHRIST'S SECOND APPEARING

1. Sears, 18–19.
2. Abraham Stanley's name has also been recorded as Abraham Standerin and Abraham Standley.
3. Henri Desroche has suggested the possibility that Meacham led a party of New Light Baptists into the wilderness to escape the war. *The American Shakers*, 90.
4. Stein, 13–14.
5. Sears, 21–23.
6. Albanese, 182.
7. Muncy, 18–19.
8. Desroche, 102.
9. Muncy, 20.
10. William Sims Bainbridge, "Shaker Demographics 1840–1900: An Example of the Use of U.S. Census Enumeration Schedules," *Journal for the Scientific Study of Religion* 21.4 (December 1982): 360.
11. Quoted in White and Taylor, 321.
12. Henri Troyat, *Tolstoy* (New York: Grove Press, 2001), 476.
13. White and Taylor, 3.

CHAPTER 7: THE ERA OF MANIFESTATIONS

1. Stein, 167.
2. Frederick Evans in the *Atlantic Monthly*, May 1896. Quoted in John Humphrey Noyes, *History of American Socialisms* (New York: Dover, 1966), 596.
3. Emma Hardinge, *Modern American Spiritualism: A Twenty Years' Record of the Communion Between Earth and the World of Spirits*, 3rd edition (New York: Published by the author, 1870), 27.

CHAPTER 8: AMERICA'S BEST-KNOWN MYSTIC

1. William James, *Varieties of Religious Experience: A Study in Human Nature.*

Centenary edition (New York: London, 2002), 15*n*.

2. Whitney Cross, *The Burned Over District: The Social and Intellectual History of Enthusiastic Religion in Western New York, 1800–1850* (New York: Harper & Row, 1950), 56.

3. Joseph W. Slade, "Historical Sketch of Thomas Lake Harris, Laurence Oliphant, and the Brotherhood of the New Life," in *Thomas Lake Harris and the Brotherhood of the New Life: Books, Pamphlets, Serials, and Manuscripts. 1854–1942*, ed. Jack T. Ericson. A Guide to the Mircofilm Collection (Glen Rock, NJ: Microfilming Corporation of America, 1974), 2.

4. W. P. Swainson, *Thomas Lake Harris and His Occult Teaching* (London: William Rider & Son, 1922), 11.

5. Herbert W. Schneider and George Lawton, *A Prophet and a Pilgrim: Being the Incredible Story of Thomas Lake Harris and Laurence Oliphant; Their Sexual Mysticisms and Utopian Communities Amply Documented to Confound the Skeptic* (New York: Columbia University Press, 1942), 4; Robert V. Hine, *California's Utopian Colonies* [1953] (Berkeley: University of California Press, 1983), 13.

6. Quoted in Schneider and Lawton, 5.

7. Swainson, 12.

CHAPTER 9: THE POUGHKEEPSIE SEER

1. Eric T. Carlson, "Charles Poyen Brings Mesmerism to America," *Journal of the History of Medicine and the Allied Sciences* 15.2 (April 1960), 121.

2. Horowitz, 33.

3. Ibid., *37–38*. On Poe's witness to Jackson Davis's phenomena, see Robert W. Delp, "Andrew Jackson Davis: Prophet of American Spiritualism," *The Journal of American History* 54.1 (June 1967): 44.

4. Edgar Allan Poe, "Review of *Human Magnetism,*" *Broadway Journal*, April 5, 1845. Reproduced by the Edgar Allan Poe Society of Baltimore and available online at https://www.eapoe.org/works/harrison/jah12co8.htm.

5. Edgar Allan Poe, "Mary Gove," July 1846. *The Literati of New York City, Part III.* Reproduced by the Edgar Allan Poe Society of Baltimore and available online at https://www.eapoe.org/works/misc/litratb3.htm#govemary.

6. Delp, "Andrew Jackson Davis," 44–45.

7. George Bush, *Mesmer and Swedenborg; Or, The Relation of the Development of Mesmerism to the Doctrines and Disclosures of Swedenborg* (New York: John Allen, 1847).

8. Andrew Jackson Davis, *The Magic Staff: An Autobiography of Andrew Jackson Davis*, 8th edition (Boston: Bela Marsh, 1867), 342.

9. Delp, "Andrew Jackson Davis," 45.

10. "Progress in Cincinnati," [USP], April 15, 1848, 312.

11. Ibid., 313.

12. Ibid.

13. Ibid.

CHAPTER 10: THE FOX SISTERS

1. For accounts of the Fox family saga, see E. W. Capron, *Modern Spiritualism: Its Facts and Fanaticisms, Its Consistencies and Contradictions, with an Appendix* (Boston: Bela Marsh, 1855); Hardinge; and Joseph McCabe, *Spiritualism: A Popular History from 1847* (New York: Dodd, Mead and Company, 1920).

2. Testimony reproduced in Capron, 39ff.

3. See Capron, 33–38.

4. Eliab W. Capron and Henry D. Barron, *Singular Revelations. Explanation and History of the Mysterious Communion with Spirits, Comprehending the Rise and Progress of the Mysterious Noises in Western New-York, Generally*

Received as Spiritual Communications,
2nd ed. (Auburn, NY: Capron and
Barron, 1850), 14.

5. Capron, 54.
6. Ibid., 51.
7. Capron and Barron, 45.
8. Ibid., 82–83. Margaretta Fox notoriously "exposed" the fraud she and her sisters committed, but later retracted her confession.
9. Hardinge, 10.
10. Capron and Barron, 96.
11. Albanese, 189.
12. Ibid., 217.
13. Horace Greeley to undisclosed recipient. Reprinted in Hardinge, 71.
14. Capron and Barron, 29.
15. Ann Braude, *Radical Spirits: Spiritualism and Women's Rights in Nineteenth-Century America* (Boston: Beacon Press, 1989), 23.
16. Capron and Barron, 92.
17. Braude, 89 and *passim.*

CHAPTER 11: THE APOSTOLIC CIRCLE

1. In *Spiritualist Magazine,* 1856, 60–63. Cited in Schneider and Lawton, 9–10, 11*n*10.
2. McCabe, 30.
3. Hardinge, 209.
4. Capron, 124–25.
5. C.f. John Benedict Buescher, *The Other Side of Salvation: Spiritualism and the Nineteenth-Century Religious Experience* (Boston: Skinner House, 2004), 79; and Capron, 118.
6. "Chosen vessels," Hardinge, 209. Accounts of this invitation vary slightly; it is unclear whether Harris summoned Mrs. Benedict in order to offer his services or whether she sought him out at the request of the apostolic spirits, as Hardinge and Capron suggest. Capron's original recounting of the Auburn–Mountain Cove adventure suggests there may have been

two meetings between Benedict and Harris in Brooklyn: the first in 1849 and the second after Harris's return to Brooklyn in 1850. C.f. Hardinge, 208; Albanese, 268; Capron, 117, 124–25.

7. Capron, 119.
8. Hardinge, 209.
9. I. S. Hyatt, "Modern Inspiration, at Mountain Cove," *Spiritual Telegraph,* October 16, 1852, 4.
10. Quoted in Hardinge, 210.
11. Capron, 125.
12. Ibid., 126.
13. Ibid., 127.
14. See Melissa Daggett, *Spiritualism in Nineteenth-Century New Orleans* (Jackson: University Press of Mississippi, 2017), 25. Schneider and Lawton, 20.

CHAPTER 12: POET IN NEW YORK

1. Hardinge, 213.
2. *The Spiritualist Register,* 1857, Compiled by Uriah and Eliza Clark, Auburn, NY.
3. Thomas Lake Harris, *The Wisdom of Angels* (New York: New Church Publishing Association, 1857), v–vi.
4. Ibid., 12–14.
5. Ibid., 15–16.
6. In fact, it was an audience member at one of Collyer's public lectures who first suggested that he magnetize a phrenological organ. See Taylor Stoehr, "Robert H. Collyer's Technology of the Soul," in *Pseudo-Science & Society in 19th-Century America,* ed. Arthur Wrobel (Lexington: University Press of Kentucky, 1987), 23, 32.
7. Albanese, *A Republic of Mind and Spirit,* 195.
8. Harris, *The Wisdom of Angels,* 18–24.
9. Hardinge, 214.
10. Thomas Lake Harris, *Song of Satan: A Series of Poems Originating from a Society of Infernal Spirits and Received, During Temptation Combats* (New

York: New Church Publishing Association, 1858), 4.

11. Schneider and Lawton, 38.

CHAPTER 13: THE BROTHERHOOD OF THE NEW LIFE

1. The first twelve disciples included individuals of American, English, Irish, and Scottish nationality. Arthur A. Cuthbert, *The Life and World-Work of Thomas Lake Harris. Written From Direct Personal Knowledge by Arthur A. Cuthbert, An Almost Life-Long Associate* (Glasgow: C.W. Pearce & Co., 1908), 17.

2. Requa died in 1868. "The Brocton Community," *Milwaukee Daily Sentinel,* December 12, 1873, Issue 294, 3.

3. Cuthbert, 27.

4. "An Autobiographic Sketch," [HOP], Box 4, Folder 2.

5. Cuthbert, 10.

6. Margaret Lockwood Carden, *Oneida: Utopian Community to Modern Corporation* [1969] (New York: Harper Torchbooks, 1971), 84. It was a stance common even to men of such conscience as Ralph Waldo Emerson, who wrote, "I have quite other slaves to free than those negroes, to wit, imprisoned spirits, imprisoned thoughts, far back in the brain of man." Quoted in Philip Lee, *Against the Protestant Gnostics* (New York: Oxford University Press, 1997), 124.

7. Cuthbert, 10.

8. This was more terminology that Harris adopted from Swedenborg.

9. "Experiences of a Sister in the New Life." Extracts of this document are recopied in letters between undisclosed recipients dated May 1, July 12, and October 19, 1881, [VVP], Folder 0000.9.1.4.

10. Cuthbert, 18.

11. Letter from Mrs. Cuthbert to unknown recipient, [HOP], Box 1, Folder 6.

CHAPTER 14: SALEM-ON-ERIE

1. "An Autobiographic Sketch," [HOP], Box 4, Folder 2.

2. "Successful" see William Alfred Hinds, *American Communities* [1878] (New York: Corinth Books, 1961), 141; initial speculations in Brocton began in 1865 according to William S. Bailey, "The Harris Community: Brotherhood of the New Life," *New York History* 16.3 (July 1935): 279; land purchases were not complete until October 1867, per Harris's letter to H. C. Taylor, reprinted in H. C. Taylor, *Historical Sketches of the Town of Portland, Comprising also the Pioneer History of Chautauqua County, With Biographical Sketches of the Early Settlers* (Fredonia, NY: W. McKinstry & Son, 1873), 170–74.

3. "A Peculiar Community," *Santa Rosa Democrat.* Reprinted in *St. Louis Globe-Democrat,* February 2, 1879; "The Brocton Community," *Milwaukee Daily Sentinel,* December 12, 1873, Issue 294, 3.

4. "The Brocton Community," [MDS], December 12, 1873, 3.

5. Taylor, 35–36.

6. Schneider and Lawton, 160–61.

7. "The Brocton Community," [MDS], December 12, 1873, 3.

8. Taylor, 171–2.

9. Bailey, "The Harris Community," 279. See also Schneider and Lawton, 14, 36–37, 148.

10. Alexander Gordon claims "two Indian princes" joined the colony. See Alexander Gordon, "Harris, Thomas Lake," *Dictionary of National Biography, 1912 Supplement,* ed. Sidney Lee (London: Smith, Elder & Co., 1912), 216–17. Facsimile and transcript accessed at Wikisource. News reports on which Alexander based his entry had initially established the presence of Indians at Brocton. See "A Peculiar Community."

11. Schneider and Lawton, 155.

12. Transcript of a letter from nine Japanese former members of the BNL, dated June 17, 1868, aboard the steamer *H. Chauncy*, [HOP], Box 1, Folder 6.

13. Schneider and Lawton, 148.

14. The names of the Japanese residents of Garden House did not pass into the historical record.

15. Ibid., 229.

16. Ibid., 185–88.

17. Ibid., 181.

18. Ibid., 190–92.

19. Laurence Oliphant to Mr. Cowper, January 3, 1869; reprinted in Schneider and Lawton, 237–38.

20. As part of his 1873 history of the nearby town of Portland, Dr. Horace Clefton Taylor interviewed Harris by mail regarding the Lake Erie settlement. See Taylor, 169–74.

21. Laurence Oliphant to Mrs. Cowper, April 5, 1869; reprinted in Schneider and Lawton, 239.

22. Quoted in Schneider and Lawton, 124, 127.

23. Bailey, "The Harris Community," 282.

24. Robert V. Hine estimates the oft-repeated figure of $90,000 as the Oliphants' total contribution, probably based on the amount Laurence Oliphant eventually recovered from the Brotherhood coffers. Hine, *California's Utopian Colonies*, 20.

25. Schneider and Lawton, 128–33. 2 letter to Cowper is excerpted on page 133.

26. Schneider and Lawton, 264–65.

CHAPTER 15: CALIFORNIA IDYLL

1. Thomas Lake Harris, *The Wisdom of the Adepts: Esoteric Science in Human History* (Santa Rosa: Privately printed, 1884), 86–87.

2. See, for example, the letter from Jane Lee Waring to Mrs. P[arting] and Miss N, "May I not say, Beloved Sisters," March 18, 1883, [OCC], Harris correspondence file.

3. Respiro, *The Brotherhood of the New Life. An Epitome of the Work and Teaching of Thomas Lake Harris*. 3rd ed. Vol. 1: Internal Respiration, or The Plenary Gift of the Holy Spirit (Glasgow: C.W. Pearce & Co., 1914), 74.

4. "Experiences of a Sister in the New Life."

5. Ibid.

6. Letter from a brother to undisclosed recipient, January 21, 1879, [HOP], Box 1, Folder 5.

7. Arthur A. Cuthbert to Mr. C—, September 13, 1880, [HOP], Box 3, Folder 3.

8. "Letter to a Shaker Friend," Fountain Grove, Santa Rosa, July 5, 1877, [HOP], Box 1, Folder 3.

9. Hinds, 148.

10. Ibid., 142.

11. Ibid., 146.

12. Ibid., 147.

13. Thomas Lake Harris, "BG," [HOP], Box 7, Folder 13.

14. "Private Property and Social Life in the Light of the Christ," Typewritten, undated, [HOP], Box 4, Folder 14.

15. Jane Lee Waring to the Brothers and Sisters, 1877 Paris, [HOP], Box 1, Folder 6.

16. Hine, 19.

17. Letter to Sam Swan, quoted in Schneider and Lawton, 474.

18. Letter from "ER" to "MH," [VVP], 00009.1.1.

19. Quoted in Respiro, 80.

20. The thousands of manuscript and typewritten pages in the archives of Columbia University stand as testament that Harris took his role as prophet and bard of the new dispensation quite seriously. A full account of Harris's literary endeavors has never been attempted.

CHAPTER 16: PARADISE LOST

1. Schneider and Lawton, 339–41.

2. Arthur A. Cuthbert to "Violet," Dated Fountain Grove, November 16, 1881, [HOP], Box 1 Folder 6.

3. Because it was a sum roughly equal to what the Oliphants were believed to have invested in the Brocton colony, Oliphant was said to have "recovered" his assets. "Current News and Comments," *Daily Evening Bulletin* [San Francisco, CA], Issue 88, January 20, 1882. C.f. Schneider and Lawton, 340.

4. Dr. Swan to Dr. Berridge, New York, January 23, 1882, [OCC], Harris correspondence file.

5. Schneider and Lawton, 377.

6. "Hypnotic Harris," *San Francisco Chronicle*, December 13, 1891. Reprinted in Schneider and Lawton, 534.

7. Ibid.

8. Quoted in Schneider and Lawton, 539.

9. Quoted in Schneider and Lawton, 538.

10. Thomas Lake Harris to Dr. Thompson, February 18, 1892, Quoted in Schneider and Lawton, 549.

11. Schneider and Lawton, 558.

12. "Thomas Lake Harris Married," *The Daily Inter Ocean* [Chicago, Ill.], Issue 346, March 4, 1892, 2.

13. Letter from Arthur A. Cuthbert to "My dear friends in the New Life" dated at Criccieth, April 8, 1906, [VVP], 00009.1.1.

CHAPTER 17: A MESSIANIC MEETING

1. "Chevallier's Malicious Charge Against T. L. Harris," [TFS], 3.2, January 2, 1892, 1.

2. "Miss Chevallier Again," [TFS], 3.5, January 30, 1892, 2.

3. Teed discusses Thomas Lake Harris at length in a letter to A.W.K. Andrews, March 20, 1885, [KUC], Box 226, Folder 22.

4. "Spiritual and Temporal Combination, [CDT], February 25, 1892, 2; "A Celibate Combine: Cyrus W. Teed and Thomas Lake Harris. No Messianic Partnership Proposed." *San Francisco Chronicle*, February 26, 1892, 5.

CHAPTER 18: KORESH, SHEPHERD OF GOD

1. See Isaiah 44:28. David Koresh, the messianic leader of the Seventh-Day Adventist Sect of Branch Davidians murdered by the FBI at Waco, Texas, would later adopt the same name.

2. Sources diverge over whether Teed's middle name was Reed, Read, or Reade, and he occasionally used an additional middle name, Romulus, that he appears to have invented himself. Reed is the spelling used by the Florida State Archives, but Read is the name Teed signed on his 1904 membership card to the Koreshan Unity, and which appears on medical licenses issued to Teed by Onondaga and Oneida Counties in upstate New York. However, the Read surname was also the one by which Teed wished to establish lineage dating to the seventeenth-century American colonists, which casts some doubt on its authenticity. See Howard D. Fine, "The Koreshan Unity: The Chicago Years of a Utopian Community," *Journal of the Illinois State Historical Society (1908–1984)* 68.3 (June 1975): 213.

   Some sources state Teed was born on July 3, 1839, but Teed later always insisted his birth date was October 18. If this is true, it likely has to do with his preference for the astrological chart based on a birthdate of October 18. See Nick Wynne and Joe Knetsch, *Utopian Communities of Florida* (Charleston SC: The History Press), 14.

Sources also diverge with respect to Teed's precise birthplace. In its first article about Teed, the *New York Times* listed Walton, New York, a hamlet in Delaware County, as Teed's birthplace. Other sources, including official Koreshan documents, list his birthplace as Teedsville, near to Walton, and today called Trout Creek, NY. See Fine, 213; and Joscelyn Godwin, *Upstate Cauldron: Eccentric Spiritual Movements in Early New York State* (Albany, NY: Excelsior Editions, SUNY Press, 2015), 218.

3. Claude Rahn, aka Brother Claude, *A Brief Outline Of the Life of Dr. Cyrus R. Teed (Koresh) and the Koreshan Unity* (Estero, FL: Koreshan State Historical Society—BK-0003, 1963), 18.

4. Lyn Millner, *The Allure of Immortality* (Gainesville: University Press of Florida, 2015), 15.

5. Wynne and Knetsch, 16.

6. Millner, 16.

7. The New York Eclectic Medical College was also a cog in the New York Democratic Party machine. "Boss" William Tweed was named to the College's board of trustees. See New York Public Library, Art and Picture Collection, Image ID #801198.

8. Godwin, 219.

9. According to documents licensing him to practice in Onondaga and Oneida Counties, the diploma he presented to licensing authorities was dated February 8, 1869, [KUC], Box 230, Folder 1. His biographer states Teed graduated in 1868, in the college's second class. See Millner, 16.

10. Millner, 18.

11. Koresh. *The Illumination of Koresh* ([Chicago], n.d.), 1.

12. Arthur Versluis, *The Esoteric Origins of the American Renaissance* (New York: Oxford, 2001), 4.

13. Ibid., 5.

14. Koresh, *Illumination*, 3–4.

15. Ibid., 4–5.

16. Ibid., 8, 10–11.

17. Ibid., 12. The reference to Egyptian mythology indicated the ambitious reach of Teed's emerging syncretic belief system, which embraced elements of Hermeticism, Kabbalah, and Rosicrucianism. Teed likely wrote the recollection of this vision after encountering Theosophy.

18. Ibid., 12–16.

19. Ibid., 17–18.

20. Ibid., 21.

21. Teed's discovery of his female spiritual counterpart was strongly redolent of Harris's identification of Queen Lily (also called "Christa") as his counterpart. However, the reference to Enoch and Elijah suggests another route through which Teed acquired his knowledge of Hermetic science: as it developed to include higher degrees and multiple orders, Freemasonry had incorporated Hermetic lore into initiation rites beyond the seventh degree of the Royal Arch. Much of it had to do with the construction of Solomon's temple, an obsession the Freemasons shared with Rosicrucians, for whom Enoch the Prophet was a vessel of knowledge. See Albanese, 135–6.

22. Rahn, 24.

23. Letter to W. S. Sickels, Moravia, February 1878, [KUC], Box 232, Folder 5.

CHAPTER 19: THE NEW AGE

1. Teed to A.W.K. Andrews, December 16, 1878, [KUC], Box 225, Folder 42.

2. Teed to A.W.K. Andrews, July 19, 1879, [KUC], Box 225, Folder 53.

3. Stephen Pearl Andrews, *The Basic Outline of Universology* (New York: Dion Thomas, 1872).

4. "Preliminary Covenant of Consocia-

tion." July 24, 1877, [KUC], Box 230, Folder 25.

5. *The Herald of the Messenger of the New Covenant.* No. 1. Moravia. NY, November 1877. Typewritten facsimile, [KUC], Box 232, Folder 13.

6. "Prospectus of the Herald," 1877, [KUC], Box 230, Folder 26.

7. *Herald of the Messenger.*

8. Letter from Henrici Lenz to A.W.K. Andrews, Binghamton NY, dated April 29, 1880. [KUC], Box 234, Folder 1. See also Rahn, 23.

9. Letter from Teed to A.W.K. Andrews, May 5, 1880, [KUC], Box 225, Folder 65.

10. Ibid.

11. Here, Teed developed a hyperbolic variant of the Shakers' belief that celibacy led to longevity and spiritual purity. Teed often pointed out that "virgin" is a word derived from the Latin *vir* for man and *gune,* a Greek word for woman. See Teed's novel *The Great Red Dragon* (Estero: Guiding Star, 1909), 129.

12. The framework of civilizational ages characterized by the Zodiac was not unique to Teed, who modeled his schema on the one popularized by H. P. Blavatsky, a founder of the Theosophical Society.

13. Cyrus Teed to Emma Norton. June 26, 1881, [KUC], Box 228, Folder 49.

14. Godwin, 220.

15. Millner, 34.

16. Patent No. 282,431; filed on June 20, 1883, and granted jointly to Teed and Andrews on July 31, [KUC], Box 232, Folder 18.

17. "Sure He Is the Prophet Cyrus: A Doctor Obtaining Money on the Ground That He Is a New Messiah," [NYT], August 10, 1884, 1.

18. Millner, 35–36.

19. "Sure He Is the Prophet Cyrus."

CHAPTER 20: DR. TEED'S BENEFACTRESSES

1. Millner, 38.

2. Sarah E. Patterson to A.W.K. Andrews, January 17, 1885, [KUC], Box 234, Folder 2.

3. Cyrus Teed to A.W.K Andrews, March 14, 1885, [KUC], Box 226, Folder 20.

4. Cyrus Teed to A.W.K. Andrews, March 20, 1885, [KUC], Box 226, Folder 22.

5. Koresh, "Woman's Mission in the Kingdom of the New Age," *Healing Voice* 1.7 (April 1885): 281.

6. Leonard ran on the National Equal Rights Party ticket helmed by Belva Lockwood's second presidential bid in 1888.

7. *The Alpha*, 10.9 (May 1, 1885).

8. Beryl Satter, *Each Mind a Kingdom: American Women, Sexual Purity, and the New Thought Movement, 1875–1920* (Berkeley: University of California Press, 1999), 183–84.

9. Ibid., 186–87.

10. Cyrus Teed to A.W.K Andrews. June 11, 1885, [KUC], Box 226, Folder 24.

11. Cyrus Teed to A.W.K. Andrews, June 18, 1885, [KUC], Box 226, Folder 25.

12. Sheridan Paul Wait, "Elizabeth Thompson," *The New England Magazine* 6.3 (March 1888): 231.

13. Letter from Teed to A.W.K. Andrews. June 23, 1885, [KUC], Box 226, Folder 26.

14. Cyrus Teed to A.W.K. Andrews, September 22, 1885, [KUC], Box 226, Folder 29.

15. Letter from Teed to A.W.K. Andrews. July 2, 1886, [KUC], Box 226, Folder 35.

CHAPTER 21: TEED GOES MENTAL

1. Satter, 60.

2. Millner, 46–47.

3. See Thomas Lake Harris, "Probable

Grounds of Christian Union, a Lecture, Delivered in the Cairo Street School-Room, Warrington," October 19, 1859 (Manchester: Johnson and Rawson, 1859).

4. "mercenary" and "sophistical," Cyrus Teed, "What Is Christian Science?" *Guiding Star* 1.1 (December 1, 1886): 1.

5. "Metaphysics" course brochure, World's College of Life, chartered October 1886, [KUC], Box 231, Folder 7.

6. "Held to the Grand Jury: Dr. Teed Practiced Medicine Without a License," [CDT], February 23, 1888, 12.

7. Millner, 65.

CHAPTER 22: THE KORESHAN UNITY

1. Gustav Faber, "The Message," Part 2, [KUC], Box 234, Folder 38.

2. "Cyrus, The Son of Jesse: The Successor of Adam, Moses, Abraham, and Eli," [CDT], April 10, 1887, 6. These theories are also expounded at length in Teed's books *The Cellular Cosmology* and *The Immortal Manhood*.

3. Godwin, 223.

4. Silverfriend later authored a book on palmistry titled *How to Read Character: The Science of Cheirology*. It was published at Estero by Guiding Star Publishing House in 1911.

5. Millner, 61.

6. Victoria Gratia, "Woman's Restoration to Her Rightful Dominion." Address delivered before the Koreshan Convention at Central Music Hall, October 8, 1888, by Annie G. Ordway, President of the Society Arch-Triumphant (Chicago: Guiding Star), 1893, 2–6 [OCC], Box 57.

7. Attendance book for the Society Arch-Triumphant, [KUC], Box 30, Folder 28.

8. "Blasphemy and Folly: Chicago the Scene of a Pretended New Dispensation," [CDT], July 20, 1890, 26.

9. T. Jackson Lears, *No Place of Grace: Antimodernism and the Transforma-tion of American Culture, 1880–1920* (New York: Pantheon, 1981), 41–42; and Chris Lehmann, *The Money Cult: Capitalism, Christianity, and the Unmaking of the American Dream* (New York: Melville House, 2016), 171–72.

10. "Teed's Trip to Heaven," [CDT], May 17, 1891, 35.

11. "Appeal to Ballots," [CDT], August 3, 1894, 5. "Invasion and Ovation: Pittsburg Does the Handsome Thing by Coxey's Army," *Washington Post*, April 4, 1894, 1.

12. Arthur Lipow, *Authoritarian Socialism: Edward Bellamy and the Nationalist Movement* (Berkeley: University of California Press, 1982).

13. "How Can Social Order Be Established?" [TFS], 3.6, 6. *The Flaming Sword* also published an excerpt from Thomas Lake Harris's *The New Republic*, in which the Poet praised Edward Bellamy.

CHAPTER 23: MESSIAH ON THE MOVE

1. "A New Religion: Heavenly Promises Direct from Chicago: Professor Spear's College of Life," [SFC], November 27, 1890, 2.

2. See [KUC], Box 228, Folder 34.

3. *The Plowshare & Pruning Hook* was published in San Francisco from May to November 1891; it was briefly revived in Chicago before being absorbed into *The Flaming Sword*.

4. Leland Stanford was a sitting US senator at the time, serving from 1885 until his death in 1893. He previously was governor of California.

5. "A Convention: The Bureau of Equitable Commerce," [SFC], July 15, 1891, 10.

6. Other speakers at the event included Dr. R. H. Hunt, a Mrs. [James] Mills and Mrs. [Annie] Ordway, aka Victoria Gratia. See "War on

Capital: Opening of the Koreshans'
Campaign: The Bureau of Equi-
table Commerce and Its Purposes
Explained," [SFC], July 17, 1891, 8.

7. Ibid.

8. "Impracticable Social Reforms,"
[LAT], July 19, 1891, 4.

9. [RPJ] 12.2, August 15, 1891, 1.

10. "Left Her Husband for the Messiah:
Mrs. Mills of San Francisco Joins
the Converts of Dr. Cyrus R. Teed,"
[CDT], August 7, 1891, 8. C.f. [RPJ],
Vol. 12, No. 2, August 15, 1891, 1.

11. Millner, 100–101.

12. Millner, 72.

13. "Koreshan Messiah," [SFC], September 27, 1891, 8.

14. "Fakir Teed: The Self-Styled Messiah Finds a New Batch of Dupes,"
[LAT]. October 27, 1891, 1.

15. "Dr. Teed Talks While in Pittsburgh," [CDT], November 29, 1891, 3.

16. Millner, 78–80.

17. "An Economite Denounces Dr.
Teed," [CDT], January 3, 1892, 6.

18. "The Koreshan Home: Secession
of Secretary R. A. Spear," [SFC],
August 28, 1891, 5.

19. "Cyrus W. Teed Back in Chicago:
He Admits That He Was Accompa-
nied by a Young Heiress," [CDT],
March 16, 1892.

20. The building was sometimes referred
to as Sunlight Flats.

21. Millner, 104; "The Police Protect Dr.
Teed and His People," New-York Tribune, May 20, 1892, 1.

22. "Dynamite for Dr. Teed: Bomb
Found in Front of the Self-Styled
Messiah's House," [NYT], May 16,
1892, 5. The veracity of this report is
open to question, since it also reports
that Teed led a "free-love colony."

23. Anonymous death threat from "A
friend of woman," Address to Cottage Grove Avenue, [KUC], Box 239,
Folder 1.

24. "Dr. Teed Is Badly Scared," [SFC],
May 20, 1892, 1.

25. Millner, 106–10.

26. Koresh, "Source and Fountain of the
Potency Upon Which Depends the
Organization of the Coming King-
dom," [TFS], 3.1, January 2, 1892, 1.

27. Virginia Andrews diary, [KUC], Box
236, Folder 6.

CHAPTER 24: ANOTHER NEW
JERUSALEM

1. Sara Weber Rea, The Koreshan Story
(Estero, FL: Guiding Star, 1994), 19.

2. Wynne and Knetsch, 22–23.

3. Millner, 116.

4. Ibid., 117–18.

5. George Leposky, "The Bastion of
Koreshanity," Floridian, November 2,
1975, 7.

6. Berthaldine Boomer's typewritten
MS history of the Boomer family,
[KUC], Box 234, Folder 16, 3–5.

7. As Millner explains, Damkohler was
a follower of Charles Taze Russell
and his Zion's Watch Tower Tract
Society. He was therefore in some
ways primed to accept that the Messiah had returned. Millner, 119, 123.

8. Rea, 20.

9. Ibid., 22–26.

10. Ibid., 26–32.

11. Ibid., 27–33.

12. "Ready to Talk Two Hours or Weeks:
Long-Winded Debates Threatened
by the Rival Messiahs at Pittsburgh,"
[CDT], August 12, 1895, 8.

13. Susan Acker, "The Koreshan's
Concave Ocean," Unpublished m.s.
October 1971, 2–3, [KUC], Box 115,
Folder 1.

14. The account of this journey to
Washington is reconstructed from
loose journal notes dated November
21 and 23, 1896 AK 58, [KUC], Box
230, Folder 3.

15. Rea, 40.

16. See drafts of articles in the *American Eagle* contained in [KUC], Box 234, Folder 80.

17. Millner, 147.

18. Ibid., 148–50.

19. Morrow's contributions to the *Fort Myers Daily Palm Leaf* are held in [KUC], Box 234, Folder 82.

CHAPTER 25: A TEST OF IMMORTALITY

1. "Teed Defies His Foes," [CDT], March 9, 1896, 2.

2. Millner, Chapter 12.

3. See Adam Morris, "Perils, Gold and Yellow," *American Communal Societies Quarterly* 11.4 (October 2017): 191–217.

4. Abby to Sister Jennie, December 1908, [KUC], Box 234, Folder 18.

5. Ibid.

6. Ibid.

7. Thomas Gay to Koresh [Cyrus Teed], May 11, 1908, cc: Victoria Gratia; Victoria Gratia to Thomas Gay, May 17, 1908 [KUC] Box 235, Folder 30.

8. Ezra Stewart to W. A. Hinds, October 17, 1909, [OCC], Box 57.

9. [Gustav Faber], "History of Victoria Gratia," as copied by Richard B. Dumbleton, [KUC], Box 234, Folder 37. For Peissart's personal history, see Jane Shaw, *Octavia, Daughter of God: The Story of a Female Messiah and Her Followers* (London: Jonathan Cape, 2011), 124–30.

10. Hedwig Michel to Guiding Star Publishing House, Estero FL, February 15, 1940. Hedwig Michel to Mr. Manley and Mrs. Manley, April 5, 1940, [KUC], Box 30, Folder 19.

CHAPTER 26: DIVINE TRANSFORMATIONS

1. See Bloom, *The American Religion*, and Lehmann, *The Money Cult: Capitalism, Christianity*.

2. Mother Divine, *The Peace Mission Movement* (Philadelphia: Imperial Press, 1982), 28.

3. Ira De A. Reid, "Negro Movements and Messiahs 1900–49," *Phylon* 10.4 (1949): 362–69. The others included the movement led by Mary McLeod Bethune's National Council of Negro Women to transition from pan-Africanism to global Third World consciousness.

4. William J. McLoughlin, "The Resurrection of Father Divine," *American Studies* 26.2 (Fall 1985): 92.

5. This was Judge Lewis Smith. See Robert Weisbrot, *Father Divine and the Struggle for Racial Equality* (Chicago: University of Illinois Press, 1983), 31n1.

6. My account of Father Divine's biography draws from: Jill Watts, *God, Harlem, U.S.A.* (Berkeley: University of California Press, 1992); Robert Weisbrot, *Father Divine and the Struggle for Racial Equality*; Robert Allerton Parker, *The Incredible Messiah* (Boston: Little, Brown, 1937), and to a lesser extent, John Hoshor, *God in a Rolls-Royce* (New York: Hillman-Curl, 1936).

7. Watts, 1–13.

8. Ibid., 6, 10–11, 19–21.

9. See Lavere Belstrom, *Rediscovering God, Our International Treasure* ([Gladwyne, PA]: International Peace Mission, 2014), 43.

10. "Spermatic economy" is a concept coined by Ben Barker-Benfield to describe nineteenth-century attitudes about sexual expense, particularly as they related to phobias of masturbation. See "The Spermatic Economy: A Nineteenth Century View of Sexuality," *Feminist Studies* 1.1 (Summer 1972): 45–74.

11. Watts, 25.

12. William M. Kephart, *Extraordinary Groups. The Sociology of Unconven-*

tional Lifestyles (New York: St. Martin's, 1976), 115.

13. Cyrus Teed to Myron Baldwin. February 3, 1882, [KUC], Box 232, Folder 4, 5.

14. Cyrus Teed to Emma Norton, December 29, 1893, [KUC], Box 239, Folder 4.

15. Cyrus Teed, Draft MS of "The High Priest of the Levitical Order," [KUC], Box 232, Folders 14–15.

16. Cyrus Teed to "Golden Gate KU," [Washington Heights] January 29, 1894, [KUC], Box 239, Folder 5.

17. Cyrus Teed, Unattached handwritten manuscript, [KUC], Box 231, Folder 1.

18. Ibid.

CHAPTER 27: THE MESSENGER

1. Jill Watts suggests that Divine's celibacy instruction was influenced by Charles Fillmore, but its combination with communal lifestyles and the equality of the sexes suggests that Divine knew something about Shaker theology. Ann Lee would later surface in Father Divine's sermons. Watts, 35.

2. Weisbrot, 20.

3. Hoshor, 33–34.

4. A. J. Liebling and St. Clair McKelway, "Who is the King of Glory," Parts 1–3, *New Yorker*, June 13, 20, and 27, 1936; and Carleton Mabee, *Promised Land: Father Divine's Interracial Communities in Ulster County, New York* (Fleischmanns, NY: Purple Mountain Press, 2008), 14.

5. Equally creative verbiage was later required in Harlem, where an artery through the neighborhood became known to Father Divine's followers as "Amsterbless Avenue."

6. Sara Harris, "'House of Joy' Caused Stir in Sayville; 'Every Sunday Was Like Christmas,'" [NYT], February 23, 1954, 8.

7. Weisbrot, 28; Watts 58–59.

8. John Lamb, *The Word of God Revealed: Father Divine's Words from the Notebook of John Lamb* [n.d., Private Printing], 194.

9. Ibid., 193.

10. Ralph Waldo Trine, *In Tune with the Infinite, Or, Fullness of Peace Power and Plenty* (New York: Thomas Y. Cromwell and Co., 1897).

11. Trine, 11.

12. Lamb, 24.

13. Ibid., 141, 36, 22, 8.

14. Ibid., 35.

CHAPTER 28: TROUBLE IN PARADISE

1. Jill Watts, "'This Was the Way': Father Divine's Peace Mission Movement in Los Angeles During the Great Depression," *Pacific Historical Review* 60.4 (November 1991): 480.

2. Watts, 64; and Sara Harris, *Father Divine: Holy Husband* (New York: Doubleday, 1953), 25.

3. Lamb, 203. Angelic names were another technique Divine allegedly borrowed from the Vine's church. See Harris, *Father Divine: Holy Husband*, 19.

4. R. Marie Griffith, "Body Salvation: New Thought, Father Divine, and the Feast of Material Pleasures," *Religion and American Culture: A Journal of Interpretation* 11.2 (Summer 2001): 133.

5. Harris, "'House of Joy' Caused Stir in Sayville."

6. Ibid.; Parker, 10–12; Watts 63–68. Hadley's investigation was conducted in April 1930. See also Lamb, 56.

7. Lamb, 51–55.

8. Ibid., 1.

9. Harris, "'House of Joy' Caused Stir in Sayville."

10. Jill Watts suggests that the number was sometimes as high as 3,000 per week prior to his 1931 arrest. See Watts, "'This Was the Way,'" 479.

11. Father Divine, Sermon of September 26, 1931. Recorded in Lamb, 14–17.

12. Father Divine, Sermon of October 6, 1931. Recorded in Lamb, 24.
13. See Lamb, 14.
14. Ibid., 39.
15. Mabee, 111.
16. Weisbrot, 48.
17. Lamb, 107–109.
18. The so-called Faggots' Ball attracted everyone in Harlem society, from the upper class to neighborhood rogues, as well as members of the white intelligentsia and artistic circles, such as the actress Tallulah Bankhead.
19. "'Dry Judge' Finds Drunkenness Cheap," [NYT], February 1, 1931, 35.
20. Eugene Del Mar, "Noted Lawyer, Lecturer, and Teacher's Significant Pronouncements After Having Contacted Father Divine In Sayville, Long Island," November 23, 1931, Supplement to *The New Day*, December 12, 1966.
21. Ibid.
22. Father Divine, "Father Divine's Sermon Before the Verdict at Mineola, L.I., N.Y." [1932] (Philadelphia, New Day Publishing Co., n.d.), 31.
23. Ibid.
24. Ibid., 10.
25. Ibid., 16.
26. Ibid., 21.
27. Ibid., 26–27.

CHAPTER 29: THE HARLEM KINGDOM
1. Watts, 100.
2. Father Divine, Sermon of October 31, 1932, given at 67 W. 130th St., New York, NY. Reprinted as "Shakerism: Father Divine Says '. . . They bore witness to Ann the Word being the Son, the second coming,'" *New Day*, January 8, 1977, 14–18. Much later in the career of the Peace Mission, followers of Father Divine established a friendly relationship with the Shakers at Sabbath Day Lake, who would visit the Peace Mission for the annual celebration of Mother and Father Divine's wedding anniversary. See D. Wood, "Divine Liturgy," *Gastronomica* 4.1 (Winter 2004): 22.
3. David Shaftel, "The Black Eagle of Harlem," *Air and Space*, December 2008.
4. *The Spoken Word*, October 20, 1934, 16.
5. Faithful Mary's story is recounted in all the major biographies of Father Divine, and she became a minor Harlem celebrity in her own right.
6. I rely here on Faithful Mary's own account of her early life: *'God,' He's Just a Natural Man* (New York: Universal Light Publishing, 1937).
7. Faithful Mary, 3–10.
8. Faithful Mary, 9.
9. Wesibrot, 68.
10. Leonard Norman Primiano, "'Bringing Perfection in These Different Places'": Father Divine's Vernacular Architecture of Intention," *Folklore* 115.1 (April 2004): 3–26.
11. Richard Wright, *Lawd, Today!*, in *Early Works* (New York: Library of America, 1991), 76–77.
12. John Louis Clarke in Faithful Mary, xi.
13. Marcus Garvey, *Black Man*, July 1935. Reprinted in *The Marcus Garvey and Universal Negro Improvement Association Papers* 7 (November 1927–August 1940). Ed. Robert A. Hill et al. (Berkeley: University of California Press, 1990), 632–34.
14. Ibid., 632.
15. Ibid., 634.
16. Hoshor, 237–38.
17. "Divine Adherents in Court Uproar," [NYT], May 22, 1936, 16.
18. "4 Aides of Divine Defy Earthly Law," [NYT], May 9, 1936, 11.

CHAPTER 30: PROMISED LANDS

1. Watts, "'This Was the Way,'" 479.
2. Ibid., 484.
3. *The Spoken Word*, October 20, 1934.
4. Watts, "'This Was the Way,'" 496.
5. Charles P. LeWarne, "Vendovi Island: Father Divine's 'Peaceful Paradise of the Pacific,'" *The Pacific Northwest Quarterly* 75.1 (January 1984): 5.
6. Ibid., 2.
7. Ibid., 10–11.
8. Carlton Mabee counted 23 in Manhattan, 12 in Brooklyn and Queens, 21 in New Jersey, and 3 in Westchester County by the time of the Ulster County expansion. *Promised Land*, 18.
9. Figures vary. [NYT] reported 34 acres for $7,000. Robert S. Bird, "Father Divine's Movement Expands," [NYT], July 2, 1939, E10. C.f. Mabee, 18.
10. Weisbrot, 110.
11. Mabee, 27, 30–31.
12. Ibid., 27–28.
13. "Flag Row Mars Divine Pilgrimage As 1,877 Visit 'Promised Land,'" [NYT], August 21, 1936, 1.
14. Mabee, 61.
15. Ibid., 63.
16. Ibid., 117.
17. Ibid., 62.
18. Ibid., 45.
19. Ibid., 47.
20. "Divine's 'Heaven' Up-State Burned," [NYT], April 25, 1937, 1.

CHAPTER 31: HEAVEN TREMBLES

1. "Divine Is Deserted by His Head 'Angel.'" [NYT], April 22, 1937, 1.
2. Faithful Mary, 29.
3. Ibid., 28.
4. Mabee, 98.
5. "Divine Is Deserted by His Head 'Angel.'"
6. Kephart, 139. Faithful Mary, 49.

7. "Negro Flier Halts Father Divine Suit," [NYT], December 5, 1939 1.
8. Ibid.
9. Faithful Mary, 105–106.

CHAPTER 32: RIGHTEOUS GOVERNMENT

1. Watts, "'This Was the Way'" 489–90.
2. The meeting was reported in the *Times* and La Guardia's full speech was published in the *New Day*. Cited in Weisbrot, 161.
3. Faithful Mary, 45.
4. Brother William Ross to J. Edgar Hoover, May 28, 1936, [FD].
5. Faithful Mary, 43–44.
6. See, for example, letter from Louis Carter to J. Edgar Hoover, September 24, 1936, [FD].
7. J. Edgar Hoover to Senator Louis Murphy, October 19, 1935, [FD].
8. Elam J. Daniels, *Father Divine, The World's Chief False Christ*, 6th ed. (Winter Garden, FL: Biblical Echo Press, 1940), 9.
9. Ibid., 19.
10. F. Blair Mayne, "Beliefs and Practices of the Cult of Father Divine," *Journal of Educational Psychology* 10.5 (January 1937): 298.
11. Mabee, 68–77. Roosevelt quoted on p. 76.
12. Ibid., 84–86.

CHAPTER 33: PHILADELPHIA

1. Kephart, 139.
2. Mabee, 116–17.
3. P. E. Foxworth to J. Edgar Hoover, January 9, 1943, [FD], 62-3243-33.
4. Ruth Boaz, "Thirty Years with Father Divine," *Ebony* (May 1965), 89.
5. Boaz, 94.
6. Ibid., 88.
7. Kephart, 146.
8. After their marriage, her name was often abbreviated as S.A. Mother

Divine, as Father Divine encouraged those who took "affectionate names" to use their initials to avoid any arousing connotations.

9. "Woman, 81, Bequeaths $500,000 to 2 Father Divine Organizations," [NYT]. December 18, 1946, 1.

10. Harris, *Father Divine: Holy Husband*, 11.

11. R. W. Apple Jr. "Father Divine Shuns Rights Drive," [NYT], May 10, 1964, 65.

CHAPTER 34: JIM JONES

1. June Cordell, interviewed in *Jonestown: The Life and Death of Peoples Temple*. Dir. Stanley Nelson, Jr. 2006.

2. Tim Reiterman, with John Jacobs, *Raven: The Untold Story of the Rev. Jim Jones and His People* (New York: Jeremy P. Tarcher, 1982), 48–49.

3. Ibid., 48. David Chidester states the name change occurred in 1955. *Salvation and Suicide: An Interpretation of Jim Jones, the Peoples Temple, and Jonestown* (Bloomington: Indiana University Press, 1988), 3.

4. Jeff Guinn, *The Road to Jonestown: Jim Jones and Peoples Temple* (New York: Simon & Schuster, 2017), 32.

5. Ibid., 35.

6. FBI tape Q134.

7. Guinn, 29.

8. John Peer Nugent, *White Night. The Untold Story of What Happened Before—and Beyond—Jonestown* (New York: Rawson, Wade, 1979), 8; Guinn, 33.

9. Guinn, 41.

10. Reiterman and Jacobs, 30.

11. Marceline Jones, "To Whom It May Concern," [RYMUR], 89–4286-EE-1-I&J, 73–75.

12. Reiterman and Jacobs, 34–36.

13. Jones, "To Whom It May Concern."

14. This allegedly occurred in 1953. See

Judith Mary Weightman, *Making Sense of the Jonestown Suicides. A Sociological History of the Peoples Temple* (New York: Edwin Mellen Press, 1983), 18.

15. FBI Tape Q134.

16. Jim Jones to Marceline Jones, [Untitled, undated], [RYMUR], 89–4286-EE-3-LL.

17. FBI Tape Q134.

18. Reiterman and Jacobs, 44.

19. Martin Luther King Jr. on *Meet the Press*. NBC. April 17, 1960.

20. Thrash, Hyacinth, and Marian K. Towne, "The Last Survivor," *Indianapolis Monthly*, November 1998, 132.

21. Interview with Laura Johnston Kohl.

CHAPTER 35: DIVINE ASPIRATIONS

1. James W. Jones, "Pastor Jones Meets Rev. M. J. Divine, Better Known as Father Divine" (Published by the author. Indianapolis, 1959), 4.

2. Ibid., 4–6.

3. Ibid., 8.

4. FBI Tape Q356 (Philadelphia, August 1973). Jones also used the phrase "fathership degree" in Q972 (1973), Q1015 (San Francisco, July 1973).

5. Reiterman and Jacobs, 55.

6. FBI Tape Q162.

7. Mother Divine, "Rev. Jim Jones Cut Down by Retribution. Takes Hundreds with Him in Death Pact. Once Sought Control of Peace Mission," *The New Day*, December 9, 1978, 1.

8. Jones, "Pastor Jones Meets Rev. M.J. Divine," 11.

CHAPTER 36: THE MINISTER WANDERS

1. Reiterman and Jacobs, 62.

2. See *Indianapolis Recorder*, April 28, 1956, 3.

3. Weightman, 22.

4. [PTM] Collection 4126. Box 3, Folder 1.

5. Dan Burros to James Jones. July 23, 1961, [JRH], Box 4, Folder 2; Dan Burros to James Jones, July 28, 1961, [PTM], Box 3, Folder 1.

6. For "messages" see Reiterman and Jacobs, 76. "Messengers" was a term Jones used in Redwood Valley. Interviews with Garry Lambrev, 2016 and 2017.

7. Caroline Bird, "Nine Places to Hide," *Esquire* (January 1962): 55, 128–32.

8. Bonnie Malmin recalled seeing a picture of Jim and Marceline on either side of Fidel Castro, allegedly taken during the 1962 stopover in Cuba. See Weightman, 24.

9. Weightman, 25.

10. Ross E. Case to Kathy Hunter. May 11, 1978, [REC], Folder 3.

11. Garry Lambrev states that Jones never stipulated whether this was 3:09 a.m. or p.m. See Lambrev, "Joe Phillips: A Reflection," *Jonestown Report*, 2018, http://jonestown .sdsu.edu/?page_id=40205. Harold Cordell told Ross Case it would be 3:09 in the morning. See letter from Harold Cordell to Ross Case and Family, February 18, 1965.

12. Letter from Harold Cordell to Ross E. Case and family, February 18, 1965, [REC], Folder 2.

CHAPTER 37: CALIFORNIA MYSTICS

1. H. T. Dohrman, *California Cult: The Story of 'Mankind United'* (Boston: Beacon Press, 1958), 2–3, 80–81.

2. The name under which he swore his court testimony was Arthur Lowber Osborne Bell. Dohrman, 79–80.

3. Ibid., 92, 104–05.

4. Ibid., 31.

5. Ibid., 84–86, 110, 149.

6. Quoted in Ibid., 38.

7. There were eight CCGR churches in San Francisco and forty-eight in the Bay Area. Ibid., 61.

8. Timothy Miller, *The Encyclopedic Guide to American Intentional Communities*, 2nd edition (Clinton, NY: Richard W. Couper Press, 2015), 81–82.

9. Dohrman, 75–76.

10. Interview with Garry Lambrev, 2016.

11. Kohl, 25.

12. Thomas Sugrue, *There Is a River: The Story of Edgar Cayce* (Virginia Beach: A.R.E. Press, 1942), 5.

13. Interview with Garry Lambrev, 2016.

14. Chidester, 57.

15. FBI Tape Q1059–1.

16. Interview with Garry Lambrev, 2016. C.f. Leigh Fondakowski, *Stories from Jonestown* (Minneapolis: University of Minnesota Press, 2013), 31–38.

CHAPTER 38: NEW DIRECTIONS

1. Untitled statement by Carol Stahl. See http://jonestown.sdsu .edu/?page_id=18688.

2. Interview with Garry Lambrev, 2016.

3. Laura Johnston Kohl, *Jonestown Survivor: An Insider's Look* (Bloomington: iUniverse, 2010), 26.

4. "White Nights, Black Paradise," Panel discussion with Rebecca Moore, Jordan Vilchez, Leslie Wagner-Wilson, and Yulanda Williams. Moderated by Sikivu Hutchinson. Museum of African Diaspora, July 29, 2017.

5. See Kohl, 28. When asked about Jones's healings and clairvoyance, both Garry Lambrev and Laura Johnston Kohl stated they continued to believe Jones had a special talent. Interviews with the author. In a public event at the Museum of African Diaspora in San Francisco, Yulanda Williams, one of Jones's fiercest critics, also acknowledged his healing power.

6. Interview with Laura Johnston Kohl, 2017.

7. Ibid.

8. Ibid.

9. Leslie Wagner-Wilson, *Slavery of Faith: The Untold Story of the Peoples Temple from the Eyes of a Thirteen Year Old, Her Escape from Jonestown at 21, and Life 30 Years Later* (Bloomington: iUniverse, 2008), 25.

CHAPTER 39: GOING COMMUNAL
1. Kohl, 26.
2. Milmon F. Harrison, "Jim Jones and Black Worship Traditions," in Moore, Pinn, and Sawyer, 125–26.
3. FBI Tape Q612a.
4. Reiterman and Jacobs, 155.
5. Kohl, 38–39.
6. Wagner-Wilson, 25.
7. According to Grace Stoen in *Deceived*; interview with Laura Johnston Kohl, 2017.

CHAPTER 40: PEOPLES TEMPLE HITS THE ROAD
1. Kohl, 33.
2. Marceline Jones to Joy Sala, May 23, 1975, [PTM], Box 1, Folder 1.
3. [RYMUR], F-10-A-58 and numerous other sources.
4. Interview with Tommy Garcia, 2018.
5. Mother Divine, "Rev Jim Jones Cut Down by Retribution. Takes Hundreds with Him in Death Pact. Once Sought Control of Peace Mission," *New Day*, December 9, 1978.
6. Wagner-Wilson, 28.
7. Reiterman and Jacobs, 139–141.
8. Documents in the California Historical Society Peoples Temple Collection indicate that twelve angels left the Peace Mission for Redwood Valley in 1972, [PTC], Box 41, Folder 691.
9. Interviews with Kathy Barbour, Garry Lambrev, and Laura Johnston Kohl.
10. Morton Silver to Eugene B. Chaikin, August 7, 1972, [PTC], Box 41, Folder 691.
11. Letter from Dorothy Darling to Miss Valor St. John, July 26, 1971, [PTC], Box 41, Folder 691; Eugene B. Chai-

kin to J. Austin Norris, August 1, 1972, [PTC], Box 41, Folder 691.
12. Deborah Layton, *Seductive Poison: A Jonestown Survivor's Story of Life and Death in the Peoples Temple* (New York: Anchor, 1998); Rebecca Moore, "Closing the Books," chap. 13 in *A Sympathetic History of Jonestown: The Moore Family Involvement in Peoples Temple* (Lewiston, NY: The Edward Mellin Press, 1985), https://jonestown.sdsu.edu/?page_id=16590.

CHAPTER 41: BACKLASH
1. Lester Kinsolving, "Probe Asked of Peoples Temple," *San Francisco Examiner*, September 20, 1972, 1.
2. Chidester, 7.
3. The published and unpublished articles from Kinsolving are available from the Jonestown Institute. See https://jonestown.sdsu.edu/?page_id=14081.
4. The term "niggerized" was used on Merrill Collett and his wife. Guinn, 267.
5. Ibid., 338.
6. Interview with Laura Johnston Kohl.
7. Tanya Hollis, "Peoples Temple and Housing Politics in San Francisco," in Moore, Pinn, and Sawyer, 86.
8. George R. Moscone to Jim Jones, December 2, 1975, [PTC], Box 2, Folder 34.
9. George R. Moscone to Eugene Chaikin, January 30, 1976, [PTC], Box 2, Folder 34.
10. Marshall Kilduff and Phil Tracy, "Inside Peoples Temple," *New West* (August 1, 1977), 30.
11. Shiva Naipaul, *Journey to Nowhere: A New World Tragedy* (New York: Simon & Schuster, 1980), 40.
12. Guinn, 335.
13. Letter to Jim Jones from John Biddulph, Walter Wayne Pietila, Vera Biddulph, Mickey Touchette,

Hulena M. Flowers, Tom Podgor-
ski, Terri Pietila, and Jim Cobb, aka
"The Eight Revolutionaries," 1973.
Jonestown Institute. See https://
jonestown.sdsu.edu/wp-content/
uploads/2013/10/g8.pdf.

14. FBI Tape Q612a.
15. Kilduff and Tracy, 34.
16. Ibid., 30.

CHAPTER 42: JONESTOWN

1. Interview with Laura Johnston Kohl,
   2017.
2. Interview with Kathy Barbour, 2017.
3. Mervyn Dymally to George R.
   Moscone, June 7, 1977, [PTC], Box 2,
   Folder 27.

4. Patricia Houston to Phyllis Houston, March 26, 1978, [PTC], Box 2,
   Folder 44.
5. Deborah Layton, *Seductive Poison:
   A Jonestown Survivor's Story of Life
   and Death in the Peoples Temple* (New
   York: Anchor, 1998).

EPILOGUE

1. James D. Tabor and Eugene V. Galla-
   gher, *Why Waco? Cults and the Battle for
   Religious Freedom in America* (Berkeley:
   University of California Press, 1995).
2. Ray Kurzweil, *The Age of Spiritual
   Machines: When Computers Exceed
   Human Intelligence* (New York: Pen-
   guin, 1999), 150, 128.

BIBLIOGRAPHY

ARCHIVES AND SPECIAL COLLECTIONS
[HOP] Harris–Oliphant Papers. Rare Books & Manuscripts Collection, Columbia University.
[JWP] Jemima Wilkinson Papers, 1768–1872. Rare and Manuscript Collections, Cornell University Library. Collection #621.
[JRH] John R. Hall Papers. Collection 3803. California Historical Society.
[KUC] Koreshan Unity Collection. Florida State Library and Archives.
[OCC] Oneida Community Collection. Special Collections, Syracuse University.
[PTA] Peoples Temple Audio Tape Collection, Alternative Considerations of Jonestown. San Diego State University.
[PTC] Peoples Temple Records. Collection 3800. California Historical Society.
[PTM] Peoples Temple Miscellany. Collection 4126. California Historical Society.
[REC] Ross E. Case Files. Collection 4062. California Historical Society.
[VVP] V. Valta Parma Papers. Hamilton College Archives.†

PUBLIC RECORDS
[FD] Father Divine File. Federal Bureau of Investigation. Obtained by Freedom of Information Act request.
[RYMUR] Materials Related to Peoples Temple and the Murder of Congressman Leo J. Ryan.

NEWSPAPERS AND CONTEMPORARY PERIODICALS
[CDT] *Chicago Daily Tribune.* Chicago, Illinois.
[LAT] *Los Angeles Times.* Los Angeles, California.
[MDS] *Milwaukee Daily Sentinel.* Milwaukee, Wisconsin.
[NYT] *New York Times.* New York, New York.
[TFS] *The Flaming Sword.* Chicago, Illinois, and Estero, Florida. 1889–1949.
[RPJ] *Religio-Philosophical Journal.* Chicago, Illinois. 1865–1905.
[SFC] *San Francisco Chronicle.* San Francisco, California.
[SRD] *Santa Rosa Democrat.* Santa Rosa, California.
[TND] *The New Day.* New York, New York, and Philadelphia, Pennsylvania.

---

† V. Valta Parma was the professional pseudonym of occultist and congressional librarian Albert Pratt, Hamilton Class of 1901 (did not graduate).

[USP] *Univercoelum and Spiritual Philosopher.* New York City, 1847–1849. Available via the International Association for the Preservation of Spiritualist and Occult Periodicals (IAPSOP)

INTERVIEWS CONDUCTED BY THE AUTHOR
Kathryn Barbour. By telephone. November 13, 2017.
Tommy Garcia. By telephone. January 24, 2018.
Laura Johnston Kohl. By telephone. November 22, 2017.
Bryan Kravitz. By telephone. October 30, 2017.
Garry Lambrev. Oakland, California. August 11, 2016.
———. Oakland, California. July 6, 2017.

PUBLIC EVENTS
"White Nights, Black Paradise." Panel discussion with Rebecca Moore, Jordan Vilchez, Leslie Wagner-Wilson, and Yulanda Williams. Moderated by Sikivu Hutchinson. Museum of African Diaspora. July 29, 2017.

DOCUMENTARY
Deceived: The Jonestown Tragedy. Dir. Mel White. Gospel Films. [1979].
Jonestown: The Life and Death of Peoples Temple. Dir. Stanley Nelson Jr. October 2006.

PRIMARY SOURCES
Barbé-Marbois, François, Marquis de. *Our Revolutionary Forefathers: The Letters of François, Marquis de Barbé-Marbois During His Residence in the United States as Secretary of the French Legation, 1779–1785.* Trans. Eugene Parker Case. New York: Duffield & Co., 1929.
Berridge, C. M. See *Respiro.*
Boaz, Ruth. "Thirty Years with Father Divine." *Ebony* (May 1965), 88–98.
Brownell, Abner. *Enthusiastical Errors, Transpired and Detected, by Abner Brownell, in a Letter to His Father, Benjamin Brownell.* New London, CT, 1783.
Cuthbert, Arthur A. *The Life and World-Work of Thomas Lake Harris. Written from Direct Personal Knowledge by Arthur A. Cuthbert, An Almost Life-Long Associate.* Glasgow: C. W. Pearce & Co., 1908.
Davis, Andrew Jackson. *The Magic Staff: An Autobiography of Andrew Jackson Davis.* Eighth edition. Boston: Bela Marsh, 1867.
Faithful Mary. *"God," He's Just a Natural Man.* New York: Universal Light Publishing Co., 1937.
Father Divine. "Father Divine's Sermon Before the Verdict at Mineola, L.I., N.Y." [1932]. Philadelphia: New Day Publishing Co., n.d.
Gratia, Victoria. "Woman's Restoration to Her Rightful Dominion." Address delivered before the Koreshan Convention at Central Music Hall, October 8, 1888, by Annie G. Ordway, President of the Society Arch-Triumphant. Chicago: Guiding Star, 1893.
Harris, Thomas Lake. *Brotherhood of the New Life: Its Fact, Law, Method and Purpose. Letter from Thomas Lake Harris, with Passing Reference to Recent Criticisms.* Santa Rosa, CA: Private Printing, 1891.
———. "Probable Grounds of Christian Union, A Lecture, Delivered in the Cairo Street School-Room, Warrington. October 19, 1859." Manchester, UK: Johnson and Rawson, 1859.

——. *Song of Satan: A Series of Poems Originating from a Society of Infernal Spirits and Received, During Temptation Combats*. New York: New Church Publishing Association, 1858.

——. *White Roses for the Pall*, Vol. II. Glasgow: C. W. Pearce & Co., 1910.

——. *The Wisdom of the Adepts: Esoteric Science in Human History*. Santa Rosa, CA: Privately printed, 1884.

——. *The Wisdom of Angels*. New York: New Church Publishing Association, 1857.

Hathaway, Mrs. William. *A Narrative of Thomas Hathaway and His Family, Formerly of New Bedford, Massachusetts, with Incidents in the Life of Jemima Wilkinson and the Times in Which They Lived*. New Bedford, MA: E. Anthony & Sons, 1869.

Jones, James W. "Pastor Jones Meets Rev. M. J. Divine, Better Known as Father Divine." Published by the author. Indianapolis, 1959.

Koresh. *The Great Red Dragon*. Estero: Guiding Star, 1909.

——. *The Illumination of Koresh*. Chicago, n.d.

——. *The Immortal Manhood*. First edition. Chicago: Guiding Star, 1902.

Kohl, Laura Johnston. *Jonestown Survivor: An Insider's Look*. Bloomington, IN: iUniverse, 2010.

Kurzweil, Ray. *The Age of Spiritual Machines: When Computers Exceed Human Intelligence*. New York: Penguin, 1999.

Lamb, John. *The Word of God Revealed. Father Divine's Words from the Notebook of John Lamb* [n.d., Private Printing].

Lambrev, Garry. "Joe Phillips: A Reflection." *Jonestown Report*. 2018. http://jonestown.sdsu.edu/?page_id=40205.

Layton, Deborah. *Seductive Poison. A Jonestown Survivor's Story of Life and Death in the Peoples Temple*. New York: Anchor, 1998.

Lord Chester. See *Koresh*.

Matthew, James Maynard. See *John Lamb*.

Mother Divine. *The Peace Mission Movement*. Philadelphia: Imperial Press, 1982.

Ordway, Annie. See *Victoria Gratia*.

Rahn, Claude, aka Brother Claude. *A Brief Outline of the Life of Dr. Cyrus R. Teed (Koresh) and the Koreshan Unity*. Estero, FL: Koreshan State Historical Society—BK-0003, 1963.

Respiro. *The Brotherhood of the New Life. An Epitome of the Work and Teaching of Thomas Lake Harris*. Third edition. Glasgow: C. W. Pearce & Co., 1914.

Ritchings, Edna Rose. See *Mother Divine*.

Rozier, Mary. See *Faithful Mary*.

Stahl, Carol. Untitled statement. http://jonestown.sdsu.edu/?page_id=18688.

Thrash, Hyacinth, and Marian K. Towne. "The Last Survivor." *Indianapolis Monthly*. November 1998.

Wagner-Wilson, Leslie. *Slavery of Faith. The Untold Story of the Peoples Temple from the Eyes of a Thirteen Year Old, Her Escape from Jonestown at 21 and Life 30 Years Later*. New York: iUniverse, 2008.

SECONDARY SOURCES

Albanese, Catherine L. *A Republic of Mind & Spirit: A Cultural History of American Metaphysical Religion*. New Haven, CT: Yale University Press, 2007.

Andrews, Stephen Pearl. *The Basic Outline of Universology.* New York: Dion Thomas, 1872.

Bailey, William S. "The Harris Community: Brotherhood of the New Life." *New York History* 16.3 (July 1935): 278–85.

Bainbridge, William Sims. "Shaker Demographics 1840–1900: An Example of the Use of U.S. Census Enumeration Schedules." *Journal for the Scientific Study of Religion* 21.4 (December 1982): 352–65.

Barker-Benfield, Ben. "The Spermatic Economy: A Nineteenth Century View of Sexuality." *Feminist Studies* 1.1 (Summer 1972): 45–74.

Belstrom, Lavere. *Rediscovering God, Our International Treasure.* Gladwyne, PA: International Peace Mission, 2014.

Bird, Caroline. "Nine Places to Hide." *Esquire* (January 1962): 55, 128–32.

Blankenship, Russell. *And There Were Men.* New York: Alfred Knopf, 1942.

Bloom, Harold. *The American Religion: The Emergence of the Post-Christian Nation.* New York: Simon & Schuster, 1992.

Braude, Ann. *Radical Spirits: Spiritualism and Women's Rights in Nineteenth-Century America.* Boston: Beacon Press, 1989.

Bronner, Edwin B. "Quakers Labor with Jemima Wilkinson." *Quaker History* 58.1 (Spring 1969): 41–47.

Buescher, John Benedict. *The Other Side of Salvation: Spiritualism and the Nineteenth-Century Religious Experience.* Boston: Skinner House, 2004.

Bush, George. *Mesmer and Swedenborg; Or, The Relation of the Developments of Mesmerism to the Doctrines and Disclosures of Swedenborg.* New York: John Allen, 1847.

Capron, E. W. *Modern Spiritualism: Its Facts and Fanaticisms, Its Consistencies and Contradictions, with an Appendix.* Boston: Bela Marsh, 1855.

Capron, Eliab W., and Henry D. Barron. *Singular Revelations. Explanation and History of the Mysterious Communion with Spirits, Comprehending the Rise and Progress of the Mysterious Noises in Western New-York, Generally Received as Spiritual Communications.* Second edition. Auburn, NY: Capron and Barron, 1850.

Carden, Maren Lockwood. *Oneida: Utopian Community to Modern Corporation.* [1969]. New York: Harper Torchbooks, 1971.

Carlson, Eric T. "Charles Poyen Brings Mesmerism to America." *Journal of the History of Medicine and the Allied Sciences* 15.2 (April 1960): 121–32.

Carmer, Carl. "The Woman Who Died Twice." *New Yorker,* May 9, 1936.

Chidester, David. *Salvation and Suicide: An Interpretation of Jim Jones, the Peoples Temple, and Jonestown.* Bloomington: Indiana University Press, 1988.

Cross, Whitney. *The Burned Over District: The Social and Intellectual History of Enthusiastic Religion in Western New York, 1800–1850.* New York: Harper & Row, 1950.

Daggett, Melissa. *Spiritualism in Nineteenth-Century New Orleans: The Life and Times of Henry Louis Rey.*

Daniels, Elam J. *Father Divine, the World's Chief False Christ.* Sixth edition. Winter Garden, FL: Biblical Echo Press, 1940.

Delp, Robert W. "Andrew Jackson Davis: Prophet of American Spiritualism." *The Journal of American History.* 54.1 (June 1967): 43–56.

Desroche, Henri. *The American Shakers: From Neo-Christianity to Presocialism.* Translated by John K. Sacavol. Amherst: University of Massachusetts Press, 1971.

Dohrmann, H. T. *California Cult: The Story of 'Mankind United.'* Boston: Beacon Press, 1958.

Donnelly, Ignatius. *Caesar's Column: A Story of the Twentieth Century.* Middletown, CT: Wesleyan University Press, 2003.

Fine, Howard D. "The Koreshan Unity: The Chicago Years of a Utopian Community." *Journal of the Illinois State Historical Society (1908–1984)* 68.3 (June 1975): 213–27.

Fondakowski, Leigh. *Stories from Jonestown.* Minneapolis: University of Minnesota Press, 2013.

Garvey, Marcus. *Black Man* [July 1935]. Reprinted in *The Marcus Garvey and Universal Negro Improvement Association Papers.* Volume 7. November 1927–August 1940, edited by Robert A. Hill et al. Berkeley: University of California Press, 1990.

Godwin, Joscelyn. *Upstate Cauldron: Eccentric Spiritual Movements in Early New York State.* Albany, NY: Excelsior Editions, SUNY Press, 2015.

Gordon, Alexander. "Harris, Thomas Lake." *Dictionary of National Biography, 1912 Supplement.* London: Smith, Elder & Co., 1912. pp. 216–217. Facsimile and transcript accessed at Wikisource: https://en.wikisource.org/wiki/Page:Dictionary_of_National_Biography,_Second_Supplement,_volume_2.djvu/236.

Griffith, R. Marie. "Body Salvation: New Thought, Father Divine, and the Feast of Material Pleasures." *Religion and American Culture: A Journal of Interpretation* 11.2 (Summer 2001): 119–53.

Guinn, Jeff. *The Road to Jonestown: Jim Jones and Peoples Temple.* New York: Simon & Schuster, 2017.

Hardinge, Emma. *Modern American Spiritualism: A Twenty Years' Record of the Communion Between Earth and the World of Spirits.* Third edition. New York: [Emma Hardinge], 1870.

Harris, Sara. "'House of Joy' Caused Stir in Sayville; 'Every Sunday Was Like Christmas.'" *NYT.* February 23, 1954.

———, with Harriet Crittenden. *Father Divine: Holy Husband.* New York: Doubleday, 1953.

Harrison, Milmon F. "Jim Jones and Black Worship Traditions." In *Peoples Temple and Black Religion in America*, edited by Rebecca Moore, Anthony B. Pinn, and Mary R. Sawyer, 123–38. Bloomington: Indiana University Press, 2004.

Hendricks, Mrs. Walter A., and Arnold J. Potter. "The Universal Friend: Jemima Wilkinson." *New York History* 23.2 (April 1942): 159–65.

Hinds, William Alfred. *American Communities* [1878]. New York: Corinth Books, 1961.

Hine, Robert V. *California's Utopian Colonies* [1953]. Berkeley: University of California Press, 1983.

Hollis, Tanya. "Peoples Temple and Housing Politics in San Francisco." In *Peoples Temple and Black Religion in America*, edited by Rebecca Moore, Anthony B. Pinn, and Mary R. Sawyer, 81–102. Bloomington: Indiana University Press, 2004.

Horowitz, Mitch. *Occult America: The Secret History of How Mysticism Shaped Our Nation.* New York: Bantam, 2009.

Hoshor, John. *God in a Rolls-Royce.* New York: Hillman-Curl, 1936.

Hughes, Langston. *The Collected Works of Langston Hughes, Vol. 3, The Poems, 1951–1967.* Columbia: University of Missouri Press, 2001.

Hudson, David. *Memoir of Jemima Wilkinson, A Preacheress of the Eighteenth Century;*

Containing an Authentic Narrative of Her Life and Character and of the Rise, Progress and Conclusion of Her Ministry. Bath, NY: R. L. Underhill & Co., 1844.

James, William. *Varieties of Religious Experience: A Study in Human Nature.* Centenary edition. New York: London, 2002.

Kephart, William M. *Extraordinary Groups: The Sociology of Unconventional Lifestyles.* New York: St. Martin's, 1976.

Kilduff, Marshall, and Phil Tracy. "Inside Peoples Temple." *New West* (August 1, 1977): 30–38.

Leposky, George. "The Bastion of Koreshanity." *Floridian,* November 2, 1975.

LaWarne, Charles P. "Vendovi Island: Father Divine's 'Peaceful Paradise of the Pacific.'" *The Pacific Northwest Quarterly* 75.1 (January 1984): 2–12.

Lears, T. Jackson. *No Place of Grace: Antimodernism and the Transformation of American Culture, 1880–1920.* New York: Pantheon, 1981.

Lee, Philip J. *Against the Protestant Gnostics.* New York: Oxford University Press, 1997.

Lehmann, Chris. *The Money Cult: Capitalism, Christianity, and the Unmaking of the American Dream.* Brooklyn, NY: Melville House, 2014.

Liebling, A. J., and St. Clair McKelway. "Who is the King of Glory," Parts 1–3. *New Yorker,* June 13, 20, and 27, 1936.

Lipow, Arthur. *Authoritarian Socialism: Edward Bellamy and the Nationalist Movement.* Berkeley: University of California Press, 1982.

Mabee, Carleton. *Promised Land: Father Divine's Interracial Communities in Ulster County, New York.* Fleischmanns, NY: Purple Mountain Press, 2008.

Marlin, Charles Lowell. "Jemima Wilkinson: Errant Quaker Divine." *Quaker History* 52.2 (Autumn 1963): 90–94.

Marx, Karl. "Introduction" (1844). *A Contribution to the Critique of Hegel's Philosophy of Right.* Trans. Annette Jolin and Joseph O'Malley. Cambridge: Cambridge University Press, 1970.

Mayne, F. Blair. "Beliefs and Practices of the Cult of Father Divine." *The Journal of Educational Psychology* 10.5 (January 1937): 296–306.

McCabe, Joseph. *Spiritualism: A Popular History from 1847.* New York: Dodd, Mead and Company, 1920.

McLoughlin, William G. "The Resurrection of Father Divine." *American Studies* 26.2 (Fall 1985): 91–94.

——. *Revivals, Awakenings, and Reform: An Essay on Religion and Social Change in America, 1607–1977.* Chicago: University of Chicago Press, 1978.

Miller, Timothy. *The Encyclopedic Guide to American Intentional Communities.* Second edition. Clinton, NY: Couper Press, 2015.

Millner, Lynn. *The Allure of Immortality.* Gainesville: University Press of Florida, 2015.

Moore, Rebecca. "Closing the Books." Chap. 13 in *A Sympathetic History of Jonestown: The Moore Family Involvement in Peoples Temple.* Lewiston, NY: The Edward Mellin Press, 1985. https://jonestown.sdsu.edu/?page_id=16590.

Moore, Rebecca, Anthony B. Pinn, and Mary R. Sawyer, eds. *Peoples Temple and Black Religion in America.* Bloomington: Indiana University Press, 2004.

Morris, Adam. "Perils, Gold and Yellow." *American Communal Societies Quarterly* 11.4 (October 2017): 191–218.

Moyer, Paul B. *The Public Universal Friend: Jemima Wilkinson and Religious Enthusiasm in Revolutionary America*. Ithaca: Cornell University Press, 2015.

Muncy, Raymond Lee. *Sex and Marriage in Utopian Communities. 19th-Century America*. Bloomington, IN: Indiana University Press, 1973.

Naipaul, Shiva. *Journey to Nowhere: A New World Tragedy*. New York: Simon & Schuster, 1980.

Noyes, John Humphrey. *History of American Socialisms*. New York: Dover, 1966.

Nugent, John Peer. *White Night: The Untold Story of What Happened Before—and Beyond—Jonestown*. New York: Rawson, Wade, 1979.

Parker, Robert Allerton. *The Incredible Messiah. The Deification of Father Divine*. Boston: Little, Brown and Co., 1937.

Poe, Edgar Allan. "Mary Gove." July 1846. *The Literati of New York City, Part III*. Reproduced by the Edgar Allan Poe Society of Baltimore. Available online at https://www.eapoe.org/works/misc/litratb3.htm#govemary.

———. "Review of *Human Magnetism*." *Broadway Journal*, April 5, 1845. Reproduced by the Edgar Allan Poe Society of Baltimore. Available online at https://www.eapoe.org/works/harrison/jah12c08.htm.

Primiano, Leonard Norman. "'Bringing Perfection in These Different Places': Father Divine's Vernacular Architecture of Intention." *Folklore* 115.1 (April 2004): 3–26.

Rea, Sara Weber. *The Koreshan Story*. Estero: Guiding Star, 1994.

Reid, Ira De A. "Negro Movements and Messiahs 1900–49." *Phylon* 10.4 (1949): 362–69.

Reiterman, Tim, with John Jacobs, *Raven: The Untold Story of the Rev. Jim Jones and His People*. New York: Jeremy P. Tarcher, 1982.

Rochefoucauld-Liancourt, François-Alexandre-Frédéric. "Anecdotes of Jemima Wilkinson." *Travels in North America. The Monthly Visitor and New Family Magazine*. January 1801.

Satter, Beryl. *Each Mind a Kingdom: American Women, Sexual Purity, and the New Thought Movement*. Berkeley: University of California Press, 1999.

Schneider, Herbert W., and George Lawton. *A Prophet and a Pilgrim: Being the Incredible Story of Thomas Lake Harris and Laurence Oliphant; Their Sexual Mysticisms and Utopian Communities Amply Documented to Confound the Skeptic*. New York: Columbia University Press, 1942.

Sears, Clara Endicott. *Gleanings from Old Shaker Journals*. Harvard, MA: Fruitlands Museum, 1944.

Shaftel, David. "The Black Eagle of Harlem." *Air and Space*, December 2008.

Shaw, Jane. *Octavia, Daughter of God: The Story of a Female Messiah and Her Followers*. London: Jonathan Cape, 2011.

Slade, Joseph W. "Historical Sketch of Thomas Lake Harris, Laurence Oliphant, and the Brotherhood of the New Life." In *Thomas Lake Harris and the Brotherhood of the New Life: Books, Pamphlets, Serials, and Manuscripts. 1854–1942*, edited by Jack T. Ericson. A Guide to the Mircofilm Collection. Glen Rock, NJ: Microfilming Corporation of America, 1974.

Stein, Stephen J. *The Shaker Experience in America*. New Haven: Yale, 1992.

Stoehr, Taylor. "Robert H. Collyer's Technology of the Soul." In *Pseudo-Science & Society in 19th-Century America*, edited by Arthur Wrobel, 21–45. Lexington: University Press of Kentucky, 1987.

Sugrue, Thomas. *There Is a River: The Story of Edgar Cayce*. Virginia Beach: A.R.E. Press, 1942.

Swainson, W. P. *Thomas Lake Harris and His Occult Teaching*. London: William Rider & Son, 1922.

Tabor, James D., and Eugene V. Gallagher. *Why Waco? Cults and the Battle for Religious Freedom in America*. Berkeley: University of California Press, 1995.

Taylor, Horace Clefton. *Historical Sketches of the Town of Portland, Comprising also the Pioneer History of Chautauqua County, with Biographical Sketches of the Early Settlers*. Fredonia, NY: W. McKinstry & Son, 1873.

Trine, Ralph Waldo. *In Tune with the Infinite, Or, Fullness of Peace Power and Plenty*. New York: Dover, 1910.

Troyat, Henri. *Tolstoy*. New York: Grove Press, 2001.

Vanderhoof, E. W. *Historical Sketches of Western New York*. Buffalo: Matthews-Northrup Works, 1907.

Versluis, Arthur. *The Esoteric Origins of the American Renaissance*. New York: Oxford, 2001.

Wait, Sheridan Paul. "Elizabeth Thompson." *The Bay State Monthly* 26 (1888): 222–39.

Watts, Jill. *God, Harlem U.S.A.: The Father Divine Story*. Berkeley: University of California Press, 1992.

———. "'This Was the Way': Father Divine's Peace Mission Movement in Los Angeles during the Great Depression." *Pacific Historical Review* 60.4 (November 1991): 475–96.

Webber, Everett. *Escape to Utopia: The Communal Movement in America*. New York: Hastings House, 1959.

Weightman, Judith Mary. *Making Sense of the Jonestown Suicides. A Sociological History of the Peoples Temple*. New York: Edwin Mellen Press, 1983.

Weisbrot, Robert. *Father Divine and the Struggle for Racial Equality*. Chicago: University of Illinois Press, 1983.

White, Anna, and Leila S. Taylor. *Shakerism: Its Meaning and Message, Embracing an Historical Account, Statement of Belief and Spiritual Experience of the Church from Its Rise to the Present Day*. Columbus: Fred J. Heer, 1905.

Wisbey, Herbert A. Jr. *Pioneer Prophetess: Jemima Wilkinson, the Publick Universal Friend*. Ithaca: Cornell University Press, 1964.

Wood, D. "Divine Liturgy." *Gastronomica* 4.1 (Winter 2004): 19–24.

Wright, Richard. *Lawd, Today!* In *Early Works*. New York: Library of America, 1991.

Wynne, Nick, and Joe Knetsch. *Utopian Communities of Florida. A History of Hope*. Charleston, SC: The History Press, 2016.

ADDITIONAL SOURCES

Primary Sources

Brownell, Fannie. "Recollections of the Life and Work of Thomas Lake Harris." *Azoth* 6.1 (January 1920): 20–23.

Evans, F. W. *Shakers and Koreshans Uniting.* Mt. Lebanon, NY: [1892].

Harris, Thomas Lake. *Juvenile Depravity and Crime in Our City. A Sermon by Thomas L. Harris, Minister of the Independent Christian Congregation, Broadway, N.Y. Preached in the Stuyvesant Institute, Sunday Morning, January 13th, 1850.* New York: Charles B. Norton, 1850.

Respiro. *The Man, the Seer, the Adept, the Avatar; or, T. L. Harris the Inspired Messenger of the Cycle.* 2nd edition London: E. W. Allen, 1897.

Spear, R. O. [Prof.] *Koreshan Astronomy. The Earth a Hollow Globe! We Live Inside It! Truth Stranger than Fiction!* Chicago: Guiding Star, 1889.

Wilkinson, Jemima. "The Universal Friend's Advice. To Those of the Same Religious Society." Philadelphia: Printed by Francis Bailey, 1784. Facsimile of 2nd edition, University of Rochester Special Collections.

Secondary Sources

Adams, Grace, and Edward Hutter. *The Mad Forties.* New York: Harper & Brothers, 1942.

Barkun, Michael. *Disaster and the Millennium.* New Haven: Yale University Press, 1974.

Black, E. "Addendum 3: Bishop St. John the Divine, George Hickerson, the Apostate and Dissident." Alternative Considerations of Jonestown and Peoples Temple. 2015.

Brown, Edward M. "Neurology and Spiritualism in the 1870s." *Bulletin of the History of Medicine* 57.4 (Winter 1983): 563–77.

Carmer, Carl. *Dark Trees to the Wind.* New York: William Sloane Associates, 1949.

Crumb, C. B. Jr. "Father Divine." *American Speech* 15.3 (October 1940): 327.

Delp, Robert W. "Andrew Jackson Davis and Spiritualism." In *Pseudo-Science & Society in 19th-Century America,* edited by Arthur Wrobel, 100–21. Lexington: University Press of Kentucky, 1987.

———. "A Spiritualist in Connecticut: Andrew Jackson Davis, the Hartford years, 1850–1854." *The New England Quarterly* 55.3 (September 1980): 345–62.

Dombrowski, James. *The Early Days of Christian Socialism in America*. New York: Columbia University Press, 1936.

Fogarty, Robert S. *All Things New: American Communes and Utopian Movements, 1860–1914*. Chicago: University of Chicago Press, 1990.

Fuller, Robert C. "Mesmerism and the Birth of Psychology." In *Pseudo-Science & Society in 19th-Century America*, edited by Arthur Wrobel, 205–22. Lexington: University Press of Kentucky, 1987.

George, Henry. *Progress and Poverty. A New and Condensed Edition*. London: Hogarth, 1953.

———. "What the Railroad Will Bring Us." *The Overland Monthly* 1.4 (October 1868): 297–306.

Gin Lum, Kathryn. *Damned Nation: Hell in America from the Revolution to Reconstruction*. New York: Oxford University Press, 2014.

Greenway, John L. "'Nervous Disease' and Electric Medicine." In *Pseudo-Science & Society in 19th-Century America*, edited by Arthur Wrobel, 46–73. Lexington: University Press of Kentucky, 1987.

Hardy, Clarence E., III. "'No Mystery God': Black Religions of the Flesh in Pre-War Urban America." *Church History* 77.1 (March 2008): 128–50.

Jenkins, Philip. *Mystics and Messiahs: Cults and New Religions in American History*. Oxford: Oxford University Press, 2000.

Johnson, Paul E., and Sean Wilentz. *The Kingdom of Matthias: A Story of Sex and Salvation in 19th-Century America*. New York: Oxford University Press, 1994.

Kring, Hilda Adam. *The Harmonists: A Folk-Cultural Approach*. Metuchen, NJ: Scarecrow Press and American Theological Library Association, 1973.

Landing, James E. "Cyrus Reed Teed and the Koreshan Unity." In *America's Communal Utopias*, edited by Donald E. Pitzer, 375–95. Chapel Hill: UNC Press.

Lause, Mark A. *Free Spirits: Spiritualism, Republicanism, and Radicalism in the Civil War Era*. Urbana: University of Illinois Press, 2016.

Laughlin, J. Laurence. *The History of Bimetallism in the United States*. 4th edition. New York: D. Appleton and Company, 1897.

McCully, Richard. *The Brotherhood of the New Life and Thomas Lake Harris: A History and Exposition Based Upon their Printed Works and Upon Other Public Documents*. Glasgow: John Thompson, 1893.

Moore, Rebecca. *Understanding Jonestown and Peoples Temple*. Westport, CT: Praeger, 2009.

Moorhead, James H. "Between Progress and Apocalypse: A Reassessment of Millennialism in American Religious Thought, 1800–1880." *The Journal of American History* 71.3 (December 1984): 524–42.

Morris, Celia. *Fanny Wright: Rebel in America*. Urbana: University of Illinois Press, 1984.

Newton, Huey. *Revolutionary Suicide* [1971]. Deluxe edition. New York: Penguin, 2009.

Noyes, John Humphrey. *John Humphrey Noyes on Sexual Relations in the Oneida Community*. Edited by Anthony Wonderley. Clinton, NY: Richard W. Couper Press, 2012.

———[Assumed author]. *Mutual Criticism* [1876]. Syracuse: Syracuse University Press, 1975.

Oakes, Len. *Prophetic Charisma: The Psychology of Revolutionary Religious Personalities*. Syracuse: Syracuse University Press, 1997.

Oliphant, Laurence. "Wild Elephants." Selection from *Journey to Khatmandu* (1852). *New England Review* 27.4 (2006): 213–17.

Oliphant, Margaret W. *Memoir of the Life of Laurence Oliphant, and of Alice Oliphant, His Wife*. 2 vols. New York: Harper & Bros., 1891.

Oved, Yaacov. *Two Hundred Years of American Communes*. New Brunswick: Transaction, 1993.

Oxley, William. *Modern Messiahs and Wonder Workers. A History of the Various Messianic Claimants Special Divine Prerogatives, and of the Sects That Have Arisen Heron in Recent Times*. London: Trübner & Co., 1889.

Pavlos, Andrew J. *The Cult Experience*. Westport, CT: Greenwood Press, 1982.

Pitzer, Donald E., ed. *America's Communal Utopias*. Chapel Hill: UNC Press, 1997.

Podmore, Frank. *Mesmerism and Christian Science. A Short History of Mental Healing*. Philadelphia: George W. Jacobs and Co., 1909.

Satter, Beryl. "Marcus Garvey, Father Divine and the Gender Politics of Race Difference and Race Neutrality." *American Quarterly* 48 (March 1996): 43–76.

Scheeres, Julia. *A Thousand Lives. The Untold Story of Hope, Deception and Survival at Jonestown*. New York: Free Press, 2011.

Sherman, M. L. and William F. Lyon. *The Hollow Globe: Or, The World's Agitator and Reconciler. A Treatise on the Physical Conformation of the Earth*. Chicago: Sherman and Lyon [self-published], 1875.

Standish, David. *Hollow Earth: The Long and Curious History of Imagining Strange Lands, Fantastical Creatures, Advanced Civilizations, and Marvelous Machines Below the Earth's Surface*. Cambridge, MA: De Capo, 2006.

Starka, Deborah A. "Koreshan Unity: Vision, Experience, Aftermath." MA Thesis. California State University Dominguez Hills. Summer 2006.

Tawney, R. H. *Religion and the Rise of Capitalism. A Historical Study*. New York: Harcourt, Brace, and Company, 1926.

Tuveson, Ernest Lee. *Redeemer Nation: The Idea of America's Millennial Role*. Chicago: University of Chicago Press, 1968.

Wisbey, Herbert A. "Portrait of a Prophetess." *New York History* 38.4 (October 1957): 387–96.

INDEX

Note: Page numbers after 363 refer to Notes.